CHILE: UNDER MILITARY RULE

RICHARD GOTT, MARLISE SIMONS, PHILIPPE LABREVEUX, RICHARD J. BARNET, TOM WICKER, DALE L. JOHNSON, MAPU, JOYCE HORMAN, EDMUND C. HORMAN, DEAN PEERMAN, MRS. JOSE TOHA, MARCEL NIEDERGANG, NACLA, GEORGIE ANN GEYER, CLASCO, MIGUEL CABEZAS, CHICAGO COMMISSION OF INQUIRY, MARTIN GARBUS, AMNESTY INTERNATIONAL, JOHN POLLOCK, LAURENCE R. BIRNS, ROBERT O. TIERNAN, HARALD EDELSTAM, INTERNATIONAL COMMISSION OF ENQUIRY, WILPF, EDWARD M. KENNEDY, RAUL CARDINAL SILVA HENRIQUEZ, BERTRAND RUSSELL TRIBUNAL II, GEORGE E. BROWN, NATIONAL COUNCIL OF CHURCHES, BISHOP CARLOS CAMUS, DONALD M. FRASER, CANADIAN MISSIONARIES IN EXILE, U.S. CATHOLIC CONFERENCE, CHRISTOPHER ROPER, HELMUT GOLLWITZER, JAMES BECKET, WORLD COUNCIL OF CHURCHES, ECOSOC, FRED HIRSCH, RUY MAURO MARINI, PABLO NERUDA, AND OTHERS.

A dossier of documents and analyses compiled by the staff of IDOC/International Documentation with the special assistance of guest editor Gary MacEoin

IDOC/North America

CHILE: UNDER MILITARY RULE

A dossier of documents and analyses compiled by the staff of IDOC/International Documentation with the special assistance of guest editor Gary MacEoin.

WITHDRAWN

IDOC/North America
235 East 49th Street, New York, New York 10017

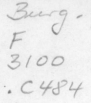

Chile: Under Military Rule

Staff for This Book

Diana Calafati-Coben, *IDOC Editor*
Gary MacEoin, *Guest Editor*
Pat VanHeel Gaughan, *Production and Marketing*

Acknowledgements

The editors gratefully acknowledge the advice and
assistance of Laurence R. Birns, William L. Wipfler,
Thomas Quigley, and David Broad and extend their
gratitude to those persons who submitted original essays,
to those editors who granted permission to reprint
materials from previously published works, and to those
groups and individuals listed in the source list whose
cooperation and support have been invaluable.

Cover design donated by Terrence J. Gaughan,
art by Liam Roberts

About IDOC

IDOC/North America, the publisher of this volume
and the monographic series IDOC/International
Documentation, is a nonprofit educational and religious
organization incorporated under the laws of New York
State. It aims primarily to generate, validate, and
transmit to the English-speaking world documentation and
analyses on international issues of justice, order and
liberty—social, political, economic, educational, and
religious—with a special commitment to gathering from
the Third World information not readily accessible to
North American readers.

For further information on IDOC/North America
publications, also available by subscription, please write
to IDOC/North America, 235 East 49th Street,
New York, New York 10017. *Représenté au Canada
par* Jonathan Wenk, 630 Prince Arthur W., #6,
Montreal, Quebec.

IDOC/North America is affiliated with IDOC/
International in Rome, which publishes:
the *IDOC Bulletin* (in English), a monthly source of
alternative documentation and communication
($10/year from IDOC, 30 Via S. Maria dell'Anima,
00186 Rome, Italy); the *Future of the Missionary
Enterprise Series* (in English), bimonthly dossiers on
Christian mission problematics, with mission-oriented
issues of the *IDOC Bulletin* in the intervening months
($30/year, $50/two years, $75/three years, same address
as above); and *IDOC/Internazionale* (in Italian), a
fortnightly review of documents and documentary
studies ($18/year from IDOC-Ora Sesta, 25 Via Molina
delle Armi, 20123 Milan, Italy).

CHILE UNDER MILITARY RULE

CHILE TO THE THIRD CIRCLE

". . . superbia, invidia e avarizia sono
le tre faville c'hanno i cuori accesi."

(La Divina Commedia, Canto VI)

Nearly a year after the destruction of the Allende regime in an orgy of savagery without parallel in Latin America's history, the elements are available not only for a record of the events but for an informed evaluation of what the Chilean counterrevolution means for the people of Chile and for all victims of the institutionalized violence of contemporary capitalism.

IDOC/International Documentation assembles in this publication that record and evaluation. Section one opens with several analyses of the strategy of the Popular Unity government, some pointing to one moment, some to another, at which the course of events might have been changed. Perhaps the most realistic evaluation is that of Richard Gott, who argues that, regardless of what scenario might have developed, the end result would have been the same. What that means is that the wealthy who monopolize power will use that power to prevent the growth of counterpower—that there is no peaceful way to alter the social balance.

The material in the next two sections, which deal with life under the Junta and with military justice, gives strong support to this view. All the values of Western civilization have been sacrificed to the objective of destroying the basic structures by means of which Chile's have-nots had been acquiring a modest participation in political, economic, cultural, and social power. A tradition of constitutionality was callously ruptured, then the Constitution itself tossed into the ashcan. Innocent people were slaughtered. Refugees from other dictators were chased out of the country. Chileans were rounded up by the thousands, brutally tortured physically and psychologically, held indefinitely as "prisoners of war" without charge or trial. The rule of law has disappeared. The U.N. Declaration of Human Rights and other international codes by which Chile is bound are ignored.

The mentality of the armed forces as revealed in the planning, execution, and institutionalization of the counterrevolution is profoundly disturbing. The International Commission of Enquiry into the Crimes of the Military Junta declared in Helsinki, in March 1974, that a conspiracy constituting high treason had been in progress since early 1972. On September 11, 1973, the Army —in Pinochet's own words—came into the streets "to kill." It behaved then, and continues to behave, like an army of occupation, like the Nazis in France in 1940. We have had many examples in the past decade—Brazil, Uruguay, the Dominican Republic, Guatemala, and others—of the impact on Latin American armed forces of the indoctrination provided by the Pentagon's instructors at centers in the United States and in the Panama Canal Zone, as well as in the war colleges of the various countries. The brainwashing introduces the Mylai syndrome, transforming the "enemy" into a "gook," proper material for "wasting." It denationalizes and McCarthyizes the military, giving them

a destiny complex. They see themselves as the repositories of the wisdom of their respective countries, entitled to judge all things, but themselves above judgment. All of this was previously on the record. What Chile has done is to carry the process, as never before, to its logical conclusion. No Latin American can now trust his own armed forces. All of them have gone through a like denaturing. Nor does the threat stop at the Rio Grande. What about us? Are the armed forces of the United States any different?

In the section on the church in Chile, the central document is the statement issued by Cardinal Silva on behalf of the entire body of bishops at Easter. It shows that, after a period of vacillation and ambiguity, the church leaders have finally decided they must take a stand against the gross and continuing violations of basic human rights. But the conflict within the ranks of the church is far from over. A recent meeting of Catholic journalists at Santiago went on record as condemning the "self-censorship" to which most Catholic publications are submitting themselves, even to the extreme that "important episcopal documents have been published in mutilated versions by the decision of the bishop of the diocese." About the same time, the Federation of Students of the Catholic University of Santiago was criticizing the bishops on the ground that they had issued their Easter message without due reflection. In their view, the bishops should all have behaved like the bishops of Valparaíso and La Serena. These two leaders of reaction continue to praise the Junta and to call on all Chileans to join the crusade against the evils of Marxism.

The analysis of the economic situation in Chile and the direction in which the country is moving raises deep issues for all Third World countries. Just as the Junta is not returning workers and peasants to their pre-1970 condition, but is stripping them of all the political and social advances won over a century, neither is the economy resuming the developmental forms of the 1960s. Things in fact are working out quite differently from the projection made by the military when they were plotting the counterrevolution. They then counted on the total support of the international business community, the global corporations, and the governments of the dominant capitalist countries. They reasoned correctly that the Allende regime posed a mortal threat to all those interests, because its success would produce a domino effect throughout Latin America and around the world.

They got all the help they needed to eliminate Allende. But once that was done, they had lost their leverage. The computer is not grateful. It is realistic. Instead of the gush of capital the Junta expected, all it is getting from the rich nations and the global corporations is a trickle calculated to prevent total collapse while the sweat of the poor is being converted into gold to repay the debts of the past, debts accumulated mainly not by the Allende regime but by its predecessors.

Chile must consequently abandon the dreams of industrial development which it entertained in the 1960s.

There is room in South America, within the global strategy of the Nixon-Kissinger pax americana, for only one sub-imperial power—and that is Brazil. Chile must be content with supplying the raw materials—copper today and, hopefully, oil later. In consequence, prospects are bleak for the mass of Chileans. Already they have been pushed far below the level of the 1960s through the simple mechanism of controlled wages and free prices, combined with the elimination of independent labor unions and other structural means to express grievances. The business community supports this policy. The middle sectors welcomed it for a time. It benefitted them by returning to them the consumer goods which under Allende they had been forced to share with workers and peasants. Soon, however, with the failure of the Junta to control inflation, the squeeze expanded to many in the middle sectors. They, too, must now be controlled, dragooned, and terrorized into acceptance.

What seems to be emerging in Chile is a new approach to population control, or rather, a new application of an old approach. The global corporations, the decision-makers of today's and tomorrow's world economy, are committed to use of capital-intensive technology in the exploitation of regions with surplus labor as well as those where labor is scarce and dear. They believe they can make most profit by concentration on ever-higher levels of consumption by those who already consume excessively, while ignoring the masses at subsistence level whose productivity is so low that they can afford only minimal consumption. Within a philosophy which reduces man to the categories of producer and consumer, this effectively excludes from the human race a half to two thirds of mankind, including a half to two thirds of Chileans. Already it has been noted that the Junta's economic policies assume a population of six million in a country that today has ten million and an excess of births over deaths.

Malthus recognized war, disease, and hunger as the final controllers of population. The logic of the East-West détente as practiced by Nixon and Brezhnev excludes war from the equation, at least as a major factor. Their approach assumes minor wars and ensures the growth of guerrilla and sabotage activities all around the world. But the main task of controlling population must be left to disease and hunger, and the Junta has already put them to work fulltime by eliminating the health services for workers and peasants and by denying work to millions of Chileans and simultaneously proclaiming that whoever does not work does not eat.

Will the next step in Chile and throughout the Third World be to limit human fertility by force, perhaps by treatment of water supply systems? Gunnar Myrdal not long ago expressed the opinion that the conscience of mankind would not stand for such interference with a basic human right. It is by no means clear that he is correct. The savagery already committed in Chile in defense of the rich against the poor has indeed evoked wide condemnation around the world, as this present volume also attests. But the protest has been only marginally effective. Power in Santiago is arrogant, as it is in Wash-ington, confident of its ability to beat into the ground all who do not voluntarily lie down.

Where then do we go from here? First of all, we have to accept that the prospects for improvement in Chile and elsewhere are dim. As Rubem Alves has said, this is no time to plant pumpkins. To think we can achieve a quick victory is folly. After Chile, the prospect of either a peaceful or military road to socialism in this generation must be discounted. Instead, says Alves, let us plant fig trees, which grow slowly but solidly. Even if we do not live to taste the fruit, it will nourish our children and grandchildren. The arrogance of power flouts public opinion but fears it. Witness the vast expenditure of effort devoted to distorting and confusing people's minds. The first objective must be to counter this by searching out and proclaiming the truth, by developing in the minds and hearts of courageous people a commitment to human solidarity and a repudiation of inhumanity no matter how clothed. This volume is offered as a modest contribution to that long struggle.
—Gary MacEoin

Gary MacEoin, a man of towering talents, is author, journalist, lecturer, lawyer, poet, philosopher, and social scientist. Born in the west of Ireland, he earned degrees at the University of London and the National University of Ireland and edited two Irish dailies before becoming an American citizen 20 years ago.

As Guest Editor, he brings to IDOC a rare sensitivity to Latin American culture and history, a deep personal commitment to the liberation of its people, and 30 years' experience covering news and trends in that area for Time, Life, and Reuters, to name but a few. His books on Latin America include Revolution Next Door, Latin America: The Eleventh Hour, and Colombia, Venezuela and the Guianas. He won the 1974 Journalism Award of the Catholic Press Association for his "Brazilian Bishops Fight for Human Rights." The citation reads: "Out of deep experience with the poor of the world and through direct reporting in Northeast Brazil, the author draws a clear and grim account of the Church in conflict with the ruling rich who use legal and economic power to starve helpless millions."

June 1974 saw the publication of two new books: Northern Ireland: Captive of History (Holt), called "the best book to date on embattled Northern Ireland," and No Peaceful Way: The Chilean Struggle for Dignity (Sheed & Ward). "MacEoin has got the facts," said one reviewer, and another, "No Peaceful Way is well-documented, plainly honest, and therefore devastating." Reviews unanimously hail his careful research and consistently high standards of analysis and reportage, but it is MacEoin's humanity which lifts his work beyond the mere scholarly. His words carry weight because he never loses sight of the poor. It is their struggle which informs and illumines his writing, and his life.
—D.C.C.

GLOSSARY

AIFLD: American Institute for Free Labor Development

callampa: slum or shantytown

campamento: improved slum, working-class community

CNT: Confederación Nacional de Trabajadores (Chilean National Workers' Confederation), Junta-approved affiliation of 26 small unions, the "new alternate" to CUT

CODELCO: Corporación del Cobre (Chilean Copper Corporation), state company formed in 1955

CODESEC: Corporation for Social, Economic, and Cultural Studies, propaganda wing of the PDC

COMACH: Confederación Marítimo de Chile (Chilean Maritime Federation)

comando comunal: neighborhood command/committee

cordones industriales: industrial belts

CORFO: Corporación de Fomento (State Development Corporation), created in 1939 during the Popular Front

CUPROCH: Confederación Unica de Profesionales (Central Confederation of Professional Workers)

CUT(CH): Confederación Unica de Trabajadores (de Chile) (Central Labor Confederation), militant leftist group organized in 1953; now dissolved and "replaced" by CNT

DINA: Dirección de Investigacion Nacional, plainclothes paramilitary intelligence group established by General Pinochet in December 1973

ECLA: Economic Commission on Latin America, one of the U.N.'s five regional bodies created to provide a forum for continual discussions of economic questions; an embryonic OECD (see "Paris Club")

ECOSOC: U.N. Economic and Social Council, a 54-rotating-member body including the Commission on Human Rights

empleados: low-level white-collar workers

Eximbank: U.S. Export-Import Bank, a federally funded bank established in 1934 to promote U.S. exports by lending purchase money to overseas buyers

FDU: Federación Democratica Unida (United Democratic Federation), a combination of PDC and PN in opposition to the UP coalition

gremio: a guild or society, usually an association of employers, professional or tradespeople, which can include both workers and management

IMF: International Monetary Fund, an independent international organization formed in 1945; manages world's reserve currencies with the object of preserving international liquidity and currency exchangibility

latifundi: rural estate employing 12 or more workers; system of land concentration in *latifundios* is denoted by *latifundia*

ley de fuga: right to shoot a prisoner while fleeing

MAPU: Movimiento de Acción Popular Unido (United Movement of Popular Action), formed by non-Marxist leftist defectors from the PDC in 1969; joined UP coalition

MIC: Movimiento Izquierdista Cristiana (Movement of Christian Left), formed in mid-1971 by PDC leftists and joined by some MAPU members

MIR: Movimiento de la Izquierda Revolucionaria (Movement of the Revolutionary Left, formed 1965; now best-organized, most significant group left of the UP

Operación Charlie: Operation Charlie, codename of campaign, probably designed by CODESEC, to discredit former Army commander-in-chief, General Carlos Prats

OPIC: Overseas Private Investment Corporation, a quasi-governmental agency, guaranteed by the U.S. government, to insure private corporations operating in lesser-developed countries in case of loss or damage by war, expropriation, or inconvertibility of currency

"Paris Club": Organization of Economic Cooperation and Development, established after WW II to distribute Marshall aid and now a consultative and economic coordinating body for the world's 12 richest nations

Patria y Libertad: Fatherland and Freedom, a right-wing vigilante organization

PC: (sometimes CP) Partido Comunista (Communist Party), formed in 1922 as outgrowth of Chilean Socialist Workers' Party; officially recognized in Chile in 1931; banned in 1948; legalized in 1958; joined UP coalition

PDC: (sometimes CDP) Partido Democrata Cristiana (Christian Democrat Party), most recently in power under Eduardo Frei (1964-70), its co-founder in 1933

Plan Z: Plan Zeta, codename for alleged left-wing insurrection supposedly developed by Joan E. Garces and ultimately used as justification for the coup

PN: Partido Nacional (National Party), extreme rightist party informally allied with the PDC in opposition to the UP

Poder Feminino: a conservative organization of housewives, professional and businesswomen famed for the anti-Allende "March of Pots and Pans," December 1971

población: synonym for campamento

poblador: resident of población

PR: Partido Radical (Radical Party), centrist party formed in 1862; included in the Popular Front of the 1930s and the UP coalition

Protección Comunal: Neighborhood Protection, a right-wing vigilante group

SIM: (sometimes MIS) Servicio Inteligencia Militar (Military Intelligence Services)

SOFOFA: Sociedad de Fomento Fabril (National Manufacturers' Association)

UNCTAD: U.N. Conference on Trade and Development, including the 135 members of the General Assembly

UP: Unidad Popular (Popular Unity), a coalition of Radicals, Socialists, Communists, and MAPU which agreed on a common program in December 1969 and elected Salvador Allende president in 1970

World Bank: International Bank for Reconstruction and Development, founded in 1946 to aid economic recovery in Europe; now provides capital for short-term, well-defined projects in developing countries, with control remaining in hands of principal donor countries

COUNTERREVOLUTION

In order to draw the correct conclusions from the Chilean experience, it is essential to differentiate between factors which would come into play in any attempt to change over from a capitalist to a socialist society and those special factors which came into play in Chile because of the existential condition of that country's society and economy.

The first piece below, written by a Chilean living in Chile, is particularly useful for this purpose. It stresses, for example, the peculiarly Chilean elements in the belief of Allende and those close to him that their opponents would remain within the juridic framework, causing them to make no adequate preparation for the appeal to force which the opposition in fact chose. Also significant in this article are two very positive conclusions: that "the economic and political structures of dependent and peripheral capitalism do not permit the general well-being of the popular masses"; and that the Chilean experience "has been nothing if not a powerful argument for socialism."

The role of the military constitutes another crucial element still frequently discussed in stereotypes and unwarranted generalizations. The essay The titled "The Military as Agent of a Fascist Revolution" here offers important insights, stressing, for example, the fact that the military, as a vital part of the society, "were full participants in the contradictions and spectrum of choices faced by their fellow citizens." But the seizure of power solved those contradictions dialectically, if not constructively. Once the longstanding restraints on violence imposed by the so-called rules of the game had been eliminated, "there were no checks on the action of those who saw their enemies as totally outside the accepted range of discourse, and—by extension—outside the pale of civilization." All the subsequent and continuing savagery followed logically.

Certain aspects of the international conspiracy to topple Allende, such as the role of ITT, have been widely reported. Some remarkable details of the process are documented in the article in this section entitled "The Brazilian Connection." Of particular significance is the description of the propaganda techniques used to play on the fears of women and mobilize them by appeals to their sense of duty and religious training. Here once more it becomes evident that the claimed objectivity of the media of communications is a mere façade, that all the vaunted principles can be tossed overboard when expediency so dictates.

Reflections on the Chilean Experience

Many analyses of the three years of Popular Unity and the genesis of the military takeover have appeared since the September coup—very few of them by Chileans. The following essay, written in December, 1973, was received at the Pacific Studies Center in East Palo Alto, California, translated by Paul Bundy and Deborah Shreve, and published in the Center's Pacific Research and World Empire Telegram, *January-February, 1974. The Chilean author must, for obvious reasons, remain anonymous.*

For many people the military coup in Chile has left a bitter aftertaste. The Unidad Popular (UP) period had in many ways been a totally new experience: a challenge, not to say an attack, against both historical experience and traditional theory on the transition to socialism. As some of the European press has pointed out, Allende's attempt caused as much stir as Dubcek's in Czechoslovakia. But both had bleak outcomes—in the Chilean case, one which has been infinitely more repressive and bloody. For some, these experiences prove the absolute incompatibility between socialism and democracy. For others—those who have looked more carefully—the lesson lies elsewhere: an economic base that attempts to become socialist is incompatible with the rules of a bourgeois parliamentary democracy and vice versa. In other words, recent historical experience only reemphasizes an elementary theoretical principle—one recognized equally by functionalists and Marxists: the essential monism of all societies, the need for a direct *correspondence* between economic and political structures. In Chile there was an attempt to move towards socialism while simultaneously maintaining the traditional state apparatus and bourgeois democracy. This attempt to run counter to theoretical principle provoked the results we have all witnessed.

Nevertheless, these more general abstract conclusions should come at the end of this paper. For the moment the urgent task is to analyze the specific dynamic of the Chilean experience. To begin with, we should ask a few basic questions. Among others: Why did the Unidad Popular triumph in Chile? What course did the UP Government follow? Was the military coup inevitable?

The notes that follow are a modest attempt to answer at least some of the elements within these questions.

I. The Reasons for the UP Victory
A. The Restructuring of the Ruling Class

The roots of the UP victory lie in the type of growth Chile experienced in the '60s and the social conflicts that emerged in the process. Synthesizing, we can identify two key elements: the insufficiency of the inner-directed development advocated by the popular front economic plans of the '40s and early '50s, and the new tendencies of foreign investment.

After the crisis of the '30s, Chile was one of the few Latin American countries to launch industrial import substitution. Nevertheless—and this was to become the rule in Latin America—the process exhausted itself fairly soon. On the one hand, the backward agrarian structures remained unchanged (during the Popular Front government of Aguirre Cerda, 1938-1941, the watchword was "a truce with the countryside"), which obviously even further reduced the size of the industrial market, already limited by the country's low overall population. On the other hand, external commercial dependency increased: capacity to import grew very slowly, and yet the pressures to import doubled. The agricultural trade balance ran a deficit from 1937 on, and now the country needed capital goods and intermediate goods. Furthermore, the new industrial pockets, primarily producing non-durable consumer goods for the internal market and enjoying an almost natural oligopoly, were rapidly integrated into the ruling class. In the '50s the industrial bourgeoisie was becoming predominant, the political system was discredited (the "Ibáñez earthquake" of 1952, a sharp indicator of the trend, cancelled the period of radical administrations that began in 1938) and economic stagnation became progressively more acute. For example, between 1940 and 1952, the industrial product grew at an annual rate of 5.3%, while between 1952 and 1960 it dropped to 2.3%. In per capita terms, this amounted to stagnation of the industrial product. In the same period, assembly industries offered almost no new jobs. Simultaneously there were signs of peasant revolt in the countryside.

At the beginning of the 1960s it was clear that a broadening of the capitalist base demanded important changes in the existing economic structure. It meant pushing through a capitalist reform program, which would have to include: a) an agrarian reform that would stimulate agricultural supply, cheapen labor costs without lowering real wages and therefore raise industrial profits, save foreign exchange and transfer the surplus to the financing of industrial development; b) an advance to a second industrial phase that would include durable consumer goods and an important part of the means of production (intermediate and capital goods) that the process demanded; c) an increase in import capability by exporting more ("export or die" was the slogan used by Jorge Ahumada, director and "brains" of Frei's economic plans), and also through foreign aid. If, in the 1940s, industrialization was seen as the foundation for national economic independence, now, in the 1960s, with the accumulation of experience, it was thought that the *new industrializing phase,* along with related reform measures, would definitely lead to dynamic and autonomous growth.

It was the Christian Democratic Party, led by Frei, that represented these ideas politically. Its leaders were different from those who had led the first wave of import substitution. They were modern businessmen closely connected with a dynamic techno-bureaucracy anchored in the private sector—in short, a modern and development-oriented industrial bourgeoisie. Two other characteristics differentiate it from the one that led in the 1940s: a) it had an economic ideology—the one from ECLA (the U.N. Economic Commission for Latin America) that was rational and that had been well assimilated; b) it possessed a socio-philosophic ideology (Christian social humanism) drawn from Papal encyclicals and Maritain, which allowed it to project a longer-range model of society (anti-capitalist and anti-communist, according to its spokesmen).

This program found support especially among petit bourgeois sectors, but also attracted peasant and proletarian segments.

At first this new and modern industrial bourgeoisie gave the impression that it would function like a *national bourgeoisie* (in the classic sense, that is, as a bourgeoisie that would implement anti-oligarchical and anti-imperialist tasks). On one side, it included an agrarian reform program that was supposed to liquidate the traditional *latifundio* (landed estate); on the other side, an industrial development program that would supposedly eliminate dependency and generate the necessary preconditions for a dynamic, autonomous, self-sustained growth. And, to tell the truth, the traditional right, a part of the left, and many militants of the Christian Democratic center believed that things in fact would turn out that way.

However, the evolution of the international situation was to determine a very different course. In the metropolitan centers—and I am referring especially to the United States—there were at least three processes going on that have to be kept in mind: a) a long economic "boom" that stretched to 1968 (this is all the more important to note if one recalls that periods of economic rise in the center are not favorable to reformism in the periphery); b) the 1960s were characterized by the vigorous rise of multinational corporations. Through these corporations the metropolitan center began to map out a new international division of labor, in which the less sophisticated industrial sectors are transferred to those regions where there is cheap labor. Changing its traditional pattern, foreign investment began to step into the industrial sector in the periphery; c) paralleling this, there was a tendency on the part of foreign capital to begin a "strategic retreat" from the traditional primary and extractive sectors; d) on a broader horizon there was a definite *regional* displacement of U.S. foreign investment, away from the Third World—especially Latin America—to more developed capitalist areas like Europe.

From this sketch we can immediately draw a first conclusion: the interests of this *new* foreign capital tend to go in the same direction as the interests of the modern industrial bourgeoisie represented by Frei and his supporters. But as these local strata are in a manifestly weak position—financially, commercially and technologically—when compared with the *new* foreign capital, instead of a confrontation, there is a merger. The *new* foreign capital, now that it is serving the internal market at least partially, is also interested in agrarian reform. This is the element that most decisively influences the viability of the changes in the agricultural sector.

In other words, in Chile the modern industrial bourgeoisie (located fundamentally in the durable consumer goods and means of production sectors), instead of functioning as a national bourgeoisie, functioned as an *anti-latifundio, but pro-imperialist, bourgeoisie*. The first characteristic makes it appear a national bourgeoisie; the second, a *comprador* [buyer] or intermediary bourgeoisie. But in fact it is neither the one nor the other. What we have is a new phenomenon which reflects the new conditions under which the relationships between the center and the periphery are structured at the present time.

Clearly these new phenomena should cause a serious restructuring within the ruling class bloc and, in the process of the shake-up, a serious *political crisis*. In the 1950s the ruling class was made up of: a) "old" foreign capital, located in the primary export sector (especially copper); b) the financial-commercial bourgeoisie; c) the monopolistic industrial bourgeoisie, producing essentially non-durable consumer goods; d) the traditional landowners or *latifundistas*. The new 1960s model presupposed important breaks and displacements. First of all, it spelled the more or less rapid demise of the traditional landowners and their complete displacement from power.[1] In the second place, it meant that there were sharp internal frictions and struggles as certain groups within the ruling class became more important while others were displaced. Among other displacements: a) traditional foreign capital loses weight (although in Chile it is not displaced or superceded) in relation to *new* foreign industrial capital; b) within the domestic industrial bourgeoisie, traditional sectors are displaced by more modern ones who, in turn within the national context, become the leaders of the ruling class.

In short, there was an important redefinition of the power structure. This process of redefinition created serious internal conflicts within the ruling class and—given the bourgeois democratic characteristics of the Chilean political system—the continual recourse to popular mobilizations. And, as one can find in a quick reading of the *Communist Manifesto*, interbourgeois conflicts, to the extent they overflow and use other classes, greatly contribute to the development of the political consciousness of the proletariat and the masses of the people. All of this happened in Chile, and to a large extent explains the conflicts within the ruling class and the rise in mass consciousness that Chile experienced in 1970 and which led to the Allende victory.

B. The Explosiveness of the Economic Model

In the new economic program advocated by the Frei administration, capital accumulation within industry was to be directed fundamentally into the development of durable consumer goods and some fairly complex means of production. The organic and technical structure of investment—imposed by the industrialized center—determined certain aspects of the accumulation process that are important to remember: a) the capital-product relationship in new investments was higher than the national average. In other words, unless there were a rise in the rate of investment, the rate of productive growth would fall. In fact, the rate of investment dropped from 16.4% to 15.6% between the first and second halves of the 1960s; b) the new industrial projects, as they absorbed large doses of capital in an overall context where there were greater drops in investment, necessarily promoted a greater concentration and therefore an increase in the degree of monopoly. This process generated the conditions for: 1) a redistribution of aggregate industrial value at the expense of salaries; 2) intra-industry surplus value transfers that favored the more oligopolistic sectors; c) more visible foreign capital in the new and more dynamic sectors. And, as is common, these firms actually provide very little new capital. In the majority of cases they buy out and/or merge with already established domestic firms, and they finance themselves predominantly by using the Chilean capital market. In other words, the new guidelines for industrial growth led to a situation where there were additional pressures on the balance of payments; d) the capital density (capital per employed worker) in the more dynamic sectors was very high. Each additional dollar invested contributes very little to solving the serious unemployment problems in the country. The more dynamic industrial sectors, those with the highest productivity, had a very modern employment structure: a high percentage of engineers and technicians, etc. The majority of their blue-collar workers were highly skilled. In both the type and number of jobs, the investment in labor tended to become more and more regressive.

Those are some of the more important features of the new pattern of industrialization. It created strong tendencies towards the concentration of capital, production and profit. As Pedro Vuskovic, later Minister of Economy in the Allende government, so aptly put it: it was a model that promoted both "concentration and exclusion."

In general, because it tended to aggregate the structural heterogeneity of industry and the Chilean economy, it brought about a regressive redistribution of income. In more concrete terms, its results were highly explosive.

On one side, there was the behavior of that segment of industry which produced services and non-durable goods. During this period it was classified as a traditional or non-dynamic industry, which involved some distortion. In this branch of industry the oligopolistic sectors retained control while medium and small industry saw their positions deteriorate. The latter clearly had to find an anti-monopolistic outlet that would stimulate their markets and increase mass consumption. As a result, it's not surprising that Allende received important support from these sectors.

Secondly, there was the behavior of the petit bourgeoisie in both its salaried and non-salaried sectors. In the case of the salaried sector there are two important things to note: a) those in the public sector (e.g., white-collar workers, teachers, etc.), in the traditional private sector and in the more traditional professions in most cases saw their levels of income stagnate. In almost all cases their expectations were frustrated; b) the educational system—especially the universities—went through quantitative and qualitative changes. Enrollment increased and reforms were initiated that promoted modernization. Given the new tendencies in industrialization the latter was functional, but the former was dysfunctional. The outcome was growing unemployment among skilled professionals and progressive impoverization of the petit bourgeoisie. Consequently, it's not surprising to find an extreme radicalization of students, both in the universities and the secondary schools, in the face of an economic development incapable of absorbing them. And when you add the fact that traditionally, the educational system in Chile had been a viable means for upward mobility, it is easy to understand the critical impact the evolution of these new trends had on the salaried petit bourgeoisie.

However the hopes and reactions of the petit bourgeoisie, in its traditional sense, vary according to its ties to larger economic sectors. If connected, productively and commercially, with the more dynamic sectors it may have experienced a relative boom. However, many in this group felt the impact of the monopolization process. In fact, the vast majority of the petit bourgeoisie was not linked to the dynamic sector and as a consequence was hit both by the monopolies and the low level of demand.

To sum up, the new model carried minority sectors of the bourgeoisie and the petit bourgeoisie to the top of a more or less typical consumer society. And the same process tended to exclude and marginalize larger and larger sectors of the population.

These objective conditions made it much easier for the proletariat and its political representatives to unite in a broad class front. However, there were other developments.

We have already pointed out that there was increasing social unrest in the countryside towards the end of the 1950s. Frei's agrarian reform, among other things, tried to absorb and channel the unrest. The goal was to eliminate the traditional *latifundio,* support the more sophisticated capitalist sectors and develop family farms, which—along with other more strictly economic objectives—would assuage the "hunger for land." The parliamentary debate over the Agrarian Reform Law lasted more than two years and when it was finally implemented, the results were meager. It affected less than 25% of the land which had an adequate water supply and helped only about 10% of the peasant families. What it actually did was accelerate the development of large scale agrarian capitalism and therefore increase the ranks of the rural proletariat. The problem of the *minifundio* (miniature farm) sector wasn't solved at all. A parallel development, in many respects promoted by the government itself, was the considerable growth of peasant unions. Between 1966 and 1970 the number of peasant unions rose from 201 to 510 and the active membership jumped from 10,700 to 114,000. Rather than calming things down, the reform actually spurred on the peasant movements in the Chilean countryside. Between 1964 and 1968 peasant strikes were multiplied by 11 and there were increased extralegal actions and open struggles that led to direct occupation of lands. In 1969 there were 150 land seizures, while in the period 1960-1969 the yearly average was only 6. Given the increase in land seizures, the possibilities for a worker-peasant alliance grew much stronger.

Finally—last, but not least—we have to mention the behavior of the urban proletariat. They were also affected; and their conduct reflected the ups and down of a reformist program that was rapidly turning into its opposite. The first two years of the Frei administration were characterized by a three-faceted process: a rise in the levels of economic activity, a slowing down of inflation and a progressive redistribution of income. From a political angle this was a reflection of the rising support in its struggle against more traditional groups—especially the *latifundistas*—entrenched in the power structure. This boom was shortlived. By mid-1966 the dynamic and redistributive push began to subside and from 1967 on the real characteristics of the new model came to the fore with a vengeance. Real wages dropped and unemployment—especially hidden unemployment—went up. These were the immediate objective consequences. Among the subjective consequences, we should at least note that Christian Democratic reformism initially tried, at the expense of the left, to absorb and channel certain working class sectors. In this new situation the competition for influence on the urban proletariat (actively contested by the left), the intensity of inter-bourgeois conflicts, the unfulfilled political promises and the corresponding expectations they had created, and the rapid deterioration of the reformist program, precipitated the rise of an unparalleled and uncontrollable workers' movement. Between 1966 and 1970 the number of unionized workers rose from 351,000 to 551,000, or 60%. While in the period 1963-1964, the number of striking workers were 256,000, in 1969-1970 it reached 922,000 workers, an increase of 260%.

In short, by 1970 there was a spectacular and deeply conscious popular movement in Chile.

C. The International Context

Obviously, internal political events, especially in Latin America, are not independent of developments on a global scale. The Chilean case was no exception to this rule.

It has been said that capitalist development is characterized by the law of unequal development. In this specific case the beginning of the 1970s was replete with tendencies and patterns that were particularly favorable to the Allende movement.

In the first place, there was the beginning of what we could call the strategic crisis, or the long-term crisis, of U.S. capitalism. U.S. hegemony, which was almost unchallengeable at the end of World War II, has been increasingly undermined both by the vigorous resurgence of other capitalist centers (Europe, Japan) and by the growing rise of "independent" forces in the Third World. To paraphrase Nixon, the U.S. can no longer impose its will as in the past. This hegemonic crisis which is a long-term process and therefore full of ups and downs, opens up a period which in the long run is favorable to reformist movements.

Simultaneously, especially between 1969 and 1971, the U.S. economy was plagued by a serious recession. Certain features of the post-war cycle, like "stagflation," were accentuated and the balance of payments problems reached record levels. This situation considerably weakened the State Department's room for maneuvering and, as a result, favored almost any attempt to renegotiate the terms of dependency. And finally, there were the extremely serious economic, military and political problems that beset the U.S. because of the war in Vietnam. As Nixon put it in his 1971 message to Congress on foreign policy:

The American people have grown somewhat weary of 25 years of international burdens. This weariness was coming in any event, but the anguish of the

Vietnam war hastened it, or at least our awareness of it. Many Americans, frustrated by the conflict in Southeast Asia, have been tempted to draw the wrong conclusions.[2]

In the face of an organic and politically powerful popular movement, it was not a situation where you could blithely send in the Marines and then wash your hands. The Indochina War and its "frustrations and wrong conclusions" demanded a more cautious and flexible policy.

Finally, and as a complement to what previously has been discussed, there was the growing power and expansionism of the European powers and Japan. If you add to this the world recession which affected all the countries in the center (although with different degrees of intensity), one finds a sharp inter-power conflict both for markets and for investment spheres. In this type of situation the weak countries find themselves strengthened in relative terms and this favors those programs that seek a greater degree of national independence. And yet these international conflicts are also reflected in the internal political scene in the corresponding struggles between the different ruling class groups according to their international ties.

To sum up, internationally there was a weakening of the U.S.—the hegemonic power of the system—and a sharpening of inter-imperialistic conflicts. This in turn had a decisive impact on internal Chilean conflicts and favored attempts to change the economic and political structures of the country.

Why did the Unidad Popular triumph? That was our initial question. We can answer it briefly by stating that towards 1970 there was a crisis in the restructuring of the Chilean ruling class. Simultaneously, a vast popular movement demanding substantive changes rose. The struggle of the masses aggravated the conflicts within the ruling class. Some (Radomiro Tomic) tried to absorb the popular movement with a reformist program; the others (Jorge Alessandri) wanted to wipe out the popular movement with a repressive and conservative program. Furthermore, as the ruling groups failed to perceive fully the chances of a total break within the system (partly because of the UP program, partly because of the effective control the UP leadership had, at the time, over the mass movement—a point stressed by Allende in his speeches during this period—they failed to settle their internal differences. All of this, together with the very favorable international situation, provoked the electoral split within the right, the electoral victory of Allende, and, finally, his later assumption of power, or, to be more precise, access to the executive branch of the existing State apparatus.

II. The Unfolding of an Experiment

A. The Conditioning Factors of the Point of Departure

One of the key choices in any strategy for economic development involves the options between accumulation and consumption. The alternatives are not absolute (in the sense that greater accumulation necessarily implies less consumption) but relative. What matters are the relative percentages by which one or the other variable is increased in relation to given variations in income.

In Chile, as in other underdeveloped countries, the choice is indisputable from a theoretical point of view:

surplus must be directed primarily toward an increase in productive investment.

In a general sense this view has been reflected in the early *concrete* situation of those countries that have begun to build socialism. Two crucial factors should be stressed here. In the first place, the construction of a socialist movement followed bitter, massive, and more or less prolonged armed struggle, a fact which has resulted in both a highly politicized consciousness among those who fought for change, and in a close unity between the leadership and the base. Economically, austerity and frugality have been basic ingredients. In a sense armed struggle has played the role that Calvinism played in the birth of capitalism. Thus, pressure for increased consumption has not been particularly strong.

Second, there is another decisive element: the building of the new economy has always followed the making of a political revolution. The classical sequence of events in socialism has been opposite to that of capitalism: first the old ruling-class state apparatus has been destroyed, then a *new* state apparatus has been created and the long and arduous task of economic construction has begun. Political security, therefore, is crucial, as it allows for long-term planning which automatically favors investment, especially the long-term investment most needed in poor countries.

Neither of these factors was present in the case of Chile. The old state apparatus remained intact, the Chilean left having at best assumed control of *one branch* of it, and that through an electoral process. The election returns reflected a pretty shaky victory—around 36% of the vote. One could more or less anticipate that the favorable conditions that allowed for victory would give way to difficulties in the future.

Two important elements should be added to the picture. First, the right forced Allende to sign a restricted agreement on constitutional guarantees before his confirmation as President, thus effectively blocking still further the possibilities for any attempt at "legal" transformation. Second, there was a factor rooted in the Unidad Popular's own political program. To quote Allende, the dictatorship of the proletariat is but *one of the forms* for building socialism. "Chile, today, is the first country in the world called upon to develop and undertake a second model of transition to a socialist society."[3] The use of existing legality was the basic presupposition for the beginning of the transition to socialism. And beneath that presupposition lay another: the change in the social and economic system would come about without open class confrontation.

These are some of the basic elements that should be kept in mind.

B. Expansion Through Consumption

The basic choice that Allende made in the political economy was to favor consumption, a decision taken not only on the basis of the factors previously discussed, but also because of the acute economic depression that hit the country towards the end of 1970, coupled with the existence of considerable unused productive capacity. There were also theoretical influences which—from a methodological point of view—tended to favor distribution and consumption to the detriment of production.[4]

The UP's stated objectives in political economy were to reactivate the levels of economic activity, to effect a substantial redistribution of income in favor of the poorest sectors of society, and to initiate changes in the forms of property by establishing a dominant state economic sector. The new policies on salaries, prices and public spending were the key levers for the achievement of the first two objectives. There was substantial readjustment of basic salaries, outstripping the previous increase in the cost of living, and inflation was slowed down significantly. The result was a notable increase in real salaries and, as a consequence, a veritable explosion in the level of popular consumption. For example, the consumption of foodstuffs went up more than 27% in the period 1971-1972. The increase in supply and the considerable expansion of public deficit spending, on the other hand, led to the belief that gross profit would not decline in 1971, or at least not by much. However, this didn't spur greater investment. The capitalists increased their own consumption and savings (of foreign exchange). As one might expect, private investment contracted.

At the end of the first year the results were spectacular. The GNP rose by 8.3% (the highest rate in fifteen years), industrial production rose by 14.6%, unemployment dropped from 8.3% to 3.9% (subsequently it dropped to 3.1%), and the annual rate of inflation went down from 35% in 1970 to 22% in 1971.

Nevertheless, the picture wasn't totally rosy. Consumption, particularly of foodstuffs, showed an elasticity towards income that was well above what was expected. This fact, along with the rising demand for imports caused by the increase in economic activity, and the disastrous fall in the world price of copper, created serious difficulties in the balance of trade. Inflow of foreign capital fell precipitously, the cost of servicing the foreign debt grew, and no massive foreign aid from the socialist bloc was forthcoming. In short, the export sector was in a critical situation and could no longer be used, as had been the case in the first few months, as the variable that would guarantee success.

In the area of distribution, wages and salaries, according to two official estimates, amounted to 59% or 63% of national income. Bearing in mind that, according to the UP's six-year plan, wages and salaries were to have constituted 61% of national income by 1976, the conclusion is obvious: consumption was rising too fast.

This, in turn, generated a sharp contradiction between the new level and composition of demand and the level and composition of supply. As we know, it's not particularly difficult to promote changes in demand, but once more immediate reserves have been exhausted, it's extremely difficult to change the level of supply. In the case of Chile there was an additional problem: one could expect little from the private sector and it was precisely this sector that controlled the bulk of the supply. In other words, the evolution of the economy demanded an emphasis on accumulation, a fact which in turn demanded a vigorous effort to establish the productive state sector.

A marked imbalance manifested itself: while consumption increased beyond all bounds, the state's capacity to control basic avenues of surplus production and appropriation grew very slowly. Three factors stood in the way of this essential objective: legal problems, a united parliamentary opposition, and the government's own legalistic penchants. Unless this economic model were capable of solving the state's problems of accumulation, it ultimately threatened to bring about an explosive situation.

C. The Second Year: "The Year of Accumulation"?

The conflicting factors which stood in the way of economic evolution were clear by the first quarter of 1972. Before the close of 1971, the Government had already announced that 1972 would be "The Year of Accumulation." However there were conflicting views on the necessary steps and measures that would have to be taken. Those who had been managing the economy up to that point proposed to accelerate the process of expropriation of industry and distribution so as to achieve a dominant state sector as quickly as possible. At the same time, there was strong criticism of the endless bureaucratic twists and turns in the implementation of political and economic policy, and emphasis was put on the necessity for vigorous and thorough popular control of production, distribution and consumption. In a strictly political sense, however, those to the left of Allende didn't really have very clear or well-defined objectives.

By contrast, the political leadership of the UP decided on an opposite policy. They wanted to slow down the process of expropriation, seek a political understanding with the Christian Democratic opposition, and clearly define "the rules of the economic game" as an incentive to the private sector. They also emphasized labor discipline and increased efficiency in the management of the state sector.

The resulting polemic may be somewhat crudely summed up by the two slogans: "move forward in order to consolidate," and "consolidate first, then move forward."

As always happens, politics triumphed over economics and there was a "change in direction": economic policy changed and implementation of the second position began. Its proponents maintained the presupposition that the tide was turning against the left.

The economic results were poor and totally opposite those hoped for. Although exact figures are not available, the rate of investment dropped even by comparison to 1971. Consumption did increase again, but only slightly. The growth rate (overall, industrial and agricultural) dropped alarmingly, and labor productivity fell. By the end of 1972, the symptoms of serious economic disequilibrium were acute. In October 1971, the annual rate of inflation was 16%; in October 1972, it was 144%. And by January 1973, it was 183% At the same time the repeated attempts for an agreement with the Christian Democrats failed.

In short, the new alternative was a total failure and 1972 was far from being the hoped for "Year of Accumulation." To mention but one possible reason for the failure: the view that the tide of popular support had turned away from the government was a misconception. The popular rise that began in 1968 continued to grow in depth in 1972. While it is true that some middle sectors (but by no means all) turned to the right, by way of compensation, there was a growth in the strength of the most decisive sectors in the progressive bloc, especially among the urban proletariat in large industry. The owners' lock-out of October 1972, which failed, was a clear index of this trend.

D. An Elusive Surplus

At an equal rate of profit the monopolistic firms, because of their greater capital, reaped much larger profits. But precisely because they were monopolies their rate of profit was higher than average. The transfer of surplus implicit in this situation can be explained by two mechanisms: the increased formation of social value in one branch of industry, at a time when there were uneven levels of productivity within that branch, and price differentials between the more oligopolistic branches and those bound at least somewhat by free competition. Given the typical intra/inter-branch heterogeneity that exists in underdeveloped countries, the appropriation of surplus by the large monopolies tends to be highly concentrated. As a consequence, if those forms are nationalized it is logical to suppose that the State would now control the greater part of national surplus and could therefore promote a vigorous process of accumulation.

In Chile, a good number of monopoly firms, although by no means all, came under State control. However, the low level of saving continued and became worse. In fact, in government circles, the common question was: where is the surplus? It seemed to have vanished magically. Even the new nationalized firms began to show signs of financial weakness.

There were obviously some concrete reasons. In the first place, a fact no one could miss, consumption was expanding at a much greater rate than income. In the second place, there was the behavior of private investment. The latter not only contracted abruptly, but diverted its liquid assets either into foreign exchange or into speculative investments, both of which aggravated the economic situation. This may not have been decisive, especially as there were other factors that clearly limited the State sector's capacity to accumulate.

A key factor was the policy on prices. All the available studies indicated that prices in the private sector rose much more quickly than those in the State sector. As it was much easier to control prices in the State sector than in the private sector, the main effort to hold down prices was shouldered by the State-controlled firms. This different behavior over prices provoked a massive transfer of surplus from the State sector to consumption and private firms. The newly nationalized monopolistic sector wasn't acting as it had in the past, and as a result the possibilities for accumulation dropped substantially. The way in which the system of multiple exchange rates was run also reinforced this same tendency.

To the above we should add two, more political, factors: 1) the absence of popular control of production, distribution and consumption, all of which (along with objective conditions) allowed both speculation and the rises in prices which ultimately favored the private sector, and 2) the growth of non-productive expenditures (under the heading of "general expenses") in the State firms. Not only was the surplus transferred, there were also wasteful, non-productive expenditures within these State firms.

Finally, there were the real obstacles that limited greater investment. In this context it wasn't enough to have capital savings. What were needed were *real* resources that could be used to augment the means of production. Since in dependent countries the productive capacity of this sector is very small, everything depends on import capacity, and, as we have seen, restrictions on this possible source were extreme. The price of copper had dropped by almost 1/3, imports more than tripled between 1970 and 1973, and the foreign financial and commercial blockade reached critical limits.

E. The Economic Crisis and the Reliance on Politics

In the first half of 1973, the economic situation deteriorated until it was untenable. Inflation approached an annual rate of 250%. Production, when it didn't actually fall, remained stagnant. Shortages, speculation and the black market spiraled and there was a sharpening of class conflict. In this context, the parliamentary elections of March 1973 marked a decisive turning point. On the one hand, in spite of the poor economic situation, the results revealed the strength and depth of the popular mass movement that wanted social change, and, in fact, showed that large popular sectors placed their political beliefs and long-term interests before their economic and short-term interests. On the other hand, the opposition forces, given the election results, made a strong and unified decision in favor of a coup d'etat.[5]

Towards the second half of the year the economic situation threatened to become completely unmanageable. Probably the only area where there was national unanimity was on the need to bring the economy under control. Naturally, the solutions proposed were radically different from one another.

The right's anti-crisis program boiled down to the following essential points: a) a freeze of wages and salaries; b) drastic cuts in public spending; c) a general readjustment of the pricing system and price levels, in other words an added push—although supposedly for a short period only—to the already rampant pace of inflation; d) denationalization of the State sector; e) a desperate search for financing from abroad (loans and investments). In short, it was a question of readjusting total supply and demand by drastically restricting the latter and by providing incentives for private investment that would restore necessary confidence and security.

The right was forthright about the political conditions needed to make this program viable. It would require a change "in the accepted rules of the political game," and the imposition of a "strong government" that would be capable of "guaranteeing the economic activity of the private sector for a long time to come." Without mincing words they proposed a clear-cut rightist dictatorship.[6]

The more radical left proposed something quite different. In economics, they called essentially for the following measures: a) a confiscatory monetary reform; b) rationing of consumer goods to be decided and implemented by the masses; c) complete nationalization of the industrial sector and the distribution monopolies, and, in the countryside, a lowering of the maximum allowable land holding not subject to possible expropriation to 98.85 acres of irrigated land; d) suspension of foreign debt payments; e) worker management of the State sector and workers' and popular control within the private sector of production, distribution and consumption. Among other measures they called for an end to commercial secrecy, open audits of all accounts, single bank accounts, work cards (enrollment), and compulsory unionization of managers and businessmen by industry and region, etc. In strictly political terms the organizations that would carry out the program would be bodies of the "Poder Popular" (People's Power or People's Government). They would be directly elected democratic organizations, both legislators and executors, with delegates—at all levels—subject to popular recall at any time. This overall program would become the "Asamblea Popular" (Popular Assembly), the form of the new State structure. The proposal was unmistakable: it meant a straightforward Democratic-Popular dictatorship.[7]

Finally there was the centrist position, proposed and supported mainly by the Government and the leadership of the UP. In economics, it essentially repeated the program the Government had tried to implement since mid-1972, after the so-called "change in direction." The main emphasis was on the "battle for production," an increase in efficiency and discipline in production, the launching of an effective planning system and the definition of clear game rules that would promote security and confidence in the non-monopolistic private sector. Its political slogan was "avoid civil war." Its viability depended on the success of the conversations leading to an agreement with a sector of the opposition.

The rules of the bourgeois democratic game, as it existed in Chile, would have been preserved if this centrist program had been successful. We all know the result. As the saying goes, the road to hell is paved with good intentions. The same can be said for the road that culminated in the September fascist coup.

F. The Recourse to Foreign Aid

The problem of accumulation remains the key aspect of economic growth. In the last analysis, the chances for a government to consolidate itself depend on its capacity to develop productive forces. From this perspective, the viability of the UP's economic-political model was chancy in the extreme.

In Chile, in a broad sense, one can isolate four economic sectors: a) services and non-durable goods; b) durable consumer goods; c) the export sector—essentially the large copper industry; d) the agricultural sector. Intermediate forms of production can be included, depending on their specific character, in the first two sectors. As import substitution in Chile has been extensive but superficial (it has advanced horizontally rather than vertically), its inclusion in the first two sectors makes sense. We can assume the non-existence of machine and heavy capital goods production.

As we have seen, the attempted model began with a large expansion of popular consumption, which put pressure on sectors (a) and (b). Given the agrarian reform program it was unrealistic to expect a short or even medium-term adequate response from the agricultural sector (d). As for goods and services (a), once it had reached the limits of its productive capacity it needed heavy investments. At the same time, the country needed to develop an industry that would produce means of production (a long-term program which, by transferring the expanded production base to the country itself, spells a break from dependency), or have to resort to imports. Clearly, at a given moment, both approaches require imports, but in one case the need is for capital-capital goods (machines to produce machines), and in the second case, capital-consumption, which means the investment process remains tied to, and dependent upon, the metropole.

The latter alternative was chosen, a fact which struck many people as inevitable given Chile's relatively small size. As a result, the dynamic of both investment and consumption depended completely on the behavior of the highly industrialized supplying countries. In other words,

the country's real capacity to accumulate depended on its capacity to import fewer consumer and intermediate goods. And so, in the case of these goods, it was a vicious circle: either you tried to produce them within the country, with the consequent pressures on investment that would entail, or you had to import them. In conclusion, the inelasticity of the internal supply of goods and services created a clear contradiction: either you had an import capacity that was growing at a high rate, or you had to drastically slow down the expansion of consumption. The latter solution, as we know, wasn't the case, and the first alternative was far from being reached. Export levels varied slightly, and deteriorating terms of trade caused a loss of about $500 million in 1971-1972. In the last analysis the viability of the model depended on a single mainspring: massive foreign aid. Obviously, this would not come from capitalist countries. This explains Allende's trip to the U.S.S.R. However, the aid wasn't forthcoming, or at least not in the quantities required.

In other words, the times are not yet ripe for "easy economic take-off." The hard road of original capital accumulation is still a necessary stage in the process. Or, as Chou-en-Lai wrote in a letter to Allende, "one has to rely on one's own forces."

III. An Inevitable Outcome?

A. The Reasons for Disagreement

As we have noted, the institutional regime would have prevailed if and when there had been a successful political agreement between the Government and the Christian Democrats. But this turned out to be impossible. Why?

In the first place there were decisive trends that deepened in 1973. One of these was the steady rise of the masses in a context of general economic contraction. The majority of the popular sectors, especially the urban proletariat, redoubled their economic and political demands and even began to form their own ad hoc organizations. Simultaneously, there were progressively lower surplus margins to meet these economic demands without damaging, or even destroying, the combined ruling class.

In the second place, there was the character of Christian Democracy. Its leadership (Frei and his group) represented the interests of the modern industrial bourgeoisie allied with U.S. foreign capital. The Tomic and Fuentealba group was more closely connected to sections of the middle and petit bourgeoisie and to European capital. The party's base was predominantly petit bourgeois. As this constituency, given the economic situation, was moving to the right, the Frei sector was almost guaranteed control of the party. As a consequence, the basic tasks

---

"The founders of Christian Democracy in Chile were convinced, as they are still convinced, that a deep crisis was destroying the foundations on which the so-called civilization of the West rests.

"They rejected capitalism as a system. They believed, and they continue to believe, that it was in its origins materialistic and inhuman; and that, even though it represented a technique of previously unknown dynamism for economic expansion, it did not constitute a true undertaking of civilization."

—*Eduardo Frei in* Un Mundo Nuevo
(Ediciones Nueva Universidad, Santiago),
written July 1973, published September 1973

---

for the Frei group were to promote a further deterioration of the economic situation and to boycott all attempts at an agreement with the Government.

In the third place agreement with the Christian Democrats would mean that a decisive part of the surplus would remain in the hands of the ruling class. In the conditions of economic stagnation and/or retraction that prevailed, this would have called for both a political and economic sacrifice, especially from the industrial proletariat. And the latter showed no interest—in fact quite the contrary—in accepting such concessions.

If there are unused productive resources, both profits and salaries can go up. That's what happened during the euphoria of 1971. But by 1973, along with lower profits, used capacity was at a peak. In this case Ricardo's assertion—"salaries go up and profits decline"—was completely valid.

Furthermore, the Government, to successfully arrive at an agreement with the opposition, would have had to impose coercive restrictions on the proletariat. That would have been tantamount to political suicide, a Government coup again its own constituency. Meanwhile the industrial proletariat called for the complete removal of the ruling class and, in anticipation of the task, began to create and promote an alternative People's Power. According to its spokesmen, this alternative would also have won over a good number of the middle class who otherwise would have succumbed to the right.

The demands of the ruling bourgeoisie and the demands of the proletariat were mutually antagonistic.[8] The Government was in the middle trying to work out a compromise (or, if you like, a program of class collaboration), while objective conditions made that approach impossible.

B. Was the Coup Inevitable?

Put in such a way the question seems totally gratuitous. After all, if the coup triumphed, it was obviously as a result of something, of processes that objectively came together and produced it. There is no point in getting bogged down in a lot of metaphysical clap-trap. The outcome *was* inevitable. What is compelling is to analyze *what conditions* led to its being so. Since we have already set down some of the elements basic to an understanding of the process, at this point we can be rather sketchy.

First of all, there is an essential fact, discernible at a glance: the Unidad Popular leadership proposed a legal and peaceful transitional program. This is what it was prepared for, and it was fundamentally around this concept that action was taken in a coherent and honest fashion. When the course of events called for a different approach, the leadership was clearly unprepared. It was incapable of acting otherwise. As Gramsci wrote, and it fits the situation perfectly, "a State wins a war to the degree that it has meticulously and technologically prepared for it in peacetime." That is, to struggle for peace one must be prepared for war.

In the second place, we come face to face with a fundamental oversight. In any transition period the State is the principal lever of political economy, and in Chile, the State was never completely controlled by the Allende Government. But even this wasn't the decisive factor. The key "oversight" was that the existing bourgeois State apparatus simply doesn't work as a launching pad for a transition to socialism. A qualitatively different State apparatus is an essential precondition. This "oversight" was like trying to go to the moon by passenger car.

Given these conclusions, was it *really* a case of moving forward towards socialism? Or, as so frequently happens in our countries, was it something else under that guise?

We may tentatively assume that it was in fact something else. Objectively, what was sought was a democratic, dynamic, and relatively independent model of State capitalism. It was a kind of peripheral capitalism oriented towards the welfare of the popular masses.

If that be the case, the experience had simply and conclusively shown that the economic and political structures of dependent and peripheral capitalism *do not permit* the general well-being of the popular masses. Possibly this goal could be achieved by the highly industrialized capitalist countries. In the periphery it is a closed option that is no longer feasible.

In conclusion, and in a way that is neither curious nor surprising, the Chilean experience, even if its outcome had been different, has been nothing if not a powerful argument *for* socialism. That, clearly, is its fundamental lesson.

Footnotes

1. There are two clearly distinguishable sectors within the traditional right that makes up the National Party. In general, both have agrarian interests, but in one case these are connected in a subordinate way to industrial-banking-commercial interests. In the other case purely agricultural interests are uppermost. The first sector wound up recognizing the Frei leadership. The other sector rejected this leadership and supported putschist attempts even during the Frei administration.

2. "United States Foreign Policy for the 1970s: Building for Peace. The President's Report to Congress February 25, 1971," in *Weekly Compilation of Presidential Documents*, VII, No. 9 (Monday, March 1, 1971), p. 310.

3. Salvador Allende, *Chile's Road to Socialism*, ed. by Joan Garces (Harmondsworth: Penguin, 1973), p. 140.

4. See a key article: Pedro Vuskovic, "Distribucion del ingreso y opciones de desarrollo," *Cuadernos de la Realidad Nacional*, No. 4 (1970).

5. The rise in copper prices suggested an economic recuperation that would not help the right in forthcoming elections. Moreover, and this was clearly the decisive factor, the development of what was called "Poder Popular" (People's Power) suggested that there would be a complete left assault on the system before 1976.

6. In this respect it's worth rereading the economic and political commentaries that appeared in *El Mercurio*, especially between May and August, 1973.

7. The best and most useful material on this appeared in the magazines *De Frente, El Rebelde* and *Punto Final* during May-August, 1973.

8. This should be stressed. That the positions were expressed in such a way clearly indicates that the *basic and essential* contradiction of the *whole* system had become the *principal contradiction*. Under these circumstances, a definitive resolution of the contradiction meant the elimination of capitalism as the dominant mode of production in Chilean society. Lack of resolution, or a temporary resolution, whatever the nature of the postponement, meant opting for the maintenance of capitalism as the dominant form.

Recommended Sources (for the preceding article)

Laurence Birns, "The Death of Chile," *The New York Review of Books*, XX, No. 17 (November 1973).

"Chile: The Story Behind the Coup," NACLA's *Latin America & Empire Report*, VII, No. 8 (October 1973).

Gabriel García Márquez, "The Death of Salvador Allende," *Harper's* (March 1974).

Mishy Lesser and Steve Volk, "Ambush on the Peaceful Road," *Liberation*, XVIII, No. 3 (November 1973).

Ralph Miliband, "The Coup in Chile," *The Socialist Register 1973*, ed. Ralph Miliband and John Saville. (London: Merlin, 1974).

Betty and James Petras, "Ballots into Bullets: Epitaph for a Peaceful Revolution," *Ramparts*, XII, No. 4 (November 1973).

James Petras, "Chile After Allende: A Tale of Two Coups," *Monthly Review*, XXV, No. 7 (December 1973).

David Plotke, "Coup in Chile," *Socialist Revolution*, No. 16 (July-August 1973).

Paul M. Sweezy, "Chile: The Question of Power," *Monthly Review*, XXV, No. 7 (December 1973).

Maurice Zeitlin, "Chile: The Dilemmas of Democratic Socialism," *Working Papers*, I, No. 3 (Fall 1973).

Andy Zimbalist and Barbara Stallings, "Showdown in Chile, *Monthly Review*, XXV, No. 5 (October 1973)■

No Through Road to Socialism

Richard Gott is Latin American editor of The Guardian *and general editor of the Latin American Library of Penguin Books. Writing in a* Guardian Extra *on November 21, 1973, he analyzed the forces that led to the Chilean coup and the tradition to which the new regime is heir. He maintains that the fall of the Allende government was inevitable and that "the Junta's victory . . . may well go down in history as the first defeat of the Soviet-American alliance."*

On September 11, the Chilean road to socialism came to an abrupt halt. But was the fall of Salvador Allende inevitable? Would some other policy have produced another, less disastrous, result? If the hand had been dealt afresh, could the game have turned out differently? The three years of the Popular Unity government have now passed into history, to be smothered by myths and wishful thinking, but the questions remain and will be reexamined for many years to come.

The basis of Allende's coalition was an alliance between the Communist Party and the Socialist Party, both Marxist parties with a long and respectable history of political agitation on behalf of the Chilean working class. In Santiago today, adherents of each party are blaming the other for the disaster on September 11. The Communist argument is roughly as follows: the Chilean road to socialism was conceived as a reformist plan that would seek to make as many gains for the working class as was possible within the institutional framework inherited from the past. Allende would continue as President until his legal term expired in 1976, and if necessary the reform process would be slowed down to gain the support of the opposition Christian Democrat Party. After 1976 the process would have continued, possibly with General Carlos Prats, the "loyal" commander-in-chief, as the new presidential candidate of the left.

This policy of reform rather than revolution was certainly that favored by the Soviet Union (and probably by extension desired by the State Department—though not by American business), and indeed the Russians refused to give anything other than token economic support to Allende until he showed signs of consolidating his power.

With the Russians putting pressure on the Communist Party, and the Americans and the Vatican doing the same to the Christian Democrats, there would appear to have been the basis for a Super Power agreement to solve the Chilean problem—leaving Allende in power but effectively emasculated. The Junta's victory, which spoilt this scheme, may well go down in history as the first defeat of the Soviet-American alliance. In this context it is certainly no surprise to find the Chinese maintaining their embassy in Santiago.

As supporters of this policy of rapprochement with the Christian Democrats, the Chilean Communists of course blame the Socialists and their allies in the MIR yet further to the left for chasing after an illusory revolution—a pursuit that was bound to end in catastrophe.

The Chilean Socialist Party, for its part, by nature far more revolutionary than the Communists, with distinct traces of anarchism and Trotskyism in its historical make-up, feels that the Communists, by their moderation, sabotaged the revolution. The Socialists believed that a policy of permanent conflict with the institutions of the bourgeoisie, coupled with mobilization of the working class—exacerbated class struggle—would make a Leninist revolution possible. And in the last few months it looked as though they might have been right. There was a vast mobilization of working-class strength in the industrial areas surrounding Chile's big cities. The slogan "popular power" was fast becoming a reality. It was not altogether fanciful to believe that revolution was on the agenda.

Yet when all is said and done, very few people believed in it. There was never a moment when a Socialist leader could plausibly have gone to Allende and said: "Look, drop your maneuverings with the military and rely on the people instead." The only man who hinted at such a solution was Fidel Castro.

Castro thought that the strength and combativity of the Santiago working class could swing the balance in Allende's favor, "even though other circumstances are unfavorable." Perhaps he was right. But Allende did not take his advice. My own feeling is that the balance of forces against the left was too strong for any insurrectionary attempt to have proved successful. By refusing to make a presidential coup, Allende saved Chile from a civil war that the left could not have won. There were groups in the army sympathetic to Allende, but they supported him as a constitutional President, not as a revolutionary socialist. The small minority of progressive officers in the Chilean armed forces wanted reform, not revolution.

The military Junta is now making great play with the so-called "Plan Zeta," a plan for a left-wing insurrection in September alleged to have been drafted by Allende's Spanish speechwriter, Joan E. Garces. It is the kind of plan that revolutionary groups might well have been idly considering, but there is no real evidence that they were, or that they were intending to put it into effect. In any case it would have had little chance of success. (It is worth noting too that the generals admit that they knew nothing of the alleged plan before they made their coup. It was in no sense the cause of the coup —though of course it has subsequently been used to justify it.)

The degree of popular mobilization in Chile could not have promoted a successful revolution. On the other hand, it was also too great to allow the Communist plan of cooperation with the Christian Democrats to bear fruit. The paladins of "popular power" could not conceivably have linked hands with a Christian Democrat Party moving daily farther to the right. This plan would only have worked—and perhaps not even then—if Allende had been prepared to mount a fierce onslaught against the left, which he was in no position to do.

It is now the task of the generals to pick up the pieces. To give them credit, they have a fairly profound knowledge of the nineteenth-century history of Chile. (General Pinochet, the president of the Junta, has even written books about it.) But their understanding of contemporary economics is small. General Leigh admits that he is no economist. Only Admiral Merino has claimed some expertise in this field. He wants to do away with the policy of import substitution and to concentrate instead on mining and agriculture. The twenty-five years of study and research by the economists of the United Nations Economic Commission for Latin America, which made such a tremendous impression on the Peruvian generals, have clearly passed the Chilean armed forces by. Their understanding of their own country is minimal.

"The country must return to what it used to be," sighs Admiral Merino, as though in some way it were possible to return to an era when the landlord and the small capitalist and the foreign investor plundered the country to their heart's content. The ambition of the generals is to return to a system of unadulterated free enterprise. As their civilian advisers they have dug out Raúl Sáez and Orlando Sáenz from the private sector, Carlos Massad from the International Monetary Fund, Jorge Cauas from the World Bank, and Sergio Molina from the Ford Foundation. The economic prospects are not very encouraging. The immediate result of the coup has been huge price rises, no compensating wage adjustments, collapse of demand, and massive unemployment. No one complains any longer about how difficult it is to get a maid, but even the jubilant middle class has been shocked by the economic price it is being asked to pay for the "restoration." In the shanty towns, people are close to starvation.

The growth of middle-class unemployment—people thrown out of work for supporting Allende—will be bad enough, but lower down the social scale it will certainly result in a huge increase in the robberies and crimes of violence which characterize most Latin American countries except Cuba and from which Chile has hitherto been relatively free. The generals maintain that they are worried about poverty, and General Oscar Bonilla, the Minister of the Interior, makes frequent expeditions to the shanty towns to win their support. But there is no evidence that the generals understand the causes of poverty or have the remotest idea of how to eradicate it.

The men the shanty town dwellers would most like to see dead are ex-President Eduardo Frei and Leon Vilarin, the leader of the lorry-owners strike that preceded the coup. They are regarded as being among the intellectual authors of the coup, through Frei has not yet

proved to be a beneficiary. Selective assassination and vengeance killing seems an almost inevitable sequel to the unprecedented violence unleashed in the past two months, though it is unlikely to be officially sanctioned by what remains of the left-wing parties.

The problem facing the revolutionary left is that their faces are well known, the country is scared, and the economic oppression has only just begun. Chile, geographically, has little to recommend it as a place to start a guerrilla war. A less revolutionary possibility is that the generals will quickly make themselves so unpopular that they will be forced to give way to civilians, as happened this year in Argentina and in Chile in the time of General Ibañez. A more likely probability is that they will remain in power for a generation.

They have begun to put up wooden scaffolding around the Moneda, the pretty eighteenth-century palace that two Hawker Hunters bombed two months ago when the Chilean armed forces decided to overthrow one of the last remaining democracies in Latin America. Plans are already in hand to restore the presidential palace to its former reticent splendor. The rubble will be removed from its quiet courtyards. The broken ironwork will be rewelded. The injured masonry, where shells smashed into the carefully proportioned Italianate facade, will be built afresh. New tapestries will be found for the walls, and one day soon the fountains will play again.

It will not be so easy to restore the Chilean body politic. What happened on September 11 has already had a huge impact both in Europe and on the rest of Latin America. But in Chile, the coup has given a mortal blow to a certain aspect of the country from which it seems unlikely ever to recover. Everything for which Chile was known outside, not just during the years of the Popular Unity but for decades before, has been swept away. Over the past hundred years Chile had seen the steady growth of a democratic tradition, the incorporation into political life of the middle and working class, and the growth of a working class movement unequalled in Latin America. These considerable gains have all been lost.

More recently Chile had become a center of intellectual research and activity unparalleled for its size in much of the world. Its research centers, particularly in the social sciences—CEREN, CESO, ICIRA, FLASCO, CIDU, CEPAL itself—attracted intellectuals of immense distinction. Amid the maelstrom of Latin American politics, Chile was a civilized haven where human rights were respected, democracy was honored, and ideological discussion flourished. Catholic and Marxist magazines of a high standard jostled each other on the newsstands. Political debate, even in the highly charged atmosphere of the past three years, still took place essentially between friends. Only three weeks before the coup, the Marxist president dined with the Christian Democrat leader in the house of the Cardinal.

This civilized atmosphere has disappeared. The liberal, democratic, international aspect of Chile has gone forever, smothered beneath an avalanche of xenophobia, racialism and anti-intellectualism, which must always have existed at some level in the Chilean character, but until now had been conveniently cloaked. Bolivian students have been killed, not because they were involved in politics, but simply because they were Bolivians, regarded by a certain stratum of Chilean society as "indios"—an inferior race.

Books are burnt and libraries ransacked not just because the military want to stamp out Marxism, but because they resent intellectuals. The speeches of Frei and the writings of Paulo Freire have all found their way to the bonfire. The universities have all been handed over to the military to control. The Chilean motto is "By reason or by force," and if the first orginally prevailed, the second has now very clearly taken over. Whereas Allende and his Popular Unity, perhaps Utopians, were seeking an independent socialism, the generals are returning to the dependent capitalism of the nineteenth century, which is certainly an important historical strand in Chile's development. A week after the coup, the fifteen leading British businessmen in Santiago met over whisky in the British ambassador's drawing room and expressed their unanimous enthusiasm for the downfall of Allende. They and their peers will undoubtedly do their best to help the generals along the path they have chosen—the "restoration" of a Chile which many people had forgotten existed.

This re-emergent Chile has been hidden under a weight of myths, the principal one being that the armed forces are non-political. Yet it only needs a cursory glance through Chilean history to realize that this has never been true. Since the time of independence, the Chilean soldiers have backed governments that supported their class interests. When this support has been lacking or weak, the armed forces have not hesitated to intervene directly. In 1891, and at moments in the 1920s and 1930s, Chile's soldiers controlled the country and were the arbiters of its destiny.

Indeed, apart from the brief War of the Pacific, when Chile wrested the nitrate fields and copper mines of the Atacama desert from Peru and Bolivia, the Chilean armed forces have had no role other than to maintain an internal order that protects their existence as a caste. Their origin is after all that of a conquering Spanish army that was forced to spend its time putting down the revolts of the indigenous inhabitants. The "state of internal war" that has been visited on Chile since September 11 is only a formalization of a situation that has existed in the country since the days of Pedro de Valdivia—its original Spanish conquistador.

One should not have been surprised by the coup—though everyone was—only by the fact that it took so long to stage. Serious planning of it only seems to have begun after the congressional elections in March. With 44 percent of the vote, Allende believed that he had done well, and he considered that he had a mandate to continue fulfilling his election program. The military on the other hand noted the fact that the opposition had polled more votes and concluded that Allende should march no further down the road to socialism. Later they also came to believe that the elections had been a fraud. According to General Gustavo Leigh, the head of the Air Force and the toughest politician in the current four-man Junta, the military became convinced that Allende was intentionally leading the country to economic breakdown.

This has become a constant theme of the Junta's propaganda. They have frequently singled out Pedro Vuskovic, Allende's first minister of economics, for criticism. Vuskovic, they claim, a distinguished United Nations economist (now in an embassy seeking a permit to leave the country), was not lacking in technical ability. Therefore he must have purposely planned the country's economic ruin.

General Leigh has also cited the disgust of the military for the way in which they felt that Allende was buying them off. "People began to hate the soldiers because they were privileged," he says, "which in reality we never were." Allende did certainly try to buy the confidence of the officer class. He played off one against the other and to the end seems to have believed personally that important sections of the armed forces and the police would remain faithful to him. But this was a game that could not go on indefinitely, and in the end he was betrayed.

The pressure on the armed forces to act, from right-wing civilians, was also extremely powerful. A secret report of the private enterprise industrialists' association, SOFOFA, written before the March elections, warned that if the Popular Unity secured more than 42 percent of the vote, it would undoubtedly consolidate itself in power. The government secured more than 44 percent. According to General Leigh, the military felt that these would be the last elections in Chile. The vocal complaints of angry businessmen did not fall on deaf ears.

In addition a strong influence on the generals on the active list were their companions-in-arms in retirement who have their own lobbying organization. They had warned Allende on a number of occasions of their preoccupation with the danger to "national security" of some of his policies. These retired officers, who form a powerful middle-class pressure group, were among the most important organizers of the coup, bridging the gap between fascist civilians and coup-minded generals. Since the coup they have proved indispensable in carrying out numerous vital tasks for the Junta, running universities, copper mines, state industries, and government agencies.

The coup itself had a precursor on June 29, when a tank regiment led by Colonel Robert Souper surrounded the presidential palace. It was a failure, since at that stage there were still a sufficient number of generals in key positions to prevent Colonel Souper from receiving support. But this coup—the "tanquetazo" as it was called in Chile—certainly crystallized the situation, leaving the left uncertain and divided as to how to react and reinforcing the determination of the right to be more effective next time. The immediate result was the occupation by their workers of a large number of factories that had not hitherto been expropriated—an event which further enraged the right.

The green light for the September coup was given when General Carlos Prats, the commander-in-chief loyal to Allende, was forced to resign at the end of August. He was followed into retirement by two generals who actually commanded troops in the Santiago area. Those three generals were the last dike against the coup. The two principal coup-makers were General Leigh, who took over the Air Force in August, and Admiral José Merino, who was in charge of the garrison at Valparaíso. On Sunday, September 9 they decided to act. They presented General Augusto Pinochet, Prats' successor, and a somewhat vacillating figure, with an ultimatum, whereupon he agreed to join the coup. The head of the Navy, Admiral Raúl Montero, was abruptly deposed, as was the head of the police, General José Marie Sepulveda, and the half dozen police generals. And with this purge in their own ranks at the top, the Junta emerged on September 11 to lead their forces united against the elected president. Within 24 hours the situation was under control, taking the military themselves by surprise.

The fact is that the Chilean military now dominate the scene, unrivalled in power. They have taken control at every level, occupying every single post of importance throughout the land. If they could have appointed a retired general as the Cardinal, they would have done so. If progress and development could be brought about merely by the existence of an all-powerful executive, the Chilean military would have a unique chance to change their country for the better. But the Chilean nation constitutes a delicate, complex mechanism, accustomed to political guile, not to the military bludgeon. So far the changes have all been for the worse. ■

The Military as Agent of a Fascist Revolution

The author of the following article is a Chilean sociologist presently living in the United States who must remain anonymous. The essay was received by IDOC in May 1974.

The military coup in Chile can best be understood as the result of a conflict in values. This conflict raged over the terms of Chile's adjustment to the historical contradictions of capitalism and shaped both the circumstances which permitted the coup to take place and the intensity of the Junta's repressive acts.

To understand this conflict, we need to recall that Chile had experienced at the turn of the century a growth of its industrial and urban society on the one hand, and the concomitant extension of the possibilities for political participation, on the other. With the return of a representative and democratic system in the 1930s (after a brief period of military rule), the political parties and movements within Chile, as they sought to achieve and utilize power, endeavored to deal with the complex forces of economic growth, the redistribution of wealth, and the growing amount of social and political participation by the lower sectors of the population. Each succeeding government had laid emphasis on a different aspect of the body of problems and demands generated by the emergence of a more mature urban and industrial order.

The process culminated and reached a crisis with the coalition government of the Unidad Popular (UP). Its electoral victory in 1970 came after a series of experiments aimed at redressing the grievances of those—still the majority of the population—who had been effectively excluded by the formal democratic process from real participation, either in power or in the benefits of increased national wealth. The UP electoral program had appealed to many in this grouping. The crisis produced by Allende's victory was caused by the attempt of the new government to advance the democratization of the nation's political, economic and social structure and, at the same time, to maintain the existing power arrangements. To understand this we must look in a schematic fashion at the course of events.

The UP sought to alter the terms of distribution of the benefits of economic development *within* the context of the existing formal representative democratic system. Its attempt at this was, admittedly, ineptly executed—its

failure, a product of its romantic political and economic approach, compounded by the burdens of sabotage from political opposition within and boycott from without to which it was subjected. The UP should have adequately anticipated that any profound reordering of Chilean society through the mechanism of an alteration in control over significant sectors of the economy would produce a clash within the dominant classes. The upper- and middle-class elements who had been both the beneficiaries and directors of the society, who had long espoused "democratic" government and, at the same time, wanted to preserve their economic hegemony, could not be expected to submit docilely to a curtailment of their power.

The clash was preordained from the very start, but initially was promoted by only the wealthiest portion of the dominant class. But as the process of government-directed change continued, and as the structure of formal democracy proved to be no impediment to the UP in its pursuit of that change, the unrest became increasingly more widespread among the dominant classes. The formal democratic process and its accompanying ideology had served as a means of national integration which had papered over class and value differences. But now those differences were sharply felt.

The conflict between the traditional bourgeois interest in national integration *and* in maintaining its particular economic privileges developed into an all-embracing struggle over the fundamentals of social organization (a *true* value conflict) and was resolved by the dominant classes in favor of a return to the status quo ante and its narrow ranks of societal participation. That resolution in turn was translated into a willingness to sacrifice a political order which no longer served to defend the existing system of distribution. In effect, faced with a choice between defending capitalism and defending democracy, they elected to defend capitalism by whatever means necessary.

As the early months of the Allende administration passed, the heated language of public discourse, the press, radio and television, as well as the intense debates of politicians in Congress or in public presentations; the politics that displaced impartial justice in the courts; the clashes in the streets and the pleas for more dialogue on the part of the constantly diminishing minority of those who subscribed to political legitimacy, all bore witness to the growth of this value conflict. The period from October of 1972 to the September 1973 coup saw its acceleration and foredoomed conclusion.

The relationship between this conflict in values and the military is three-fold. The military, as a vital part of the society, were full participants in the contradictions and spectrum of choices faced by their fellow citizens. As an institution, they were subjected also to the pressures of those who sought to utilize them as an instrument of their own political interests. Finally, and most important to the actual setting in motion of the coup, the spread of the value conflict, with the consequent breaking down of a national consensus (signalled as it was by widespread civil disobedience, as well as the pronouncements of authoritative figures and professional organizations), permitted the military to act with a reasonable security that it would be successful.

The division between enemies and friends, the rejection of neutrality, in short, the polarization of the society which characterized the situation prior to the coup, continued afterwards. But here a distinction began to exist.

Whereas prior to the coup, the restraints of existing rules of the game limited the violence of the situation, once these rules had been eliminated, there were no checks on the action of those who saw their enemies as totally outside the accepted range of discourse and, by extension, outside the pale of civilization. The violence of the military's repression of all it defined as enemy and foreign reflected the intensity of the conflict and the unleashing of two antithetical universes of discourse.

The clash of values provided the energy for the reaction of the military to the government of the UP, but other fundamental elements contributed to the style and skill with which it operated. To begin to understand this, we need take note of the ideological influences coming from both outside and within the continent in recent decades. If we go back to the start of the postwar era, the first important influence can be seen in the image of the Cold War. The associated spectres of external intervention and internal subversion, reinforced by the international implications of McCarthyism in the United States, set the terms of the Chilean military's understanding of its role. Convinced of the importance of national security, the military had moved from a symbolic participation in hemispheric defense to a more durable concern with the internal (i.e., communist) threat and the possibility of internal strife. It is this national security role which has prompted the military to train for guerrilla warfare, both of the urban and rural variety, and to acquire more sophisticated police techniques.

Such concerns were promoted by the military in the United States who in the postwar period had developed a special relationship with their counterparts in Chile. Through the efforts of the United States, dramatically symbolized by the U.S. Army training facilities in Panama (where courses in internal war, interrogation and the communist threat are offered), Chilean military officers and enlisted men acquired and continue to acquire competence in these various skills. It is this notion of national security which became the explicit justification for the Chilean coup, while the concept of internal war became a central feature of the regime's continuing self-legitimization.

The national security mentality is linked as well with the rejection of democracy, another part of the prevailing ideological climate. From the onset of the Brazilian regime in 1964, the most prominent feature of Latin American political evolution has been the rejection of formal representative rule. That rejection has been buttressed by the actions of the United States, both implicitly and explicitly. The culmination of the latter was the Rockefeller report, the principal statement of U.S. posture toward Latin America under the Nixon administration. For the first time in the history of inter-American relations, the government of the United States publicly condoned the rejection of democratic principles and inferentially approved the terms of the technocratic state, which in the case of Chile was the outcome of the value-and-class conflict that had brought about the termination of democracy.

It is in this rejection of democracy as a necessary feature of the new political order that we may find the significance of the military's action for the future of Chilean politics. Denying the thesis that all should participate in the making of social decisions, they argue that what is essential for the well-being of the society is the preservation of national integrity and the promotion of economic growth. The latter is, in essence, a technical problem whose solution depends on the application of appropriate techniques and skills. In this view, the making of the decisions in this area cannot be left to the whims of an erratic public opinion or the corruption and inefficiency of formal parliamentary democracy. Only those organizations with sufficient technical capacity and with an adequate notion of hierarchy, such as the armed forces, can possibly provide the basis for ordering and directing the society. For the rest, there are places in the hierarchical order that correspond to their capacities.

For the above school of thought, not only is a hierarchial order of a technocratic nature more efficacious, it is far less dangerous. Democracy in Chile was not merely corrupt, but bears a large measure of the blame for the disaster which was the Marxist experience. Therefore, it loses all value for the future. What is needed is an orderly society which channels participation and rewards through the security, efficiency, and technical proficiency it provides.

It is here that the significance of the value conflict ultimately becomes clear. From the initial choice between particular and societal interest, the society as a whole, and the military as instruments and as shapers of that social change, have moved toward not merely the elimination of their enemies, but the shaping of a new order. That new order, characterized by an emphasis on hierarchy, authority, and techniques rather than ideas, and the forceful repression of deviants, has a name: Fascism. ∎

The Brazilian Connection

Marlise Simons is a writer based in Mexico who reports frequently from Latin America for The Washington Post. *The following article appeared in that newspaper on January 7, 1974.*

Dr. Glycon de Paiva describes himself as "a mining engineer with a number of other interests." One of his recent interests, as a leading figure in a private anti-communist think tank here, was advising Chilean businessmen how to "prepare the ground" for the military overthrow of President Salvador Allende last fall.

Aristoteles Drummond, a founding member of a Brazilian paramilitary group, says he made two trips to Chile as a courier, taking money "for political actions" to a right-wing anti-Allende organization.

De Paiva and Drummond are two of a number of Brazilians who acknowledge helping Chilean foes of Allende. Other private and business interests in this country gave money, arms, and advice on political tactics.

There is no evidence that the Brazilian government played any role in this anti-Allende effort, although its sophisticated military intelligence network must have been aware of it. Brazil was never publicly hostile to Allende. Trade between the two countries increased sharply after Allende's election in 1970, and the Bank of Brazil's branch in Santiago was the only foreign financial institution there to escape Chilean government control.

A week before the September 11 coup, however, Brazil's Minister of War, General Orlando Geisel, told the Paraguayan ambassador to Brasilia that Chile was "already in military hands."

And within two days of the coup, Brazil surprised even its own diplomats by becoming the first country to recognize the new Chilean Junta.

Brasilia also immediately sent food and medicine and dispatched secret agents to Santiago to identify and interrogate Brazilians detained there. It was reliably learned here that two planeloads of Brazilian "extremist" prisoners arrived from Chile after the coup, one plane landing at Viracopos airport near São Paulo and the other, with 22 prisoners, at Rio's Galaeo airport.

The Brazilian Model

The coup that brought Brazil's armed forces to power in March, 1964, appears to have been used as a model for the Chilean military coup. The private sector played a crucial role in the preparation of both interventions, and the Brazilian businessmen who plotted the overthrow of the left-leaning administration of President Joao Goulart in 1964 were the same people who advised the Chilean right on how to deal with Marxist President Allende.

Soon after Allende's election, thousands of Chilean businessmen took their families and fortunes abroad, settling principally in Ecuador, Argentina, Venezuela, and Brazil.

In Brazil, the well-to-do Chileans quickly found work in multinational corporations or invested their capital in new companies or on the stock exchange. And in their dealings with Brazil's private sector, they quickly established contact with the architects of the 1964 Brazilian coup.

For example, they met Gilberto Huber, the wealthy owner of Brazil's largest printing concern, AGGS. In 1961, Huber and several powerful business associates had founded the Institute of Research and Social Studies (IPES), a political think tank with the specific object of preparing to overthrow Brazil's "communist-infiltrated" civilian government. Between 1961 and 1964, IPES organized, financed and coordinated anti-government activities and served as the bridge between private enterprise and the armed forces before the coup. The executive secretary of IPES was General Goulbery Couto e Silva, who founded Brazil's political intelligence agency in 1964.

One year ago, Chilean Luis Fuenzalida, who had joined Huber's company, told friends proudly: "We are going to throw out Allende, and I am learning from Huber what they did in 1964."

Another key member of IPES and one of its founders was Dr. de Paiva. A leading conservative economist, ardent anti-communist and an admirer of the United States, which he has visited frequently, de Paiva, who also acts as a consultant to a number of U.S. and multinational companies in Brazil, believes the Allende government was a "threat to the entire continent, but it was clear he would not be allowed to stay."

De Paiva was prepared to play a part. "After Allende took over, Chilean businessmen came here and asked for advice. I explained how they, the civilians, had to prepare the ground for the military to move," de Paiva recalls. "The recipe exists, and you can bake the cake any time. We saw how it worked in Brazil, and now again in Chile."

Dr. de Paiva's "recipe" involves creating political and economic chaos, fomenting discontent and deep fear of communism among employers and employees, blocking legislative efforts of the left, and organizing mass demonstrations and rallies—even acts of terrorism if necessary.

His recipe, Dr. de Paiva recognizes, requires a great deal of fund-raising. "A lot of money was put out to topple Allende," he said, "but the money businessmen spend against the left is not just an investment, it is an insurance policy."

Based on his experiences in IPES, Dr. de Paiva recommended to his Chilean visitors, whom he declined to identify, that first they create an intelligence system to study the actions of all key people and movements. "At IPES, for example, we had files on 45,000 people. Only after you have established the central information banks can anti-government actions be properly prepared and coordinated."

Like other veterans of the "businessmen's revolt" which set the stage for Brazil's '64 takeover, de Paiva readily admits that Chile's pre-coup political panorama was vastly different from Brazil's. For example, Chile's long democratic tradition had created tightly knit political and professional organizations, which, unlike Brazil's, encompassed a large proportion of its population. The counterrevolution in Chile could therefore make use of many opposition channels already in existence. In Brazil, the cooperation of the military was also more easily ensured since they had had a much more recent taste of political power than their Chilean counterparts. Yet Brazilian observers insist that in style and techniques their coup and Chile's are "cousins in the first degree."

After Chile's coup, a prominent Brazilian historian, who asked not to be named, said: "The first two days I felt I was living a Xerox copy of Brazil 1964. The language of Chile's military communiques justifying the coup, and their allegations that the 'communists' had been preparing a massacre and a military take-over, was so scandalously identical to ours, one almost presumes they had the same author."

Following in the footsteps of IPES and using its "recipe," Chile's *gremios*, or middle-class professional brotherhoods, with business and landowners' associations, created the Center for Public Opinion Studies. In the days before the coup, I visited one of the center's meeting places, a villa in Providencia, a residential district of Santiago. On the ground floor, notices encouraged people to take karate and first-aid lessons. The upstairs meeting rooms were covered with maps of the capital, divided into action zones, and filing systems reached to the ceiling.

Public Opinion Studies was one of the principal laboratories for strategies such as the crippling anti-government strikes, the press campaigns, the spreading of rumors and the use of shock troops during street demonstrations. The Providencia villa also served as headquarters for the women's movement which was so effectively used against the Marxist president.

Similarly, Chile's main opposition party, the Christian Democrats, founded the Corporation for Social, Economic and Cultural Studies (CODESEC) to design anti-Allende campaigns. It was financed by local contributions and made use of funds from the German and Italian Christian Democratic parties.

There have been reliable reports that CODESEC, with the help of psychologists and sociologists, planned "Operation Charlie," the hate campaign designed to bring about the fall of the army's commander-in-chief, General Carlos Prats. In late August, wives of high-ranking army officers (including the wife of General Oscar Bonilla, the Junta's present interior minister) gathered in front of Prats' home with militant women of the Christian Democratic Party and the neo-Facist "Fatherland and Freedom" movement. For hours they shouted insults and demanded Prats' resignation.

And it was Prats' resignation, two days later, that opened the door to the coup. As the general later explained, the hate campaign had been an important factor in his decision to leave his post.

Mobilizing the Women

Glycon de Paiva takes particular pride in the way "we taught the Chileans how to use their women against the Marxists. We ourselves created a large and successful women's movement, the Campaign of Women for Democracy, and Chile copied it."

In Chile, the opposition to Allende created Poder Femenino ("Feminine Power"), an organization of conservative housewives and professional and businesswomen who became famous for their "marches of the empty pots." Poder Femenino took its cues, its finances, and its meeting rooms from the *gremios*, the professional brotherhoods. Despite the directives from the male-dominated leadership, Dr. de Paiva explains that "the women must be made to feel they are organizing themselves, that they play a very important role. They are very cooperative and don't question the way men do."

"Women are the most effective weapon you have in politics," de Paiva continues. "They have time and they have a great capacity to display emotion and to mobilize quickly. For example, if you want to spread a rumor like 'the President has a drinking problem,' or 'he had a slight heart attack,' you use women. The next day it is around the country."

Both in Chile and Brazil, de Paiva points out, women were the most directly affected by leftist economic policies which create shortages in the shops. "Women complain at home, and they can poison the atmosphere. And of course, they are the wives and the mothers of the military and the politicians."

Yet the women's most crucial role, according to de Paiva, is "to prove to the military that they have wide civilian support." To de Paiva, therefore, it is no coincidence that ten days before the 1964 Brazilian coup, thousands of women marched through the streets of São Paulo—and that, five days before Allende's overthrow, Poder Femenino in Santiago held its largest rally ever.

Arms and Men

As preparations for the coup began in earnest last spring, Allende's foes feared there could be armed confrontations with leftist groups, which reportedly were armed themselves to defend the government. The activists on the right needed weapons, particularly for the paramilitary Fatherland and Freedom movement and for Proteco, the right-wing neighborhood committee. One of the places they turned to was Brazil.

Senator Pedro Ibañez of Chile's conservative National Party reportedly offered to help. The senator, who owns two supermarket chains and Chile's largest instant coffee company, is a frequent trader with Brazil. In June, dockworkers in the Brazilian coffee port of Santos charged that crates of "agricultural equipment" being shipped to Ibañez companies contained machine guns.

There also was fear on the right that a division within the military might result in a civil war. This concern was reportedly expressed to Brazilian friends, who suggested contact with Brazil's Anti-Communist Movement (MAC), a paramilitary body founded in 1961 and rather similar to Fatherland and Freedom.

Last spring, Aristoteles Drummond, one of MAC's founding members, announced to his friends in Rio de Janeiro: "They are going to get rid of Allende; and we have put 500 men at their disposal."

Later, during the first week of June, the Brazilian offer of "500 men" was repeated at a meeting in Antofagasta, a town in the north of Chile. Present at the meeting were Pablo Rodriguez, founder of Fatherland and Freedom, and Roberto Marshall, a former Chilean Army major who was expelled in 1960 for "subversion of the armed forces," and since then has lived in Bolivia.

Secret service sources in the Allende government claimed that at this meeting Fatherland and Freedom was offered $8 million by Marshall, who said he was acting on behalf of "Brazilian friends."

Funds from Brazil

There appeared to be no shortage of financial offers. In Rio de Janeiro, MAC members Drummond and Faustino Porto both disclosed that they had acted as couriers for money going from Brazil to Chile.

Drummond said he had traveled to Chile twice, "to take money for political actions to high officials of Fatherland and Freedom. Porto claimed the money destined for Chile came "from São Paulo and there was a lot of it." But he refused to identify the source.

The inflow of dollars from abroad was no secret to Allende. By early August it had become public knowledge that the organizers of the transportation strike preceding the coup were paying close to 35,000 drivers and owners of trucks, buses, and taxis to keep their vehicles off the road. Two taxi drivers told me they were each receiving 6,000 escudos (the equivalent of $3 at the black market rate) for every day they were not working, and a group of truck drivers said they received a per diem of $5, paid in dollar bills. On the basis of this, Allende aides calculated that the 45-day strike cost close to $7 million in pay-offs alone.

It was also an accepted fact that thousands of Chileans abroad were raising funds and sending in contributions. Jovino Novoa, a conservative lawyer and a member of the Chilean exile community in Buenos Aires, said in an interview: "Of course money was sent to Chile. We all did what we could, each according to his capacity."

The most successful fund-raiser among Chilean conservatives was Orlando Saenz, at the time president of Chile's Association of Manufacturers (SOFOFA) and now economic adviser to the foreign ministry in Santiago. On his fund-raising campaigns. Saenz traveled frequently to Brazil, Argentina, and the United States.

Last July, he called on General Juan Peron and Argentina's interim president, Raul Lastiri. Saenz reportedly received no offer of financial help from the Argentina government, but, according to a memorandum President Lastiri sent to Argentina's secret service, Saenz informed him that a military coup was being prepared.

In addition Saenz urged the Argentina government to interrupt its crucial shipments of low-priced wheat, meat and corn to Chile because its humanitarian attitude was "saving" the Marxist government.

Although high-ranking members of the Allende government repeatedly alleged that large amounts of dollars were entering Chile to pay for strikes and anti-Allende campaigns, they never substantiated their claims in public.

Three weeks before the coup, I raised the question of "foreign financing" in separate interviews with a senior member of the secret service and with a close aide of Allende. Both men declined to disclose any details "for policy reasons."

"We are presently negotiating our debt with Washington," Allende's aides said. "These negotiations are vital to us, and we cannot afford a scandal now." ■

Armed Forces: Behind the Façade of Unity

The following article, written by French journalist Philippe Labreveux, appeared in Le Monde, *January 12, 1974. It takes a close look at the Chilean armed forces—their role in the September coup, their systematic neutralization of the people and programs of the Popular Unity government, and their ruthless intervention in Chilean life.*

"But why did you have me arrested?" the bewildered priest asked the air vice marshal, who glared at him as though trying to detect someone else—maybe a demon, but certainly a Marxist—beneath the cassock. "Why send me to the Santiago National Stadium? Why deport me?" The vice marshal replied that the reason was immaterial.

There is no arguing with the Chilean officers. They talk a lot, thus filling up the silence they have imposed on their fellow citizens, but they keep bringing out the same old tired phrases, the same unanimous criticism of Salvador Allende and his followers. Indeed, the question arises not so much as to why the Chilean Army ousted the Popular Unity government, but why it did not do so sooner.

The delay was certainly not due to any lack of inclination. The Army's constitutionalist veneer had already begun to peel away by the time Allende came to power on November 4, 1970. The insubordination of General Roberto Viaux in October 1969 at the end of Eduardo Frei's presidential term and the murder a year later of the commander-in-chief, General René Schneider—two episodes in which several roles were played by the same civil and military personalities—showed that there was already considerable unrest within the Army.

President Allende took note of this and recognized that the "professional demands" which had largely provoked General Viaux's insubordination were justified. This action probably helped him to keep the Army out of strictly political decision-making for two years.

The members of the putsch are now only too willing to forget the favors they enjoyed. But the record shows how ungrateful the Army was to a government which was particularly generous just when it had to face a serious economic crisis. Between 1970 and 1973, the national defense budget rose by 650 percent, a huge increase even when inflation is taken into account. The difference seems even greater if 1969 is taken as a point of reference. This was the last year of Eduardo Frei's Christian Democrat government, which like that of Jorge Alessandri six years

previously, showed a sudden concern for the Army's well-being just before the presidential elections.

But Señor Allende was more generous even than the right. At the end of 1970, all ranks benefited from increased wages and improved living conditions; training stints abroad—an important factor in Chilean officers' advancement—were made available to more of them; and lastly, their weapons were modernized thanks to purchases from, for instance, France and Britain. Much of this material, both heavy and light, was used with effect during the September 11 putsch.

Allende's generosity was rivalled only by that of the United States. According to the military attache of one Western country, "When the Nixon government realized that it could not make Popular Unity see reason, it adopted an attitude which one might objectively describe as neutral hostility; but this didn't stop Washington keeping up and even striving to improve its relations with the Army."

For this purpose, the United States gave Chile privileged treatment and posted three military attaches and half a dozen assistants in Santiago. In all, there were about 30 officers in the whole country who kept in close contact with the Navy and the Air Force, the Fach.

When Chile nationalized the American copper companies in 1971, Washington subjected Santiago to an "invisible blockade": it withdrew the economic aid it had lavished on previous Chilean governments and put pressure on the World Bank's agencies to reduce or eliminate their credit lines. But at the same time, it increased its military aid programmes, which cost $45.5 million between 1970 and 1973; that is twice as much as between 1964 and 1970.

One of the chief reasons why the United States and the Chilean right were able to cancel out Allende's efforts to maintain the Army's political neutrality, and finally win it over, was the constant influence exerted by American officers on their Chilean colleagues during training spells. In the special bases of the Panama Canal Zone and in American military academies, there grew up a bond between officers of both armies which naturally resulted in a convergence of view.

Two hundred Chilean officers and noncommissioned officers go every year for training in the United States and Panama. One of them, General Washington Carbasco, told me that he had benefited enormously from his visit, during which he was taught "counter-insurgency" tactics. His political convictions were merely reinforced by his visit to Cuba in 1972, though he admits he got "an extraordinary welcome."

Allende and some military leaders, particularly in the Army, were aware of the danger of an officer corps steeped in anti-Marxist propaganda. One of his closest military advisers told me that "Allende wanted to maintain the best possible relations with the United States. Any breaking off, or even re-examination, of military relations with Washington would, in his view, have introduced a political factor into an essentially professional problem. In any case, such action would have no immediate effect on the thinking of Chilean officers."

General Prats, who was appointed head of the ground forces in 1970, did, however, try to put over his view, and that of several other generals, about the role of the military, and in a series of meetings and informal "chats" did his best to convince his colleagues to respect the Constitution. His aim was to coax them into the "center of the political system," where he felt the Popular Unity and the

Christian Democrats would have to converge if Chilean society were not to collapse.

He failed. First, he could not convince Allende soon enough of the urgency of his project. Secondly, the ditherings of the government, torn between communists and far leftists, conciliators and hotheads, in addition to the Christian Democrat Party's shift to the right under the influence of Frei, prevented any such reconciliation.

General Prats, who belonged to the armed forces' left, if not the extreme left (this was the main reason for his failure), made an exit at that point. When he returned from an extended tour of Europe last May, during which he turned down a Soviet offer of tanks because of opposition from his colleagues, he found the situation critical. He managed to quell the June 29 uprising of Colonel Souper, but the conspiracy already had too many ramifications for him to be able to punish all the guilty.

Why then, did it take so long for the *coup de grace* to be given a government in the throes of an economic crisis so cleverly exploited and made worse by the rich industrialists, farmers, shopkeepers, and truckers? The putschists wanted to get rid of the last bulwarks of legalism—Admiral Raúl Montero and, above all, General Prats —so that they could project the image of total unanimity within the armed forces. In other words, they wanted to 'constitutionalize' the *coup d'état*.

When Prats finally resigned, he still hoped that his successor, General Augusto Pinochet, who had been chief of staff for three years, would be able to carry out the purge that was now necessary. His hopes were in vain.

The right-wing press resumed the offensive and was followed by a series of out-and-out attacks by the *gremios*—first the truckers, and then the shopkeepers and professional people. The Navy and the Air Force had made their positions clear, and, although there were a few recalcitrant elements in the Army, everyone on the right felt sure that they would step back into line, either voluntarily or under force.

The unity of the armed forces is of axiomatic importance in South America. Such unity in Chile meant that there would be no civil war. The Army knew this very well, as did Allende's supporters who immediately withdrew from the battle—some of them like the communists and "Mirista" in orderly fashion, and others, the socialists, in the confused manner that was their characteristic while in power.

Even so, there was a real explosion on September 11: the Army's anger was all the greater for having been so long repressed. Since the aims of the putschists were to take over "in the shortest possible time" and "with minimum loss of life," one can understand the logic of their bombardment of the presidential palace, the merciless destruction of certain points of resistance, and the "exemplary" execution of snipers. But it is extremely difficult to explain the indiscriminate repression of the Chilean people—the raids, the torture, the murders, and the endless suffering inflicted on men, women, and children.

The short document published on September 11 outlining the "reasons for the Junta" simply claims to justify "the destruction of a government which was initially legitimate, but which later lapsed into flagrant illegitimacy." The crimes of a civil war which never took place had to be justified, though not recognized, so a story was made up which claimed that the enemy was preparing a horrible massacre. Aided by a few newspapers, the public ended up believing the imaginary horrors while resolutely refusing to see the ghastly reality. One of these papers wrote: "Extremists in Osorno distributed 400 metal files to the inhabitants of the Elmo-Catalan *población* so they could sharpen their shovels and use them as people's guillotines on Army officers, policemen and opposition leaders. The speedy intervention of the Army, however. . . . " Decidedly, there's no arguing with the Chilean officers.

One month after the *coup d'état*, General Pinochet stated: "To our minds there are neither victors nor vanquished." Surely a case of wishful thinking, as can be seen when one looks at the division in both camps.

From 1970 to 1973, the Navy and the Air Force were more united and showed more hostility to Allende than their colleagues in the Army and the police: they kept in contact with the pressure groups, the *gremios* and other professional organizations, and with the parties which, as the months went by, slithered into the opposition camp. They also maintained, and even strengthened, their traditionally strong links with the United States.

When it came to splitting the booty, it was the Navy which took the lion's share. The Army (28,000 men including 9,000 regulars) now has three ministries (interior, housing, and secretariat to the government), as have the Air Force (public works, agriculture, and health) and the police (labor, land and colonial territories, and mines). The Navy, on the other hand, with its 21,000 men and 1,200 regulars, obtained four of the most important ministries: foreign affairs, defense, education, and finance; on top of that, the Ministry of Justice went to the former head of the international law department of the naval general staff.

Of the three services, the Navy is probably the best prepared for government. The number of regulars is the same as in the Army, but in the naval school there is a stricter selection, a longer period of training, and a wider range of subjects studied than in the equivalent schools for the Army and Air Force. It is hardly surprising that the Navy is the only service which seems to attract the sons of well-off parents and that it very soon backed the cause of the "momios" (the privileged) against the Allende government.

The Minister of Finance, Admiral Lorenzo Gotuzzo, has lifted price controls on the majority of products, including many essential foodstuffs; bread and oil have gone up by 256 percent, sugar by 500 percent, and tea by 1,800 percent. "The party is over," announced the Admiral. "Now the bill must be paid."

The bill will be paid by the tens of thousands of people who have been sacked for political reasons and employees whose wages are now virtually frozen. At the same time, there is rampant inflation (amounting to about 1,000 percent for 1973), and sooner or later wages will have to be increased in order to avoid both a recession and widespread unrest. This has been promised, but it seems fairly certain that within six months at the most the Junta will have neutralized the sweeping redistribution of income imposed by the previous government during its first two years in office.

The Ministry of Economy was given immediately after the putsch to Army General Rolando Gonzales, but his "populist" tendencies were not to the liking of the industrialists whose firms were nationalized from 1970 to 1973, and the ministry was transferred to Fernando Leníz, head of Chile's largest press concern, the Mercurio Group.

Admiral Ismael Huerta, the Foreign Minister, whose economic adviser is the leading industrialist, Orlando Saenz, has reassured international financial circles: the Junta is prepared to grant compensation to the American copper companies which were nationalized in 1971. The representatives of Dow Chemical whom I met in Concepción when they were inspecting the works of their subsidiary, Petrodow (nationalized in 1972), said that Admiral Huerta had contacted them himself just two days after the *coup d'état*.

As for Señor Saenz, he was the Junta's treasurer: before the putsch, he travelled the length and breadth of the "free" world in search of financial support. He apparently approached various big Swiss banks and Argentine businessmen, though both quarters, as is hardly surprising, deny having agreed to help. But it would seem that the Brazilians did supply generous amounts of money and arms to civilians of the extreme right-wing civilian group, Patria y Libertad. And in the United States, such concerns as ITT were only too willing to oblige. Anyway, wherever the money came from, someone had to finance the strikes (for a month and a half, the truckers got 2,000 escudos a day each), pay for travel, and arm the terrorists. The cost of a *coup d'état* runs into millions of dollars.

The breach of the Constitution and the downfall of the Allende government was certainly opposed by elements within the armed forces, which had to be, and were, neutralized. Even so, the policies since adopted by the Junta under the impetus of the Navy and the Air Force are not to the taste of all officers. But as they consider unity essential, they prefer to give an impression of perfect unanimity and draw a veil over any internal disagreements which may exist.

This is hardly surprising, since any protesting voice has been silenced by exemplary punishment. General Prats has doubtless received preferential treatment: he has merely been exiled. But other generals have been arrested. Squadron leader Alamiro Castillo has sought refuge in the Argentine Embassy, and flight lieutenant Raul Vergara has been arrested. Several Navy men and a retired captain are at present awaiting trial by a military court. And Colonel Cantuarias, head of a school for alpine riflemen, apparently committed suicide on October 3. The Junta is extremely irritated by any mention, public or private, of these cases.

But the real hawks in the Junta number only four, and one wonders how long they will be able to keep the upper hand. The "doves" (the term is of course a relative one) often use a different kind of language. The Minister of the Interior, General Oscar Bonilla, spends his time visiting the slums and factories of Santiago, reassuring the workers that they will not lose their social advantages and decrying the "old-fashioned employers who leave but a few crumbs to the workers."

No doubt General Bonilla can afford to adopt such populist tones: the least that could be said of such a seasoned conspirator is that he had no warm feelings towards Allende and his followers. But it could be that he is reflecting the view of an Army which has been dragged by the two other services into a process of bloody revenge, and which is trying to keep its distance in order to be able to take political control when the time comes.

For the Army seems to be more qualified to meet the wishes of the people: its officers come from relatively modest backgrounds, they travel a lot, and they are in more frequent contact with civilians than their colleagues in the Navy and Air Force. General Washington Carrasco's concern for the miners of Lota and Schwager reflects his anxiety about the social scene. Colonel Hernan Ramirez has expressed doubts as to whether the armed forces are going to be able to maintain their present level of "popularity": he is the only officer I met who does not seem to have too many illusions about the future of the regime. But the Army also has its "hawks," who share the opinions of the Navy and of Air Force General Gustavo Leigh, probably the most hawkish member of the Junta.

The rooting out of Allende supporters seems to have become more intense than ever. The political police are now better informed and coordinated and able to rely more heavily on interrogation under torture. Even the military courts have been told to be more severe: it is said in Santiago that several military leaders who toured the provinces during the second half of October criticized the laxity of certain garrisons and the "liberalism" of the judges.

As a result, some people who had already been sentenced to imprisonment were shot. And in La Serena, a group of Allende partisans (including a factory manager) who had been sentenced to 60 days in jail are said to have suffered the same fate, along with the firing squad that had refused to carry out its orders.

The ruthless intervention of the armed forces in Chilean life completely neutralized those who had occupied the political stage up until September 11. So the only hope of putting a halt to the all-destroying machinery of the military must lie within the military itself. ∎

The Nixon-Kissinger Doctrine and the Meaning of Chile

Richard J. Barnet presented the following paper to a conference of the Transnational Institute held in Amsterdam, Holland, April 22-24, 1974. A nonprofit organization devoted to research and the exchange of ideas, the Transnational Institute is a newly founded affiliate of the Institute for Policy Studies in Washington, D.C., of which Mr. Barnet is a member. Starting from the premise that "United States complicity in the overthrow of the Allende experiment is evident," Mr. Barnet examines "the new assumptions about the world that Henry Kissinger brought to the White House." Among these: (1) the Soviet Union evidently will no longer exert its power to protect another socialist experiment in the Western Hemisphere, and (2) the "rollback" of Soviet and Chinese power is impractical, short of nuclear confrontation. "Kissinger is now willing to accord legitimacy to established revolutionary power to isolate it from revolutionary movements which at all costs must be denied legitimacy." Nixon and Kissinger, he concludes, "have gambled heavily on the cynicism of public opinion across the globe. . . . betting that a world that has been convulsed by war, revolution and confrontation for three generations would welcome a generation of peace under American hegemony, however unjust, however repressive of those who resist it."

The role of the United States in the destruction of Chilean democracy offers us the first clear vision of how the Number One Nation, as Lyndon Johnson used to call the American Empire, is adjusting to the new political realities of the 1970s. The complicity of the United States in the overthrow of the Allende experiment is evident; only the extent and character of its participation remains to be analyzed. My focus this evening is not on the details of the U.S. intervention in Chile but on what that event teaches us about the evolution of the Nixon-Kissinger Doctrine and its application around the world.

It is necessary, however, to recall a few details concerning the operations of American strategy before we examine the assumptions behind it. We know that three years before the coup Henry Kissinger stated privately that the success of the Unidad Popular would present the "gravest problems" for American interests in the rest of Latin America and even in Europe. We know that the official U.S. lending agency, the Eximbank, refused to continue credits to Chile to permit the importation of vital materials, spare parts and food from the United States. We know that the United States used its dominant position in the multilateral agencies IDB and the World Bank to boycott loans to Chile (except for loans to two conservative universities). We know that U.S. aid was cut off except for a few training grants, visits of the American Institute of Free Labor Development, the AFL-CIO organization that seeks to preserve American influence in the Latin American labor movements, and military aid. (In the last pre-Allende year, U.S. military aid was down to $800,000. In 1972, it was $12.3 million.) We know that Brazilian businessmen and conservative Chileans in Brazil, some working for multinational corporations, financed the subversion of the Allende government. (The Brazilian magazine *Veja* reports the direct involvement of an official of an American business organization in this operation.) We know that ITT, Kennecott, and other multinational companies have pursued strategies to produce "economic chaos" and to squeeze the Allende government. We know that despite cautious public rhetoric the Nixon Administration has welcomed the coup and sees it as a vindication of its policies.

The Chilean catastrophe seemed, indeed, to confirm all the new assumptions about the world that Henry Kissinger brought to the White House. First, the Soviet Union will not, it appears, use its power to protect another socialist experiment in the Western Hemisphere. Probably the most important revision of U.S. Cold War theory was the replacement of what might be called the J. Edgar Hoover conspiracy theory of international communism. Today, unlike during the Acheson-Dulles-Rusk era, the Soviet Union is regarded as a modestly ambitious status quo power interested in defending its security; preserving and, where possible, cautiously expanding its power; building an industrial consumer society in its huge expanse; and controlling its own populations. In Kissinger's view, it is not interested in making a revolution anywhere—including Russia. The continuing nightmare of the Rusk era—that liberation movements were puppets on a long string from Moscow—has been replaced by a much more realistic assessment. Kissinger is confident that he can isolate the liberation movements from the Soviet Union and, in particular, can insure Soviet non-interference in American plans for the Western Hemisphere, by offering the Kremlin an ambiguous junior partnership in building

a "generation of peace." The confrontation over Cuba is not to be repeated. So encouraged was the United States by the neutralization of Soviet Power in Vietnam that it seemed virtually assured that the Kremlin would adopt a hands-off policy toward Chile. (Whether Kissinger's assumptions are valid for the future remains to be seen.)

The second new assumption that Kissinger brought to the White House was that "rollback," as Dulles used to call it, of Soviet and Chinese power was impractical. Until Nixon, it was a basic tenet of U.S. foreign policy that the continued application of massive economic and military power on the periphery of what used to be called the Sino-Soviet bloc would eventually cause the dissolution or radical transformation (in a conservative direction) of Soviet and Chinese power. To make international pariahs of Russia and China would deny them the legitimacy they would need to survive. But Nixon and Kissinger have understood that socialism cannot be dislodged from the Soviet Union and China except at the cost of nuclear war. Therefore it is time to recognize the Soviet Revolution of 1917 and the Chinese Revolution of 1949.

Kissinger is now willing to accord legitimacy to established revolutionary power in order to isolate it from revolutionary movements which at all costs must be denied legitimacy. Acceptance of Soviet and Chinese power is thus the price of preventing further revolutionary inroads into the Third World. Revolutionary power is to be managed with the judicious use of the carrot and the stick. The largest carrot is the accord of legitimacy itself. Smaller carrots include trade arrangements, wheat deals, and credits. But with respect to the Soviet Union particularly, the stick remains crucial. The United States hopes to contain Soviet power by maintaining a massive superiority of nuclear weapons, highly maneuverable strike forces (principally Air Force and Navy), and a network of Deputy Peacekeepers, such as South Vietnam, Greece, Iran, and Brazil, who are able to maintain American influence in strategic areas of the world without the direct involvement of U.S. troops. Some of these pillars of Kissinger's "structure of peace" do their job by merely surviving. Some, like Brazil and Iran, are playing an active policeman's role in other countries of the region. Brazilians helped to train and finance the September 11 coup. "Subversion against Allende was surprisingly cheap," a Brazilian businessman is quoted in an authoritative *Washington Post* report. "The money we sent would go a long way on the black market." In the Middle East the Shah of Iran is amassing one of the largest armies in the world and is playing approximately the same role in relation to South Yemen as Brazil played with respect to Chile.

But, as Kissinger has frequently pointed out in his writings, a military capability no matter how enormous is not sufficient if it is not backed up by a strong will to commit it. To counter any Soviet "misunderstanding" that as a result of Vietnam the United States is becoming passive, the Pentagon has resorted to a world-wide alert, has given new importance to tactical nuclear weapons in strategic doctrine, and has proposed once again a first-strike counterforce posture for the Strategic Air Command. The Soviet Union is to be admitted in certain parts of the world as junior partner, but it must be continually reminded not to presume upon the relationship.

The third assumption undergirding Kissinger's new view of the world is that a successful foreign policy must be based on conservative, not liberal, rhetoric. Like many writers on foreign policy of the United States, including de Tocqueville, the Secretary of State has worried since he was a graduate student about the difficulties of reconciling great imperial tasks with the hopes, fears, and prejudices of a democratic population. The anti-war movement that sprang up in reaction to the prospect of ever-escalating American casualties in a distant and uncertain war posed, in Kissinger's view, the most serious challenge to the projection of American power that had developed in the Cold War—far more serious than any threat posed by the Soviets. If the American President were unable to act because he feared the pacifism and the isolationism of the American people, then the American Century was over. American power would ebb quietly away, and other nations would move in discreetly to pick up the pieces. Thus the real danger of Chile from the perspective of the White House was that the presence of a self-acknowledged Marxist in the American Hemisphere appeared to confirm the fact that the United States had lost its hold. (Just 20 years ago the CIA sent airplanes and troops against Guatemala City to overthrow a far more tentative nationalist who had dared to expropriate some banana lands.) Were the United States to tolerate a constitutional regime prepared to move to socialism in the American Hemisphere, it would be interpreted as a license for radical change around the world. The "domino effect" of a successful Chilean experiment, Kissinger understood, was far greater than the "domino effect" of a Cuba or a Vietnam, because the conditions could be more easily duplicated in other strategic areas of the world. Liberation movements are not easily exportable, but the idea of achieving socialism through constitutional process could be spread by a successful demonstration.

For the architects of American foreign policy the principal challenge was to construct a new consensus to replace the one that had collapsed in the Vietnam war, one that would permit the United States to take the minimum action necessary to prevent Chile and future Chiles from succeeding. The traditional anti-communist consensus was broken in the late 1960s. The Soviet Union was no longer monolithic and the embodiment of evil. It had become ally as well as enemy, trading partner as well as target. The Free World had been unmasked for many Americans as a motley collection of repressive, terrorist regimes. When the pictures of tiger cages in Vietnam and of U.S. tanks being used to shoot down Greek students in the streets and accounts of torture in Brazil began to filter into American consciousness, it became impossible to repeat the John F. Kennedy rhetoric about America as the "watchman on the ramparts of world freedom." Since the days of Acheson and Dulles the U.S. had fought the Cold War under the banner of liberalism and freedom. Kissinger, the student of Metternich, has understood the dangers of this. When nations profess morality, at least some people will expect them to adhere to it. Moral inhibitions are an impossible straight jacket. The rhetoric of crusade leads to the contradictions of defending "freedom" in South Vietnam and "democracy" in Greece.

Henry Kissinger has understood that the rhetoric of peace is both more popular and more practical than the rhetoric of freedom. His vision is indeed of a "world restored," to use the title of one of his books. It is a world of the Peace of Westphalia where each sovereign is free to profess whatever he wishes within his own territory except an ideology such as national liberation or socialism which threatens to undermine the system. Established

socialist regimes, as we have seen, are accorded Westphalian treatment. Repressive regimes which are prepared to use massive brutality to suppress democratic social change no longer need to be the basis of embarrassment and apology. On Southern Africa, Brazil, and Vietnam, the position of the United States is now clear. Internal police repression carried on without pity and without restraint preserves "peace" and "stability" and obviates the necessity of direct American military involvement. To the extent that such regimes can act as their own policemen, the United States can assume a lower profile in what Dean Rusk used to call "organizing the peace."

John Foster Dulles used to talk about peace with justice, but Kissinger, to quote another of his book titles, knows that there is a "necessity of choice." He and Nixon have gambled heavily on the cynicism of public opinion across the globe, assuming that people will put up with invisible violence and the death sentence of starvation that hovers over millions and back-room torture to avoid the visible violence of war and revolution. Peace is order and order is the continuation of the status quo. Kissinger is betting that a world that has been convulsed by war, revolution, and confrontation for three generations would welcome a generation of peace under American hegemony, however unjust, however repressive of those who resist it. That he now appears as the world's most admired public figure, praised in Peking as well as Rio, shows how acute his political instinct has been. The new "realism" of this generation's "tough guy," as Nelson Rockefeller calls him, has caught on. People are prepared to be deceived in exchange for a generation of peace, and that, quite literally, is all that he has promised.

As the stumbling blocks to peace—Brezhnev, Chou, Le Duc Tho, Sadat—appear to fall in line, the Kissinger policy is greeted with almost universal admiration. "Peace with honor" in Indochina is stipulated, and the stipulation is accepted by almost everybody despite the fact that, in clear violation of the Paris accords, the United States is sending $1.7 billion in military and economic aid to the Thieu régime this fiscal year, maintains over 10,000 U.S. personnel in South Vietnam, and has supported completely Thieu's refusal to engage in a political contest for the future of Vietnam, as was clearly contemplated by the agreements. Vietnam has disappeared from the headlines, and that is peace. When the Chilean coup occurred it was front-page news in the United States for about three weeks. As predicted, once the imposition of a fascist state was a *fait accompli*, political concern in the United States virtually vanished, just as it had already vanished over Indochina. The Watergate crisis which so undermined the credibility of Richard Nixon actually enhanced the credibility of the Kissinger foreign policy. First, Kissinger himself became a hero by default, an intelligent, occasionally witty man, only peripherally involved with the cruder forms of espionage in which the rest of the Nixon entourage had specialized, who seemed unable to fail. But, more important, the barrage of Watergate revelations reinforced public cynicism. To a considerable extent the public has accepted Nixon's defense. In foreign policy at least governments *are* duplicitous. Crime *is* a traditional instrument of rule. The liberal innocence which was at the heart of much of the Vietnam protest is gone. The patriotism which took the rhetoric of freedom seriously has largely evaporated and people are both confused and numb, an ideal state of affairs for carrying on a Metternichean foreign policy. ∎

A Sad Double Standard

The following commentary by columnist Tom Wicker appeared on the "Op Ed" page of The New York Times, *Sunday, March 10, 1974. Mr. Wicker is an associate editor of that paper.*

Two items from *The New York Times*:

March 8, 1974: "Secretary of State Kissinger told a Senate committee today that he would recommend a veto of the Nixon Administration's own trade bill if Congress refused to grant trade concessions to the Soviet Union because of its restrictions on the free emigration of Jews and others."

Feb. 28, 1974: "[A high United States official] pointed out that the Central Intelligence Agency had rejected an offer by the International Telephone and Telegraph Corporation of $1 million in September, 1970, to be spent in Chile to defeat the Socialist candidate for the presidency, Salvador Allende Gossens. The offer was made to Richard M. Helms, who was then the Director of Central Intelligence, by the agency's former director, John A. McCone, who had become an ITT board member."

There is no particular connection between these two items—except that there is now an intensive effort in Congress to deny most-favored-nation trading status to the Soviet Union if it continues to restrict the emigration of Jews; and that there was in 1970, and throughout his presidency, an intense effort by ITT and others to prevent or destroy Mr. Allende's Government in Chile. But the Nixon Administration that Mr. Kissinger represented throughout the period did not threaten or disapprove the latter effort; quite the contrary.

The CIA did turn down the ITT money (although nothing seems to have been done about the scandalous attempt by a former CIA director to bribe the agency, with private money, to undertake interference in the internal politics of another country). But the Nixon Administration restricted that Government's ability to get foreign credit and cut off foreign aid to it, continuing only to supply arms and training to the Chilean military.

Thus, it was troops trained by the United States and armed with American weapons who overthrew the Allende Government last fall and—as now seems certain—murdered Mr. Allende.

There are numerous evidences that the officers who ordered the bloody coup and the later execution of what appears to have been thousands of Chileans were encouraged in their planning by American supporters, both official and unofficial. Nor did the Nixon Administration and its embassy officials in Santiago distinguish themselves in saving the lives of refugees, including some Americans.

The Chilean story is only gradually coming to light, but what is known is in sad contrast to Mr. Kissinger's position on Soviet emigration policies. He said he regards détente as of such overriding importance that the United States must not endanger it by trying to influence internal Soviet policies.

On the other hand, in pursuit of what it conceived to be the national interest, the Nixon Administration appears to have been a considerable influence in the opposition to, and overthrow of, the Allende Government. Before that, of course, various American Governments had had a hand in numerous interventions (for example, the overthrow of Guatemala's elected left-wing Government in the nineteen-fifties).

This reflects a double standard if ever there was one. It is a double standard in the sense that American interests (as perceived by the Administration in power) may require intervention in one country's internal affairs but forbid it in another. It is an even more deplorable double standard in that it seems to permit intervention for certain selfish political or economic purposes but not for the purpose of upholding human rights.

This is not necessarily to argue that Mr. Kissinger is altogether wrong on the Soviet emigration question; there is in fact much to support his position. Anyway, to take a stand for human rights in the Soviet Union might seem a bit ludicrous, since the Administration has such strong ties to Greece, the Chilean Junta, Spain, Portugal, South Vietnam, South Korea, the Philippines and other strong-arm governments.

The members of Congress who are demanding Soviet concessions on emigration, moreover, have their own double standard; they are not so vocal about Chilean refugees, of whom only a handful have been admitted to this country, or about human rights in the numerous other repressive governments to which they annually vote military and other forms of aid. The Jewish emigration question, after all, is of interest to many of them only for obvious domestic political reasons.

Under the auspices of the Fund for New Priorities, some of the same members of Congress did take part the other day in public hearings on the situation in Chile. That would be an excellent place for them to show a more general concern for human rights—as well as for the established American double standard toward those rights. ■

The Counterrevolution

Dale Johnson is Chairman of the Sociology Department of Livingston College, Rutgers University, and editor of The Chilean Road to Socialism *(Anchor Press/Doubleday, 1973). In the article below, which appeared in* Christianity & Crisis, *October 29, 1973, the author notes that the current regime in Chile has adhered to the pattern of "classic European Fascism" with a "colonial face." "Colonial economic dependence, with the multinational corporations and the U.S. government in control, generates structures of power and class privilege in the periphery nations that have been fundamental since Nazi Germany."*

Alone among Latin American nations, the Republic of Chile withstood 35 years of intense internal and external pressures for authoritarian solutions to the problems of economic underdevelopment, social inequality and injustice, and national subjugation to centers of international power. For most of this century Chile had been Latin America's only functioning democracy.

It is true that this formal democracy masked a sociopolitical reality in which the reigns of power were manipulated by the few for their own benefit. Nevertheless, the demands for social justice and social change by Chilean workers, peasants and students, the decades of struggle by men like Salvador Allende and the persistence and discipline of the working-class parties (the Communist and Socialist parties in particular) had made Chile the only country in the hemisphere where routine force and violence against advocates of change and oppressed people had been constrained to some degree by the legality of a functioning constitutional order. The historical achievement of this formal democracy insured, until the events of mid-September, the elementary rights of citizenship to most Chileans, but it did not carry with it social justice and the institutional basis for social and economic development.

After Allende's election to the presidency in 1970, Chile's formal democracy began to gain greater substance and content. For the first time a government took office that was elected by popular vote (twice confirmed in subsequent municipal and parliamentary elections), and that represented the aspirations of workers, peasants and the poor.

But Allende assumed the presidency in the midst of conspiracies to impede the continuity of the constitutional order. The Commander in Chief of the Armed Forces, General René Schneider, one of the few strict constitutionalists among high-ranking Chilean officers, was assassinated in a plot to force a military intervention. The CIA, the International Telephone and Telegraph Co. (ITT), right-wing Chilean military officers and reactionary Chilean moneyed elements unsuccessfully probed different tactics to steal the election from the left and working people.

The Popular Unity, a nonrevolutionary government based on an alliance of Socialist, Communist and other left-of-center parties, effected modest but meaningful social reforms that ameliorated the conditions of the nation's working people. These reforms—income redistribution favoring the workers, real agrarian reform, improvement of the social security systems, participation in the management of factories and farms—also gave many poor and oppressed people a greater sense of dignity and some measure of real participation in society.

Each gain by the workers, peasants and the poor was perceived as a loss by the entrenched class interests. The government nationalized key foreign-owned mines and industries, and thus it ended the transfer of the country's wealth abroad while shifting control of vital economic decisions from U.S.-based multinational corporations to the Chilean nation. Responding to Chile's economic nationalism, the affected corporations, U.S. government agencies and international banking institutions imposed a series of increasingly tough economic sanctions. Nevertheless, some measure of power did shift from the hands of wealthy (but still powerful) Chileans and the bureaucratic state into the hands of workers.

At this point (reached toward the end of 1972), the entrenched interests began serious conversations with military officers about a "total solution." Meanwhile, Chile's "free press" became so free that newspapers, television and radio stations, traditionally controlled by the most intransigent sectors of the opposition, emitted the most atrocious lies about the government and slander of the President and his supporters. For example, there was a campaign of character assassination against General Prats, former Commander in Chief and a strict constitutionalist officer. General Prats, now in exile, was an obstacle to the reactionary officers' and civilian opposition's plotting to destroy the constitutional order. This year the media began to call openly for the violent overthrow of the government.

The Allende government did not use force against its opponents, even when opposition forces carried out acts—political strikes to overthrow the government, the organization of paramilitary civilian forces and sabotage—that in any other nation would have been treated as intolerable acts of sedition against the legal order. Rather than relying upon the force of the state (in part denied to the government by the political unreliability of the military and police forces) or arming the government's working-class supporters and party militants, the governing Popular Unity coalition, especially the President himself and the Communist Party, continuously pursued the construction of democratic socialism through a policy of moderation and conciliation.

But all efforts to accommodate meaningful institutional and social changes to the intransigence of the increasingly united, militant and violent opposition failed. The Allende government was overthrown finally by the application of violence unparalleled anywhere in the bitter history of Latin American military interventions to contain and repress forces of change.

Fascism, Chilean Style

The current regime has most of the characteristics of classic European fascism, except that the Chilean variety has a clearly colonial face, as I will indicate.

(1) *The extent and style of military violence*, beginning with the razing by artillery fire and air attacks of the presidential palace and the killing of Allende and his aides. Over 1,000 were reported dead within 24 hours of the military insurrection, and the stench of burning bodies in different locations in Santiago was widely reported. A telephone report by Amnesty International to a doctor in a Santiago hospital on September 16 indicated that in the few days since the coup 5,000 dead had been processed in that hospital alone. U.S. wire services reported unofficial estimates of 2,000 to 20,000 dead by the end of September.

Early news dispatches also indicated that the repression was aimed primarily at the imprisonment or physical extermination of the militants of all left organizations and the grass roots leadership of the working class. Those who resisted in any way were killed on the spot. The Junta admitted to herding over 7,000 political prisoners into the National Stadium of Santiago; many more continue to be interned in other locations. People released from the stadium reported savage beatings of prisoners and the execution of hundreds. The number of political prisoners and atrocities have mounted daily as the military's shock troops conduct house-to-house searches and round-ups. European and Latin American news agencies reported that slum settlements with effective grass-roots organization were razed to the ground and worker-occupied factories were destroyed.

(2) *The military operation was ruthlessly calculated in the face of clearly predictable consequences*. (Systematic military operations to eliminate threats to the established order are not by themselves necessarily fascist in character.) The high-ranking officers who planned the revolt and the civilian opposition that maneuvered the preceding political crisis and openly called for military intervention were fully cognizant of the high level of resistance that would be offered by Chilean workers, peasants, young people and the organized left. They acted with the knowl-

edge that the outcome could well be fratricidal war involving thousands upon thousands of deaths and the devastation of the economy. They knew that however successful the initial repression might be the resistance would regroup and prepare itself for a long struggle.

The imposition of a totalitarian state to overcome this resistance simply transformed the history of class conflict within the institutionality of Chile's underdeveloped capitalism and democratic policy into an indefinite future of class war. The Junta itself, two weeks after the coup, declared the nation to be "in a state of war."

(3) *The Junta has attempted to whip up a chauvinist, anti-foreign phobia.* Thousands of political refugees from dictatorial military regimes in other Latin American countries (Brazil, Bolivia, Paraguay, Uruguay, Guatemala) have been singled out as special scapegoats. Refugees have been killed, interned or deported to their countries of origin where they face certain imprisonment, torture or execution. Antisemitic propaganda has been attributed to civilian right-wing sources. Military units attacked the Cuban Embassy and a Cuban merchant ship in international waters. 'Subversive" books and literature are seized and burned; citizens are interrogated and, if they are foreign nationals or in disfavor with the fascists, arrested. Such anti-foreign acts and rhetoric mask the regime's own colonial fascist essence. Already the Junta has announced that it welcomes private foreign investment and the reopening of talks about the nationalized copper mines.

Destroying Democratic Institutions

(4) The regime has *dismantled Chile's democratic institutions in order to bring about a counterrevolution.* The military has seized control of every institution of Chilean society to make it an instrument of a totalitarian state. The Junta has dissolved Congress and abolished all political parties. (The parties supporting the Allende government received 44 percent of the vote in the March 1973 congressional elections and 51 percent in the 1971 municipal elections.) Chilean unions, which were among the strongest in Latin America, and other worker organizations have been destroyed and their leadership hunted down as criminals. The democratic Constitution has been suspended, and a new one is being drafted that will give a legal face to military dictatorship. The traditionally free press and all other democratic rights of the Chilean people have been eliminated. A total police state has been established.

Moreover, the declared political motive of the military and civilian instigators of the reaction was not simply to overthrow Allende and then to place a more moderate government in power that would avert civil war and respect the changes achieved. Its purpose was and remains counterrevolutionary: to crush the left and the organized power of the working class and peasants, to "extirpate the Marxist cancer," to reverse all the forward-looking programs of the Allende government, to take away the real social and economic benefits and democratic rights gained by ordinary Chilean citizens, and to hand control of the sources of wealth and economic power back to the Chilean oligarchy and their foreign business associates. To accomplish all this requires the kind of drastic action that only the most barbaric of fascist mentalities can conceive.

Fidel Castro, at the conclusion of a visit in 1971 that had provoked considerable opposition, issued a prophetic warning to the Chilean people: "What do the exploiters do when their own institutions no longer guarantee their

domination? . . . They simply go ahead and destroy them. . . . And we have been able to verify the manifestations of that law of history in which the reactionaries and the exploiters in their desperation—and mainly supported from the outside—generated that political phenomenon, that reactionary current, fascism."

Salvador Allende and the Chilean left understood this danger very well. Nevertheless, they proceeded, in Allende's words, in "the Chilean way," that is, on the assumption that changes can be made in an externally dependent, underdeveloped capitalist society by gradualist, nonviolent and democratic means. Less than two years later the vested interests, mainly supported from the outside, chose to destroy all their democratic and civil traditions in order to preserve their most cherished institutions: private property, monopoly of power, social inequality and class privilege. Ironically, Marxist Salvador Allende and the Communist Party of Chile demonstrated themselves to be the most faithful—and probably the last—defenders of the bourgeois democratic order in Latin America.

Opposition Within Chile

The take-over would not have been possible if the military had had nothing more than its made-in-U.S.A. arms and training in "counterinsurgency" at Fort Benning, Ga., that is, if it had lacked a social basis among the civilian population of Chile. In fact, the *golpe de estado* (*coup d'état*) responded to the explicit demands of a sizable spectrum of entrenched class interests.

The real threat to the peaceful and democratic transition toward a new society built up rapidly from October 1972 (a period of crisis caused by a truck owners' strike and employers' lockout), as fascist ideology penetrated the consciousness of sectors of the nonworking class population and the organized political opposition: the National and Christian Democratic parties, the Fatherland and Liberty paramilitary organization and the trade and professional associations of the middle- and upper-level occupation groupings. The opposition reached a point of desperation following the electoral gains of the Popular parties in the March 1973 congressional elections, which resulted in impressive inroads in the opposition-controlled Congress.

Some sectors of the opposition, especially within the Christian Democratic Party, preferred a "soft coup." (The term is *golpe blanco:* Allende's resignation with a caretaker military government preceding a restoration of "moderate" civilian rule, presumably under former President Eduardo Frei, the "Christian" and "democrat" who personally bears awesome responsibility for recent events). As a whole, however, it maneuvered to strip all legitimacy from the constitutional government in the eyes of the military and those social sectors sensitive to its propaganda.

A virtual war of propaganda was unleashed during the year preceding the coup. It played upon the petty privileges, status insecurities and social pathologies of the social strata that are produced within class societies existing at the periphery of world capitalism. The opposition, despite dramatic appeals by the church hierarchy and Allende's persistent overtures for dialogue, left no quarter for reasonable accommodation between the contending, and by now sharply polarized, class forces.

The associations of businessmen and professionals and the political parties with a social basis among the middle strata were front-line forces in the anti-Allende offensive (just as sectors of the "middle class" were mobilized in Hitler's drive for power). However, the line propagated by the media in this country (especially by that organ of "responsible" opinion formation, *The New York Times*) that Chile is a "middle-class society" and that the entire middle class turned against Allende is false.

The overwhelming majority of Chileans are workers, peasants, and marginal urban poor. All the middle strata together constitute no more than about 30 percent of the population. Furthermore, segments of these strata supported Allende, while others opposed fascism and military solutions. The majority of public school teachers and health workers supported the government. Even among professionals, such as doctors, dentists, architects and engineers enjoying upper-class incomes and life styles, significant minorities (20 to 25 percent) supported the Allende government. The traditional climate of freedom in Chile nourished a vital culture of intellectual and artistic activity, and most artists, writers, and intellectuals supported the changes sought by the Allende government.

The U.S. Role

The direct and indirect U.S. corporate and government role in bringing about this colonial fascist state cannot be overemphasized. Direct U.S. intevention took the primary form of applying economic pressures that would create economic chaos. This policy developed through three distinct stages.

From September 1970 to July 1971 the U.S. government officially pursued a "wait-and-see" approach consistent with the Nixon Administration's "low profile" in Latin American policy. However, this stage actually had two components. At the level of official policy a cool but "correct" diplomacy prevailed. At the same time, even before the Allende plurality in the September 4, 1970, election, a second element developed. This consisted of covert actions by the CIA and behind-the-scenes efforts by U.S. corporations, especially ITT, to pressure the entire business community and the government first to impede Allende's election and then, in the tense months of September and October 1970, to prevent him from taking office on November 3.

In the period roughly from July to December 1971 there was a gradual tightening of the economic screws in an effort to coerce and create economic difficulties for Chile. As early as March there was a cutoff of shipments of foodstuffs under the previous aid program and the holding-up of credits for "review."

After Chile nationalized the Anaconda and Kennecott copper mines in July, the economic pressures became even more serious. The Export-Import Bank held up credits to purchase three Boeing commercial jets "pending a clarification in policies toward foreign investment." Thereafter no credits were granted by the Export-Import Bank to finance imports of U.S. goods. Measures applied subsequently by the U.S. government, private banks and international lenders, together with low copper prices and interference with Chile's copper markets in Western Europe, amounted to a de facto embargo on the import of U.S. goods. Chile's industrial economy is highly dependent upon U.S. technology and replacement parts. Large amounts of foreign exchange earned from copper exports and abundant foreign credits are needed to finance the import of hundreds of millions of dollars in food, as well as essential supplies for the economy.

By October all U.S. aid programs, *except military*, that had previously been held up for review were officially suspended, and foreign bank credits disappeared. In October the newly appointed U.S. Ambassador, Nathaniel Davis, arrived in Santiago. Davis, an expert in anti-communist affairs, was Ambassador to Guatemala, 1968-1971. There he oversaw all forms of U.S. assistance to Guatemala's repressive right-wing regime. (The "pacification" program in that country killed some 20,000 opponents of a dictatorship that had its origin in the CIA-sponsored counterrevolution of 1954.) The appointment of an ambassador with experience in dealing with and strengthening right-wing dictatorial regimes was an indication of what the Nixon Administration had in mind for Chile.

Working with Davis out of the embassy were ten known CIA agents (for names, biographies and analysis of the CIA "coup team," see the press release by the North American Congress on Latin America [NACLA], September 14, 1973). I do not believe that the CIA engineered this event in the way it did in Guatemala, the Bay of Pigs, and Cambodia. The CIA probably confined itself to financing subversion against the Allende government and providing intelligence to Kissinger's National Security Council, the Council on International Economic Policy, and other U.S. agencies.

The belatedly well-publicized machinations of ITT were not uniquely responsible either. Responsibility for U.S. economic aggression resided with the Nixon Administration and a wide range of corporate interests who together evolved a "big stick" policy that prevailed from the end of 1971 until the September coup. It was symbolized by President Nixon's "no nonsense" policy on nationalization of properties of U.S. corporations operating abroad, proclaimed in January 1972, and it was made concrete by wide-ranging measures of economic sanction that resulted in what the Chileans termed "an invisible blockade."

Trading Independence for Privilege

Meanwhile, businessmen and opposition elements within Chile, probably aided by CIA dollars, worked toward the same end: the creation of economic circumstances that could be used to precipitate a political crisis and overthrow the constitutional government.

This strategy worked to some extent. After two years of unusual economic boom (brought about by the government's economic policy and income redistribution) in an economy that had virtually stagnated for 17 years, the economy began to give way to the pressures toward the end of 1972. The short supply of dollars and restricted access to international credits to import machinery, essential supplies, and food, and the inevitable disruptions caused by economic reorganization, agrarian reform, and political turmoil coincided to produce economic bottlenecks, severe shortages, and rampant inflation. Some sectors of the "middle class"— already affected by income redistribution favoring the workers and programs of social equality symbolically diminishing their social privileges— began to see their style of life and social position as fundamentally threatened by a government that proclaimed itself a "workers' government"—and came increasingly to be viewed as such by both partisans and opponents.

Although neither the Allende government's domestic measures nor its policies of economic nationalism were in fact revolutionary, a confrontation with U.S. power was inevitable. So completely were U.S. business and government agencies involved in Chilean society, so deeply implanted were what social scientists term the "structural relations of dependence" that the modest but concrete steps toward recovering the nation's natural resources and shifting decision-making power from corporate headquarters in New York to government offices and workers in Santiago seemed to all to be either revolutionary measures or sufficiently radical to make a transition to socialism inevitable if decisive counterrevolutionary steps were not taken.

If the current regime manages to consolidate its power (the resistance will make such consolidation very difficult), U.S. investors will reinstitute the process of achieving control over the Chilean economy. Over 100 American corporations with one billion dollars invested were well advanced in that process before Allende's election. U.S. aid —unless Congress acts to end the use of aid to shore up repressive governments—will once again begin to flow in large quantities. Lines of international credit are already being reopened. The real interests the Chilean military represent are those of the multinational corporations and the Chilean big businessmen anxious to sell their nationality for the power to preserve themselves at the top of a poor nation's social hierarchy.

By the time Allende became President most of Chile's important areas of industry and finance had already passed into foreign hands, and the Chilean business oligarchy had become the local partners of international business. Of the 18 largest nonbanking corporations, all but two had participation by foreign capital. Forty of Chile's largest 100 corporations were under foreign control, while many more were mixed ventures that allowed external influence or effective control. More than two-thirds of Chilean officers and directors of the country's top 50 corporations had either personal or close family ties to foreign investors. This marriage of convenience between multinational corporations (almost entirely North American) and oligarchs was profitable to both classes of interests. It was these interconnected interests, holding Chile in a virtual state of colonial economic dependence, that the Allende government tried to move against.

This alliance of national and foreign business interests with the militarists, equipped and trained by the Pentagon and presently in control of the state, has been—and probably will continue to be—politically supported by important segments of middle- to upper-class Chilean society. These classes, long ago acculturated to the imported values of consumerism, have enjoyed an income and style of life far removed from that of workers and peasants. They are apparently willing to yield their country's economic independence and political sovereignty to foreign powers and their own humanity to fascist rule in exchange for social privilege and the ability to consume GM cars, RCA TV's (to view the "I Spy" and "I Love Lucy" programming), Dow household cleaners (for the maid's convenience), Coca Cola and the other niceties of industrial civilization —and this in a Third World setting in which the majority of people lack many of the most elementary necessities.

Colonial economic dependence, with the multinational corporation and the U.S. government in control, generates structures of power and class privilege in the periphery nations that have been the fundamental basis of authoritarian states since Nazi Germany. And Chile may prove to be the most extreme case of colonial fascism yet to emerge, outdoing even the Greek, Indonesian, Uruguayan, Brazilian, Bolivian, South African and Spanish governments.

In the end—though that end may be years in the making—the Chilean people, frustrated in their efforts to make changes gradually and peacefully within the confines of the old democratic order, will impose their revolution with the means that become available to them. Chile has the makings of another Spanish Civil War—or perhaps another Vietnam. ∎

New Tactics for the Left: MAPU Analysis

As Christians committed to the revolutionary process, the Movement of United Popular Action (MAPU) was one of the non-Marxist parties which joined the Popular Unity (UP) coalition. Originally the most progressive section of the Christian Democratic Party (PDC), MAPU came into being in 1969 when it broke with the PDC in protest against that party's rightward trend when it was in power. As part of Allende's UP, MAPU directed its chief energies toward community action in the countryside. Now outlawed, along with all Chile's political parties, MAPU's leaders have written an analysis of the coup containing a serious criticism of MAPU itself and all other groupings within the left and a projection of long-range strategy for the reorganization of its forces. Jairo Muñoz summarizes that lengthy analysis in the article below, which appeared in Latinamerica Press, *February 1, 1974.*

The United Popular Action Movement's (MAPU) recent political analysis of the Chile coup being widely circulated in Europe is surprisingly critical of the whole Chilean left.

The document, published by Chilean solidarity committees, was prepared last November in Santiago by the political committee of MAPU, which had been part of the former Salvador Allende government's Popular Unity (UP). The eight-page analysis entitled "The Fall of the Popular Government and the New Tactical Period," affirms that it was the absence of a recognized revolutionary vanguard that definitely caused the September defeat.

> The defeat of the popular forces in September was due to the breakdown of the strategy that the reformist and center revolutionaries impressed on the revolutionary process from the beginning (1970). The strategy dominated the leadership of the masses and the Popular Unity government.

The document describes the reformist and center leftist policy as gradualist, bureaucratic and incapable of orienting the people "in a revolutionary perspective." It points out that "the Chilean experience always oscillated between two strategic alternatives, and as a result it had a vacillating political course."

To summarize, the two strategic alternatives at play inside the left were "revolutionary centrism," which predominated, and the "socialist proletarian" strategy. The first was seeking to arrive at an "advanced democracy" through an anti-imperialist, anti-oligarchical and anti-monopolistic popular revolution by legal change. The second thought the character of the Chilean revolution stemmed from socialist beginnings—in other words, it was also interpreting the UP program as anti-capitalist.

After submitting the political and economic positions

and programs of both, the document concludes:

These two strategies differed in form and timing for the take-over of power by the proletariat and therefore, they implied different treatments with regard to the armed forces.

The political analysts specify that the strategy called "revolutionary centrism" was backed by the PC (Communist Party), PR (Radical Party), sectors of the PS (Socialist Party) and the IC (Christian Left), while the "socialist proletariat" grouped sectors of the PS, of the MAPU and other revolutionary groups such as the Movement of the Revolutionary Left (MIR), which did not participate directly in the government of the UP.

In an analysis of the present military government which "directly represents the interests of the national and international bourgeois monopoly," the mistakes of the left are again emphasized. The petit bourgeoisie, the professional and the non-professional petit bourgeoisie and, in general, the middle classes support the military dictatorship. However, this support, considered momentary, is "basically due to radicalization toward the right that these social sectors experienced because of strategic and tactical errors of the Popular Unity and the left."

It is, then, a support that "has no material roots but purely political ones and, therefore, susceptible of becoming global opposition," which for the capitalist development that "the dictatorship aspires to give Chile has a negative effect."

MAPU's political study of "The Present Situation" in Chapter III emphatically states: "The new situation is characterized by a correlation of forces highly unfavorable to the working class." It distinguishes three divisions in the social sectors:

1. *The Enemies:* The support of the enemy is derived from the bourgeois monopoly and imperialism, together with the professional petit bourgeoisie and the high state bureaucracy. Its political support lies in the PN (National Party), in the extreme right of Christian Democracy and in the petit bourgeoisie trade unions. The dictatorship today receives the support of broad social and political sectors (middle class and the Christian Democrat Party). However, it means only temporary support which will disappear once the dictatorship implements its fascist model. Its political representative is the armed forces. . . . which are presently very cohesive at all levels and dominated by their more fascist sectors. Its instrument is the bourgeois state.

However, the document points out, within the "enemy forces" there exists a series of contradictions. The main one is of a "political nature," in which two sectors confront each other:

those who try to reconstruct the bourgeois democratic model in Chile . . . against those who pretend to establish in Chile a totalitarian state that will dictatorially assume the interests of the dominant class. . .

2. *Middle Sectors.* These are represented socially by the non-professional petit bourgeoisie, the petit bourgeoisie and the middle classes in general; politically and ideologically by Christian Democracy and the church, who have pronounced themselves in one way or another against a dictatorship.

The MAPU's report asserts that Christian Democracy, the group to which it previously belonged and which it left to become part of the UP, is, since September 11th, in a gradual "deterioration in its positions" in the university, in the labor unions and within the state apparatus.

The church, it says,

must also have suffered, through some of its members, the repression of dictatorship and has been able to witness the violence of the regime. If it has not taken a significant position opposing the Junta, it is due to the able propagandizing of fascism.

3. *The People.* United around the proletariat and the rural and urban non-proletariat poor, the people constitute the main social force which is an enemy of the dictatorship.

The report points out that the "consciousness level, organization and combativity" of the Chilean people is "incompatible with the type of regime that the dictatorship aspires to establish, and also incompatible with the degree of exploitation that the development of capitalism requires."

However, when it mentions the people's political representatives, MAPU's political document seriously criticizes the left. It refuses to allow the slightest error or deviation. It says:

Reformism is one of the political expressions of the people and is represented by sectors of the PC, PS, PR and the IC and dominated by the PC, which is still the most important party of the left. Reformism still has strong roots in the masses although they had begun to question it before the coup and even more strongly afterwards.

It states that reformism desires above all to struggle "only for the return of bourgeois democracy" and that "it will deliver the hegemony of the anti-fascist front to the bourgeois sectors of the alliance." The revolutionary forces, says the analysis,

are another political expression of the people and are represented by MAPU, MIR, sectors of PS, PC and IC. Still weak in their political ideology and organization, without any single vanguard for expression, these sectors so far have little influence on the masses, especially the working class. Only decision, strategy-tactic correction, articulation and organization will allow them to be transformed into a significant force.

The document also considers the Chilean case in the international context.

The UP's fall has made a strong impact on the international workers' movement since it means the loss of one of the most advanced positions in the struggle for socialism.

Referring to this continent it says:

The Latin American proletariat will enter a higher stage to the degree it studies the Chilean experience and understands the need of organizing on a continental scale to struggle for socialism.

In the last part, "Some Strategical Considerations," the MAPU lays out a long-range policy for the future based on the premise that the coup and the dictatorship have not solved the problems of the poor.

This is still the key point in the class struggle. The bourgeoisie has not yet solved its problems of domination; and the proletariat, if it has lost important positions, still keeps its fundamental energy and has entered into an advanced state of reorganization of its forces.

It considers that

[D]emocratic revindications of the masses oriented toward raising their standard of living, ending monopolies and foreign capital, and defending their organizations (labor unions, industrial belts, communal commands, etc.) can only be satisfied with socialism. To struggle for democracy today is to struggle for socialism. It is not possible to go back to the former situation; bourgeois democracy is impossible in Chile today.

In its brief conclusion the political report renews its criticism of the left, stating that it is constructive criticism:

[T]he triumph of the revolution does not emerge spontaneously; it must be prepared for and won; only a solid Revolutionary Party, sufficiently strong to subordinate reformist tendencies, to set up a mass movement and lead it in a decisive struggle against dictatorship, can do this. The present non-existence of such political military leadership of the masses constitutes the main problem the Chilean working class has to face. Its absence is the main cause of the September defeat, and the future of the revolutionary process depends upon its development and consolidation.

For many political observers the document is a serious self-criticism which MAPU has undertaken along with other revolutionary groups within the left. Analysis such as this was to be expected and has been received with growing interest in the Latin American and also the European left.

For example, this report has been widely published by most of the European committees for solidarity with Chile and has been studied by the committees of each country. Sweden, which has more than 70 committees, also is giving refuge to more than 600 exiles: Uruguayan, Bolivian and Brazilian, as well as Chilean.

Meanwhile, in Chile, MAPU's General Secretary, Oscar Garreton, has taken asylum in the Colombian Embassy, but the Chilean government has denied him permission to leave the country, accusing him of public crimes. ■

LIFE UNDER THE JUNTA

When the military seized power last September, they claimed it was reluctantly and for the shortest possible period. Whatever their intentions, their methods from the outset destroyed any possibility of a quick and peaceful return to democratic forms. An army conditioned to come into the streets and kill unarmed civilians inevitably produced polarizations and conflict that quickly became self-feeding.

The form of the new society in consequence imposed itself. The people who had learned to express themselves and exercise their influence had to be pushed back into anonymity and helplessness. The media of communications had to be censored. The system of education had to be modified in favor of the upper classes, and the content of education had to be regulated to indoctrinate the masses and persuade them that slavery was freedom.

The articles that follow express various aspects of this process. It is significant, though not surprising, that the Junta spokesmen are constantly postponing elections and other trappings of liberal democracies to an ever more distant future. Meanwhile, we can anticipate two developments. The level of oppression will continue to rise, as the objective conditions of the people of Chile grow worse. The visibility of the oppression is likely to grow less, as more sophisticated techniques of silencing take the place of the crude violence which characterized the earlier period. But the reality of oppression must continue. The generals have left themselves without an alternative.

The Case of Charles Horman

"Of particular concern to groups in the United States is the evidence that has gradually accumulated that the United States Embassy and Consulate in Santiago were staffed with ideological enemies of the Allende government, and that these failed to give United States citizens whom they suspected of sympathy with that regime the protection to which they were entitled—and perhaps even passed information about them to the Junta.

"Here the most documented case is that of Charles Horman, who was in Viña del Mar when the revolt occurred and received the indiscreet revelations of what United States military and naval personnel were doing in nearby Valparaíso. On September 15, Captain Ray Davis gave him a ride back to Santiago, where he joined his wife. On September 17, in view of the continuing fighting in Santiago and the martial law, he went to the United States Embassy to ask protection for his wife and himself. Embassy officials said there was little they could do for him, and he returned to his home, where he was arrested by the military. His wife had gone into town and was caught there by the early curfew. She got home the following morning to find the house ransacked. She immediately notified the Consulate that her husband was missing. The Consulate did in fact have information that a body identified by the Chilean military as that of Charles Horman was in the morgue, but for an entire month it would not give his wife or family any clues as to his fate." (Gary MacEoin in No Peaceful Way)

His Widow's Testimony

In the testimony which follows below, Joyce Horman, Charles' widow, records the details of her month-long search for her husband in Santiago during the fearful weeks which followed the coup. Her straightforward, unadorned reporting builds a powerful case against those Embassy officials from whom she sought help and whose callous, sadistic conduct toward a citizen they were pledged to protect has never been properly called into account by any member or body of the U.S. government. The grave questions it raises of official complicity with the Junta remain unanswered.

To the best of my recollection, the following statements are true:

Charles Horman, my husband, and I arrived in Chile on June 7, 1972. We had left the United States on December 3, 1971, with plans to travel through Central and South America. When we arrived in Chile after long months of travel, we decided to stay. Our decision was based on our need for rest as well as possibilities for employment.

Charles had been in the United States during August 1973 visiting his family. He returned on August 31, 1973, to Santiago with our mutual friend of many years, Terry Simon, who was on vacation for one month and had decided to visit us. Terry and I decided to visit the ski resort of Portillo for a rest while Charles remained at home to finish moving in and straightening up our new residence. We left on September 7th and returned to Santiago on Sunday, the 9th. We learned on Monday that Terry would be unable to change her tourist visa and would be required to change $20 a day, so a quick one-day trip was planned to Viña del Mar, a nearby beach resort, after which Terry planned to leave Chile for Peru. Since I had to take care of renewing my resident's visa in Santiago, I decided to remain at our Vicuña MacKenna home. On the evening of September 10th, Terry and Charles left for Viña del Mar. The morning of September 11th, I was about to leave the house when I learned by radio of the military coup and of the orders given for all people to remain in their homes. Due to the curfew and the state of emergency, it was impossible to leave the house from September 11th to the 15th. On September 15th I left only to buy vegetables directly across the street. There was no way of contacting anyone outside of Santiago since phone communication had been cut off. I could not find out how or where Charles and Terry were.

September 16

Charles and Terry called our landlords whose home was right next to ours and asked them to advise me that they had arrived in Santiago, were safe, and were on their way over to the house. They arrived at 12 noon. Charles and I went into a room to talk and he related to me what he had experienced in Viña del Mar.

While trapped in Viña by the coup from September 10th to the 15th, Charles and Terry stayed at the Miramar Hotel. They met, by chance, several U.S. military officers. They conversed with them, were entertained by them, and were brought back to Santiago in a car driven by the chief of the U.S. Military Mission, Captain Ray E. Davis. Charles told me that the U.S. military officials exhibited much enthusiasm about the success and smooth operation of the coup. As an example of these sentiments, Charles then quoted Art Creter, a retired U.S. naval engineer, who claimed he was on a Chilean naval ship in the Valparaíso harbor during the coup. He also told me that the U.S. aides expressed a high level of antagonism towards the former Allende regime. He said that he had been told by the same military officers that the Chileans were expecting aid from the United States which was to be channeled through the U.S. Naval Mission. The three names Charles mentioned are: Captain Davis, Colonel Patrick Ryan, and Art Creter.

Later that evening we all discussed our situation in Santiago, as we saw it. Foreigners were being denounced and arrested by the military; private cars and public vehicles were being searched and any irregularities of personal or vehicle documents were sufficient basis for arrest. Books were being burned in the streets, and any literature pertaining to Chile's government of the last three years found in any home labeled the resident as an "extremist" and guaranteed his arrest. Given these circumstances, we decided that Charles should accompany Terry to the Embassy the following day to inquire about how we might all leave the country as soon as possible.

Terry expressed a desire to have a hotel room downtown in order to be closer to the necessary offices. We looked over books and papers which we had in the house to see if there was any literature which would "offend" any military person who might search our home.

September 17

Charles and Terry left for the Embassy at about 12 noon. I went out to purchase food and to visit friends to see if they were safe. Transportation was very poor, and around 6:30 p.m. it became clear that I would not be able to travel back home before the 7 p.m. curfew. At the time, I was with a friend, and we decided to go to an acquaintance's apartment which was within walking distance and spend the night there. No one was at home so we knocked on another door. The people there were too terrified to allow us to stay, since they were foreigners also and thought it would be too risky. We spent the night at the top of the stairwell of the building, hoping the police or military would not come by.

September 18

At 8 a.m. I took a bus to my home, arriving at 8:30. The front gate was unlocked, and the lock and chain were on the ground, but there was no indication that the gate had been forced open. I walked back to the house and discovered that it had been ransacked and many things were missing. Shortly afterwards, three people from the neighborhood came to tell me that the military had come to our house two or three times the previous evening. The man of the group identified himself as the owner of some nearby properties and urged me to leave immediately and to stay at another place since he thought the military would soon return. They left and I wrote a note for Charles. At the time I thought he had had the same problem I had run into the previous night and had not been able to return to the house because of curfew regulations and lack of transportation. As I headed to the front gate, someone standing in an adjacent bread line motioned to me not to exit from the front of the house. I did not understand the significance of his gesture but was frightened enough to go back and leave through the rear gate. This gate was open, although normally it was firmly closed. At that point I noticed that an adjoining house also had been broken into from the rear.

I went to a friend's house by bus and tried to call other friends to see if I could locate Charles. I was exhausted from not having slept the night, and very upset about not being able to find Charles or account for the ransacking of the house. We called still another friend, a Mr. M., who asked me to come talk to him. But since I was near collapse, a member of the family with whom I was staying went over instead. Another member of this family, a Mrs. F., a trained psychologist, decided it was crucial that I rest and she gave me a sedative.

Later, the person returned with information from Mr. M. He related how Mr. M. had been very unnerved by receiving a phone call from the military which had threatened his life if they found out he was lying. Mr. M. said that they had called Charles an "extremist" and asked how he had known Charles.

Mrs. F. called a secretary in the U.S. Consulate, who was her personal friend, and reported that she had heard that Charles Horman was missing after having been taken by the military and inquired about what could possibly be done. The secretary had replied that Charles was not registered at the Consulate and that his wife should come there to report. I later found out that another friend, a Mr. A., had received a message to report to the nearest police station to answer questions about Charles. Mr. A. reported the contents of this message to Mr. Frederick Purdy, Chief Consul of the U.S. Embassy, on September 18th.

September 19

I went to the U.S. Consulate. I told the secretary I wanted to speak to someone and report that my husband had been taken by the military. The secretary asked if Charles were registered and I replied that I was not sure. She said they did not have a card on him and asked me to fill out a form. She then asked a Mr. Hall to speak to me.

Mr. Hall came out of his office and walked over to the desk where I was seated. He explained to me that the Consul, Mr. Purdy, was busy and that he (Mr. Hall) would help me. I told him my husband had been taken by the military, that the house had been ransacked, and that I wanted help from the Embassy in locating my husband. Mr. Hall inquired about the circumstances of Charles' disappearance. He asked when Charles had been taken. I replied, "Last Monday." Then he asked: "Was there anything in the house that might have irritated the soldiers?" I said, "No, absolutely nothing," but after thinking further mentioned that Charles had a short study on the role of rightist General Viaux in the assassination of the constitutionalist chief of the army, General Schneider, shortly before President Allende took office. (It came to mind because, on the previous Sunday, we had gone through the house looking for anything that might prove offensive to the military in any way. Charles and I had decided after some discussion and after looking at the pages that all the information included on the Viaux/ Schneider case was public and common knowledge, so we had not destroyed it.) Mr. Hall seemed interested in finding out more about these pages. Mr. Hall asked what Charles had been doing in Santiago, and I gave a detailed explanation of Charles' work. He seemed especially curious about the film on Chile on which Charles had worked.

I also explained to him that a friend of mine had been called by the Chilean military and questioned about Charles. Mr. Hall gave me a form for reporting stolen articles, and I asked him if I could bring it in the next day because I did not want to do it right away.

I asked him if he had an address for Terry Simon. He located her card and told me she was staying at the Hotel Riviera. Mr. Hall did not mention calls of the previous day about Charles' seizure.

Terry had phoned Captain Davis sometime after the curfew on September 19th to ask for his help in the case. Terry explained the facts to him and mentioned that Charles' wife was very concerned. Davis replied that he did not know that Charles was married. "Yes," Terry replied, "she's here now." She went on to explain that we were good friends. Captain Davis then asked if Charles was involved in anything which would explain his arrest by the Chilean authorities, whether he was affiliated with any political party in Chile or if he had had any weapons in the house. The answers to all these questions were negative. Captain Davis then said that he would see what he could find out and that Terry and I should go to his office in the Embassy the following day. (I had now moved into the Hotel Riviera, where I stayed with Terry.)

September 20

We went in the morning to Captain Davis' office at the Embassy. Captain Davis was not there when we arrived, so we spoke briefly with a Colonel Uribe, and the secretary gave us coffee. Davis arrived and we explained what we knew to him.

We related everything we knew of Charles' capture, our home being ransacked, and my friend who had been called by the Chilean military authorities about Charles. Captain Davis called Mr. Purdy, asked that Charles' parents be notified and gave him Charles' passport number and my address at the Hotel Riviera. He then called Admiral Huidobro of the Chilean Navy and asked him to come by his house for dinner that night or, if that were not possible, to stop by for a drink. Captain Davis then invited us to come for dinner, since, he said, it would be helpful for us to talk to Admiral Huidobro. He suggested, due to the curfew, that we plan to spend the night at his house. I asked that he provide an escort for me to return to my home to pick up some of my belongings, explaining that I was afraid to go alone.

Captain Davis' chauffeur drove Captain Davis, Terry, and me to my home. We were escorted by three armed Chilean soldiers who followed us in a van. We retrieved a few personal belongings from the house.

On the way back to town Captain Davis again invited us to his home for dinner, repeating that a personal interview with the Admiral would be advantageous. Terry and I expressed our concern that perhaps we would miss telephone calls concerning Charles' whereabouts if we were not in the hotel. Captain Davis assured us that he was in close contact with Mr. Purdy on this matter and that he would be called immediately by him if there were any new developments. He said that if we wished to return to the hotel after dinner it could be arranged because he had a pass to drive after curfew. He did not recommend it, however, stating that even with a pass it would be dangerous.

Terry and I arrived at Captain Davis' house a little before 6 p.m. We had decided to spend the night there because Captain Davis had concluded that it was dangerous to travel in the streets after curfew even though he had official permission to do so. The following are a few relevant conversations which I recall from that evening.

Shortly after we arrived Captain Davis suggested we go upstairs to listen to the news, from Panama, as I recall. He had a large radio setup in a room just outside his bedroom. We listened to various reports and afterwards Captain Davis said, see—they really do not know what's happening in Chile; they don't even care. Captain Davis then asked us if we knew that the new Chilean government was getting some bad press. We replied that we had not heard anything one way or another. Comments were exchanged between us to the effect that it was impossible to know what was happening in the nation from what was appearing in the Chilean press. Captain Davis also stated that a CBS reporter in Chile had been responsible for some of the bad press.

He then asked us if we hadn't known that there would be a coup. He said everyone else knew so we must have known. I said it had seemed likely but I did not know when it would occur nor did I expect it would take place with such violence. Captain Davis said surely I could understand that the military was just protecting itself, that it had uncovered a plot against its leaders. He added that it's just like a person backed into a corner and threatened with his life, lashing out with all the power he can to defend himself. He said that I must know what a big job the military had to do here in Chile. He asked me what I thought the average Chileans felt, and then he commented on how badly the Allende administration had managed Chile's economy. He asked me what I was doing in Chile, where I had gone to college, and what I had studied. He asked the same questions of Terry.

At this point Captain Davis received a call from Admiral Huidobro, who expressed his regret that he could not come by.

September 21

In the morning we called Captain Davis at his office, and he sent his driver to get us. We dropped Terry off at a friend's, and the driver took me to my home to interview neighbors. My landlord told me that someone had followed the truck which took Charles away and had seen the truck enter the gates of the National Stadium. He also told me that he would try to arrange a meeting with this person for me. I also spoke with Neighbor A., who told me she had seen Charles being taken away by the military.

The driver then took me to the house of Mr. M., the friend who had received the call from the Chilean military.

Neither Mr. M. nor his wife was there, but his mother-in-law told me that Mrs. M. had answered the phone first and the military had told her to be careful of what she said and to tell the truth because the conversation was being taped. Mrs. M. said fine, proceed. They asked her why an extremist had her telephone number. The military then described Charles' physical appearance and occupation. Mrs. M. explained that Charles and I had lived nearby and that we used her telephone regularly because we did not have our own. At that point, as Mrs. M.'s mother described it, Mr. M. got on the phone and spoke with the military. The caller identified himself as SIM—Military Intelligence Service. SIM wanted to know who he (Mr. M.) was and why he knew the person described, where the person (Charles) worked, and if he were an extremist. The caller said to Mr. M.: "If you're lying you'll have to run for your life."

September 22

In the morning Steven Volk, a friend, came by the hotel to accompany Terry and me to the U.S. Consulate. We arrived at about 11 a.m. and were amazed that, during such a period of emergency, there were only two secretaries and Mr. Purdy working.

I asked to see Mr. Purdy and shortly thereafter was told: "Mrs. Horner [sic], you can come in now."

I told Mr. Purdy that somehow Mr. Hall had taken down the information about my husband incorrectly the previous Wednesday. I had heard that the Consulate was saying that Charles had "disappeared" on the 10th of September. I explained that when Mr. Hall had asked me on which date Charles had been taken, I had replied to Hall, "Last Monday." I had had no idea what date it was because I had been extremely upset.

Mr. Purdy asked why I had not reported in on September 20th as I had said I would. I explained that I

had been with Captain Davis, who had assured me that he was in close contact with Purdy's office and that he would receive any important communication from Purdy immediately. I had been investigating on my own to find Charles and that had seemed much more important to me than filing a stolen article report as requested.

I also asked Purdy if he had been to the National Stadium to ask about Charles. He stated that the computer lists issued by the military had not as yet included Charles' name.

At that time Mr. Purdy asked if I could give him Charles' passport number. I replied that I could, but asked if Captain Davis had not already done this. (Terry and I had been present when Captain Davis telephoned the passport number to Purdy.) Mr. Purdy replied that Captain Davis must have sent the number over by mail. When I showed surprise that he would send this by mail rather than by picking up the telephone, Mr. Purdy angrily replied, "Mrs. Horner [sic] . . . , I mean the *Embassy* mail. Now listen, you can read anything you like into what I say, but if you people don't think I've been doing my job . . . I haven't had a good lunch with my friends for the past eleven days, and I missed my baby's birthday on the 18th and I've worked late two nights."

I was extremely shaken by this hostile outburst and apologized to Mr. Purdy for anything I might have said and added that we were probably both tired and under pressure. Terry then read him the passport number, which he recorded. When Steven, Terry, and I left the Consulate, I was in tears and near hysteria.

September 24

In the late morning Terry and I went to the U.S. Consulate. This was the third time we had been to the Consulate and the third official who had met with us. We had not seen the same person twice in three visits. We now spoke with Dale Schaffer, who seemed to be an assistant to Mr. Hall.

Schaffer suggested we contact the Dutch Embassy because they had gotten a representative inside the National Stadium. He also mentioned the names of two U.S. citizens who had just been released from the Stadium. He did not offer to contact them for me; rather, he suggested that I do it myself. He then left the office to get the addresses of the two U.S. citizens and of the Dutch Embassy.

When he returned, Terry and I asked to see the note cards being kept on Charles. Schaffer had made a passing reference to these note cards earlier in the conversation. Nonetheless, Schaffer looked surprised at our request. As we looked through the cards, we noticed the following phrase: "Journalist . . . working on (maybe as) extremist." I said: "What is this?" I repeated the phrase to Mr. Schaffer, who said that that must have been a reference to Charles' study of the Viaux case, and he said that the people who killed General Schneider were extremists. I also saw that it was noted on the cards that Mr. A. had called the Consulate on the 18th and on the same day an Embassy secretary had reported another call from a friend of hers (Mrs. F.) saying that Charles was missing.

I recollect Mr. Schaffer suggesting to me that Charles was in hiding because he did not want to see me. I assured Mr. Schaffer that this was impossible.

The driver took me back to the Riviera Hotel. That evening Captain Davis called.

He asked if it were possible that Charles had been involved in some political activity without my knowing it. I said that that was absolutely impossible. He replied that I should not be so sure. He asked if I had ever heard about the most famous Russian spy who ever lived. I said I had not. He said the spy's wife had never known what he was doing. I laughed and said: "That doesn't say much for their relationship, does it?" He said, "Now look, you're an intelligent, young, pretty girl with your whole life ahead of you." He told me to look forward, not back. "Don't forget that if there is anything I can do for you, be sure to let me know."

September 25

I received a phone call from Major Luis Contreras Prieto, who said he had been contacted through a New York bank. Prieto had been told we were at the hotel and that he should come by to help us with our problem. He said he would be over shortly.

Major Prieto arrived dressed in military uniform accompanied by a man in civilian clothes. He said that he had been wounded during one of the first days of the coup, which was why his foot was in a cast. We explained our problem to him, and he said we should be calm because he would have information concerning my husband by tomorrow at the latest. He seemed very confident, and said that if I had not heard from him by tomorrow that I should call him. He wrote down his name, address, and phone number and I wrote down Charles' name in full for him.

September 26

I went to see Ambassador Nathaniel Davis a little before 1 p.m. The receptionist said that she would try to get through to his secretary but that the line was busy. I sat and waited. After fifteen minutes I requested that the secretary try to reach him again for me. Somewhat later I was taken to his office by his secretary, Joan Scott. When he entered, he said, "How do you do? . . . I understand that Captain Davis has been working with your problem. Would you mind if I call him in? If you would like a private audience, that can be arranged." I said it made absolutely no difference to me, so he then called in Captain Davis. When he entered, the three of us went into the Ambassador's conference room, where Captain Davis was asked to report on the case.

Captain Davis said he had asked his friends in the Chilean military if they knew anything of Charles Horman. He reported that Charles' name had not appeared on any of the lists at the Stadium and that his military friends had told him that the military had no knowledge of Charles Horman.

Ambassador Davis then asked me: "What more can we do for you?" And I said, "Well, has anyone from this Embassy gone in the Stadium? I understand that other ambassadors have gone to the Stadium and have gotten their people out." I asked if it were possible to arrange for someone from the Embassy or for me to go to the Stadium and look. I added that it seemed possible to me that there was such confusion there that Charles' records might have been lost or that he might have been misplaced. I wanted to look. The Ambassador then said that we didn't want to ask favors of this government—if we got favors, everyone else would expect to get them too—and we didn't wish to do possible damage to our relations with this new Chilean government. I repeated my question,

not understanding why that meant we could not go to the Stadium and inquire. Ambassador Davis asked just what I wished to do in the Stadium. Would I like to look under all the bleachers and into all the corners? I answered that that was exactly what I would like to do and that I saw nothing wrong in that. Ambassador Davis told me, in what I felt to be a cold and condescending manner, that I had to be patient. I broke into tears and said that I felt I had been more than patient.

At that point Captain Davis made a comment to the effect that I wanted results. I agreed. Ambassador Davis then agreed to ask Colonel Espinoza (at the Stadium) to check the Stadium lists again. I apologized for taking up so much of their time.

I then accompanied Captain Davis to his office, where I told him about Major Prieto's call and visit of the day before. Captain Davis reacted more quickly than he ever had before. He said that this was a very important piece of information. He said we should get on it right away. He tried calling Prieto immediately and, when he received a busy signal on the line, went to the next room and told his assistant (a man with a black patch over one eye) to telephone Major Prieto right away. I gave them Major Prieto's address and telephone number.

At 4:30 p.m. I called the Prieto home. Mrs. Prieto answered and told me that the Major was at the doctor's and that he would call me when he returned. She had heard no news from him about my husband.

At about 6 p.m. Mrs. Prieto called me back; the Major was in bed on doctor's orders. She said that my husband was alive and well but that he could not be located until they found out what charges were being made against him. I asked her if the Major had any objection to my reporting this information to my Consulate. She said none.

September 27

In the morning, I called the Consulate and gave the Major's information to Consul Purdy. He took the Major's telephone number and said he would check on the information.

At 1:30 Purdy called me (this was the first time since Charles' seizure the Consul had contacted me) to tell me that I had misunderstood the Major's wife and that, in fact, the Major had no information about my husband. Purdy said he was going to check the morgue. He also told me that he had received telegrams inquiring about Charles and that I could have a list of those who had sent them.

I called Mrs. Prieto and she told me that I had not misunderstood her previous report but that they had had the wrong name. (I had given the Major Charles' name in writing on the 25th of September.) She stated that the information had been correct but was about another person.

September 29

I returned to Vicuña MacKenna to speak with a friendly neighbor. He stated that there had been a witness to the raiding of the house and the arrest of Charles. He added that a wife of a friend of his (a colonel) had suggested that Charles might have friends on the left and might be hiding with them. He said many people had come to watch the soldiers, that it was impossible to confide in anyone these days, and that I should be very careful.

I called Captain Davis to report what I had learned, and he told me he had been assigned officially to the case and asked if I would come in the following Monday for an interview.

My neighbor called to tell me that he had heard that the Stadium would be open the following day for visitors and that I should go and ask about Charles.

September 30

Steven Volk accompanied me to the Stadium. We found out that "visitors' day" was for the soldiers who had been on continual guard duty but not for the prisoners.

October 1

I moved out of the Riviera Hotel and into the house of some friends, the Armstrongs. I then went to see Captain Davis.

When I entered, Captain Davis asked for a detailed description of Charles: his height, weight, clothes, identifying marks, beard, glasses. He said that it was very important he learn all he could about Charles. He added that he had spent some time as a research analyst for the Pentagon and that he knew how these things worked. He said it would be very helpful if I could give him a resume of all my husband's past work experience and a list of all his friends here in Chile with information about what each one was doing here. I said that I would provide the requested information but that it did not seem to be the most important information for determining where the military were keeping Charles. He asked me what Charles was really like, and I asked him what his own impressions were, since he had met Charles. Captain Davis said that he thought Charles was an introvert, semi-intellectual, and someone who did not say very much.

Later that afternoon I returned to my home and spoke with my neighbor, who had arranged for me to speak with the person who had seen the soldiers take Charles to the National Stadium.

The lady told me she had been visiting her mother, who lived across the street. She had been calling a taxi just as Charles was being loaded into the truck with the soldiers. She said she caught a taxi as the truck was pulling away. The route of the taxi to her own house accidentally coincided with the route of the soldiers' truck to the National Stadium. I asked her if she could remember anything distinctive about the truck, and she replied that it was an ordinary transport truck—nothing unusual. I thanked her for the information. I asked her if she would mind repeating this to an American official. She said she wouldn't mind, but that they wouldn't believe her, because she had supported Allende. She left to go to her home.

Before leaving, my neighbor told me that two men from the U.S. Embassy had come to interview him last Sunday (September 30th). He stated that he could not remember their names, but that one of them was blond.

I phoned the information given me by the woman to Captain Davis when I reached the Armstrong house.

October 2

General Camilo Valenzuela Godoy, who had been contacted through a Chilean friend of my father, came by the Armstrong house and introduced himself. He explained that he had been retired under the Frei regime but that he still had many friends in the Chilean military. He said he would surely be able to find Charles, so I wrote Charles' name down on paper for him.

I went to Captain Davis' office for a 1 p.m. meeting.

He asked me if I had prepared the resume and list of Charles' friends. I explained that I had not had the time. He said he thought it was important for the investigation to talk again to the lady who had seen the truck which took Charles away and had entered the National Stadium. I told Captain Davis that it seemed more important to interview neighbors to see if we could identify which military group had arrested Charles, because I had already spoken with the woman at length. (At a later date, an investigator spoke with a neighbor who confirmed my report.)

The investigator assigned to the case, Luis Blaney, arrived at Davis' office to accompany me to my neighborhood to interview the neighbors. He was a Chilean, employed for some time by the U.S. Embassy

Blaney and I left in an Embassy jeep; the next hour or so was spent in driving to another part of town for gasoline. I asked him what he knew about the case and he replied: "Everything." I asked him what he meant by "everything," and he said that my husband had disappeared. I then repeated to him what I had already told many times to the Embassy personnel, the Consulate personnel, and Captain Davis.

At about 2:30 p.m. we arrived at the neighborhood of the Vicuña MacKenna house, and we spoke with two women.

The first woman, Neighbor B., was working in a liquor store two doors away from the gate to our house. She stated that ten to fifteen soldiers had arrived in a truck. They had come to her store to ask some questions but had passed on without too much discussion. She said the truck was open, green, and that it was not a standard Chilean military vehicle, but more of a civilian transport type.

The second woman, Neighbor A., said that the soldiers had rung the bell at the front gate of our house and that no one answered. She brought them a step ladder so that the soldiers could climb over the fence. They kicked in three doors before reaching the door to our house. Shortly thereafter the soldiers brought Charles to the front gate and he unlocked it. Then they put him in the truck with a box of books and took him away. She said that she was sure they were regular soldiers, because her brother is a soldier and she knows Army uniforms. She said that Neighbor C., who lived next door, had talked with the group's commander at length. I was told that Neighbor C. worked and could only be reached very early or very late in the day.

I told a neighbor to try to contact the woman who had seen Charles taken to the National Stadium and ask her if she would talk to Embassy officials.

Before leaving I asked the investigator to meet me there again at 8:30 a.m. in order to talk to Neighbor C., who left for work early in the morning. He was very reluctant but finally agreed to do it. I returned to the Armstrongs' by bus. Captain Davis called to invite me to dinner, but I declined.

I telephoned my father-in-law, Edmund Horman, at his home in New York and asked him to please come to Santiago and help.

October 3

In the morning I went directly to the Vicuña MacKenna neighborhood. Blaney arrived late, and the woman we wanted to speak with had left for work. I attempted to speak to some other people in the neighborhood, but they were not cooperative; they said that they had seen nothing. Blaney left.

Edmund Horman called and asked me to get a report of the data acquired by the Consulate. I told him that Blaney had frightened the neighbors the previous day with his manner and that today he had not arrived on time. He suggested that I request another investigator.

I called Purdy who told me he had gotten Charles' fingerprints from Investigaciones.

He said something to the effect that there were a large number of bodies in the morgue. Purdy also said that photos of Charles were circulating in Investigaciones, INTERPOL, the Stadium, and the morgue. He told me that James Anderson was one of the men who had visited the vicinity of my home last Sunday and that he had learned that the neighbors saw the soldiers on the 17th of September and a green truck, and that Charles had not been beaten and that the military had taken a box of books with Charles when they arrested him. He added that the neighbors had been reticent about talking.

I requested another investigator and was given the name of Donald McNally and his telephone number. I called NcNally and asked him to meet me at a neighbor's house the next morning

I revisited Neighbor A. She said she would ask around to see if anyone had more information. She seemed to want to help me. I went to the home of Major Prieto. He was still in bed as the doctor had ordered.

He said they had no new information. I said that I was interviewing the neighbors to try to identify the group of soldiers who had picked up my husband. The major wrote me a letter of introduction to Colonel Ewing, the Secretary General of the government, and stated that Ewing would be able to locate the group immediately. The Major suggested that I go with a member of the U.S. Embassy military group to assure an audience. He also said that a Colonel Hon had contacted him and had gotten information on the contact orginally made through the New York bank.

I returned to the Vicuña MacKenna area and called Investigator Blaney. He said that he could not come there at 5 p.m. to meet the woman (Neighbor C.) because no one at the Embassy worked past 5 p.m.

I spoke with General Valenzuela, who reported that a personal friend of his working at the International Red Cross said that Charles had been released on September 21 and was seen heading in the direction of Curico. He said the Consulate had been notified of this. I called Purdy, who said the Consulate had not received any such notification.

The General telephoned again and his daughter repeated the same story in English and said that I should check with the downtown office of the International Red Cross.

I called McNally and asked him to meet me at 8:30 the next morning.

October 4

At 8:30 I went to Vicuña MacKenna and met Blaney and McNally. We interviewed the woman next door who con-

firmed the description of the captain of the group of soldiers and the number of soldiers. She said that Charles had not been beaten and that he had been taken with a box of books. She could not remember the license plate number of the truck and did not know the name of the captain.

October 5

I went to the International Red Cross and spoke with a Mr. Leman about the story told me by Valenzuela two days earlier. He telephoned two nurses, neither of whom had information on Charles. He said he would contact a third nurse.

I saw a letter on his desk from Mr. Purdy dated October 2. It mentioned that Charles had disappeared on the 17th, that Frank Teruggi had been arrested, and that they would appreciate any help they could get in locating either of the two men. Mr. Leman said they had received no word of Charles but they would look.

I went to the Armstrong residence and moved my things to the Hotel Crillon, where I had made reservations for myself and my father-in-law, Mr. Horman, who was arriving that day. Mr. Purdy met Mr. Horman at the airport and brought him over to the hotel. We then went to the Embassy for a meeting. Present were Mr. Horman, Colonel Hon, Ambassador Davis, Mr. Purdy, and myself.

Ambassador Davis said that the Embassy feeling was that Charles was probably in hiding. My father-in-law replied that this seemed implausible—that even if Charles had been afraid to call me directly, he could easily have passed a message through one of our friends.

Mr. Horman went on to ask what had been done to follow up on the probability that Charles had been seized by the Chilean Military Intelligence, as had been indicated by the evidence of neighbors who witnessed his arrest and of friends who subsequently had been called by the military. Ambassador Davis looked at Mr. Purdy and asked if he knew anything about the telephone calls. Purdy said. "No sir." I then reminded Mr. Purdy that two calls were recorded on the Consulate note cards being kept on Charles' case. (I had seen them during the interview I had had with Mr. Schaffer.) Purdy went to get the cards. He came back confirming that both calls had been noted. Davis wondered whether the calls had really been as Mr. Horman described them, so my father-in-law suggested that Davis have them checked immediately. The Ambassador ordered Purdy and Hon to do so. Mr. Horman also checked the calls himself. On the following day Mr. Purdy told Mr. Horman that both people involved had been interviewed. Their accounts of the calls matched the description we had provided. The Consul stated that Colonel Hon would ask Chilean Military Intelligence for a report on these conversations.

October 6

I went with Mr. Horman to see a United Nations official who had been working hard trying to locate missing persons. He told us that he would do all he could to locate Charles but that most of his efforts were channeled through the Refugee Center and we should check there. I called Mr. Leman at the International Red Cross. No one there had heard of, or had come across, Charles. He said that they were checking the lists of freed prisoners then and that they would call me the next Tuesday. He also said they were searching the National Stadium.

October 7

I do not recall the precise date, but around this time Mr. Purdy told me of an official notice from the Chilean military that Charles had been picked up on the 20th of September for infringement of curfew and released on September 21st. (These dates correspond to the arrest and supposed release of Frank Teruggi according to the report only recently issued by the Chilean military.) Purdy said, referring to this official note, that it must be mistaken, that it didn't correspond to facts, did it? I agreed that of course it didn't, and the matter was dropped.

Also around this time I requested that Mr. Purdy phone Colonel Ewing for an appointment, since I had had so much trouble myself.

I explained to him what Major Prieto had said about the possibilities of his locating the captain who had arrested Charles. Purdy asked his secretary to do so. Purdy did not seem anxious to accompany me but offered to arrange for someone else to do so. The secretary at the Consulate reported that Ewing's office said they would call back. Ewing's office never called back, and to the best of my knowledge the Consulate never attempted to make another appointment with Ewing.

October 8

I went back to Vicuña MacKenna with letters asking neighbors to call the Consulate anonymously if they had any more information about Charles' arrest. The Consulate never reported any such calls.

October 9

I went to the Embassy to speak with Public Relations Officer Halsema to see about getting information about Charles into the Chilean newspapers.

I spoke with his assistant, Mr. Don Planty, who sent me with two Chileans to the office of *El Mercurio*. I had a short interview with people there, and they accepted information about the "disappearance" of Charles (not of his arrest). They said something would go into the paper. As we were leaving, I remembered that I had forgotten to mention the reward offer. The two Chileans promised they would see to it that something to that effect got in the paper. The article about Charles' "disappearance" and our search for him appeared in *El Mercurio*, but no mention was made of a reward.

October 10

Mr. Purdy called Mr. Horman concerning a fingerprint check at the morgue. Mr. Horman and I went to the Argentine Consulate, hoping that they might know something or that Charles might be inside. We also went to speak with the Vicar General, but he had little information to offer. I went to the Refugee Center, and they had no information.

I went to see Charles' dentist, Dr. Abud Tapia, to ask for Charles' dental records. He said that he had destroyed Charles' file two days before. I explained that Charles had been arrested and had been missing since the 17th of September and that we had to check the morgue. He said he worked for the military and would ask his military friends if they had any news.

October 12

I began procedures to get a safe conduct pass out of the country. Mr. Horman went to the National Stadium.

October 15

Mr. Horman went to the Refugee Center early in the morning and told me that a woman reported to him that she had been advised by an officer at the Stadium that Charles Horman had been, but was no longer, there.

At 2:30 p.m. I went with my father-in-law to the home of Major Prieto.

The Major said that his original report, that Charles was alive and well, was based on what his sources in the military had told him, but that the military's story had changed when he called them back for more information. The Major stated that the military interrogators were supposed to have called their foreign prisoners' consulates during the interrogation.

In response to a plea for information by Mr. Horman, the Major called the Military Intelligence Service and arranged for two investigators to meet with me and my father-in-law the following morning at our hotel. The Major suggested that Charles might have been killed by left-wing extremists.

Mr. Horman then spoke with Mr. Purdy and reported to me that he had asked Mr. Purdy what he thought of the Major's assertion that Charles may have been killed by left-wing extremists. Mr. Purdy said that he doubted that either left- or right-wing groups had been involved. Mr. Horman also inquired as to the use of civilian trucks by the military. Purdy agreed that this had been common practice.

I spoke to a woman who worked at the Refugee Center. She called back later and said that Mrs. Halsema, the wife of the Public Relations Director at USIS, when asked why there had been so much difficulty locating Charles, had responded by commenting: "Yes, . . . I wonder just what naughty thing he was up to."

October 17

Mr. Horman had a meeting at the Ford Foundation and came by to meet me afterwards, around 11 a.m. One of the men he had interviewed had stated privately to him that he had heard from a friend (an officer in an English-speaking embassy) the following: that this person had been told by a friend, a Chilean general, that Charles Horman had been shot in the National Stadium on or before September 20th.

The two SIM investigators we had met on the 16th returned. They stated that a body of the same approximate height and weight as Charles had been brought to the morgue on September 18th. They described the clothes, but only the underwear was similar to clothes Charles owned. The weight was five or six pounds less than his, but they explained that might be due to loss of blood.

October 18

At 10:40 a.m., the two Intelligence investigators came to my room with a summons for me to appear at the National Police Headquarters in 20 minutes. They were harsh and frightened me. My father-in-law, after calling Mr. Purdy, who said that nothing should be done until he called him back, suggested that I go across the street to wait at the Lufthansa office. He told me to go to the U.S. Embassy and ask for protection if he did not come back in 30 minutes.

Mr. Purdy and Mr. Horman went to see Inspector Rojas. A Mr. Errol Rainess came by the Lufthansa office and took me over to the U.S. Embassy. At noon my father-in-law and Mr. Purdy returned to the Embassy. I went with my father-in-law to the National Police Headquarters but they had shifted our appointment to 4 p.m.

At 4 p.m. we returned to Investigaciones. While Rojas interviewed me, Purdy telephoned my father-in-law who afterwards informed me that the Embassy had been told by the Chileans that they had made a positive fingerprint identification of the body of a man who had been shot in the Stadium on September 18th and who had been interred in the wall of the National Cemetery on October 3rd. We telephoned and arranged to have Charles' dental records forwarded to Purdy via Charles Anderson of the State Department.

October 19

Two Military Intelligence officers confirmed the identification in a visit to my father-in-law.

Purdy also telephoned to confirm the identification on the basis of a fingerprint check by Embassy personnel. Purdy said that he considered this identification entirely conclusive and said that, although he had received the dental records, he did not believe that this further check was necessary.

October 20

Inspector Rojas of Informaciones came to the hotel and confirmed the identification and circumstances of death to my father-in-law.

Mr. Horman and I left Santiago on a 0 p.m. flight. ∎

The Case of Charles Horman

His Father's Charge

Edmund C. Horman arrived in Santiago on October 5 to search for his son Charles. Like his daughter-in-law, Joyce, he was subjected to evasions, indifference, and apparent inertia on the part of Embassy officials, and was forced to conduct his own investigations through whatever means were available to him. In the following letter sent to Senator Fulbright on October 25, Mr. Horman protests the outrageous behavior of the American Embassy and concludes: ". . . it seems apparent that it is Department policy to clear the Chilean government of responsibility and, at the same time, clear themselves of their obligation to hold a foreign government to account for killing an American citizen."

[For a fuller discussion of U.S. State Department and Embassy conduct following the coup, see IDOC No. 58, p. 65-69: "An Accusation Against the American Embassy in Santiago," by Richard R. Fagen, Professor of Political Science at Stanford University and President-elect of the Latin American Studies Association.]

Dear Senator Fulbright:

I was in Santiago, Chile from October 5th to October 20th, in search of my son, Charles Horman, who was killed by Chilean Military Forces in the National Stadium and who is mentioned in the letter sent to you by Richard R. Fagen of the Institute of Political Studies of Stanford University on October 8th.

My hope is that the telling of what I observed in Santiago and in Washington may lead to better protection of American citizens than was afforded to my son and to others by the Department of State.

Charles was seized in his rented house by Chilean soldiers at 5 p.m. on September 17th. The soldiers placed him in a truck and the truck was seen to enter the National Stadium, where prisoners were being concentrated. These events were witnessed, wholly or in part, by four people. On the following morning a Chilean industrial designer, and friend of Charles, was called by a man who identified himself as from Military Intelligence and asked questions about Charles. On the same morning a call was made to Warwick Armstrong, a New Zealander employed by the U.N.'s economic commission, CEPAL, and also a friend of Charles. The caller again identified himself as from Military Intelligence, asked questions about Charles and ordered Armstrong to go to the nearest *carabinero* station and make a statement. Armstrong discussed this with his superior at CEPAL. They decided that going to the station might be dangerous. They also decided that Armstrong should call Robert P. Coe at the American Embassy. Coe told Armstrong to speak to U.S. Consul Frederick K. Purdy, which he did. Purdy told me later that he had learned of Charles' seizure, at about the same time, from an Embassy employee who had been called by a friend of Charles.

On October 5th I arrived in Santiago and, with my daughter-in-law, met with U.S. Ambassador Nathaniel Davis, Purdy and Colonel William Hon, military attache to the Embassy. Davis said that the Embassy feeling was that Charles probably was in hiding. I said that this seemed implausible; that even if he were afraid to call his wife directly, he easily could have passed a message through one of their many friends. I asked what had been done to follow up the probability that Charles had been seized by Military Intelligence, as indicated by the evidence of neighbors who saw the seizure and friends who had been called by Military Intelligence. Davis looked at Purdy and asked whether he knew anything about the telephone calls. Purdy said, "No sir." My daughter-in-law reminded Purdy that, some days before, he had shown her some of his notes and that the call from Armstrong was on them. Purdy then remembered the calls. Davis wondered whether the telephone calls really were as I had described them. I suggested that he have them checked out immediately and he told Purdy and Colonel Hon to do so. On the next day, October 6th, Purdy told me that both people who had been telephoned had been interviewed; that their accounts matched mine; that Colonel Hon would ask Chilean Military Intelligence for a report.

On October 8th Purdy and Colonel Hon came to my hotel. Colonel Hon said that the Chilean military denied all knowledge of Charles. Repetitions of this statement were the only information given to me by the Embassy on this matter until October 18th. I gave them a letter

asking that they press on; that they investigate the possibility of prisons other than the National Stadium; that they check all foreign embassies where Charles might have gained asylum; that they make a fingerprint check of all unidentified bodies in the morgue; that news releases be given all Chilean newspapers; that reward offers be made in the newspapers. I offered to pay the rewards. All the above were approved for immediate action by Davis. Purdy, however, asked me to check the Swedish Embassy, explaining that their relations with the Swedes were not cordial because of the help given to an American woman who had said that the American Embassy had refused to help her and who had been given shelter by the Swedes. I spoke to the Swedish Ambassador [Harald Edelstam] by telephone later.

On October 10th Purdy telephoned me, saying that a fingerprint check showed that Charles was not in the morgue. At my request he confirmed this by letter. I then asked for a re-check by a recognized expert and offered to pay any fee. Several days later this was done and the same report received. On October 9th I had sent Purdy a note asking that a check be made on disposition of bodies removed from the morgue.

On October 15th, after being told by Purdy that the Chilean military continued to deny any knowledge of Charles and that our people knew of nothing further that could be done to persuade them, I visited Major Luis Contreras Prieto of the Chilean Army. I was put in touch with him by his brother, who is employed by a New York bank. I appealed to the Major on the grounds of humanity, saying that, if Charles were not alive, I hoped that they would not leave me without the truth when I returned to face his mother. Prieto immediately telephoned a Major Hugo Sala of Military Intelligence. After hanging up he told me to wait for a visitor next morning. On October 16 two men from Military Intelligence, Ortiz and Menesas by name, visited me for almost two hours. When they left, they said I would hear from them promptly. On October 17 they returned and asked many questions about the clothes which Charles wore. They asked whether I could obtain fingerprints. I called Purdy at the Consulate and he sent the prints at once by messenger. The men left with them. On the same afternoon I visited Enrique Bernstein for almost an hour. He is Foreign Minister Huerta's assistant and had been spoken to in New York by my brother-in-law, the arrangement having been made by Brian Urquhart of the United Nations. Señor Bernstein promised to do everything possible.

On the same day, a man associated with the Ford Foundation told me that a close friend of his also is a close friend of a general in the Chilean Army; that the general had said that Charles had been shot to death in the National Stadium "on or before September 20th."

On October 18th Inspector Mario Rojas, of Investigaciones, summoned my daughter-in-law to be interviewed. He showed me a letter from the Minister of the Interior directing him to devote his entire effort to finding the truth about Charles.

In the late afternoon Purdy telephoned me. He said that the Chileans had telephoned the Embassy and said that they had matched Charles' fingerprints to those of the body of a man who had been shot in the National Stadium on September 18th and had been interred in the wall of the National Cemetery on October 3rd. This report was confirmed to me formally in visits by the men from Military Intelligence and by Inspector Rojas of Investigaciones.

So, from September 18th to October 5th, the date of my arrival in Santiago, the American Embassy did *nothing* to verify the evidence which had been placed in their hands on September 18th and which proved to be the key to the truth. From October 5th to the very end, their "efforts" produced no results beyond their repeated statements that they had contacted the Chilean government, right up to General Pinochet, and had been told that the Chileans knew nothing about Charles or his whereabouts. And yet, within three days after my talks with Major Prieto and Enrique Bernstein, the truth was made plain.

I do not know the reason underlying the negligence, inaction and failure of the American Embassy. Whether it was incompetence, indifference or something worse, I find it shocking, outrageous and, perhaps, obscene.

My own observations and the experiences related to me by others convince me that the attitudes and behavior of some—not all—American State Department employees fall very short of those of the personnel of certain foreign embassies and of workers in the groups who are helping refugees in Chile. As examples I might mention:

—October 8th. Ambassador Davis directed that news releases be requested in all Chilean newspapers and that offers of reward be inserted. As of October 16th, despite my daily inquiries, one news release and no reward offers were printed. When I was referred to the Embassy press officer, I was told that I should be grateful for the one story. I then protested to the Ambassador, who put another man on the job. Another story appeared on the following day and the reward notices were prepared for immediate insertion as advertisements.

—A friend of my daughter-in-law asked the wife of an Embassy officer why there was so much delay and difficulty in locating Charles. The response, as quoted directly to my daughter-in-law, was: "He must have been doing something very naughty."

—On September 28th I was in the State Department offices in Washington. One of the men let me use his office for four hours while he attended a meeting. During this time, a friend of my son, who had literally devoted all his time to the search, called from the reception desk and asked for me. The man to whom he spoke had talked with me at length and could literally see me in the office. He told the young man that I was not there and refused to let him come up and wait for me.

—The Department issued press releases and made statements to me and to others, both in Charles' case and in that of Frank Teruggi, quoting the Chilean statements that both had been released from the National Stadium and possibly were in hiding. This seemed completely illogical at the time and was proven false in my son's case. Taking these actions of the Department together with an article printed in the *New York Post* during this past week which quoted a Department press officer by name as saying that Charles probably was seized by a leftist group, it seems apparent that it is Department policy to clear the Chilean government of responsibility and, at the same time, clear themselves of their obligation to hold a foreign government to account for killing an American citizen. The press release to the *Post* conflicts directly with the view expressed to me by Purdy. Fearing that the Chileans might disclaim responsibility by blaming Charles' seizure on rightist (the thought of leftists doing this is preposterous) groups, I had asked Purdy the Embassy view of the possibility that such groups might have been active. He confirmed what I already believed: that there was so much dissension and possible disloyalty in the Chilean Army that special armbands were issued each day and that any such irregular groups would have been in great danger.

—My daughter-in-law was treated discourteously by Embassy people. As stated earlier, until October 5th no steps were taken to follow up the evidence which was given to the Embassy on September 18th.

Very truly yours,
(signed) Edmund C. Horman

cc: Secretary of State Henry Kissinger
    Senator Edward Kennedy
    Senator Jacob Javits
    Senator Gale McGee
    Senator Adlai Stevenson
    Senator Charles Percy
    Congressman Dante Pascell
    Congressman Donald Fraser
    Congressman Paul McCloskey
    Congressman Robert McClory
    Congressman Edward Koch
    Congressman Jack Kemp
    Professor Richard Fagen

Seven Days in Chile's Climate of Fear

Managing Editor of The Christian Century, *Dean Peerman is a member of the Chicago Commission of Inquiry into the Status of Human Rights in Chile which visited Santiago on a fact-finding mission in February 1974 and whose report is published in the next section. The following article, based on his general observations of life in the Chilean capital, was published in* The Christian Century *on March 20, 1974.*

Soldiers and *carabineros* seem to be stationed everywhere we go—their submachine guns at the ready. Almost as prevalent are billboards and posters which read: *"En cada soldado hay un Chileno; en cada Chileno hay un soldado"* ("In every soldier there is a Chilean; in every Chilean there is a soldier.")

Upon arriving at our hotel, we—an ad hoc Chicago-based fact-finding commission concerned about the status of human rights in Chile—are greeted by three women from Santiago's Christian community. They warn us not to talk with Chileans on the streets—not only because the ruling military Junta encourages "patriots" to inform on "suspicious" persons, but because there are many plain-clothes intelligence agents around. We invite the three women to join us for dinner, and on the way to a restaurant we note that there would hardly be any strangers to talk with anyway; except for the military, the dimly lit streets are virtually deserted—even though curfew is several hours away.

At the restaurant one of our dinner guests expresses guilt feelings about partaking of what, by her standards,

is an expensive meal; she is acutely conscious of the hunger and suffering of the Chilean poor. Though the Junta claims to have inflation under control, the cost of a number of basic necessities has skyrocketed in recent weeks; the price of bread, for example, has risen 400 percent in less in less than than two months. We learn that many families now eat only three or four meals a week. Unemployment is widespread—about 20 percent; thousands of workers, most of them leftists, were dismissed from their jobs following the *coup d'etat* of September 11. Wages are fixed by decree, but some workers receive considerably less than the official minimum wage of 18,000 escudos ($24) a month.

As we return to the hotel, we witness the kind of happening that has become commonplace in Chile: one of our guests encounters a distraught friend who tearfully reports that her fiancé was picked up by the military three days before and that, though she has been to every place of detention in Santiago, she has not been able to locate him.

We have had a sobering introduction to Chile's siege atmosphere. More than five months after the violent putsch that overthrew the Marxist but democratically elected and constitutionalist government of President Salvador Allende, Santiago is still a fear-ridden, terror-filled city.

By day, however, Santiago has a deceptive surface calm: the streets are crowded, the tourists and the American corporation executives are reappearing, the summer weather is delightful. And one gradually grows accustomed to the ubiquitous presence of the military. The apparent tranquillity is largely a consequence of the fact that the wanton blood-letting of the early stages of the coup has given way to more sophisticated and discriminating methods; instead of the dragnet, there is the nocturnal knock at the door. Though the Junta's campaign to "extirpate the Marxist cancer" is as ruthless and relentless as ever, the September savagery is being replaced by low-profile repression. As an exceptionally candid Army colonel is reported to have remarked: "We've ended the phase of massive slaughter and entered the phase of selective slaughter." The military authorities have become much more calculating and efficient; no longer, for example, are they publicly putting books to the torch—if only because they are concerned about their credibility abroad.

One evening a young man who has heard about our commission of inquiry hazards a visit to the hotel. He is a member of the Inner Religion of Silo, a youth-oriented sect that draws on Eastern mysticism. Thirteen of the sect's leaders are in jail; Bruno von Ehremberg, the principal leader, has been badly tortured and is being held incommunicado. Because some young people leave their homes upon joining Silo, the Junta-controlled press has accused the cult of "corrupting the youth" and breaking up family life. Because the group is antimaterialist and therefore anticapitalist, the authorities have concluded that it is procommunist; actually it is apolitical. Handing me a copy of one of Silo's now-banned books, my visitor pleads with me to publicize the plight of his sect. The Junta's incarceration of these harmless young utopians leads me to wonder if it is really being "selective" after all. (But certainly it is thorough; we have discovered that several of our hotel rooms are bugged.)

Chile has a strong, well-entrenched legal tradition, and the military government has sought to give a veneer of legitimacy to its despotic operations by invoking the constitutional provision pertaining to a "state of siege" and reinterpreting it in terms of a "state of internal war." The Junta insists that accused persons have the benefit of the procedural guarantees that obtain under such extraordinary circumstances—but those guarantees amount to very little indeed. Under the "internal war" declaration, the authorities can detain, search and interrogate anyone at any time or place—and by any means. (To facilitate "interrogation," the Junta has imported Brazilians who are expert in that art.) Prisoners can be held incommunicado and without charge, and if and when a case does come to trial, the defense lawyer generally cannot see his client—or even the list of charges—until a few hours beforehand. The military officer presiding over the trial—which is completely secret—often adds many years to the sentence recommended by the prosecution. Max Silva, vice-minister of justice, freely acknowledged in an interview with our group that prisoners are presumed guilty.

In short, due process does not exist in Chile. And the Junta's claim that it is acting legally rather than arbitrarily is singularly unconvincing; for one thing, a "state of siege" decree requires authorization of the Congress—but one of the military's first moves was to abolish the Congress, along with outlawing the leftist political parties and declaring all other parties to be in "indefinite recess."

Our 12-member commission has a very full agenda; frequently we split up into groups of two or three or venture out individually in order to cover more ground. We are received by Junta officials who profess to be surprised that a group such as ours would come to Chile at a time when "we are restoring the country." We speak with professors who describe how the universities, after being seized by the military, have been decimated by large-scale expulsions of both students and faculty, and how entire departments—the social sciences, public health, journalism—have been closed down.

We meet with foreign ambassadors who inform us of the difficulties encountered in securing safe-conduct for some of the people who took asylum in their embassies after the coup. We interview "suspect," unyielding labor leaders whose union activities have been proscribed—as well as newly appointed labor "un-leaders" whose only task seems to be to pass Junta directives on the workers. We gain entry to one of the many detention centers—a gymnasium called Estadio Chile—and are permitted to talk with four prisoners on a balcony overlooking the gym floor where more than 200 others—some of them as young as 16 and 17—are confined; it is the "showcase" prison and a place of "recuperation"—but when no guards are watching, prisoners on the floor below open their shirts to show us the marks of the torture they have been subjected to in other detention centers.

And we visit with church people—courageous Catholics and Protestants who, often at great risk, are aiding the destitute families of Junta victims and who in some cases have provided hiding places for fugitives from the repression. Comments one prominent Christian: "I try to look for good things in bad people. But I cannot find one good thing that the Junta has done."

One of our commission's primary purposes, however, is quite specific: to investigate the murder of Frank Teruggi, Jr., a 23-year-old American student who was caught up in the early carnage of the coup. Frank's father, a typographer from the Chicago suburb of Des Plaines, is one of our group. He is not satisfied with the information

that the Chilean government has conveyed via the U.S. State Department prior to our trip; it contains discrepancies and hiatuses. In Mr. Teruggi's opinion, the State Department itself has been remiss; in December it assured him that inquiries were being made in Santiago "at top diplomatic levels," but the end result was a report giving the same explanation of what happened to Frank that was given in a report issued in October, shortly after he was murdered. Originally the authorities stated that Frank had been arrested for curfew violation on September 20; this was patently untrue, since he and his roommate, David Hathaway, were picked up at the same time—in their apartment. But the Junta has stood by the rest of its story: that Marxist literature was found in Frank's room; that he was held overnight at the soccer stadium for questioning, then released; that his bullet-riddled body was brought to the morgue the next day; that he was probably killed by "left-wing terrorists." Yet no other prisoner was detained for so brief a time—or released so near the curfew hour—as the Junta claims was the case with Frank. (Hathaway was held for six days.) And the Junta admits there is no record of Frank's release.

At the beginning of the week the commission has a session with U.S. Ambassador David H. Popper and four of his associates. They are cordial and, under Mr. Teruggi's polite but firm prodding, promise to try to "clear up the gaps." But they suggest no new line of investigation and even refuse to furnish Mr. Teruggi a letter of introduction to appropriate Junta officials. (They are similarly unencouraging when we press them about the possibility of our country's opening its doors to Chilean refugees.)

With step-by-step perseverance, Mr. Teruggi accomplishes more in five days than the U.S. Embassy has in five months. Followed everywhere by two men in a small blue car, he goes to the place where Frank lived and finds on a telephone book the Embassy number in his son's handwriting; he visits the police substation where Frank was first taken and learns that no inquiries have been made there. Particularly helpful is a conversation with a conservative Chilean businessman—a friend of David Hathaway's family—who says that David's girl friend notified him of the two youths' arrest on the morning of September 21, and that he immediately phoned the American consulate. (The consulate is queried and claims it has no record of any such call.) The businessman arranges an appointment for Mr. Teruggi with General Oscar Bonilla, Minister of the Interior. Visibly taken aback by the conflicting evidence Teruggi confronts him with, Bonilla vows to reopen the case and declares that the government will apologize if it is established that Frank died as a result of "negligence" on the part of the military.

Near the end of our stay, Mr. Teruggi finally finds out the appalling truth about his son's death. It comes in the form of detailed eyewitness testimony presented in a document delivered by a well-known and trustworthy Chilean woman to an embassy of a Western European country. The document "clears up the gaps" between the time Frank was separated from David Hathaway at the soccer stadium and the time his body was brought to the morgue. Young Frank was never released from the stadium while still alive. After what the authorities had done to him, they did not dare release him. "I honestly don't believe they'll ever admit they killed him," Frank, Sr., ruefully remarks.

Undeniably, the democratic process was falling apart toward the end of Salvador Allende's three-year presidency. Operating with a narrow electoral mandate and often hamstrung by the opposition-controlled Congress and courts, his Popular Unity coalition government angered the oligarchy with its efforts to redistribute wealth through agrarian reform and other measures. Attacked by the left for moving too slowly and by the right for moving too fast, Allende was very much a man in the middle. The revolutionary left resented his insistence on proceeding by means of "bourgeois legality"; the rightists resented his failure to prevent the left's illegal expropriation of a number of small farms and his "sectarian" way of handing out jobs according to party affiliation. Polarization between extreme left and extreme right led to political stalemate and social disruption—with the right doing all it could to sabotage production and to paralyze the country through strikes staged by truck owners and people in the professions. The role of the United States in Allende's downfall has been well documented; its "invisible blockade"—the termination of all aid other than military, the credit squeeze, etc.—was devastating. But whether that role was *decisive* remains a question.

The death toll from September's military coup in Chile certainly supassed 10,000 and is still rising at a rate of up to 50 a week, according to semi-official sources in Washington

Asking around Washington and New York, one can come up with the most varied estimates. The lowest comes from businessmen and pro-Junta Chileans, who speak of a few hundred dead—a figure which conflicts even with the latest official admission in Santiago that 3,500 died.

The Chilean ambassador in Washington, General Walter Heitmann, provoked an incredulous reaction when he alleged recently in a debate with the former Swedish Ambassador in Santiago, Harald Edelstam, that since he had not seen a single body he did not believe that anyone had been killed.

According to Edelstam, between 10,000 and 15,000 were killed. This tallies fairly well with the Central Intelligence Agency's reckoning — 10,800 dead by the beginning of December. A confidential memorandum from the Ford Foundation's representative in Santiago to the Foundation's New York headquarters made a comparable estimate.

Much higher figures are given by representatives of the Chilean left, who claim a figure of 40,000.

Apart from those who were killed out of hand, it has now been fairly reliably established that more than 2,000 people had been executed after secret military trials until Christmas.

When the history of this Latin American Gulag Archipelago comes to be written, the records will also have to take into account about 30,000 children left as orphans, 25,000 students who cannot complete their studies, and 200,000 people who have lost their jobs for political reasons—Edelstam's figures.

Katherine Camp, vice-president of the Women's International League for Peace and Freedom, told the recent congressional conference that there was a real possibility of famine in the coming winter. The first victims will be the orphans, the unemployed and their families.

—*Christopher Roper in*
Le Monde, April 6, 1974

Whatever the shortcomings of the Allende regime, however, there is no conceivable justification for the political genocide that is now taking place in Chile. (Estimates of the number of people executed by the Junta range as high as 20,000—though the figure we have heard most often is 40,000.) Even certain members of the Christian Democrat Party are now being rounded up—the party which was Allende's principal opposition and most of whose members supported the coup. What happens in regard to the Christian Democrats will be a key to the future: if the Junta arrives at an accommodation with them, it will have decided on a kind of populist authoritarianism; if it cracks down on them, it will probably move toward total police-statism. Ismael Huerta, the Junta's Minister of the Exterior, apparently is not prepared to deny that Chile is a fascist state; at the recent conference of foreign ministers in Mexico City he told reporters that he cannot say whether the military government "is or is not fascist." Certainly its methods are fascist; what it lacks is an undergirding ideology. And Catholic leaders sadly point to several signs indicating that the Junta plans to use the church in developing that ideology.

Throughout the week many people—Chileans, Ford Foundation personnel, and others—voice the hope that we and similar groups will appeal to the U.S. government to apply its considerable leverage with the Junta in order to bring about the restoration of fundamental human rights in Chile. But the prospects for our government's doing anything of the kind seem dim indeed, in view of its hasty resumption of aid following the September coup.

Our commission of inquiry is escorted back to the airport by a German-born, strongly pro-Junta tour guide who fought with Hitler's army in World War II. His parting words to us: "I hope you come back soon." Numb from all that we have seen and experienced—and from all the true-life horror stories that we have listened to—we can scarcely muster a smile.■

The Death of José Tohá

José Tohá was taken prisoner in the presidential palace on September 11, the day of the coup. A close friend and associate of Salvador Allende, he was the first minister appointed to office following the electoral victory of the Unidad Popular. Along with the late President, he was a member of the Socialist party and regarded as one of the most astute and effective men in the UP government during its three years in office. He served in turn as its Minister of the Interior, of Defense, and of Agriculture and was said to be one of the few government officials able to negotiate with moderate elements of the anti-Allende forces in the critical days preceding the coup.

In September, Tohá, along with 36 members of the UP government, was imprisoned in the Antarctic Dawson Island camp. In December he was transferred to a Military Hospital at Punta Arenas reportedly suffering "malnutrition" and in February to a hospital in Santiago, where he died on March 15. Members of the Chicago Commission of Inquiry who asked to see him during their mission to Santiago in February were told he could not receive visitors. Rose Styron of Amnesty International reports, "José Tohá, Minister of Defense, a man six feet four inches tall, when last seen alive was down to 112 pounds and could hardly see, hear, or walk. The Junta has listed him a suicide, but there are convincing reports he died by strangling." His widow, whose testimony follows, expresses grave doubts about the official reports of his death, as have many others. Her statement, written in exile in Mexico during April, tells of her urgent pleas to members of the Junta who were "friends" before the coup, including Generals Pinochet and Bonilla.

I'm sure that what the world expects of me is a scandalous story of the long days of fighting to save José's life. I've decided, however, to hold to the simple facts. Let the world judge.

September 11

At 8 a.m. we heard about the rebellion and that President Allende was at La Moneda Palace with his closest collaborators. José went there immediately. Around 1:15 he phoned from the State Department telling me to be calm. "I'm here following the President's orders," he said. "He's asked for a cease-fire and for a talk with the Generals in order to obtain guarantees for the workers, to assure that their living quarters and the industrial districts would not be bombed." Apparently the President was not successful. Only a little later I learned of Salvador Allende's death. That night, in despair, I phoned Almirante Carvajal. "Your husband is fine," he said. "He's a remarkable man and I'm sure he'll come through." Unfortunately I believed him. As José had been the Defense Secretary for some time, our whole social life revolved around military people and their families.

September 14

We, the Ministers' wives, received a call saying we should prepare a suitcase with heavy clothing for our husbands who were interned at the Military Academy. I included a vicuña blanket, a gift given to José by General Pinochet. I was assured there was nothing to fear because my husband was highly esteemed by the military.

September 17

We heard that our husbands had been sent to Dawson Island. I went to the Defense Department to inquire and accidently met General Pinochet. He greeted me warmly. When I requested an appointment, he gave me one for the next day. I went with Mrs. Letelier and Mrs. Almeyda. General Pinochet's humor was not the same; he was violent.

September 19

The list of prisoners sent to Dawson Island appeared in the newspaper *El Mercurio*. Having an appointment with General Bonilla, head of the Department of the Interior, I asked him, knowing the polar climate on Dawson Island, if we, the wives of the prisoners, could send more clothing to our husbands. He agreed. Our correspondence with the Island became, every day, more irregular and censored. Over a month passed without any news.

December 7

I discovered that José had been in the Military Hospital at Punta Arenas since November 24, for "malnutrition." I asked General Leigh if I could visit my husband. At Punta

Arenas I was told that I could only see him once and for only ten minutes. I firmly refused such conditions and I was finally allowed to see him four times, always in the presence of an official with a machinegun. José's physical state was deplorable. He was a tall man, well over six feet, but always very thin, and now he had lost more than 22 pounds. He told me how he, along with the other prisoners on the Island, was forced to hard labor on a very meager diet, how they were insulted and humiliated and under the tension of not knowing what they were accused of and when they would be tried.

December 22

I went back to Santiago and my five- and eight-year-old children. In January Aniceto Rodríguez, the first man to be freed from the Island, told General Arellano about José's precarious health and said that if he continued on the Island his life would be in danger.

February 1

José is transferred to the Military Hospital in Santiago.

February 2

His mother was permitted to visit him. She returned completely upset. José now weighed only 120 pounds.

February 4

I was allowed to see him alone for fifteen minutes. He could hardly see me. He was losing his eyesight. I asked the officials if I could bring the children on the sixth, his forty-seventh birthday. This was allowed us and the meeting was dramatic. After five days of adequate treatment he was noticeably better.

February 15

I arrived at the hospital with my youngest son and was told that José was no longer there. He had been taken away to be questioned, but they refused to tell me where.

February 19

I urgently requested to see General Pinochet. I was told that due to his preparation for a trip to Brazil, all appointments were canceled. I insisted and he saw me the next day at 5 p.m. He greeted me well. "I don't come to speak to you as the President of the Junta," I said, "but as Augusto Pinochet, our old friend. I ask you to give me back my husband." He answered, "You can't ask me this." He seemed nervously disturbed and his actions were violent, pacing up and down the room, mumbling that José had been friendly with him but that he couldn't promise anything.

February 28

José was taken back to the hospital and I ceded my visiting permit to his brother, who is a doctor. He was shocked when he saw his brother. We later found out that during the time José was absent from the Santiago Military Hospital he had been detained at the Air Force War Academy, where he was constantly questioned under pressure and his life was threatened. All I know is that in this lapse of time he was not the same man. "If they're going to kill me," he told his brother, "I wish they'd do it at once.

Day and night, every minute, they all keep repeating to me that I am a murderer and a thief." His mind was completely upset. The following day his mother visited him and José had a new doctor, a psychiatrist.

March 8

I saw José, not knowing it was to be the last time. He was lying on the bed, extremely weak. "They're going to try me as a murderer and a thief," he told me. I tried to make light of this. It was difficult for me to bring his spirits up with a machinegun-holding guard constantly present.

General Bachelet died in prison. I visited his widow. I desperately called Colonel Ibáñez and told him that I hoped that, after what happened to General Bachelet, urgent steps would be taken to save José. The newspaper headline that morning reported that José was in very serious condition.

March 15

At 5 p.m. I received a phone call from Colonel Aguirre. He said, "I'm calling on behalf of General Arellano. Your husband has just died." I don't remember what I said. Later, when I entered José's hospital room I saw his naked body lying on the bed. I finally saw peace in his face. I took his head in my arms and talked to him softly. I turned towards the military guards saying: "This is what we receive after giving three years of our lives working for all of you. You give me back a dead body." One of them answered: "It was his own decision. He took his own life," and showed me a belt and pointed out the slight marks on José's neck. "Whether it was his will or not," I said, "I can only say that the last time I saw him he could hardly lift a finger, and the expression in his face now does not look at all like that of a strangled man. But even if what you say is true, I want you to know that I consider it the most beautiful act of protest against unjust treatment, and that this will help save the lives of his comrades."

Until José's death, I still believed in many things—in friendship and human kindness. I do not want to judge anybody. I only hope that those who are responsible for José's death may be able to sleep peacefully. ■

Santiago, Chile—José Tohá, a key official in the government of former President Salvador Allende, and a political prisoner since Allende's fall last September, committed suicide Friday in a military hospital, official sources reported.

The sources said Tohá hanged himself in his hospital room and was found dead at about midday.

Tohá, 47, a newspaperman by profession, served as minister of both interior and defense under Allende.

A member of the militant wing of Allende's Marxist Socialist party, Tohá was at the center of innumerable political storms as the opposition repeatedly sought his ouster as an extremist.

After Allende's fall, Tohá was jailed with other Allende officials on Dawson Island at the extreme south of Chile. A month ago, he was transferred to a military hospital in Santiago for treatment of what was described as extreme nervous depression.

Along with other high ranking former Allende aides, he faced trial by a military tribunal.

—Miami Herald, *April 6, 1974*

Chile's Perpetual Dictatorship

Six months after the coup, the military Junta was taking great pains to convince world opinion that things had taken a turn for the better in Santiago. Bolstered by assurance from the Chilean Embassy in Paris that there would be no administrative obstacles to a journalist making an on-the-spot inquiry, Le Monde sent Marcel Niedergang to Chile. Mr. Niedergang arrived in Santiago, but was immediately ordered out of the country. The following report on Chile's new order was filed from Buenos Aires and appeared in Le Monde *on April 6, 1974.*

Six months after the collapse of Salvador Allende's Popular Unity government, Chile's military masters seem as determined as ever to hang on to power for as long as possible. The Junta continues its extremely punitive, though less blatant but more scientific, course of nipping in the bud any significant move to organize left-wing forces clandestinely. Diplomatic sources in Santiago say that the arrests, harassment, dismissals on political grounds, and torture continue to be the order of the day. But the most telling differences over the last month have arisen among the leaders of an army subject to some agitation and a Christian Democrat Party which finds it hard to accept the idea of all political parties being shut out of the governing process and which fears that a Brazilian-type regime may be established in Chile.

Christian Democrat hopes were in fact dashed anew by the clarification given recently by Justice Minister Gonzalo Trieto Gandara. He said that the new Constitution being drafted would officially endorse the ban on political parties suspended following the *coup d'état* of September 11, 1973. The Constitution would forbid the formation of any party or group "having links with foreign countries." Chilean Christian Democrats, who form the leading party in the country, have never made a secret of their relations and friendship with Christian Democrats in the world outside.

The party, led by Eduardo Frei, ran Chile between 1964 and 1970, and in the dying days of the Popular Unity government it took part in the clamor for Salvador Allende's head. It hailed the *coup d'état* as an act of salvation, and Mr. Frei himself said last October that the only solution for Chile was "a military government." While giving the impression that they accepted "a limited but necessary period of dictatorship," the Christian Democrats hoped the Junta would fix a timetable for restoring normal constitutional government. But as the weeks rolled by, the leaders of the armed forces kept postponing the deadline from two to three, five, and six years.

Scrubbing Minds

But General Augusto Pinochet, considered last September to be one of the most moderate of the Junta members, is increasingly beginning to use the word "never" in his speeches. In a recent address to the Chuquicamata miners, he reminded his listeners that unions were now debarred from engaging in any kind of political activity. "And that is not a decision which applies for three or four years," he emphasized. "It's valid for all time. It's a question of scrubbing minds clean."

Echoing him, the rifle corps commander General Cesar Mendoza declared that the Junta was going to stay in the saddle "for an unlimited length of time" and that all parties, whether of the right or the left, would be "indefinitely" banned. In an effort to stop or slow down this development, former Senator Patricio Alwyn, who was one of the stubbornest opponents of the Allende government, criticized—in his "private and official capacity"—what he called the "systematic and spiteful campaign against the Christian Democrats" that had been conducted since the *coup d'état*.

The former senator conceded that there was a need for "a moral, economic and social clean-up," but added: "Flouting human rights is not the best way of establishing this harmony. Tiny groups of people think that what happened in Chile will help them recover their privileges and the political and economic power they had lost during the process of democratization. But it is not fair that the savings of workers should benefit capitalist groups." And he concluded his letter in these terms: "We are convinced that it is not possible to build a lasting order on repression. We are convinced that the total political immobility of democratic sectors is likely to facilitate the clandestine activity of Marxist groups. In the absence of proper guidance from its leaders, the rank and file of the Christian Democrat Party is at the mercy of agitators, impostors and infiltrators."

Pinochet Unmoved

General Pinochet does not seem to have been moved by the arguments of a leader of the Christian Democrat right wing because, shortly afterwards, he made an allusion to the "bad Chileans" who pressed for an end to the military government. Enrique Montero, the Deputy Minister of the Interior, pointed out that on the orders of the Junta the police were going to conduct an inquiry into the matter.

There was a repetition of this dialogue at cross purposes when Mr. Alwyn obtained an interview with General Oscar Bonilla, the Minister of the Interior. The latter allowed that there had been excesses where respect for human rights was concerned, but added that there was "a daily flood of denunciations directed against the Christian Democrats" and that Intelligence Services had uncovered "a plan against the Junta" drawn up by the Christian Democrat Party. It seems clear that there is a widening gulf between the military, whose advisers all belong to the National Party, and to a group of economists known as the "Chicago Boys," and the cold-shouldered Christian Democrat leaders.

At one time General Bonilla was Eduardo Frei's aide-de-camp when Frei was president. But the former president no longer has free access to his erstwhile aide, and he confides his great disappointment to his closest friends. Radomiro Tomic, the leader of the Christian Democrat Party's left wing, who is a former ambassador to Washington and was a candidate against Allende in the presidential race, is now in the United States where he is lecturing in a university. He believes that the Junta is set "for at least ten years" of power in Chile, and that the only hope lies in a "rapprochement with the progressive or liberal element in the armed forces." Another former Christian Democrat leader, who was also a minister under Mr. Frei, is much less optimistic. "How sad," he said, "to see a big party being put to death."

In his interview with General Bonilla, ex-senator Alwyn made a reference to "an offensive directed straight at the Christian Democrats in the hope of creating a political vacuum which would favor the installation of the National Movement in civilian and military life." A former military aide of Allende's is perhaps thinking of the same men when he refers to "a civilian shadow cabinet working hand in glove with the Junta." ■

Marcel Niedergang, the Latin American specialist of the Paris newspaper *Le Monde,* was recently denied entry at [Santiago's] Pudahuel International Airport.

The incident, coming on the heels of a several-day detention of a British newsman, George Roth, correspondent for the Canadian Broadcasting Corporation, is fresh evidence, say observers here, that Chile's new military government is smarting from overseas criticism and has become suspicious of foreign newsmen.

For *Le Monde,* however, the Niedergang incident suggested that Chile's military were trying to hide something. "When a government refuses entry to a journalist," the paper asked, "how can one not conclude that it has something—perhaps many things—to hide?"

Whatever the reason, the denial of entry to Mr. Niedergang is another example of the Chilean military Junta's attitude toward the press and toward newsmen. At home, the Junta has muzzled the few remaining newspapers, radio stations, and television channels—putting them all under stiff censorship.

There was a time when Santiago's newspapers were the most freewheeling, controversial, and entertaining papers in all of Latin America. But that was before the military came to power last September, overthrowing the Marxist government of Salvador Allende Gossens.

The military immediately closed five newspapers that had supported Dr. Allende, including the Communist Party's *El Siglo* and the highly politicized *Puro Chile,* which represented an extremely leftist point of view.

Two other papers have folded since then—the rightist *La Tribuna,* which the military closed for publishing a story that later proved false, and *La Prensa,* official organ of the centrist Christian Democrat Party, Chile's largest. *La Prensa* was closed down by its publishers since it was under heavy censorship, and "there seems no point in putting out a political newspaper when politics are banned," as a spokesman said.

That leaves only five papers now publishing—three put out by the conservative *El Mercurio* organization, *La Patria* (which uses the presses of the onetime *La Nacion,* the government paper), and *La Tercera de la Hora,* a tabloid with the largest circulation in Chile, about 400,000 copies daily.

Instead of the lively, controversial press of earlier days, these five papers are "in some ways very little more than house organs for the military," as a local newspaper here put it. "They certainly are not newspapers doing the job that newspapers ought to do—searching for the truth. They merely print whatever the government permits them to print."

The same is true for the radio and television stations and for magazines. *Ercilla,* a weekly newsmagazine long considered one of Latin America's best, is read by censors before it goes on the newsstands.

Another magazine here appeared recently with a page torn out—pulled out by the military censors.

The military-imposed censorship prohibits stories critical of the military, those that mention price increases not announced by the government, and those about members of the Allende government unless the information has been officially released. All mention of politics is taboo.

Military officials here are reluctant to give reasons for the censorship. But one officer said some days ago that "we are going to restructure the country, and we can't have criticism." . . .

—James Nelson Goodsell in
The Christian Science Monitor,
April 4, 1974

The Marginal Poor

The poblaciones which ring Santiago and house a quarter to a half of the city's nearly 4,000,000 inhabitants have been an area of major concern to the Junta and the object of especially cruel and immediate repression during the coup. They were the element of Chilean life which had responded most enthusiastically to the efforts of the UP government and its allies to politicize their natural constituency. From their original condition of shantytowns, many had developed into integrated neighborhoods with simple but solid homes and with previously unimagined facilities for food distribution, child and health care, and education for young and old. Now the leaders have been killed or imprisoned, or are in hiding. The food-distribution centers have been closed, as have the health centers and other community centers.

The following two pieces trace the history of one such población before and after the coup. It has been variously called Ranquil, then Nueva Habana, and now, grotesquely, New Dawn.

Los Sin Casa

The following *is an excerpt from the North American Congress on Latin America (NACLA) publication* New Chile, *1973 edition.*

There are many homeless people in Chile's cities, as in the cities of other Latin American countries, where migrations of peasants from the impoverished countryside have led to the mushrooming of shanty towns. Called *callampas* (mushrooms), these shanty towns are grim sores where people live in tents, cardboard shacks or in the open. MIR (Movement of Revolutionary Left) began to organize among those people in late 1969, urging groups without land or homes to unite in concerted action to improve their lives. In at least eight cases, groups did act, and eight revolutionary "*poblaciones,*" or "*campamentos*" (poor towns, or camps) grew out of those actions.

Ranquil was one of these *poblaciones.* The result of a land invasion undertaken in mid-1970, *Ranquil* contained about 1,000 families and several *Miristas* from the organization's sub-group called *Los Sin Casa.* At first glance, *Ranquil* resembled the *callampas* most of its inhabitants had fled. There were few wood homes; most of the *pobladores* (inhabitants of the *población*) lived in

tents or in tiny shacks made of wood and cardboard. But *Ranquil* was different. Armed guards admitted visitors only if they had passes or special permission from *Ranquil's* governing body. Posters, flags, and political information brightened dark walls and replaced non-existent windows. A nurse, a former nun, ran a clinic, which was staffed by volunteer MIR medical students from the University of Chile. Everywhere one looked, there was evidence of tight organization and high political consciousness. When the people's militias—composed of men and women—started drilling, it was clear that the people of *Ranquil* meant to defend their land.

Pobladores explained their community organization: the *población* is divided up into blocks and each block sends a popularly elected delegate to a *población* "*directorio.*" Further, *pobladores* take part in various work fronts, such as the *frente de salud* (health front) or the *frente cultural,* which oversees all cultural and educational projects, as well as sports events. Each Front also sends a delegate to the "*directorio.*"

No one starves in *Ranquil.* Though most of the *pobladores* cook and eat in their own homes, there is a community kitchen where rotating members of the community prepare food each day for those who need it. Strict rules govern social life. Drinking, wife-beating, child-beating, and gambling are forbidden, and a system of people's courts deals with these and other problems. Men and women share almost equally in the governing bodies, the courts, and in the militias. Nevertheless, most household work is still done by women.

Under Frei, the MIR *pobladores* lived under constant threat of attack. After all, they had taken over land from the state or from private interests; and the Frei government saw the revolutionary *poblaciones* as havens for criminals and guerrillas. But under the UP government, *Ranquil* had grown and become stronger. For the first time in their lives, the children of *Ranquil* have milk every day. The clinic, now called Doctor Ernesto Che Guevara, was recognized by the National Health Service, and university-trained nurses, a mid-wife and a general practitioner were assigned to work there. Every child in the *población* from three to fifteen years attends school; during the regular school year, they go to state-supported schools, but during the summer months of 1970-1971 (November-January), all *Ranquil* children attended special schools staffed by the *pobladores* themselves, aided by university students.

In January, 1971, the inhabitants of *Ranquil* celebrated their growing solidarity: they re-named their *población* *Nueva Habana.*

Life in Chile's "New Dawn"

The following article by Georgie Anne Geyer, Chicago Daily News, *appeared in* The Washington Post, *April 7, 1974.*

Two years ago, camp boss German Arriaga stood amid the incredibly patched shacks of the "New Havana" and explained how the Marxists had built this budding shantytown.

The sprawling, muddy settlement on the outskirts fo Santiago then was the purest example of the most far-left experiments that were taking place under the Marxist government of President Salvador Allende.

"They were all workers with no place to live and nothing to eat," Arriaga said. "People came from all over and organized themselves."

Before, many of them had rented parts of farms. But now people live differently. Here they are organized in health groups, in schools and in vigilantes. "We have our own political meetings and our own system of justice. If a wife is mistreated by her husband, for instance, she can go to the block court and they will try to change him."

That was March, 1972, when the Revolutionary Leftist Movement (MIR), which even Allende could not control, ruled scores of experimental shanty towns like this all over Chile.

As they experimented with virtually every form of leftist social organization, socialists came from afar to watch.

Today, the 1,400 or so persons of New Havana—newly christened "New Dawn"—show clearly what the military takeover of Chile has meant on an individual level.

When the military overthrew the Allende government last September 11, MIR leaders here fled or were rounded up and killed. The new people of New Dawn will not speak of them.

Today, these piteously poor people stand around in the sun, some buying doodads from a street peddler, women carrying water to the shacks. They talk about the cost of living.

"I make $10 a week," said Carmen Munoz, mother of six who came from the poor coal mining town of Concepción to work as a maid in Santiago. "A loaf of bread now costs half a day's salary and a small carton of milk costs a day's salary."

In her tiny wooden shack is only one bed, where she and her 9-year-old son, the only child with her in Santiago, sleep at opposite ends. "In the winter it is worse," she said. "You burn a little charcoal in a pan and go right to bed. I really feel desperate here. Life is a misery."

New Dawn is living these days in a kind of limbo. There are still the elected delegates for some of the blocks, the people say, but there is no over-all organization. The police, who did not dare enter when it was New Havana, now come in regularly.

Men of the camp, most unemployed now that the assured higher salaries and the social programs of Allende's time are gone, talk hesitantly, but they do talk.

"Allende is not dead," said one, his eyes narrowed. "He is overseas somewhere. They'll never tell where he really is."

Asked if he missed the former political meetings, another young man said he did not.

"They never solved anything," he said. "They never brought enough work for us either. But now we not only have to live off our families and friends, we also have to keep our mouths shut." He made a gesture as if to zip up his mouth.

One, his voice falling to whisper, says, "Yes, at heart, we do miss one thing." What? "The President," he says, and he glances around as he talks.

At the corner, standing in the folds of mud that are the road, a shirtless young man with bulging muscles says bitterly: "Well, it's all about the same as it was before. Before, we had money and no food. Now we have the food and no money to buy it."

The military Junta that now rules Chile has put food back in the market but at exorbitant prices. The generals have decided that the people simply have to "take it."

"It is difficult, I know,'" said General Gustavo Leigh Guzman, one of the Junta members, in an interview. "But they will just have to sacrifice."

Other military men think the people of the shantytowns and poor rural areas, probably 40 to 50 percent of Chile, are happy with the change.

"Before, I would never drive through a shantytown," said Captain Carlos Ashton, assistant to the minister of foreign affairs. "But the other day I drove through one, and people were just the way they had been before.

"Before, under Allende, if you drove through they would turn your car over—they hated anyone who had cars. Now they are even noble again."

Noble or whatever, the poor people of Chile, like so many of the Latin American poor, now seem to be statistics on economic drawing boards.

But they are still here, and history cannot forget that virtually all of them voted for Allende, making him the first freely elected Marxist president in history.

The new way may work better than the old way, or it may not. While leaving, one cannot help wonder what will be the next name of New Dawn. ∎

Restructured Universities

Purged Professors, Screened Students, Burned Books

The situation of the universities in Chile since the coup has been the subject of three reports sent by Enrique Oteiza, executive secretary of the Latin American Council of Social Sciences, Buenos Aires, to the Council's member institutions and other related groups throughout Latin America. The most recent, dated March 20, 1974, is reproduced in translation. Dr. Oteiza stresses that only fully verified incidents are reported. The purpose, he adds, is not only to inform the member groups concerning the outrages committed against the universities and their academic personnel, but to stress the gravity of the resulting situation in order to obtain the greatest possible support for the efforts being undertaken by the Council on behalf of the victims.

The Junta on September 28 assembled the rectors of Chile's universities and revealed its plans of reorganization. It named for each university a rector who would be a delegate of the government, armed with plenary powers to restructure, appoint administrators, set up councils and committees, and formulate university policy. The new rectors are officers of the armed forces, all of them retired with the exception of Colonel Eugenio Reyes T., named to the State Technical University, Santiago.

Admiral Hugo Castro Jiménez, the new education minister, announced in a nationwide radio and television speech on October 2 the Junta's policy for university education. "The Junta," he said, "does not intend to destroy the autonomy of authentic university values, but on the contrary to strengthen them by eliminating those who shelter under this autonomy for the purpose of getting rid of the essence and function of the university."

The decree named the following delegate rectors: University of Chile, Santiago, General César Ruiz Danyau, former Air Force chief; Catholic University of Chile, Santiago, Admiral Jorge Sweet Madge; State Technical University, Santiago, Colonel Eugenio Reyes T.; Catholic University, Valparaíso, Admiral Luis de la Maza; Federico Santa Maria Technical University, Valparaíso, Captain (naval) Juan Naylor Wieber; University of Concepción, all branches, Captain (naval) Guillermo González Bastías; Southern University (Universidad Austral) of Chile, Valdivia, Colonel Gustavo Dupuis P.; Northern University, Antofagasta, Colonel Hernán Danyau Quintana. General Ruiz Danyau was also named president of the Council of Delegate Rectors.

For the purposes of restructuring the universities, the Council of Rectors created by the decree is shaped in the direction of a top-level organ for coordinating and planning all higher studies. It will integrate under a single control the institutes of higher education of the armed forces alongside the universities. It has plenary powers to restructure the universities, establishing and eliminating at will courses and campuses; evaluating, approving, or suppressing study programs; and representing the universities both nationally and internationally.

Decree-law No. 139 of November 21, 1973, authorizes the delegate rectors of the University of Concepción, the Federico Santa Maria Technical University, and the Southern and Northern universities to fire employees when this may be "necessary for the interests and the restructing of the universities."

University of Chile

Immediately after the generals seized power, Elgardo Boenninger—who was then rector—tried to gain control of the university, apparently to avoid a military take-over. He named men he could trust as heads of each campus, all of them closely allied to the Christian Democrats. Extreme right-wingers in the university, organized as the "University Front," fought this policy vigorously with the object of forcing the armed forces to come in. They won a first round when the Junta named a vice-rector for the Valparaíso campus. In response, Boenninger resigned, and the Junta named General Ruiz Danyau as delegate rector of the principal university of the country.

The university's highest collegial authority, the Normative Council, was dissolved. The members who represented leftist interests had to seek asylum in friendly embassies or escape from the country by other means. One of the most prominent, Professor Enrique París, was seized, taken to the National Stadium, and there tortured to death.

General Ruiz Danyau named new vice-rectors for the Western, Northern, and Southern campuses in Santiago and set up a committee to restructure the Eastern Campus. Simultaneously, he named 36 public prosecutors to bring to summary trial (drumhead court-martial) in the emergency military courts those professors, employees, and students who were charged with having leftist leanings. The charges went far beyond anything established in the previously existing University Statutes, including such offenses as "having altered in any way the established functioning of the university," or of "having infringed the moral rules inherent in the position." Charges are anonymous and require no proofs.

As regards the Eastern Campus of Santiago, the professors, administrative staff, and students left it peacefully on September 11. That evening it was raided and ransacked by military units who destroyed various buildings. The library of the School of Journalism was burned on the ground that it contained "subversive literature." Students living in the two university residences were expelled, and their personel effects were transferred to the Air Force Logistic Command. This campus remains closed. Its employees are obliged to sign in each day at the military control post, a requirement used on various occasions to arrest one of them.

The restructuring committee has announced that teaching activities will be resumed only for the final years of some courses, and even in these courses all materials or branches related to the social sciences have been eliminated. Those most affected are sociology and psychology, both being closed for at least this year. The same is true of the Department of Political and Social Action. Its programs and courses, especially training for social service, have been radically altered. All registrations of students have been canceled. Anyone who wants to continue must re-register in person. Activities in the lower courses are to be resumed this year. All teachers and researchers will have to submit to a process of re-evaluation, including the filling in of a special "curriculum vitae" form.

Eastern Campus officials particularly affected include the former vice-rector, Eduardo Ruiz, who received asylum in the Embassy of Panama. Almost all sociology professors have been expelled. José Balmes, dean of Fine Arts, former dean Pedro Mira, and Professor Alberto Pérez were placed under house arrest but later managed to reach a friendly embassy. Other Fine Arts professors have been expelled. The entire staff of 40 persons of University Extension, University Planning and Integral Wellbeing has been dismissed. In global terms, some 90 percent of the teaching staff and 70 percent of the administrative staff have been eliminated.

The faculty of Fine Arts is being completely restructured. The military authority has named Matías Vial as dean and Lily Garafulic as general secretary. Many teachers have been cited for summary trial, several of them on the basis of charges brought by the new dean. The Education faculty also is being restructured under a new dean, a new secretary-general, and new department heads. Only 220 of the 3,562 registered students are authorized to attend classes. New heads have similarly been named to Philosophy and Letters, with 200 of 2,489 students authorized to continue, and to Social Sciences, in which the social service and sociology programs have been totally eliminated and only 70 of the 2,224 students allowed to continue in the other programs. The faculty of Medicine is being partially restructured, with 880 of the 1,369 students authorized to attend classes. The faculty of Sciences is being restructured, with 60 percent of the students attending classes. Thirty-five professors were expelled, 25 of them because they were foreigners. Finally, the faculty of Natural Sciences and Mathematics is being restructured, with 250 of a total of 2,503 students attending clases.

The Northern Campus, Santiago, has been less affected. The former heads of the School of Dentistry have been retained, but 20 professors and 110 students were expelled. Similarly, in the Chemistry faculty, the heads were kept, but 37 professors and 200 students were expelled. The heads of the faculty of Juridical and Social Sciences also survived. Thirty-four students, including the president of the Student Center, were expelled. The Political Sciences building was closed because it adjoined the School of the National Police *(Carabineros)*. The president of the Law Center and 136 other law students were expelled. All professors suspected of leftist leanings were cited for summary trial on the basis of lists drawn up in each department.

The faculty of Musical Sciences and Arts is being restructured. The former heads were removed, and 350 professors and 340 administrators were expelled. The faculty of Political Economy was suppressed. Its dean, Roberto Pizarro, had to leave Chile. Only 200 of the 1,800 students were allowed to register in other departments. The professors were subjected to a variety of pressures, and many of them had to seek asylum in embassies. The heads of the Architecture faculty were removed, as were 36 professors and 150 students. The faculty of Medicine was ransacked by troops several times, especially at the J.J. Aguirre Hospital, many of the doctors and administrators in the hospital being interned. The Medical Technology course has been suppressed. Forty-five professors were expelled. Dr. Alfredo Jadresic, a former dean, was arrested and taken to the National Stadium, then told he must leave Chile within 10 days or be sent to the Chacabuco prison camp.

The Southern Campus, Santiago, consists of the faculties of agronomy, veterinary and forest sciences, and medicine and the departments of natural and exact sciences, chemical and physiological sciences, social sciences, agro-industry and food sciences, and animal production. The entire campus was ransacked by the military. All registrations were canceled, and re-registration requires personal attendance. Fulltime professors and researchers were all cited for summary trial, and all halftime personnel were dismissed. The result was that 24 professors and 34 administrators were expelled from the faculty of Veterinary, 40 professors from Medicine, 48 professors and 86 students (including the president of the Student Center) from Agronomy, 8 professors and 46 students from Forestry, 12 professors from Natural Sciences, 17 professors from Social Science (the department proportionately most affected, so that it will probably disappear), two professors from Chemistry, and three from Animal Production.

The Western Campus, Santiago, is clearly the least affected, undoubtedly because of the open support of the Junta expressed by those in charge. Enrique d'Etigny, the vice-rector, was confirmed in his post and also named pro-rector of the University of Chile. The students, nevertheless, were subjected to extreme harassment. Foreigners were expelled from the university, and most of them had to leave Chile. Chileans were subjected to a variety of punishments, ranging from suspension for a semester to expulsion from the university. The Engineering School was raided and ransacked several times in the search for wanted students.

The situation of the regional campuses of the University of Chile is even more critical than for those in Santiago. Many professors are held in regional prison camps, and little can be learned about them. Many professors have simply disappeared.

The Arica campus is being restructured, with new heads for five of the six departments. There are no classes or other student activities.

Iquique is similarly being restructured, and all student activities have ceased. The shooting of Professor Freddy Taverna has been confirmed.

Two professors of the La Serena Campus were shot, Riquelme Zamora and Jorge Peña, who was director of the La Serena Children's Orchestra attached to the university and the only one of its kind in Chile.

Valparaíso is being restructured, half the students having been expelled. After Pedro Uribe was named vice-rector, 500 professors were fired. Many professors and students, including the president of the Student Federation, have been interned. Pady Ahumada, professor of mathematics, was shot. All activities of several academic divisions have been suspended. They include the Center of Historic and Philosophical Studies, which has been dissolved and from which some 25 persons have been fired. Also suspended are the faculties of Economics and Architecture and of the Pedagogic Institute, which included a school of journalism, a school of social service and a department of sociology. Ten members of the department of sociology were fired and its director was imprisoned.

All student activities are suspended at the Osorno Campus, and the programs of social service have been suppressed. Student activities are also suspended at Antofagasta, Talca, Chillán, Temuco, and Osorno, and all these campuses are being restructured.

Catholic University of Chile

The Catholic University has shared the same fate as all other universities. It has been, taken over and is being restructured. Admiral Jorge Sweet M., the delegate rector, has named new heads of faculties and departments.

Four specialized centers have been eliminated as such, the Center of Studies of the National Reality (CEREN), the Center of Agrarian Studies (CEA), the Institute of Sociology (IS), and the Center of Urban and Regional Development (CIDU).

Created as part of the university five years ago, CEREN was intended to promote "interdisciplinary investigation, teaching, and extension services in relation to the analysis and critical interpretation of Chilean and Latin American society seen as a totality." It was later integrated into the university's Cluster of Interdisciplinary Social Studies, and its director was dean of the Cluster. Its five years of work are recorded in the 17 issues of the review *Cuadernos de la Realidad Nacional* (Memoranda of National Reality), a learned journal with a substantial impact at home and abroad. Decree No. 154/73 of the Delegate Rector's office dissolved the Center and canceled the work contracts of both fulltime and parttime professors. This meant the expulsion from the university of 23 professors and researchers.

Decree No. 154/73 dissolved CEA and canceled the contracts of all 11 fulltime professors and researchers.

Decree No. 151/73 restructured the IS, canceling the contracts of five professors and researchers and reassigning six others to administrative duties.

When the new university authorities took over control of CIDU, Guillermo Geisse resigned as director, and a reorganizing committee was named, with Patricio Chellew as acting director and Ricardo Jordán and Gobriel Pumarino as the other members. Although CIDU survives, its programs will be modified and reoriented. Seven professors have already had to leave the university, and the remaining parttime professors, four in number, will have to leave at the end of the year.

Decree No. 153/73 canceled the work contracts of

10 professors of the School of Journalism. In the School of Social Work, the contracts of 20 of the 31 fulltime professors were canceled, and many parttime professors and assistants were also fired.

The Department of Economic and Social History, which was responsible for major programs of research and teaching, was suppressed. Contracts of all its academic staff, including five professors and researchers, were canceled.

The general situation of Catholic University can be summed up under two heads. First, there is the closing of academic units and cancellation of work contracts en masse (CEREN and CEA), or alternatively the expulsion of individual professors (IS). Secondly, instead of canceling the contracts, in some cases professors were assigned to other units. This in practice was the same as a delayed expulsion, because the other units refused to accept those transferred.

Military search parties invaded and ransacked various buildings. On September 11, the studios and offices of the university's television transmitter, Channel 13, were occupied by soldiers at dawn. They remained for several days. CEREN was thoroughly searched in the last week of September. The Eastern Campus, seat of the Cluster of Social Studies, was ransacked by the National Police three times; the residence of the Rector, Fernando Castillo Velasco, twice.

Various members of the teaching and administrative staffs, as well as students, were arrested. Some of these are still held. The most serious confirmed case is that of Professor Leopoldo Benítez (Architecture). He was denounced to the authorities by an informer and taken to the Chile Stadium on September 18. There he was shot dead, without trial or judgment of any kind. The military in charge said he had "tried to escape while being interrogated."

As with the regional campuses of the University of Chile, little information is available about those of Catholic University. The Maule Campus (Talca) is being restructured. All courses of the Center of Agrarian and Peasant Studies (CEAC) were suppressed, and 10 professors were fired. This put an end to the programs of the Peasant School, Rural Administration, and Rural Development. The Frontera Campus (Temuco) is also being restructured. Father Mauricio Hebert, academic assistant director, was expelled to Canada. One effect of the restructuring is the elimination of six professors and six assistants from the education department.

State Technical University

The Central Campus in Santiago was occupied after a violent onslaught in which the armed forces used heavy artillery. Professor Enrique Kirberg, the rector, was arrested, as was his wife. All persons found inside the buildings were taken to the National Stadium. Professor Kirberg was moved later to Dawson Island, and he is still there without any charges having been formulated against him. Ten other members of the governing body are also still held.

The Technical University has suffered more than any other in the process of "ideological purification." It is the only one given an officer still on active duty as rector. The purging calls for total restructuring. Sixty percent of the academic personnel have been dismissed or must soon leave, and many of them are being held. The evening

and night courses which allowed workers to get higher education have been suppressed. The agreements for training workers between the university and the Central Labor Confederation (CUT) and other entities have been canceled. Fewer than a third of the 15,000 students are allowed to attend classes. Many of them, including the president of the Student Federation, are held.

Luis Flores Sierra, a lawyer, has been named as delegate vice-rector of the Talca Campus, with Captain Jorge Zucchino Aguirre designated to keep a close watch on his every action. They have announced that classes will be renewed "with the total exclusion of all Marxist students."

Luis Christen, delegate vice-rector of the Valdivia Campus, has said that the campus is "being reorganized and experiencing a process of political purification." Forty-five professors and administrators have had their contracts canceled. The president of the Student Federation and 64 other students have been expelled.

Northern University

Campuses are located in Arica, Antofagasta, Vallenar, and Coquimbo. They had previously a total of 9,000 students. Colonel Hernán Danyau Q., the delegate rector, has told the press that university activities had quickly returned to normal, after the expulsion of the foreign professors from the country and the internment of Chileans found guilty of extremist activities. The courses in anthropology, sociology, and journalism will continue, he said, but no students will be admitted this year because the former "Marxist indoctrination" makes a total restructuring necessary. Not only these courses but the entire university will be restructured, and the teaching staff will be reorganized in order to ensure the depoliticization of the university's activities. The students have been treated very harshly. Daniel Trigo, president of the Student Federation, is held at the Cerro Moreno airbase, but nothing is known of his condition. The university residences are frequently ransacked.

The purge initiated by the delegate rector has hit the academic staff most acutely. All 25 foreign professors were expelled, as were 10 Chileans. There is no firm count of the number of those shot by the military authorities, but it is known that they include Luis Muñoz, president of the Union of Non-Academic Personnel; Elizabeth Cabrera, Social Visitor of the Division of Student Services; Nesco Teodorovic, a student in Social Communications; and Francisco Donoso, professor of sociology.

Valparaíso Catholic University

The delegate rector, Admiral Luis de la Maza de la Maza, is in charge of restructuring. As in other universities, the greatest stress is in the area of the social sciences. Units whose activities are suspended while the staff is being investigated include the Institute of Social Sciences, the School of Education, the School of Social Work, and the Center of Studies of Training for Work (CESCIA). All teaching and administrative staff of these units have been denied access to their offices since the military took over and are not allowed to take out their work materials.

Michael Woodward, a professor in CESCIA, reportedly died of injuries sustained while being interrogated in prison.

All professors suspected of leftist leanings were cited for summary trial and given the option of resigning or being expelled. They were not allowed to offer any defense at their trials. Adequate justification for expelling a professor, according to the authorities, is that he had shown sympathy for the ideology of President Allende's constitutional government, or that he had acted against "university values." More than 30 professors failed these tests. The students were compelled to re-register, a process in which 200 were excluded.

Federico Santa Maria Technical University

Restructuring by the delegate rector has included the dissolution of the social sciences group and the cancellation of all student registrations. The re-registration must be in person, and it involves procedures completely different from before.

Concepción University

Various buildings were invaded by troops and police on September 11. Many professors, administrators, and students were arrested, and many of them were later transferred to the island of Quiriquina. The university authorities then in office immediately dissolved the Institute of Sociology, the School of Journalism, the Department of Theater, and the Council of University Extension. They canceled all work contracts for teachers and administrators in these departments as of September 20, with no compensation whatever. Students, except those in the final year, lost all credit for the work they had done.

Restructuring continued under the delegate rector named on October 2. Details are not known, but it is confirmed that activities of the Institute of Anthropology have been suspended and four professors expelled. Two of these were held for nearly a month before being expelled from Chile as foreigners. Twelve students picked by the delegate rector on the basis of their right-wing militancy formed a committee to rule on applications for re-registration. They accepted 11,000 of the former 23,000 students. Only 400 of the 2,400 students living on campus were readmitted. Many students were arrested and imprisoned. The most appalling of the confirmed cases is that of Antonio Leal, secretary general of the Student Federation. Tortures applied by the interrogators while in prison caused him to lose an eye and to have a gangrenous leg amputated.

Southern University

Armed forces occupied the buildings on September 11. Activities were partially resumed on September 17. Supporters of the previous government were immediately subjected to an organized campaign of denunciation. The dean of Philosophy and Letters, who had been a candidate for rector in the previous university elections, was imprisoned, as were Grinor Rojo of the Spanish Department and Carlos Opazo of the Department of Languages. Many foreign professors and researchers were jailed, mistreated, and forced to leave the country. It is believed that about a fifth of the 500 teaching staff risk losing their jobs. This situation has resulted already in the disappearance of the licentiateship (master's degree) in Spanish Philology and of a recently started graduate course in the faculty of Philosophy and Letters. When Colonel Gustavo Dupuis P. was named delegate rector in October, he continued Omar Henríquez, Fernando Morgado, and Rafael Pesbi in their posts as vice-rectors and Hernán Poblete Vargas as secretary-general. ■

"Scrubbing Minds"

Reprinted from The New York Times, *March 24, 1974*

"They're much more strict. Maybe it's like the Army."

The rumple-haired, 11-year-old youngster was commenting on his first week of the new school year under Chile's military regime. In the southern hemisphere the season is now the the equivalent of fall in the northern hemisphere.

The military Junta has reinforced measures intended to eliminate politics from the schools and establish "order and discipline." Primary and secondary schools opened with bans against long hair for boys and miniskirts for girls. Courses have been revised, and Chile's superintendent of secondary education, Gilberto Zarate, announced that six textbooks have been removed from high schools, and one was "modified."

Several teachers claimed that at least twice that number of texts had been removed from courses in both primary and high schools, including some that had been introduced during the three years of Allende's left-wing administration.

Uniforms Required

School uniforms are required. Boys must have haircuts short enough "so that their shirt collars can be seen" and girls are barred from wearing jewelry. Though the wearing of school uniforms has been traditional here, the rule was ignored by many pupils in recent years. Blue jeans replaced gray trousers for boys or dark skirts for girls.

The cost of new uniforms and school supplies has cut into the March budget of many poor and middle-class families. Prices soared when the regime adopted a free-market policy, eliminating the rigid price controls established by the Allende government. Notebooks that cost the equivalent of two cents a year ago are now 30 cents. Basic uniforms went up from about $4 to nearly $30. The minimum monthly salary decreed by the Junta is 18,000 escudos, or $24. The average is nearly 75,000 escudos, $100. A father with four youngsters observed that it cost him more than a month's pay to send his children off to classes.

Universities Purged

School bells rang for nearly 2.6 million youngsters in lower schools last week. Classes won't resume until next week in most of the universities where the military purge cut much deeper. . . .[See "Restructured Universities" above.]

The Junta's education minister, Rear Admiral Hugo Castro Jiminez, said "anarchy reigned" in the colleges with professors using classes to indoctrinate their students in Marxism. He said courses have been revised to promote the "moral and spiritual values of our Chilean Christian tradition."* ■

*Admiral Hugo Castro, named education minister after he had demonstrated his zeal as book burner at the Technical University of Valparaíso, says his objective is to destroy Marxism first, then "every kind of politics." The Santiago press, without humor and apparently without irony, stressed Castro's outstanding qualifications for his ministerial tasks: he had graduated from special courses—in the United States—in artillery, combat communications, torpedoes and sonar.—The Editors

How They Killed a Poet

Plegaria a un Labrador

Levántate
y mira la montaña
de donde viene el viento, el sol y el agua.
Tú que manejas el curso de los ríos,
tú que sembraste el vuelo de tu alma.

Levántate
y mírate las manos
para crecer estréchala a tu hermano,
juntos iremos unidos en la sangre,
hoy es el tiempo que puede ser mañana.

Líbranos de aquel que nos domina en la miseria,
tráenos tu reino de justicia e igualdad,
sopla como el viento la flor de la quebrada
limpia como el fuego el cañon de mi fusil.

Hágase por fin tu voluntad aquí en la tierra,
danos tu fuerza y tu valor al combatir,
sopla como el viento la flor de la quebrada
limpia como el fuego el cañon de mi fusil.

Levántate
y mírate las manos,
para crecer estréchala a tu hermano,
juntos iremos unidos en la sangre,
ahora y en la hora de nuestra muerte, amén.

Song: Prayer to a Peasant

Get up
And look at the mountain
From whence come the wind, the sun and the water,
You who plot the course of the rivers,
You who have sown the flight of your soul.

Get up
And look at your hands.
Give one to your brother in order to grow.
We will go together, united in blood.
Now is the time, which might be tomorrow.

Free us from that which rules us in poverty,
Bring us your reign of justice and equality.
Blow, like the wind, the wildflower;
Clean, like the fire, the barrel of my gun.

Do, at last, your will here on earth.
Give us your strength and courage to fight.
Blow, like the wind, the wildflower;
Clean, like the fire, the barrel of my gun.

Get up
And look at your hands.
Give one to your brother in order to grow.
We will go together, united in blood.
Now and in the hour of our death, amen.

Victor Jara's ordeal and death in Estadio Chile is well known—documented by Amnesty International and the Chicago Commission and related by eyewitnesses. His widow reports, "Since December 1973 it is forbidden to mention his name in Chile. A few days after his death, somebody working in the Junta's television station risked his life to insert a verse of the song above over the soundtrack of an American film." The following is excerpted from an eyewitness account by Chilean journalist Miguel Cabezas, writing in La Opinion, an Argentinean newspaper.

Victor Jara was one of the leaders in the wave of the creative "people's culture" which reached far beyond Chile's borders in the first years of the seventies. He was a composer, singer, guitarist, and poet, loved even by people who did not share his radical political involvement. He was connected to the left like Pablo Neruda.

When the news reached Jara that the military had demanded Allende's exit, he left for the Technical College in Santiago, a leading center of leftist support. He had worked with the students during the transportation strike, handing out food in the poor areas. Now he was taking part in the students' preparations for resistance at the college.

Many of the students were killed or wounded during the shooting of September 11. They finally gave up to avoid a total massacre. They were forced to lie down with their faces to the ground and their hands behind their necks. The slightest movement was punished with a bullet. Many of the wounded bled to death. To help a comrade at one's side meant the helper's own death.

Jara was one of those who lay until 6 p.m. Then he and hundreds of others were transported to the football stadium. At the stadium, guards fired their machineguns regularly every quarter of an hour. Loudspeakers spit out insults constantly: "Perverted wretches, traitors, you are our hostages of war. If you do anything you'll be killed on the spot."

Many were shot by soldiers. Prisoners were shot while they sat in the grandstands under blazing spotlights. People were tortured in sight of everyone. Over 20 bodies lay unmoving on the field—people who had thrown themselves from their seats above, unable to stand living any longer.

Victor Jara went around and tried to calm his comrades. At one point he found himself facing the commandante, who, upon seeing Jara, made some motions as if he was playing the guitar. Jara nodded, surprised.

The commandante called four soldiers who grabbed Jara and conducted him to a table at a point where the maximum number of people could see what was to happen.

Jara was ordered to lay his hands on the table. The officer then took an axe and in two hacks cut off the fingers of both hands. Jara slowly collapsed.

The officer began to kick the body, shouting: "Sing, damn it, sing!" Somehow Jara managed to get to his feet and stumble towards the grandstand. There was a total silence. Suddenly, Jara's voice was heard:

"Yes, comrades, let us obey the commandante." He swayed back and forth until he found his balance again. He lifted his maimed hands and began to sing a revolutionary song which everyone knew. The whole stadium sang with him. The sound roared out over the concrete as Jara led the beat. It became too much for the soldiers. They shot Jara, and when he had fallen they turned their machine guns toward the grandstands and began to shoot wildly. ■

HUMAN RIGHTS AND JUSTICE

In one area, at least, the United Nations has made a permanent contribution to man's self-understanding: Its Universal Declaration of Human Rights, adopted in 1948, set standards against which the actions of states will henceforth be judged. For example, when the Catholic and Protestant churches in Brazil wanted to mobilize opinion against the excesses being committed by the military rulers of their country, they chose in 1973 to build their campaign around the observance of the 25th anniversary of the UN document.

And now the worldwide challenge to the behavior of the Chilean Junta toward Chileans and toward foreigners who had found asylum in Chile before it seized power is likewise focused on this Declaration. As one international commission of enquiry after another has testified, its most elementary rules have been and continue to be openly and flagrantly violated. It specifies that nobody can be sentenced unless found guilty by a properly constituted tribunal of an act which was a crime when committed. It prescribes speedy trial, clear formulation of charges, and free access to defense lawyers. It forbids torture, whether physical or mental.

The documents presented below are for the most part formulated in the detached language of lawyers. They include testimony from the International Commission of Jurists, from Amnesty International, from observers sent to Chile by leading bar associations of different states and countries. Notwithstanding the formal language, the message comes through loud and clear. The Junta in Chile has set itself in open and continuing opposition to the conscience of mankind. It stands condemned at the bar of history.

Chicago Commission of Inquiry

"The Chicago Commission of Inquiry into the Status of Human Rights in Chile (henceforth referred to as the Commission) was constituted as an ad hoc group of Chicago citizens concerned about the conditions of human rights in Chile after the military takeover of September 11, 1973. The Commission was formed upon the initiative and with the assistance of the Chicago Citizens' Committee to Save Lives in Chile, a loose coalition of groups and individuals. Members of the Commission hold differing political views and religious beliefs. They also vary in their attitudes toward the policies of the Popular Unity government headed by the late President Salvador Allende.

The members of the Commission are:

Ernest DeMaio, *General Vice President, United Electrical Radio and Machine Workers of America*

Abraham Feinglass, *International Vice President, International Meatcutters and Butcher Workmen*

Geoffrey Fox, *Instructor of Sociology, University of Illinois, Chicago; Vice President, Chicago Circle Federation of Teachers*

Father Gerard Grant, S.J., *Professor of Philosophy, Loyola University*

George Gutierrez, *Counselor, Change Program, Northern Illinois University; Member, Human Relations Committee, DeKalb, Illinois*

Dean Peerman, *Managing Editor,* The Christian Century

Joanne Fox Przeworski, *Pre-doctoral Fellow, Committee for the Comparative Study of New Nations, University of Chicago*

Jane Reed, *Associate General Secretary, Board of Church and Society, United Methodist Church*

James Reed, *Pastor, Parish of the Holy Covenant, United Methodist Church*

Doris Strieter, *Village Trustee, Maywood, Illinois*

Frank Teruggi, Sr., *father of Frank Teruggi, Jr., murdered in Chile*

The members unanimously endorse the full contents of this Report." [*Reprinted below by IDOC, with only minor abridgements in the introductory section. Part II of the Report, "Analysis," is reprinted in full.*]

The Purpose of the Commission

The purpose of the Commission was to examine the current state of human rights in Chile. Of particular concern to the Commission were also the circumstances surrounding the death of Frank Teruggi, Jr., and the role of the Embassy of the United States in protecting U.S. citizens. It is the hope of the Commission that this report will focus the attention of public opinion on the plight of political prisoners in Chile and in particular that it will serve to orient and facilitate aid to the victims of persecution.

Human rights are understood in the light of the United Nations Charter which, in the opinion of the 1971 Declaration of the World Court, imposes direct obligations as to human rights; the Universal Declaration of Human Rights; the International Covenant on Civil and Political Rights; the Chilean Constitution and the appropriate laws. The report presents and documents several cases which fall under the above definitions. . . .

Summary of the Findings

Given the limitations of time and resources, the Commission cannot estimate the frequency of detentions, torture, and executions in Chile. Moreover, because of the necessity to protect several of its sources, no documentation can be made public with regard to several cases of searches, seizures, detentions, and torture. These limitations will be discussed in detail below.

The principal findings of the Commission are the following:

(1) The campaign of terror developed by the Junta seems to have assumed a systematic and organized character;

(2) Cases of politically motivated detentions are numerous: (a) the estimate of the number of persons detained as of January 20, 1974, exceeds 18,000; (b) an estimated total of 80,000 have been detained in the past six months; (c) a single list, made available to the Commission, of persons who have been detained and are presently missing contains over 250 names.

3. No legal procedures are followed on a systematic basis, not even those appropriate for the "state of war and the state of siege" in the light of Chilean laws. Detentions continue indefinitely without charges being preferred. The access of lawyers to their clients is curtailed in violation of the *Codigo de Justicia Militar (Code of Military Justice)*, Libro II. Tituto IV, Art. 184. Proceedings of military tribunals are secret in contravention of Art. 196. The request of the Commission to observe a trial was denied by the Vice-Minister of Justice. Additional sentences are arbitrarily imposed after military tribunals pronounce their sentences.

(4) The use of torture continues. The Commission has obtained (a) written depositions of family members, (b) eyewitness accounts, (c) testimonies of released prisoners detailing the nature of wounds inflicted. As of December 11, 1973, there have been at least 42 published reports of more than 410 persons killed "while attempting to escape."

(5) The use of economic sanctions with regard to those suspected of sympathies toward the government before September 11 is widespread: our estimate is that a total of approximately 160,000 were expelled from their work for this reason. An unknown number has been forced to retire prematurely, forfeiting the accumulated social security and retirement benefits. Those on the government blacklist are barred from other employment.

(6) Of 137 national unions, 30 of the less important are functioning; the rest were either dissolved or suspended. The national and regional bodies of the Central Federation of Workers (CUT) were disbanded. All delegated labor bodies and meetings of such bodies were abolished and prohibited. Several union members were picked up at random and shot in the presence of other workers, for example, 11 railway repair and maintenance workers in San Bernardo.

(7) Unemployment is estimated to have reached 20 percent. The work week was extended by four hours. Inflation since the takeover has been 1,000 to 1,100 percent. Wages were raised by decree from 200 to 300 percent depending on work category on January 1, 1974. Unemployment compensations are based on 75 percent of the average wage during the past 12 months, but because of the inflation, such compensation, even when provided, is below the level of subsistence; hunger is widespread.

(8) All universities and several private elementary and secondary schools are under military administration. Several university schools and departments are closed. Police and non-uniformed agents are often present in classrooms. No extracurricular activities are allowed. Tuition has been instituted, and access to education made much more difficult. The estimated number of students expelled reaches 20,000 (6,000 in Concepción alone); 300-400 professors are seeking employment and many more of those expelled have left the country. New educational programs are expected to drastically curtail the study of the social sciences, journalism, and public health.

(9) All periodicals which the Junta views as opposition have been closed. Of the 11 major newspapers which appeared daily in Santiago prior to September 11, only six continue to be published. Of these six, three are controlled by the Edwards family. Moreover, *La Prensa*, the Christian Democratic newspaper, recently announced that it will discontinue publication. Copies of newspapers (1971-September, 1973) sympathetic to the Popular Unity government were removed from the National Library and other libraries. After a period of self-censorship, prior censorship has been reinstituted by the Junta. Some bookstores were closed, their books confiscated and burned. Most of the books dealing with philosophy, politics, and social problems are dangerous to own. Many people voluntarily burned their books, journals, and posters out of fear.

(10) From the early days of the takeover, there was an intense campaign against foreign residents in Chile. As of February 17, according to *El Mercurio*, 3,647 foreigners were given safe conduct passes to leave the country. A total of 7,317 persons obtained safe conduct passes, while 243 persons are said to remain in foreign embassies. All embassies party to the right of asylum (Montevideo Convention, 1961) are carefully patrolled, and access to them is prohibited.

(11) The Embassy of the United States seems to have made no serious efforts to protect the American citizens present in Chile during and after the military takeover. It refused to aid Charles Horman, directing him to seek assistance from his local police; it maintains not to have known anything about the arrest of Frank Teruggi, Jr., until notified by Steven Volk on September 24, 1973. This must be contrasted with the conduct of several Western European embassies which threatened to break diplomatic relations if any of their nationals suffered at the hands of the military. The U.S. Embassy is one of the embassies where no asylum was given. The U.S. consular officers

continue to reject those seeking refuge in the United States whom they consider to have leftist sympathies.

(12) Contrary to the assertion of the Chilean Junta, Mr. Frank Teruggi, Jr., was murdered while in military custody at the National Stadium. He was tortured and shot 17 times. Contrary to the statements of the U.S. Embassy, protection was sought on his behalf the morning after he was detained and before he was murdered. Contrary to the assertions by the Embassy, no thorough investigation has been made with regard to the circumstances of his death by the Junta. Actually, the information concerning his death was unearthed by Frank Teruggi, Sr., while in Santiago.

(13) The Church high schools and Catholic University have been placed under military control along with state schools. At least 130 priests have been forced to leave Chile; at least three were killed and many tortured. Right-wing priests, notably Father Raul Hasbun, director of the Catholic University television station (Channel 13), are now attacking priests who are critical of the Junta. The Junta campaign in the press includes "letters" to the editor which denounce the Church as infiltrated by Marxists and as being an agent of international communism. . . .

Organization of the Report and the Evidence

The Report is organized topically to cover the subjects listed above. As its purpose is exclusively to present the findings of eight days of investigations and interviews, no attempt is made to reach any summary judgment concerning these findings. The Report represents the findings of the twelve members of the Commission and may include information available elsewhere. Such duplication is unavoidable and in fact corroborates the findings.

On the other hand, it must be emphasized that this Report is in no way intended to provide complete information on the present state of human rights in Chile. It covers only the information obtained *first hand* by the members of the Commission during their stay in Chile. No attempt has been made to draw upon any other source.

The presentation of the evidence must be greatly circumscribed by the considerations of safety for the sources from which some of this evidence was obtained. The Commission had to weigh with utmost care whether the publication of a particular piece of evidence would jeopardize its source. It therefore sacrificed the evidence whenever doubt appeared. The evidence is classified as follows:

(I) Official interviews in which the name of the person or organization, the date and place can be identified;

(II) Interviews with persons known to members of the Commission but whose names cannot be made public. These interviews will be numbered and referred to in Part II by broad categories, e.g. deposed labor union official, a prisoner at Estadio Chile Prison;

(III) Interviews with persons unknown to members of the Commission, principally chance encounters;

(IV) Written documents, lists of missing, prisoners and dead; signed accounts of house searches, torture; examples of letters summarily suspending workers, students, etc. as well as summaries of specific situations by knowledgeable Chileans;

(V) Written documents which cannot be identified in any way but which have been and will be shown to selected persons in the United States and abroad.

A Comment on Interviews with the Junta Representatives

During its stay in Santiago, the Commission had various interviews with official representatives of the Junta. It is the impression of the Commission that the Junta representatives made no attempt during these interviews to present us with a portrayal that would be in any way compatible with the situation known to them and easy to observe by anyone outside their offices. To the contrary, we were impressed by the fact that those Junta representatives felt most assured that they can present obviously transparent lies with utmost impunity. We were told, for example, that every prisoner is given the charges against him (Vice Minister of Justice Max Silva, Lieutenant Colonel Mario Rodriguez) and even that the former Minister of Foreign Affairs, Clodomiro Almeyda "is in his house." (Taped interview with Max Silva.) Upon telephoning Almeyda's wife, the Commission learned that he had been held on Dawson Island and removed to Santiago military hospital for treatment. He is allegedly no longer in the hospital, but she has no idea of his whereabouts. When the Commission requested to see José Tohá, former editor of *La Ultima Hora* and former Minister of Interior, Defense and Agriculture, the Minister of Justice responded that he was in a military hospital and could not receive visitors. (He has since been reported dead under mysterious circumstances.)

It is clear that the Junta is bewildered by the fact that anybody might actually be concerned about the status of human rights in Chile. Anyone who does not uncritically accept the pronouncements of the Junta is regarded as an enemy. Their vilifications range from the U.S. Senate ("infiltrated by Marxists"), Senator Edward Kennedy ("agent of international communism"), the Ford Foundation ("not only infiltrated but controlled by Marxists, including admitted communists—*La Segunda*, December 20, 1973) to Ambassador Harald Edelstam of Sweden ("The Red pimpernel"—*La Segunda*, February 22, 1974).

Following is the complete, unabridged Part II, "Analysis," from the Chicago Commission Report. The citations in parentheses within the text are to the five appendices to the Report cited above, under "Organization of the Report and the Evidence." We are sorry that space restrictions prohibited IDOC from reprinting all 31 pages of material included in these appendices, but we have reproduced, following this analysis, two documents which provide shocking examples of the mind of the Junta as translated into official policy. Please consult the "Source List" at the back of this book for information on obtaining complete copies of the Report and Documents.

A. General Atmosphere of "State of War," "State of Emergency," "State of Siege"

The campaign of terror developed by the Junta seems to have assumed a systematic and organized character. Repression is more selective than during the first months following the takeover, but it is thorough and well prepared. Names of prisoners, their locations, and details of arrest are computerized; it is assumed that these lists include potential prisoners as well. For example, while persons who spent three months or more in Cuba were arrested during the first wave of detentions, persons who spent two months there were arrested subsequently, and those who were one month in Cuba are being detained at present. (II, 13)

Official reasons cited for continuance of the "state of war" include reports of assaults, enemy plans, sabotage, resistance, arms caches, etc. People in general said there is no way of knowing the truth since the mass media are completely controlled and carry primarily local news. Arbitrary arrests and seizures are known only to the family affected and neighbors; people are afraid to report those missing for fear of casting suspicion on themselves.

The terror is sustained by the following means.

1. Propaganda Campaigns: Enemy Plans and Sabotage

a. The military continually publicizes enemy plans and assaults against military installations to justify the continued "state of internal war," deaths, and indiscriminate roundups of people. As of February 23, 1974, there are five such purported plans: Plan Z (used as justification by the Junta for forcibly taking over the government), Plan Zulu, Plan Mariposa, Plan Lautaro, and Plan Leopard. (IV, 9)

Plan Z is a most effective instrument of propaganda, and it is widely believed by the middle class. Lists of persons who allegedly were going to be killed by the Popular Unity coalition are shown selectively to private individuals. These lists include even some leftists and a large number of persons completely apolitical, such as women without any record of political activity. A middle-class housewife told a member of the Commission: "It existed. They were going to kill us. My sister saw the list —our names were on it." (II, 13) Released prisoners reported that soldiers, while beating and torturing, screamed, "You bastard, you savage, you were going to kill me." (II, 19).

The Commission has obtained several items of evidence concerning another of these plans, Plan Leopard. According to *El Mercurio* of December 23, 1973, five persons were apprehended and killed the previous night while trying to assault an electrical tower station near Santiago. In the pocket of one, the military found the "Plan Leopard," a document carefully detailing instructions for blowing up electrical towers. The persons were Luis Alberto Canales Vivanco, 27 years; Jocista Carlos Alberto Cuevas, 21; Pedro Rojas Castro, 21; Alejandro Patricio Gomez Vega, 22; and Luis Orellano Perez, 25.

According to our evidence, they were arrested at gunpoint in their homes between December 18 and 22 by plainclothesmen, apparently from the Air Force, and taken in white Bresler refrigerator trucks with license plates removed. In the case of Luis Alberto Canales Vivanco, we have further evidence that his family was informed that he would be taken to the local police station. After a short time his brothers went to this police station where they were told that no order of detention had been issued that day. His family searched for him for three days, to no avail. On Saturday, December 22, they inquired at the Medical Institute for information and were told to return the following day. On Sunday they identified his body, which had numerous lacerations and bullet wounds in different areas. That same day the family heard in a news bulletin the official version of Luis Alberto's death. (IV, 9; V)

b. A recent article in *El Mercurio* claimed that a forest fire near Valparaíso had been started by communists because the fire burned in the shape of a hammer and sickle. (II, 20)

c. Seven persons were officially reported to have been killed during an alleged attack on the Temuco Regiment on the evening of November 10, 1973. According to the evidence obtained by the Commission, all men had been taken prisoner prior to this date; their wives made repeated attempts to save them between November 5 and 10, including the afternoon of the very day they were killed. Alberto Molina Ruiz, 56 years old, who was named in the official communique as the leader of the assault, had lost his right arm, from the shoulder, in a mine accident at Lota some years ago. (II, 3; IV, 20)

2. Curfew and Freedom of Movement

a. Curfew in Santiago during our stay was from 1 to 5 a.m. Its effect might be best illustrated by a remark of Colonel Espinoza, Chief of Detention Camps. When the Commission requested permission to visit various prisons, he replied, "If you want to go to the Estadio Chile, just stay out after curfew and we'll take you right there."

b. During the first week of February an Italian woman tourist was shot dead in Viña del Mar over a misunderstanding with a policeman who requested documents. (II, 11)

3. Cadavers Found in Rivers and on Streets

a. There is widespread talk among the population about bodies being found in the Mapocho River in Santiago and elsewhere. The Junta authorities are anxious to discredit such accounts. However, we learned from numerous sources that this was true. For example, a resident of a high-rise apartment building overlooking the Mapocho River confirmed shootings on the river bank with the bodies falling into the water. (III, 14)

b. Seven Brazilians were routed from their apartment in September; only one had been engaged in politics. They were shot on the river bank; one of them was not killed. Falling into the water, he remained there, floating down the river until nightfall, when he managed to find refuge. (II, 2)

c. A Spanish priest of the Salesian order, Juan Alsina, 29 years old, was arrested at San Juan de Dios Hospital, where he was the director of hospital personnel. His body was found in the Mapocho River and claimed through the help of the Spanish Embassy. He had died from torture. (II, 2; II, 12)

d. On January 8, 1974, the bodies of five prisoners were found in the Pilmaiquen River. (IV, 9, 22)

e. Two bodies were found lying outside an elementary school. One victim died with his identification card in his extended hand. Some Army men passing by commented to the teachers and students gathered in front of the bodies, "It must have been the police. We take our cadavers to the morgue." (II, 22)

4. Searches and Seizures

In spite of General Oscar Bonilla's television speech in November during which he explained the rights of citizens during search and seizure operations, the military and paramilitary patrols enter homes with no search warrants, make arbitrary arrests, and take articles of value. Many searches occur during the night, but they are equally common in daytime.

a. Evidence includes a detailed account of a house search and arrest by unknown individuals on January 30, 1974. There members of the family were taken away after the family and their factory employees were terrorized. In addition various personal items and valuables were stolen. As of February 23, there is no news of the whereabouts of the father, son and daughter who were taken. (IV, 3)

b. In the working-class areas, periodic searches are common. For example, in La Legua area of Santiago, military arrive every two or three days; some 20 to 30 prisoners are taken each time; some are released. (II, 12)

c. When the military searched a home in Las Barrancas, Santiago, the wife apparently complained that it was the third such search and asked that they please leave her family in peace. As the military departed, they said to the little boy outside, "So long, kid, you won't be seeing us around anymore." The child, surprised, inquired, "You mean you found my Daddy hiding in the roof?" The military reentered the house, brought the father downstairs, and shot him in front of his family. (II, 20; III, 12)

5. Documents Problems

a. In many cases personal identification cards were carried by the head of the household. A detention or death often leaves the family without any documents and thus paralyzes its movements. The military will detain persons who, when stopped, can produce no identification. For example, Ricardo Octavio Lopez Elgueda, 14 years old, was detained September 20, 1973, in his residential area for not having his ID card. (IV, 30)

b. In order to reclaim and trace these lost identification cards, the family must present an official solicitation. For example, in La Legua a worker was taken January 17, 1974, with family documents on him. His body was found two days later. A request has been made by the members of his family to recover their papers. (V)

c. Without official death certificates for heads of families, the legal situation, official financial assistance, etc. becomes complicated. For example, in the case of Dr. Enrique Paris, psychiatrist at the University of Chile, his wife claimed his body at the morgue one month following the takeover, but the authorities would not issue a death certificate. According to Chilean law, passports for her two small children could not be issued because the father's authorization is needed. Finally, after three months, the death certificate was issued. (II, 8; IV, 13)

6. Turning Oneself In

a. According to Decree 81 of November 6, 1973, any person cited for presentation in the *Diario Oficial* must appear before the authorities within five days. Failure to comply is punishable by prison sentence regardless of the verdict on any other charges that may be pending against the person.

b. Among the persons who did turn themselves in, the fate of three is known. Pediatrician Jorge Mario Jordan Domic was killed October 16. Dr. Jorge Avila, young and recently married, turned himself in September 19 or 20; shortly thereafter, he disappeared; his death was confirmed in December. (IV, 6; IV, 13) On September 22 a high school student, 17 years old, turned herself in after hearing her name over the radio. She was four months pregnant. Electric current was applied to her genitals during interrogation. She was afterward treated

at a hospital where the prognosis was grave brain damage to her unborn child. She remains a prisoner in Santo Domingo. (V)

7. Denunciations

Despite General Augusto Pinochet's repeated statement, "We want all Chileans united" and a poster campaign "Let's Build Chile Together," newspaper advertisements and radio announcements have exhorted people to denounce suspicious activities and strangers. Fear of plainclothesmen spying in church, school classrooms, and crowds is widespread.

On its first day in Santiago, the Commission received a visit from a person sent by friends to caution against speaking with Chileans on the streets or openly on buses, in taxis, etc. We were told that the Junta encourages "patriots" to inform on suspicious persons and that there are many plainclothesmen, Military Intelligence officers, around.

a. A neighbor denounced a party of eight young teachers as a political meeting. As the police arrived, the denouncer was standing in the doorway. For violating curfew, he was taken along with the other eight. All men (including the denouncer) were shot; the women were raped at the police station by drunken policemen and released. (II, 6)

b. Family members turn each other in: for example, the case of a Communist Party activist whose fiancée's brother-in-law wanted to denounce him. The fiancée and her mother pleaded with the would-be denouncer; the fiancé sought asylum in a Western European country. (II, 3)

c. In the cases of both North American students killed, Charles Horman and Frank Teruggi, Jr., the reasons for arrest are attributed to denunciations by neighbors. (II, 21)

d. Two minors, Sergio Manuel Castro Saavedra, 16 years old, and Victor Vidal Tejeda, also 16, were detained in October because of denunciations. The former is presumed dead; the latter was shot, his body claimed on November 29 in the morgue. (IV, 30)

e. A Salesian priest, Father Gerardo Poblete from Iquique, was denounced by a Fatherland and Freedom student for criticizing the Junta in his classroom. His body was found at the Santiago morgue and burned October 25, 1973. (II, 12)

8. Economic Pressures

a. According to Decree 6 of the Code of Military Justice, during a "state of war" everyone is only provisionally employed.

b. Workers, political leaders, and intellectuals find themselves in the most distressed situation economically. The number of those dismissed for political reasons exceeds 150,000. Under the *Law of Desahucio*, prior to September 11, 1973, a fired worker was entitled to severance pay for a determined period of time. Junta decrees permit firing employees without this compensation. Further, in limited cases where payments are made, the effects of inflation (between 1,000-1,100 percent from September to February) outweigh the compensation which is determined by the average income for the previous year.

c. Workers are being fired or forced to resign, thereby losing all rights to pension plans provided by the state system and retirement benefits.

9. Unlimited Military Authority

The clear authority under which military patrols operate is best illustrated by the following cases.

a. During the House Search and Arrest of three family members on January 30, 1974, the following items were taken by plainclothesmen, agents of the Military Intelligence Service (SIM) Phillips tape recorder with stereophonic earphones and microphone; Phillips electric shavers; two cameras; feminine articles of value; underclothing; shirts; interior bags, etc. No inventory of articles was given to the family as is the case with formal requisition by the Army. (IV, 3)

b. When a military plane returned to Chile from Panama, loaded with electrical appliances, the officers were asked to pay customs duties. The military put customs officials and police to the wall and threatened them, so the military were allowed to take the goods and leave freely. (II, 24)

B. Detentions and Executions

The Commission found that the National Congress building now houses the Bureau of Detention and Prison Camps which is in charge of all prisoners.

1. Frequency and Manner

a. It is not part of Junta policy to inform families where prisoners are taken; if they do find out, it is through their own means. Letters to prisoners at Estadio Chile from their families indicate that many relatives did not know where prisoners are being held. (III, 8) There are hundreds of cases of missing persons, either those taken at home or those who never returned home after leaving for work or an errand; whereabouts is unknown. (IV, 30; V)

b. There are numerous case of multiple re-arrests by different groups. Of particular importance is the seeming arbitrariness of these arrests and the autonomy of different branches of the armed forces. For example, X (name known to us) was interrogated five times. First, his house was searched; a day later he was arrested by Military Intelligence; the third time, a month later, he was arrested by policemen; the fourth time, by a patrol of military and policemen. His present whereabouts is unknown. (V) Y (name known to us) was arrested on three different occasions and is presently missing. Z (name known to us) was arrested four times, the last time by plainclothesmen. (V)

c. There are several cases of people who are told their arrest was ordered by a local commander. When inquiries are made by family, the local military officer says no order was issued for such an arrest. For example, the case of Luis Alberto Canales Vivanco. (IV, 9; V)

d. The newspapers *La Patria* and *Tercera de la Hora* on February 16, 1974, carried stories about a con-man masquerading as a soldier and preying on fearful people. He told them that they were in danger of arrest and for a certain sum he could fix things—a scheme that could not have worked if people were not being picked up by the military.

e. On its first evening in Santiago, the Commission, accompanied by Chilean friends, encountered by chance one of their acquaintances. Her fiancé, a bookstore owner and Spanish citizen, had been arrested by the military on Wednesday, February 13, at 6 p.m. She had arrived just as he was being taken away but was not allowed to speak to him. Neither she, his father, nor the Spanish consul has been able to locate him in any place of detention. (III, 2)

2. Charges and Sentencing

Those arrested are presumed guilty. Interrogation and torture are used to extract confessions. Often, only after such methods are used, the prisoner is released because no charges are placed. Those released are generally threatened with death if they reveal maltreatment; they frequently must sign releases which certify that they have been well treated.

a. Lieutenant Colonel Mario Rodriguez told members of the Commission: "Only the guilty are being detained."

b. Vice Minister of Justice Max Silva said that under "the state of siege and/or internal war," the government can apprehend people without warrants, hold them without charge (and incommunicado). Prisoners can be held up to six months, though this can be extended. With reference to former government officials, he commented that the people on Dawson Island are criminals who destroyed democracy and the sovereignty of the country. They will be thoroughly investigated before they are brought to trial. It must be a careful procedure for the historical record, because the Chilean people find it difficult to believe that their leaders would commit such crimes.

c. Most of the 223 prisoners at Estadio Chile are being held without charges. None seemed to know what charges might be leveled at them. Their relatives, waiting outside the prison to deliver messages, are not aware of any charges. For some the military was in the process of gathering charges; according to Rodriguez, these would be for crimes under the previous regime as well as acts deemed criminal by the decrees and laws instituted by the new government [applied retroactively].

d. A worker in the South of Chile turned himself in the week following the takeover. He was held six weeks, during which time he was tortured by electric shock applied to four parts of his body. He was eventually released because there were no charges against him. (V)

3. Incommunicado

Prisoners are held incommunicado both from families and lawyers as well as from each other. At the Estadio Chile prison, about five men sat high in the bleachers. They were incommunicado. Red Cross workers help medically and deliver messages back and forth, but families normally cannot visit prisoners. (II, 4; III, 4, 8, 13)

4. Legal Counsel

a. We were told repeatedly that the involvement of lawyers usually begins when charges are already drawn up and the case is ready. The lawyer can see the statement of charges against the defendant some 24 to 48 hours prior to sentencing. We were told that, in the north, lawyers are given one to two hours. Frequently the only opportunity for lawyer and client to meet is the moment of sentencing. Hence the only recourse of the lawyer is to request clemency. In the case of a student from Arica, his meeting with his lawyer took place three hours before the trial and lasted three to five minutes. (II, 4, 5, 11, 18; III, 8; IV, 16)

b. Further, lawyers are appointed from a roster of the Chilean Bar Association and tend to be ultra-conservative (see its document "Illegal Acts Committed under the Allende Government and the Bar Association Support for the Junta"). Lawyers who would be sympathetic to the client's case are threatened. Trials are absolutely secret. (II, 4, 11, 18; III, 8)

c. Committee No. 2 (*Comite de la Paz*) is an official group which attempts to help families with detained relatives and/or those who need financial and legal assistance. It advertises its services in local newspapers. Apparently there is a problem trying to find lawyers who will participate in this work. (II, 5, 18, 19; III, 8)

d. If a lawyer will take the case, a writ of *habeas corpus* is presented in an attempt to locate a missing person. There are difficulties in getting a lawyer to do this, but even more in obtaining a response. For example, Andres Alywin, the brother of the president of the Christian Democrat Party, submitted an *habeas corpus* on behalf of seven farm workers who disappeared. Apparently in a rare move, the Court reacted. In November 1973 it requested information from all military sectors as to the whereabouts of these [men]. The response was negative; therefore the *habeas corpus* was thrown out. (II, 5, 9, 19)

e. At the Estadio Chile, several prisoners said they would not be allowed legal counsel until the process of investigation was completed. One of them reported that he had seen a lawyer once, but he added, "I was lucky." (II, 4) From the floor of the gymnasium prisoners shouted up, "No charges." (II, 4)

5. Torture

The use of torture is widespread, although treatment depends on various factors: who the prisoner is or is thought to be, the individual in charge of the local or regional center, and the branch of the armed services conducting the interrogation. It is the general opinion of people interviewed that the Chilean Air Force is the most brutal, the most likely to torture and kill. In contrast, the prisoners and populace in general regard the *carabineros* or national police force as more humane.

a. The most striking evidence came from some of the prisoners at Estadio Chile. Although Lieutenant Colonel Rodriguez had arranged formal interviews with seven prisoners, there was a covert opportunity to communicate with other prisoners by leaning over the balcony. This was at first done by signaling: (pointing) what happened to X's arm (in sling). This person would then casually walk by the balcony and let his arm hang down, limp, while making a slicing sign indicating it had been broken. As the men got bolder, more and more walked by, lifting shirts, showing inside of arms to indicate electric shock burns. They told us where they had been tortured: Tejos Verde, Cerros de Chena. (These places were later confirmed as sites of torture by our evidence.) By the end of the hour and one half, they were carrying on a full conversation, in English or French, once they learned of our other languages. (II, 4)

b. There is widespread belief that Brazilian military, skilled in the use of methods of torture, were brought in immediately following the military takeover to interrogate Brazilian prisoners and Chileans as well. A number of sources told us that U.S. and Brazilian torture equipment is used; electric shock units, nail bar, etc. [unconfirmed]. Other sources indicated that training in such methods was received by the military prior to the takeover in U.S. training schools in Panama and in Texas. (II, 24)

c. Methods of torture being used include electric shock applied to various sensitive parts of the body, fingernail extraction, shooting off guns next to the ear—along with more "conventional" brute methods—beating with gun butts, knife-slashing, cigarette burns, sexual molestation, and rape.

d. The cases are numerous: that of Victor Jara, internationally famous folksinger and artist is well known. (IV, 1, 2) Documents which would compromise the sources are being shown to selected persons in the United States and abroad. These documents include several testimonies of persons who were tortured and released. For example, X was exposed to electric shocks; a gun was shot next to his ear drum; and he was blindfolded for a week. Y was given electric shocks and was blindfolded 14 days. Z's death certificate said he died of bronchial pneumonia. Upon exhumation several lacerations were discovered on his body. (V)

e. The torture is being used at the present time. A mother found the body of her son on February 13, 1974. His hands and genitals had been cut off. His body was covered with burns from cigarettes and slashed with knives. (II, 8)

f. According to a letter dated February 14, 1974, which was smuggled out of X prison and given to the Commission, a man was arrested the middle of January and tortured until he signed a confession. (IV, 17)

6. Executions and the "Ley de Fuga"

When pressed by the Commission for an estimate, Vice Minister of Justice Max Silva stated that, in the early days of the military government, there were some 30 persons executed, but there are none now. [Interview taped; available from Ms. Anna Langford] The evidence makes this statement ridiculous.

a. An unusually large number of escapes by persons under police custody is reported. This usually occurs in the following manner: "While being transported from X prison to Y, the following prisoners attempted to wrest guns from their guards (or simply, to escape) during a breakdown of the vehicle. They were shot by the guards." However, it is generally known that prisoners are bound and under heavy guard while being moved.

b. According to 42 separate newspaper accounts, approximately 410 persons were shot while "attempting to escape" as of December 12, 1973, or during [the] three months [following the coup]. The latest evidence is as of January 31 in *Puerto Montt*, which reports the names of four prisoners "shot while attempting to flee." This seems to indicate that this method is still being used. (IV, 7, 9)

c. There are repeated cases of alleged suicides of prisoners. Most recently, former Minister José Tohá allegedly hanged himself in the military hospital to which he had been transferred for medical care. Toha, who was six feet, four inches tall, reportedly weighed less than 112 pounds when brought to Santiago from Dawson Island. In another case of an alleged suicide while in custody, X was said to have hanged himself with his shirt. He was dressed in a short sleeve cotton shirt; his body when claimed at the morgue was found covered with lacerations on the stomach and legs. (*The New York Times*, March 17, 1974; V)

d. Many cases are reported of prisoners being executed after military tribunals have sentenced them to a definite period of time. While some of these cases could be attributed to the responsibility of local commanders, a series of such assassinations was the result of a direct order from Santiago carried personally by Chief of the Santiago area General Arellano Stark. This mission of death started in mid October in La Serena, where 15 people were shot on October 16. The source of the order became public knowledge in La Serena after Jorge Washington Peña Hench, a respected musician and founder of La Serena's Symphony Orchestra, Conservatory and Children's Symphony, was killed. As there are 80 families in the symphony, his assassination became known. When the townspeople protested in outrage, the district military commander, Lieutenant Colonel Ariosto Lapostol, published a statement in *La Provincia* newspaper saying that he was under orders from Santiago. (III, 11; IV, 6) A case widely known in Santiago concerns the death of Carlos Berger Guralnik, a lawyer and journalist in Calama. He was among 26 shot "while attempting to escape" during a vehicle breakdown on October 20 or 21, 1973. According to *El Mercurio* of October 2, Berger had been sentenced to two months in prison by a military tribunal. (IV, 6)

e. The estimates of the total number of executions between September 11 and the visit of the Commission range very broadly. The official Junta figure is 2,170 including military men killed in the takeover (*Chicago Daily News*, February 27). Aside from Max Silva's figure of 30, the most conservative estimate encountered was 1,000 given by Gil Sinay. Informed foreign observers say that at least 5,000 deaths have been accounted for. The prevailing figure among our sources was 20,000 to 25,000, but the range reaches 80,000 according to Mrs. Hortensia Allende Bussi, to 150,000 if we are to accept the estimate of a conservative Chilean businessman. (II, 2, 5, 11, 12, 14, 25) Some names of those murdered were obtained by the Commission. (IV, 31)

7. *Partial list of those persons detained by military or paramilitary and whose present whereabouts is unknown is appended.* (IV, 30) [Not included in this reprinting, but available from the Commission.]

C. Economy

1. Salaries

a. In January, wage and salary levels were readjusted with an estimated increase which may or may not be the real increase after February changes. The long-announced "readjusted" salaries were scheduled for February, 1974. But no one knows what this will mean, in fact. Guesses are that salaries will approximately double or even triple. Minimum salary per month will be about 18,000 escudos. The following figures [top, opposite column] are approximate and change monthly but nonetheless provide an idea of the economic situation as of January 31, 1974.

b. The work week was increased by Junta decree a mandatory four hours. This means a 48- to 52-hour work week for workers, a 40-hour in-school week for teachers and university professors. (II, 6, 22, 23)

2. Prices

a. The Commission noted that the stores seem to have a plentiful supply of goods, although few people can afford to do much buying. The Junta is running an economic campaign with such slogans as these: CHILEAN, LEARN TO BUY! and FREE COMPETITION IS A JUST PRICE.

Work Classification	Wages per Month (in escudos)
Unskilled worker	10-15,000
Skilled worker	20-30,000
Piece worker (piece work now discontinued)	20,000+
Doctors working for government hospitals	40,000+
Readjusted wages, new doctors	80,000
Bank clerk	40-60,000
Social worker	50-60,000
University professor, 5 years' experience	80,000
Hotel maid	5,000+ %
Newspaper vendor	5% of sales
Ice cream vendor, summer season	(up to) 20,000

b. The economic situation and purchasing power can be seen by the following examples: (1) According to *El Mercurio*, February 15, 1974, the price of rents was allowed to increase five times over January 1974; (2) One family of five which the Commission interviewed spends an estimated 9,000 escudos on bread and milk alone. (II, 13); (3) The Commission was impressed by the fact that:

A worker who takes one bus to and from work, six days/week, four weeks/month (based on bus fare, one way, no transfer system, at 30, 45, or 90 E. if only one bus is needed) spends for his average bus fare: *90 E./day x 24 days*	2,160 E.
If he buys 1½ kilos of bread for his family per day (based on bread at 130 E./kilo) spends: *1.5 kilos x 130 E./kilo x 30 days*	5,850 E.
	8,010 E.
If he should be a pack-a-day cigarette smoker and smoke the cheapest brand (based on range of 130-220 E./pack) spends: *130 E./pack x 30 days*	3,900 E.
approximate total	12,000 E.

In other words, just for minimal transportation to and from work and bread for his family, a worker spends approximately 44 percent of what will be the minimum wage. Should he be a smoker, the cigarettes and bus fare (just for himself) and bread for his family will total 67 percent of the minimum wage.

(4) Articles of clothing have gone beyond the means of reach for the average worker. A blouse costs (average) 3,000 escudos; a man's shirt, 4,500; shoes, 5-8,000; children's shoes, 3-5,000.

D. Trade Unions

1. The Central Federation of Workers (CUT) has been closed; any union activity whether written or by any other means is outlawed as of September 17, 1973. (Decree no. 12 of the Junta) The Commission found a padlock on the doors of the CUT offices. Funds of unions have been frozen. All delegated labor bodies and meetings of such are abolished and prohibited. (II, 1; IV, 4)

2. Of 137 national unions, only 30 of those less important are functioning. The remaining 25 percent do not exist as unions because there can be no grievances filed, no collective bargaining; and union meetings cannot be held except with prior approval of the agenda by the police. Such meetings are limited to an explanation of military decrees. Election of union officers is also forbidden. The Junta has been attempting to replace former union officials by their own approved men. (II, 1; IV, 4)

3. Many workers are not entitled to any compensation because they were not fired but left "voluntarily" when their employers threatened to denounce them to the authorities as "extremists." Many other workers are dead or missing. (IV, 30) There is no official fund for widows and orphans. Trade unionists who collect funds for widows, orphans, and unemployed run a grave risk of punishment.

4. It seems the military are trying to physically eliminate union leaders. Leaders of CUT have been imprisoned, harassed, killed, or forced into exile (IV, 4). Two men were shot during searches of their homes: Luis Rojas Valenzuela, regional secretary of CUT in Arica, and Luis Almonacid, provincial secretary of CUT in O'Higgins. In the case of the General Secretary of CUT, Rolando Calderon, the military tried to shoot him near the interior of the Swedish Embassy; he received facial wounds in the forehead and eyes. (IV, 4)

5. Six leaders of the Longshoreman's Union in San Antonio were shot "while attempting to escape during a breakdown of the vehicle transporting them." They had been detained in mid September for alleged strike activity. Their names are Fidel Alfonso Bravo Alvarez, Raul Bacciarini Zotrila, Héctor Rojo Alfaro, Samuel Núñez Núñez, Armando Jiménez Machuca, Guillermo Alvarez Cañas. (IV, 27)

6. The following table [opposite column] illustrates the status of the trade union movement in Chile at the present time.

Union	Total No. Workers	Total Dismissed
Health workers (laborers)	45,000	18,000
Health, professional, technical[1] (doctors, nurses, etc.)	18,000	6,000
Municipal workers	16,000	3,500[2]
Teachers (Sindicato Union de los Trabajadores de la Educacion) primary through university[3]	130,000	26,000
Textiles	35,000	15,000[4]
Metals	35,000	12,000
Construction	125,000	30,000[5]
State transports (buses)	8,000	1,800
Copper workers	35,000	4,700 +
Mine workers (small and medium sized mines)	65,000	20,000
Internal revenue workers	7,000	1,000
Electrical workers	8,450	500
Railroad workers	27,000	1,200
Bank workers	16,000	1,500
Newspaper reporters (not unionized)	(est.) 6,000	2,000[6]

[1] These were dismissed for not participating in a doctors' strike against the Popular Unity government.

[2] In Santiago alone 2,000 were dismissed. More than 1,000 have been replaced by government informers.

[3] The declared intention of the military Junta is to dismiss 20 percent of the educators. A union leader remarked that this was easy to do because they had already dismissed so many students that the classes were much smaller.

[4] This is a conservative figure; there may have been as many as 20,000 dismissals.

[5] In one place alone, 10,000 were dismissed.

[6] One union leader told us he personally knew of eight reporters working as pick-and-shovel laborers on the subway construction.

E. Health and Social Services

There are systematic campaigns of persecution against the doctors, medical personnel, and students who did not participate in the strike of professionals and who were politically active prior to September 11. Many physicians and hospital functionaries were tortured and killed. Many more were expelled or suspended from the medical profession (Chilean Medical Association and National Health Service). (IV, 13)

1. For example, the gardener at Barros Luco hospital was arrested on December 21, 1973; he is presently missing. (IV, 30) The secretary at the same hospital was arrested January 18, 1974; her whereabouts is unknown. (IV, 30) A female hospital employee was tortured for information. (IV, 21)

2. A detailed plan of persecution was designed by Dr. Augusto Schuster Cortés [see complete text following] and followed by military prosecutors. (IV, 11; IV, 12) Details of this persecution are given in statements by these prosecutors citing charges against professors, students, and functionaries and the subsequent suspensions and firing of same. (IV, 14; IV, 15) Similar measures were taken in all branches of the School of Medicine in Santiago, the School of Veterinary Medicine, and the National Health Service.

3. Among the many physicians and personnel of the health services arrested are the director of the Linares Health Zone, Dr. Carlos Azmorano; the former Minister of Health Dr. Mario Lagos; nutrition expert Dr. Giorgio Solimano Canturias; director of Health for Greater Santiago, Dr. Gustavo Molina; director of the 3rd Health Zone, Dr. Asbalon Werner V. Other names are appended to the Report. (IV, 30)

4. In the Social Service Institute, the school was closed for a period of time. When it reopened, a new rector, Pilar Alvarino, was named. He with three professors chosen by him reassessed all the students. They were divided into four groups: (1) unacceptable; (2) acceptable but given stern warning with very probationary status; (3) acceptable with conditions; (4) acceptable. Through such methods many students were dismissed and social workers fired. (II, 5)

5. The military seems to be initiating a campaign against socialized medicine to the effect that the practice of medicine cannot be good quality unless services are "paid for." The charges for services are presently 3,000 escudos for a visit with a doctor of nine years' experience or less; 4,000 if 10 years or more; 5,000 if 20 or more years. (II, 7, 8)

F. Education

1. All universities and several private elementary and secondary schools, including the pontifical Catholic University, are under military administration; rectors have been replaced by military officers. The Rector of the University of Chile, a Christian Democrat, protested the violation of university autonomy; he is presently in exile. St. Georges School, one of the most progressive institutions in Chile and run by the Holy Cross Fathers, has been intervened by the military; the gymnastics teacher was made principal. (II, 6, 12, 15, 20, 22, 23)

2. The Junta is attempting to develop an elite educational system. Access to education has been made much more difficult since tuition is being instituted: 18,000 escudos [unconfirmed]. The work-study programs have been abolished; moreover, many students who participated in them have been suspended or expelled on the grounds that "they did not demonstrate a sufficient interest in their subjects." Students must now show means of support (e.g., working wife, family support) in order to attend the university.

3. The most conservative estimate that the Commission heard was that 10 to 20 percent of the professors, functionaries, and students were suspended, forced to resign, or expelled. However, this figure does not accurately reflect the situation in the universities, because some departments were particularly hard hit. For example, in Concepción, between 200 and 300 university professors (of 1,200) were suspended; approximately 6,000 of 18,000 students were suspended and/or expelled. (II, 7, 16, 20, 23, 25)

4. In the School of Public Health, which had an outstanding reputation in Latin America, 70 of 120 persons have been suspended; it is not clear how many will be allowed to return. Charges against those dismissed or expelled are vague; for example, students and faculty in the Department of Economics, School of Political Economy, were cited "for one of the above mentioned charges" after a listing of four or five counts was given. (IV, 10)

5. The Junta has instituted changes in curriculum and dress code. Uniforms and briefcases are required for all students. According to one educator, "the military doctrine for all high schools and elementary schools will be reduced to discipline, cleanliness, obedience and uniforms." (II, 23) There also will be decided emphasis on military history and nationalism. (II, 15)

6. No group meetings are allowed on university campuses. When the State Technical University reopened, the new rules included no talking outside of the classroom. The universities are continually patrolled by the Chilean police. Within the classrooms, intellectual dialogue is inhibited by fear of plainclothesmen and right-wing students, etc. (II, 15, 20)

7. Publishing will be under strict guidelines; scholars are fearful even to present a manuscript which might contain material anathema to the military censors. There has been evidence of pressure on the substance of teaching and of writing, particularly in the social sciences, social work, and education. (II, 7, 23)

8. Educators have been taken prisoner, tortured, and killed; they are still being arrested. The day the Commission was leaving Santiago, it received the news that a Professor Meruane from the Catholic University had been taken at 4 p.m. the previous day. (II, 23; IV, 30)

G. Mass Media

Freedom of the press, radio, and television has been effectively crushed by the Junta. All communication systems have been seized, leftist publications banned and offices closed. Of the 11 major newspapers which appeared daily in Santiago prior to September 11, only six continue to be published. Of these six, three are controlled by the Edwards family. Moreover, *La Prensa,* the Christian Democratic newspaper, recently announced that it will discontinue publication. Prior censorship has been reinstituted.

1. Copies of the newspapers shut down have been removed from the historical records of the National Library and other libraries throughout the country. Selected books and works of certain authors are being removed from the library collections. (II, 10)

2. Leading bookstores of radical and leftist literature, records, and posters (such as PLA, Prensa Latina-Americana) are closed and their property confiscated. All bookstore owners must present a list of inventory for review. Those books censored must be removed, at a loss to the owner. Even if the newly ordered books are confiscated at customs, the owner must repay the bank for dollars advanced for the order. All political science books, right or left, are banned, as are social science books relating to Chile and any Marxist literature pertaining to Chile. (II, 9)

3. Since some books are dangerous to own, and this category remains undefined, many people have burned their libraries. A sociology professor told a member of the Commission that he burned his doctoral thesis because it pertained to aspects of the Popular Unity government. (II, 23) A middle-class woman, communist, burned her entire library out of fear: her first husband was in exile; her second husband, a communist, had been killed; her father had been killed as a "political extremist." (II, 20)

4. Of 6,000 people employed in the mass media, approximately 2,000 have been fired, and most of these are unable to find other work. Even foreign correspondents have been given harsh treatment; a few have been taken into custody for up to 11 days; some have been held at gunpoint while their quarters were searched. (II, 11)

5. A Chilean student, just returned from graduate study in Poland in June, went to retrieve his shipment of books at Chilean customs in mid September. He was told that all his books would be confiscated (1,000 books, about 600 pounds) unless he wished to make a special petition. Rather than draw attention to his situation, the student forfeited his books. (II, 16)

6. The price of periodicals has increased five or six times since September; newspapers cost 60, 80, or 100 escudos. For example, *El Mercurio* bought daily for one month would cost 3,000 escudos or one sixth the average minimum wage. Magazines range in price from 200 to 400 escudos. The Junta decrees which affect all Chileans are available in book form, but the cost is high: *Code of Military Justice,* 1,200; *Decrees of the Junta* in two volumes, 720 and 2,000. (III, 3)

H. Minority Group Treatment

1. Foreigners

Apparently, immediately following the military takeover, there was a concerted campaign against foreigners which equated those notably foreign with subversion, Marxism, and armed revolution. As the effect of this propaganda, denunciations by neighbors and co-workers were common as well as brutal maltreatment once in military custody. Upon the impetus of the United Nations Commissioner for Refugees and the World Council of Churches, an official committee was instituted to deal with the evacuation of foreigners as refugees. This Committee No. 1 (as distinguished from Committee No. 2 which deals with Chileans) established refugee camps, processed visas and employment offers, found transportation to countries of asylum, etc. According to the Executive Secretary of this Committee No. 1, Samuel Nalegash, the refugee work is almost completed.

a. As of February 21, 1974, 4,442 refugees have been processed; about 200 remain in embassies and should be out of Chile within 30 days. In addition, there are still 92 in detention camps and six in prison, three of whom soon be facing trial (10 lawyers are working on these cases). (Nalegash)

b. Over 130 priests have been expelled from Chile. The tactic of the Junta is to force the Cardinal's office to expel the priests deemed undesirable by the military; in this manner the Junta assumes no blame. Case of Irish Franciscan priest in Limache who was expelled at the end of January: He had been under house arrest because in a church sermon he had criticized large landowners for the way they treat their tenants. Because he was a foreigner and much pressure was applied, he was allowed to leave.

2. Silo

Silo is an apolitical, utopian youth cult with religious, especially Eastern mystical, overtones. The authorities claim that the group "corrupts youth," has ties with leftist extremists, breaks up family life, etc. The group is anti-materialistic and anticapitalistic; therefore, according to the Junta, it must be pro-communist (*Tercera de la Hora*, February 21, 1974). Thirteen of the group's leaders have been imprisoned; the main leader of Silo, Bruno von Ehremberg, has been tortured and is being held incommunicado.

3. Jews

According to Gil Sinay, head of the organized Jewish community in Chile and Director of the Bank of Israel, and Leon Dobry Folkman, manager of the bank, there is no campaign of anti-semitism by the Junta. Mr. Sinay feels that the Junta is afraid of projecting a fascist image abroad, and he has received assurances from General Leigh that there will be no anti-semitism.

I. Investigations of the Murder of Frank Teruggi, Jr.

On February 17, Mr. Frank Teruggi, Sr., visited the house (at Hernan Cortes 2575, Santiago) where his son had lived while studying economics at the University of Chile. There he found on a telephone book the U.S. Embassy number in his son's handwriting. (Beside the Embassy number was an extension number which could not have been obtained from the directory itself.) The new tenants of the house indicated that the place had again been searched by the military on February 10; they found nothing.

At the U.S. Embassy on February 18, the Commission members met with Ambassador David H. Popper, Consular General Frederick Purdy, and three other Embassy officials. [Tape recorders were not permitted] Mr. Teruggi presented Ambassador Popper with letters from Congressman Samuel Young and Senator Adlai Stevenson; the Ambassador did not open them. Mr. Teruggi pointed out some of the discrepancies in the information received from the Junta authorities, e.g., the Junta claims that Frank was arrested on September 20, held overnight at the National Stadium for questioning, and released at 6 p.m. on September 21. Yet no other prisoners were held for so brief a time, nor were any others released so near the 7 p.m. curfew hour. Also, the Junta has admitted that there is no record of Frank's having signed release papers. The initial claim that Frank was arrested for violation of curfew is obviously false, since his roommate, David Hathaway, was arrested at the same time—at their house. In response, the Embassy officials promised to try to "clear up the gaps." However, they suggested no new line of investigation and refused to give Mr. Teruggi a letter of introduction to appropriate Junta representatives.

On February 19 Mr. Teruggi visited a Chilean businessman who is a friend of David Hathaway's family. (II, 21) The businessman stated that David's girl friend, who had witnessed the two youths' arrest, notified him at about 11:00 a.m. on September 21 as to what had happened and that he immediately called the American consulate. (When queried, Mr. Purdy contended that the Consulate had no record of any such call.) The businessman offered to arrange an appointment for Mr. Teruggi with General Oscar Bonilla, Minister of the Interior.

On the afternoon of February 20, Mr. Teruggi went to the training school for noncommissioned officers near Plaza Zanartu, where Frank was taken when first arrested, and was told that the contents of Frank's arrest record could not be disclosed. The commandante asserted that the foreign ministry had never requested information concerning Frank's arrest.

Accompanied by the Chilean businessman, Mr. Teruggi met with General Bonilla on February 21. The General seemed puzzled by the evidence Mr. Teruggi presented—in particular, a letter from David Hathaway—and by the fact that David was released into the custody of the U.S. Embassy, whereas Frank was not; he inquired of his aides why he had not been given such information previously. Bonilla promised to reopen the investigation and declared that if it revealed that Frank died as a result of "negligence" on the part of the military, he was deeply sorry.

On February 22, Mr. Teruggi visited Mr. Purdy and told him of his session with General Bonilla. Mr. Purdy seemed surprised, confused, defensive; he declared that he did not consider the case closed and insisted on his personal integrity ("I am honest; I am honest to the point of making trouble for myself.") (Taped interview) That afternoon Mr. Teruggi had a brief meeting with Ambassador Popper, who expressed apprehension that on returning to the United States and giving an account of his trip, Mr. Teruggi would put the Embassy in a bad light.

Toward the end of the Commission's stay in Chile, Mr. Teruggi obtained convincing evidence pertaining to his son's murder. The evidence was in the form of detailed, signed testimony presented in a document delivered by a well-known Chilean woman to the embassy of a Western European country. (IV, 5) The document "clears up the gaps" between the time Frank was separated from

David Hathaway at the National Stadium and the time his body was brought to the morgue. Frank was not killed by "left-wing terrorists," as the Junta claims was probably the case. According to the document, Frank was badly tortured. He was never released from the stadium while still alive.

It is Mr. Teruggi's opinion—and that of the Commission as a whole—that U.S. officials never made a concerted effort to find out what happened to Frank, Jr. The State Department assured Mr. Teruggi in December that inquiries were being made in Santiago at "top diplomatic levels," but the end result was a report giving the same explanation of what happened to Frank that was given in a report issued in October, shortly after he was murdered. ■

The Pathology of the Fascist Mind

The two documents reprinted below (from the Chicago Commission Report) are grim samples of the apparatus of terror set in motion by the Junta to silence all expression of political life in the country, to crush the left, and to dehumanize those "deviants" singled out for physical extermination. The doctor's directives are all the more sinister because they cannot be dismissed as the isolated fanaticism of one zealot. They are, indeed, words made incarnate in the acts of the military toward the people of Chile.

The Irredeemable

It is believed that the Popular Unity contingent in the country reached, in the period of its height, a percentage close to 50 percent of the voters, a figure which was progressively diminishing until it reached 33 percent in the elections of March 1973. Those who formed part of this contingent can be classified, in decreasing order of dangerousness and activism, in several categories.

In the first place we have the *extremists,* unbalanced elements, fanatics, highly dangerous for their aggressiveness and capable of killing without qualms. They may be foreigners or Chileans; they have serious mental instability and no spirit of self criticism nor any clear understanding of their actions. Generally they are not intelligent and do not possesss good technical preparation. THEY ARE IRREDEEMABLE.

The second group is made up of *activists of high dangerousness and intelligence,* who are technically skilled and exert a crazing influence over their work groups. At a given moment they can become violent. THEY ARE IRREDEEMABLE.

The third group is composed of *ideological activists,* who while resembling the previous group in their characteristics and dangerousness, hate direct violence, preferring to exercise it through third parties. In administrative posts, the majority committed grave misuses of public or private goods, and acted with tremendous sectarianism. This group should be analyzed very meticulously to determine which of them could be made use of technically, under-

standing that they be under strict surveillance. Their place of work should be changed, and those who are not usable should be neutralized.

The fourth group is made up of the *militants of the Popular Unity parties,* who strictly carried out all the orders of their leaders, carrying out their proselytizing without much enthusiasm. Even if they are not immediately redeemable, it is possible that in time they may take stock, to reconsider their (party) membership. They constitute a labor force that is important and highly usable in this country, that is not going to require very rigorous control from the political point of view and that can be won over by the various achievements gained in time.

The fifth group is that of *sympathizers with Popular Unity,* that without any dangerousness and with more reason than the prior group, can be won over with an intelligent and successful policy. The great mass of these sympathizers are groups defrauded and duped with promises that were never fulfilled. They were only seeking their own well-being and that of their families, through achieving *job stability, minimal housing conditions, timely and humanely delivered health care, and finally the possibility of education for their children.*

Analyzing the different groups into which the Popular Unity contingent was divided, one arrives at the conclusion that it is necessary to apply a different conduct with each group. No one has any doubt about the absolute application of the norm that establishes that any officeholder in the leadership, identified with Popular Unity, whatever the degree of his involvement, should be removed from his post. Nor is there any doubt about those who must answer to justice for criminal or dishonest acts. THE COUNCIL OF WAR will determine each particular case. There remain an important number of *activists of great danger and ideological activists,* who apparently have not committed criminal or dishonest acts to answer for, but who nevertheless, because of the function they carry on in PRIMARY, INTERMEDIATE OR UNIVERSITY LEVEL TEACHING or in the NATIONAL HEALTH SERVICE, where some 80,000 Chileans work, constitute a very grave danger to the policy of NATIONAL RESTORATION promoted by the JUNTA. If we desire a wholesome fatherland, with neither winners nor losers, concerned only with its rapid restoration and to recover in as little time as possible, the three lost years, THERE SHOULD NOT REMAIN IN THE COUNTRY OR AT LARGE ANY EXTREMIST OR ACTIVIST, WHETHER CHILEAN OF FOREIGN.

The most dangerous extremists or activists should be deported, others neutralized in some place within the (national) territory. Those who are usable because less dangerous and because of their greater technical training should have their place of work changed.

The groups made up of *militants and sympathizers of the Popular Unity,* who form part of the labor force of the country at all levels, should be incorporated immediately into the task of NATIONAL RESTORATION. Let it be seen that we have a firm and inexorable attitude to eliminate all THE UNBALANCING ELEMENTS FROM OUR FATHERLAND, and at the same time, sufficient understanding to know that an important group of those who, taking advantage of their enormous trust, used them for their muddled purposes and petty interests.

(signed) Professor Dr. Augusto Schuster Cortés
MILITARY PHYSICIAN

Santiago, October 11, 1973.

The Redeemers

The citizenry and especially those who suffered the Marxist persecution during the last three years, are concerned about the different criteria to be applied in the Public Administration Services with respect to each of the groups in which UP officials were classified. They desire a uniform criterion, with firm but just measures, applied without exception at all levels. The JUNTA should not give the image of progressive weakening by diminishing the severity in judging UP officials classified as IDEOLOGICAL ACTIVISTS. They more than any other group have in their favor the apparent lack of dangerousness, since they generally did not demonstrate compromising attitudes. Not to take measures against them is going to mean, sooner or later, a reorganization of Marxism and the progressive increase of CIVIL RESISTANCE. All of which will be joined to the natural discontent that is beginning to be produced by the measures that the JUNTA is taking to cure the economy of the country. If to all this is added the insidious campaign of discrediting [the Junta] which a certain sector of Christian Democracy is carrying on at all levels, it is fertilizing the field so that the patriotic mission which the Armed Forces and Carabineros have taken upon their shoulders will be made tremendously difficult and unnecessarily prolonged.

Those who knew intimately the Marxist methods and saw their names on the lists of execution of Plan Z in their work places fear that a misguided HUMANISM IN THE POLICY COMMANDED BY THE JUNTA may undermine the solid trust that the majority of the citizenry has in it [i.e., in the Junta]. The Marxist tactic at this moment is to touch the Christian sensitivity of those who today govern and hold positions of responsibility. They try to appeal to humanitarian sentiments so that, "since nothing has been clearly proven about their guilt," measures will not be taken against them, permitting them to remain in their work sites and thus to carry on underhandedly a slowly deranging but no less destructive mission. One should always remember that the Marxists would not have hesitated an instant in executing us, our wives and our children. A great part of the sacrifice of the brave soldiers and carabineros, who gave their lives to liberate our Fatherland, from the claws of Marxism, will be lost if we do not keep fresh the memory of their cruel, dehumanized and sordid procedures. So that if they managed to fool us once and for a while, NEVER AGAIN WILL THAT HAPPEN. May we have the wisdom to carry out fully the mission that each of the Chileans who love their Fatherland and the History have set out for us: TO HAND OVER TO OUR CHILDREN A COUNTRY WHICH IS SPIRITUALLY AND MATERIALLY CLEANSED AND WITH A CLEAR CONSCIENCE THAT ITS MORAL VALUES CONSTITUTE ITS MOST PRECIOUS TREASURE.

(signed) Professor Dr. Augusto Schuster Cortés
MILITARY PHYSICIAN

Santiago, October 12, 1973.

The above two documents, translated from the Spanish originals, appear as (IV, 11) and (IV, 12) in the Documents appended to the Chicago Commission Report. Please see the "Source List" at p. 153 for information on obtaining the complete Report.

International Commission of Jurists

A three-member mission visited Chile from April 19 to 28, 1974, on behalf of the International Commission of Jurists (ICJ) to enquire into the legal situation with regard to human rights. The delegation was composed of: Mr. Niall MacDermot, Secretary-General of the ICJ and former Minister of State in the U.K. government; Professor Covey Oliver, Professor of International Law at the University of Pennsylvania, former U.S. Ambassador to Colombia, and former Assistant Secretary of State for Inter-American Affairs in the U.S. State Department; and Dr. Kurt Madlener, specialist in Spanish and Latin American penal law at the Max Planck Institute of International and Comparative Penal Law, Freiburg-im-Breisgau, West Germany. The delegation met various Ministers, judges, advocates, academic lawyers, and others concerned with human rights, including Cardinal Raúl Silva Henriques, and on May 17, 1974, released the following preliminary report. The recommendations contained in the report have been forwarded to the Chilean authorities.

1. We visited Chile on behalf of the ICJ from April 19 to 28, 1974, to enquire into the legal situation concerning the protection of human rights. The principal purpose of our mission was to investigate the legal safeguards at present in force in Chile for the protection of persons detained for political and security reasons.

2. We had meetings with the Minister of the Interior, the Minister of Justice, the Members of the Supreme Court, the Council of the College of Advocates, Cardinal Raúl Silva Henríquez, and a large number of other persons including many practicing lawyers and professors of law with experience of the problems we were enquiring into. We were greatly assisted by the Staff of the Committee of Cooperation for Peace in Chile. This is an inter-denominational organization sponsored by the Catholic, Protestant and Jewish communities to provide legal and other assistance to detainees and their families. They have an unparalleled knowledge of the situation with which we were concerned.

3. We will first make a few brief remarks about the context within which the present legal system is operating.

4. It became increasingly evident to us that Chileans are still deeply and passionately divided by the events leading up to and following the military coup on September 11, 1973, and that it will take some time to heal the wounds of the past, but we hope that the Junta will before long indicate the period of time within which they expect to be able to return the country to civilian rule. It is to us, and we believe to all Chileans, unthinkable that Chile should be numbered among the totalitarian states. It is a country with a deep and long tradition of respect for democratic freedom under the rule of law. An expression of intent to restore democracy within a definite and reasonably short period would, we believe, have a stabilizing effect, help the process of healing to which we have referred, and enable a phased restoration of basic human rights.

5. Chile is at present ruled by decree following the proclamation by the military Junta of a "state of seige" and "state of war." Following these proclamations all normal democratic liberties are suspended, including press freedom, the rights of association and assembly, freedom of speech, trade union rights, the right to strike and freedom of education. No political activity is allowed. The political parties of the former coalition government have been declared illegal, and other parties have been suspended. A curfew at night is in force.

6. The explanation given for these and other severe restrictions on traditional freedoms is the need for a temporary period of control in order to reduce the divisions of the past, and to enable the security authorities to overcome the potentially violent forces of opposition which are believed to exist underground, and across the national frontiers, with substantial supplies of weapons clandestinely imported under the previous regime.

7. In examining the legal system now in operation we have accepted the hypothesis that an emergency situation prevails in Chile and we have looked to see whether there are those minimum legal safeguards and protections of individuals rights which are to be looked for even in a serious state of emergency. More particularly, our concern has been to ascertain whether, in accordance with Chile's international obligations in time of internal war (under Article 3 of the Geneva Conventions, 1949), there are in force those "judicial guarantees which are recognized as indispensable by civilized people."

8. Our enquiry focussed in particular upon the legal aspects of the arrest and trial of persons suspected of having committed offenses for political reasons and the arrest of persons whose preventive or administrative detention is thought necessary on grounds of internal security. No official statistics are published of the number of persons arrested and held in custody for these purposes. We are satisfied that the total has been very greatly reduced in the last three months, perhaps by as much as 50%. On the other hand, substantial numbers of arrests continue to be made. On the information we have received, the best estimate we can make is that there may now be between 6,000 and 7,000 persons in detention. Of these probably about a third are awaiting trial and the remainder are being detained without charge on security grounds. The conditions in many places of detention are bad, and we welcome the announcement made while we were in Chile that detainees on Dawson Island will be transferred to the central area of Chile.

9. In addition, at any given moment there may be as many as a further 3,000 people under arrest at any one time who are being held for questioning in military barracks, police stations, or other interrogation centers by one of the four security intelligence authorities of the armed forces (Army, Navy, Air Force, and Carabineros). Sometimes these arrests are made anonymously by persons coming in plain clothes in vehicles with no number plates. No one is able to find out who has arrested them, or where they are held. Many are held incommunicado for long periods. Some are later transferred to camps or prisons for detention or for prosecution. Others are released, perhaps to be re-arrested later. It is, we believe, under interrogation at this stage that most of the cases of ill-treatment occur. We received most convincing evidence to support the declaration of the Catholic bishops on April 24, 1974, that there are "interrogations with physical and moral pressure." We believe that the various forms of ill-treatment, sometimes amounting to severe torture, are carried out systematically by some of those responsible for interrogation and not, as many people sought to persuade us, in isolated instances at the time of arrest. Habeas corpus *(amparo)* and similar remedies have not been effective to deal with these problems.

10. Under the state of war, those accused of offenses against internal security are tried before military courts martial called Councils of War. The procedure is very summary, and the role of defense lawyers is severely restricted. In addition, and most seriously, there is no appellate tribunal, and the Supreme Court has renounced any power to supervise or review their decisions. This results in a serious lack of uniformity in procedure and sentencing policy. We have received abundant evidence that many serious errors in law and procedure by these military courts have occurred, and there is no judicial procedure by which these errors can be remedied.

11. We are of the opinion that the present judicial procedures and safeguards do not meet with Chile's obligations under Article 3 of the Geneva Conventions referred to above. We respectfully put forward the following recommendations to meet what are, we consider, the minimum requirements.

12. We recommend that the military procedures available under the Code of Military Justice in time of peace should be introduced, if necessary by decree law. This would provide an appeal system and other necessary procedural safeguards.

13. To reduce the risk of ill-treatment of suspects under interrogation, we recommend that: (i) the maximum permitted period of "incommunicado," which we were told by General Bonilla, Minister of the Interior, is three days or up to eight days in exceptional circumstances on the authority of a senior officer, should be strictly enforced; (ii) relatives should be informed of the arresting authority and place of detention at the time of arrest, or as soon as possible thereafter; (iii) lawyers should have access to their clients at any stage after the period of "incommunicado," whether they are charged with an offense or not.

14. We are preparing, and propose later to publish, a full report explaining our findings and comments upon the present legal system in Chile.

15. We also enquired into the situation of foreigners in Chile, in particular refugees from other Latin American countries, about which a great deal of international concern was expressed after the coup. We consider that the government has fully met its obligations under the various relevant conventions to which Chile is a party. Nearly all of those wishing to leave have been permitted to do so, whether they sought asylum in foreign embassies, or were resettled with the help of the United Nations High Commissioner for Refugees, or left on their own by lawful means. Others, perhaps fearing they might be arrested, have left clandestinely. Only two foreigners are known to have been sentenced by military courts, and about 20 others are awaiting trial, of whom half are released on bail. Some hundreds of the original 10,000 or so aliens still remain, and a small number (about five or six each week) are still coming forward asking to be resettled as refugees.

16. We were in Chile during the week of the notable call for Christian toleration and national unity by Cardinal

Raúl Silva and the Catholic bishops of Chile. As this was also the first week of the Air Force trials, some other non-Chilean groups were showing by their presence their interest in human rights and democracy in Chile. In undertaking this mission for the International Commission of Jurists we were motivated by a deep interest in Chile's great people. We leave with hope for their future and the assurance that Chileans today, as always, cherish their finest traditions. ■

Ramsey Clark's Congressional Testimony

Former U.S. Attorney General Ramsey Clark and New York Criminal Court Judge William Booth flew to Chile on May 20, 1974, at the request of the National Council of Churches to observe the military trials of 67 former officials and armed forces officers of the duly elected Allende government. "We must show concern about the overthrow of democracies," Mr. Clark said. "This trip is part of a continuing effort both to protect human rights and to help the United States develop a foreign policy that is based on defense of freedom and democracy." Mr. Clark and Judge Booth have made similar trips in recent years to investigate possible violations of fundamental human rights around the world.

Judge Booth recently served as an observer for the International Commission of Jurists at the trials of striking contract workers in Namibia and, representing the Episcopal Church, observed the trial of Dean G. Q. French-Beytagh in Johannesburg.

In 1969, Mr. Clark was refused entry to the Soviet Union to attend the Leningrad trials of Soviet Jews who were charged with unlawfully seeking to leave the country. In 1971, he observed the Pass Courts trials in South Africa, and in 1972, the trials of the Carabanchel 10, a group of trade unionists who were imprisoned for organizing workers in Spain. In other trips to investigate violations of human rights, Mr. Clark has tried to gain, but was refused, entry to Greece and Brazil and has traveled to Ireland and North Vietnam at the request of the American Civil Liberties Union, the National Council of Churches, Amnesty International, and other organizations addressing specific forms of repression. On July 3, 1974, under the auspices of the International Committee of Concern, he flew to Paris to observe the plight of Syrian Jews.

On June 11, 1974, following his May trip to Chile, Mr. Clark testified before a joint meeting of the House of Representatives Foreign Affairs Committee's Subcommittee on International Organizations and Movements and the Subcommittee on Inter-American Affairs. On July 23 he gave testimony on Chile to the Senate Judiciary Committee's Subcommittee on Refugees.

The following is an account of his activities while in Chile.

On Sunday, May 19, 1974, I flew from Los Angeles to Mexico City. There I spent half a day in meetings with a small number of Chileans in exile including relatives of former government officials, a lawyer and law professor, relatives of persons killed or held prisoner by the military government and others. The purpose of the visit was to obtain briefings on the law and reported status of persons and conditions in Chile.

Flying overnight from Mexico City I arrived midday Monday May 20 in Santiago. Judge William Booth of the Criminal Court of New York City, arriving earlier directly from New York, met me at the airport, with a Chilean lawyer and relatives of a former high government official presently a prisoner.

We remained in Santiago until the morning of Saturday, May 25, 1974. While there our principal activities included the following:

1. Attendance throughout five separate trials of Air Force personnel charged with crimes ranging from treason to unprofessional conduct.

2. Discussions on the law and specific cases with Chilean lawyers engaged in the defense of Air Force cases or retained by families to represent prisoners formerly held on Dawson Island.

3. Discussions with prisoners charged with crimes in the Air Force proceedings including several for whom death penalties are sought.

4. Discussions with U.S. Embassy officials, including Ambassador David Popper and three key officials in the political section of the Embassy.

5. Conferences with officials of the military government including General Oscar Bonilla, the Minister of the Interior, General Orlando Gutiérrez, the *fiscal* or prosecutor in the Air Force trials, the head of the prison system and warden of the Carcel Publico in Santiago, a judge of the Court of Appeals.

6. Discussions with Enrique Iglesias, the Director of the U.N. office in Santiago.

7. Inspection of the Carcel Publico in Santiago, including military, political and the general prison population, solitary confinement facilities and prisoner interviews.

8. Discussions with officials and visits to several foreign missions in Santiago that have offered asylum and processed thousands of refugees and others.

9. Visits and discussions in the homes of citizens whose relatives are prisoner, have been killed or mistreated under the military government.

10. Discussions with church leaders, lawyers and others working to expose violations of human rights, wrongful arrests and imprisonment, torture and executions.

11. Meetings with persons who have been arbitrarily arrested, tortured and released.

Since returning, Judge Booth and I have held a joint press conference and testified before the Congress together. Separately we have spoken on Chile; interviewed for press, radio and television (including Latin American and Western European press); and written.

The full text of Mr. Clark's statement to the House Subcommittee follows.

Your concern is human rights. What nobler purpose can foreign or domestic policy pursue than the fulfillment of human rights? There are no human rights in Chile today in the only sense rights have value. The military government of Chile can transgress any human right with impunity; for any reason it chooses, or no reason at all. Rights are unenforceable. Arbitrary, uncontrolled will governs.

Democracy died in Chile on September 11, 1973. No fiction agreed upon can alter that fact. All who love democracy must mourn its passing. The death of any democracy diminishes all.

Nor is democracy unrelated to human rights. Reinhold Niebuhr told us, "Man's capacity for justice makes democracy possible, but his inclination for injustice makes democracy necessary." Injustice, including the denial of human rights, is largely unrestrained in the absence of democracy.

Chile has a longer history and higher commitment to democracy than most nations of the Americas. Article 1 of its constitution provided "The state of Chile is unitary. Its government is republican and representatively democratic." No electorate chose the military Junta that now rules Chile. By what it calls Law Decree 27, it dissolved the Congress on September 21, 1973 and transferred legislative power to itself. By Law Decree 128 it assumed the power to modify the Constitution on November 12, 1973. These were, of course, laws in name only. They represented the exercise of military power; that is all.

Constitutional government with its promises of freedom, the rule of law and integrity in governmental activity also died September 11. Chile's constitution was a nobly conceived allocation of the powers of government and rights of a people. It was born of legal process and served its nation well for nearly half a century. It did not guarantee easy times and Chile has not known easy times. It did offer democratic government. It was rendered meaningless by the violence of armed force. Among constitutional provisions directly violated are the following:

Article 4. No magistracy, or person, or assembly of persons, not even under the pretext of extraordinary circumstances, is empowered to assume any other authority or rights than those that have been expressly conferred upon them by the laws. Every act in contravention of this Article is void.

Article 11. No one can be sentenced unless he be legally tried in accordance with a law promulgated prior to the act upon which the trial is based.

Article 15. In case an authority orders the arrest of any person, he must, within the forty-eight hours following, make report thereof to the proper judge and place at his disposal the person detained.

Article 16. Every individual who may be arrested, charged or imprisoned contrary to the provisions of the foregoing articles may apply, for himself, or by anyone in his name, to the judicial authority designated by law, petitioning that the legal requirements be observed.

Article 18. In criminal cases the accused shall not be obliged to testify under oath about his own actions nor can his ascendents, descendents, spouse, or relations within the third degree of consanguinity or second of affinity, inclusive, be obliged so to testify.

Torture shall not be applied . . .

Article 22. The public force is constituted solely and exclusively by the Armed Forces and the *carabinero* guards, which entities are essentially professional, organized by rank, disciplined, obedient and non-deliberating.

Article 23. Every resolution the President of the Republic, the Chamber of Deputies, the Senate or the Courts of Justice may agree to in the presence of or on demand of an army, a commandant at the head of an armed force, or of any assembly of people, with or without arms and in disobedience of the authorities, is null in law and cannot produce any effect.

Article 66. When the President of the Republic in person commands the Armed Forces, or when from illness, absence from the territory of the Republic, or from any other weighty reason, he cannot exercise his office, the Minister whom the order of precedence as fixed by law may designate shall substitute for him, under the title of Vice President of the Republic. In default of such, the Minister who follows in the order of precedence, and in default of all the Ministers, the President of the Senate, the President of the Chamber of Deputies or the President of the Supreme Court successively, shall substitute for the President.

In case of death, or declaration of cause for resignation, or other kind of absolute impossibility, or disability that cannot be ended before the completion of the time remaining of the constitutional period, the Vice President in the first ten days of his incumbency shall issue the proper orders to proceed, within sixty days, to a new election of President in the manner prescribed by the Constitution and by the electoral law.

Article 72 (17). Special attributes of the President are: To declare in a state of assembly one or more provinces invaded or menaced in case of foreign war, and in a state of siege one or several points of the Republic in case of foreign attack.

In case of internal disturbance the declaration of one or more places being in a state of siege belongs to Congress, but if Congress is not in session, the President may make it for a determined period.

Through the declaration of a state of siege, there is conceded to the President of the Republic only the authority to transfer persons from one department to another and to confine them in their own houses, or in places other than jails, or intended for the confinement or imprisonment of ordinary criminals.

Measures taken on account of the state of siege shall have no greater duration than the siege, but the constitutional guarantees granted to deputies and senators shall not be infringed thereby.

Article 80. The power of judging civil and criminal cases belongs exclusively to the tribunals established by law.

The five trials I witnessed conducted by the Air Force under the authority of the military government were lawless charades. Whether there was in fact justification for the State of Siege and Plan Z on which it was predicated or the Junta had seen too many movies is not relevant. Nor are metaphysical references to the differences of the legal system. One need not be a scholar of Chilean law, or have witnessed trials in Spain and other continental countries as I have done, to know the trial was not governed by either pre-established principles and procedures uniformly applied or an effort to determine truth.

First it is not possible to trace power from the constitution to this court. Perhaps this is why posted outside the courtroom which was formerly the chapel of a Catholic convent was a rain-spotted carbon copy of a typed memo saying no attorney shall challenge the jurisdiction of the court or the procedures it uses. A lawyer who dared to question whether his client had been tortured was banned from further practice there among other penalties.

General Orlando Gutiérrez, the Air Force Fiscal, or prosecutor, presented his entire case by reading from the Dictamen, or indictment and witness statements, nearly all by defendants and their co-defendants. All were elicited under circumstances so inherently coercive, whatever the techniques employed, as to make them questionable by any standard. No witness testified. No prosecution witness was present to be challenged by cross examination. No defendant presented a single witness in his defense or spoke a word himself in "open" court. While the trials were called open, no family was permitted to be present and whatever the reasons, the room was virtually empty except for one morning when a first-year law class from the University of Chile attended a single trial. The press, nearly all Chilean, sat in the balcony. A few foreign observers attended part time, and personnel from the Army monitored the trials.

The serious offenses charged, treason and sedition, for which death was demanded for some, could not be applied by any stretch of logic or twist of legal reasoning to the facts alleged, which uniformly referred to activity prior to September 11, 1973, nor support jurisdiction in a military court at a later date. Thus the statute itself could not support the prosecution even if the court had jurisdiction and the application of law was not *ex post facto*.

No system seeking *objective* fact-finding permits the trier of fact to be the persons threatened by the acts alleged; yet here the very court personnel were potential victims of the conduct allegedly planned, though admittedly not executed. The absence of any legal officer to guide the court, instruct it in the law or determine procedures—only one member of the seven man court was a lawyer, the prosecutor was not—made the trial a game of soldiers playing prosecutor, judge and jury, which is to law as children playing soldier is to war, but deadly yet.

The ultimate wrong, however, was the fact that the members of the court had participated in the very violent overthrow of government that they accused some of the persons they tried with planning, but not executing. It can only be assumed that these mock trials, demeaning legal institutions and due process, were brought about as a justification for the *golpe*. Even if the charges were true, a planned overthrow of government by one Junta cannot justify an actual one by another. Subjecting these defendants to this Kafkaesque show trial is itself a denial of human rights.

The denial of human rights in Chile on and since September 11, 1973 is widespread and continuing. Life is the first right of every human. We do not know how many humans have lost their lives to lawless acts of the military. We know one of the first was the constitutional President, Salvador Allende. We know deaths must be measured in the thousands. Tens of thousands have lost their liberty. Thousands remain in detention today. Thousands more have been tortured.

Among the fundamental human rights protected by the Universal Declaration of Human Rights and the International Covenant on Civil and Political Rights ratified by Chile which have been flagrantly violated are:

1. Right not to be subjected to arbitrary arrest or detention (Article 9 U.D.H.R. and Article 9 I.C.C.P.R.).

2. Right not to be subjected to torture or to cruel, inhuman or degrading treatment or punishment (Article 5 U.D.H.R. and Article 7 I.C.C.P.R.).

3. Right to a fair and public trial with all the guarantees necessary for one's defense before an impartial and independent tribunal. Respect for the principle of non-retroactivity (Articles 10 and 11 of the U.D.H.R. and Articles 14 and 15 of the I.C.C.P.R.).

4. Right to life, liberty and the security of person (Article 3 of the U.D.H.R. and Article 6 of the I.C.C.P.R.).

5. Right not to be subjected to arbitrary interference with one's privacy, family, home or correspondence, nor to attacks on one's honor and reputation (Article 12 of the U.D.H.R. and Article 17 of the I.C.C.P.R.).

6. Right to freedom of movement and of residence within the borders of a State. Right to leave any country including one's own and to return to one's country (Article 13 of the U.D.H.R. and Article 12 of the I.C.C.P.R.).

7. Freedom of thought, conscience and religion, freedom of opinion and expression, and freedom of peaceful assembly and association (Articles 18, 19 and 20 of the U.D.H.R. and Articles 18, 19, 21 and 22 of the I.C.C.P.R.).

8. Right to work and to a just and fair remuneration and to protection against unemployment. Right to form and join trade unions (Article 23 of the Universal Declaration and Articles 6, 7 and 8 of the International Covenant on Economic, Social and Cultural Rights).

As we have seen, the military seizure of power in Chile destroyed democracy and constitutional government. No rationalization can alter that. It brought a violent and lawless reign of arbitrary power dealing death to thousands, imprisonment and torture to tens of thousands and terror to hundreds of thousands. It established authoritarian government controlling the people by military force and threat of force, seizing university administration, abolishing labor organizations, suspending political parties and burning books. It continues today a state of siege, holding former high officials of civilian government and thousands of others, many since September, yet not charged with crime. On page 5 of its White Book explaining the seizure of power it says it has governed since September 11 "in an atmosphere of absolute peace and normality."

We can rage at what has been done to rights and humanity in Chile, but rage rarely solves problems and rarer still is the solution wise. Rather we should look at our own conduct. Finally it is our own conduct that is our responsibility. What has the United States of America done in Chile?

Our nation praises democracy and constitutional government, extols the rule of law and proclaims the primacy of human rights. How then do we explain our policy and conduct in Chile? For we witnessed, condoned and may have been an agent in the fall of constitutional democracy, subversion of law and the death and torture of thousands. If we care why do we not speak out and act? You cannot make the world safe for hypocrisy.

I urge your committees to find the truth to the following questions and act upon that truth. An open, democratic society must know what its government and other agencies and instrumentalities of its society do. For their acts are our responsibility.

1. Did the Departments of State, Defense, the CIA or other federal agencies discriminate against, or directly or indirectly act to cause or encourage the overthrow of constitutional government in Chile?

2. Did U.S. economic or military aid to Chile or its withdrawal contribute to the fall of that government? Does the pattern of total aid from 1965 to date suggest a failure to value democratic government over military government?

3. Did corporations owned and operated by U.S. interests or multinational corporations dominated by U.S. interests contribute to the military seizure?

4. Do government records reveal a discriminatory policy by U.S. or U.S.-dominated business which contributed to economic instability in Chile? Do American corporations prefer to do business with the military government in Chile?

5. Why has our government not protested a military seizure of power and urged an immediate return to constitutional government?

6. Were there units of the U.S. Navy off the shores of Chile or other U.S. military presence in the area on September 11, 1973, in unusual numbers? If so, why?

7. What has our government done to protect human rights in Chile? Have we acted to prevent or protested killings, torture, arbitrary incarceration? When? How?

8. How many persons did the U.S. Embassy grant asylum to on or after September 11, 1973? What are the policy reasons for failing to protect persons whose lives were in danger as many other nations did?

9. How many persons from Chile have we offered permanent residence rights here? How does this policy contrast with our policy toward Cuba? What are the reasons for the difference?

10. Have we restricted persons exiled from Chile in visiting, traveling, or speaking freely in the United States? Why?

11. What economic, political and moral sanctions can the United States and its people bring to bear on totalitarianism in Chile?

12. What can the United States do to stimulate the United Nations, international banks, and other organizations to bring economic, moral, and other pressures to restore human rights in Chile?

If we revere life and democracy, we must pursue such questions with a passion and through them forge a foreign policy based not on military power or economic profit, but on the way governments treat their people—on the quality of human rights. Then we can hope for the realization of Benito Juarez's faith that "a respect for the rights of others is peace." ■

A U.S. Lawyer's Observations on the Junta's "Courts"

Martin Garbus, the author of this article, is a member of a Lawyers' Committee on Chile, formed under the auspices of the New York City Bar Association, to investigate reports of repression in Chile at large and the atmosphere surrounding the mass trial of fifty-seven Air Force officers and ten former officials in the government of the late Salvador Allende. The military court-martial which began on April 17, 1974, was the first trial open to the press and legal observers since the September coup and Chile's largest mass trial of the century. Mr. Garbus and other members of the Lawyers' Committee, including New York City Council President Paul O'Dwyer and Orville H. Schell, President of the Association of the Bar of the City of New York, spent ten days observing the proceedings of the military court at the Air Force War College in a suburb of Santiago. The following article appeared in the May 17, 1974, issue of the New York Law Journal *under the title "Justice in Chile: Backlash of the Military Coup."*

With other attorneys from this country, Germany, Switzerland and England, I saw the Chilean government's first open political trials. Observers were invited by the Junta to watch the trials of leading officials of the Allende regime and Air Force officers accused of conspiracy, in order to show that the proceedings were fair to the defendants, six of whom face the death penalty. The trials, now in their fourth week, are being conducted on the outskirts of Santiago in the Air Force Academy, a training school for Air Force officers.

Only those in Chile can know the atmosphere of the trial. Each morning, as our car approached within 250 feet of the academy, we were stopped by four soldiers dressed in fatigues with machine guns over their shoulders, fingers on the triggers. After they checked our credentials, we walked down the road to the academy between lines of soldiers, seeing more soldiers, tense and armed, behind embankments, trees and bushes watching us and everything that might be moving toward the academy.

At the academy entrance, we passed another checkpoint, a dozen more soldiers, and then were led to a small gatehouse where we emptied our pockets, took off our jackets and were given a finger search on each part of our bodies. On the first day of the trial, I saw an eminent extreme right-wing defense lawyer refuse to go through the search because "it was degrading." He was excluded from the courtroom. Leaving the gatehouse, we walked fifty feet down a path, guarded by soldiers, and into the academy auditorium, now a courtroom. Three guards stood along the sides of the auditorium, three more at the entrance, all with their fingers on the triggers.

The Chilean Military Code governs the trials, the government having suspended the Constitution and the lower courts after the September 11 coup. The government presents its case without live witnesses—the prosecutor relies solely on the confessions of the defendants to prove his case. Confessions have been taken from each of the sixty-seven defendants. In cases where the penalties are twenty and thirty years, it takes the government twenty minutes to one hour to present its case. Before the trials were opened, the Military Tribunal (seven judges, one is a lawyer) felt that by sitting four hours a day, the sixty-seven trials could be finished in a week to ten days. However, now it appears it can't be done that quickly and the Tribunal expects the trial to take six weeks—each murder trial according to the new schedule will take two hours.

Physical Appearance

I was surprised at how well the defendants looked in court after hearing of the torture and after seeing their jails, where eight men were crammed into six-by-eight-foot cells. All the defendants originally had great difficulty in obtaining lawyers; they were unrepresented for months. Nearly all of their present lawyers are from the right or center, originally supporters of the Junta, and former opponents of Allende. At lunch one day during the trial, a colonel, high in the administration, told me these lawyers were Marxists, for if they weren't, they would not be representing these defendants.

Some of the lawyers who feel they must raise issues that will displease the regime, are thinking of sending their wives and children out of the country. Many feel they ought to do this before the defense seeks to prove that the confessions were obtained by torture.

On the first day of the trial, one of the lawyers told the press the defendants would raise the question of mal-treatment—he was then advised by one of the officers present that he would be arrested for treason. He hasn't raised the issue again. A few days later a defense lawyer contested in court the legal validity of the trials—he said the Junta could not bootstrap the legitimacy of the Military Tribunal by saying that the civilian courts could be ignored because it declared a state of war, for, he said, the Junta under the Chilean Constitution did not have the right to declare a state of war. The prosecutor got furious when this defense was urged. He asked that the defense lawyer be immediately removed from the case. He was. The lawyer is in the process of being disbarred and does not know what will happen to him next.

Judges' Discretion

Under the Chilean Military Code, the judges have the discretion as to whether to allow defense witnesses. Thus far, the judges have emphasized their discretion in favor of the defendants, allowing character witnesses to testify. When the first defense witnesses were called and walked from the witness room in the back of the auditorium to sit before the Military Tribunal and testify that the defendant was of good character and one whom he had known and spoken to, it was an act of great courage. I held my breath as I watched the defense witnesses testify—a store-keeper who lived near the defendant, a soldier who served in his unit—for I felt their lives were at stake.

What is now happening in Santiago all seems part of a concerted effort to keep the Chileans agitated and to make the defendants and their followers appear to be dangerous. Soldiers, in readiness, are everywhere in the streets, and after the 1 a.m. curfew, the night rings with shots. During the second week of the trial, Reuters, the news service, was threatened with being closed because the Junta did not like its reporting of the trials. Radio Ballaceria, a non-political radio talk show station, was actually closed down for commenting on the trials.

Newsman Disappears

A Swiss newsman who the Junta thought was not reporting fairly disappeared for five days. The Junta claimed they did not know where he was. He was last seen, under military escort, being put on a plane at the Santiago airport. As a result of these incidents the foreign press must consider its desire to stay in Chile and report the events and the trial each time it writes a story.

The allegations of the prosecutors in the trial are each day interspersed with the front page news in the press—in order, it seems, to justify the prosecutor's claims at the trial. The second day of the trial there was announcements of the arrests of thousands of extremists in the workers' quarters in Santiago. The third day of the trial the government announced that 10,000 extremists were massing on the Argentine border to invade Chile. The story disappeared the following day—there was now a new story that those confined in prisons had arms and were planning other revolutionary acts.

Secret Trials

Even while this trial goes on, hundreds of secret trials are going on throughout Chile. A lawyer representing one of the defendants in this trial told me about another case: "I was called Monday at eleven in the morning and told to represent a defendant. I said I couldn't, I knew nothing about the case. They said unless I was there at noon, the trial would start without a lawyer. The defendant, Marcos, was a nineteen-year-old boy charged with a political speech. The prosecutor claimed this was treason and sought the death penalty. I went there, the prosecutor read the defendant's confession.

"Marcos refused to allow me to raise the question of torture, feeling the tribunal would get angry if I did. I said only that the confession was not true. The trial took a half an hour. The judge said he would call me and give me the verdict. By Thursday, I hadn't heard. I called the tribunal, and was told he was shot on Tuesday. The death sentence was handed down in the afternoon of the trial. I found his parents and fiancée and told them. They had not heard from him in months and did not even know that he was arrested, or charged."

Cardinal's Position

The week the trials opened, the Cardinal of Chile, Raúl Cardinal Silva Henríquez, expressed his concern for the Junta's limitations of human rights in Chile by issuing a public statement. The church had been quiet since the coup. That day the Junta in front page headlines, advised there was an extremist plot to kill the Cardinal and said he was to be given a four-man bodyguard. Notwithstanding the "bodyguard," the Cardinal went into retreat with fellow members of the church and, in the second week of the trial, issued a statement mildly critical of the government, saying a climate of fear existed in Chile, which the government claimed showed the church was part of a Marxist conspiracy. [See "Chilean Bishops Speak Out" on p. 124.]

As long as the trials are kept open, the defendants on trial have the benefit of knowing that whatever happens to them will not be done in secret. While this trial goes on, the government acknowledges there are thousands of political prisoners being held incommunicado since the early months of the coup. Many political prisoners have been killed in secret. The conservative news media estimates 5,000 to 10,000 killed since September 1973 (the

CIA's estimate given to Senator Kennedy's committee is 25,000) in a country with approximately the same population as New York City. It means that Chile, not involved in a war, has lost a greater percentage of its population than Israel lost in its recent war with the Arab states.

Henry Kissinger's upcoming trip to Chile moved the trials off the front pages for the first time. The Junta hopes that this trip, along with the "open" trials now in progress, lays the foundation for its claim of legitimacy.■

U.N. Commission on Human Rights

On behalf of the United Nations Commission on Human Rights, the Commission Chairman sent a telegram to the government of Chile on March 1, 1974, calling for "the immediate cessation of human rights violations" and insisting that certain prominent persons and other citizens and foreigners in similar situations "should not be prevented from leaving the country." Twenty-nine of the 36 members of the Commission endorsed the telegram or expressed concern regarding activities of the Chilean government.

The Chilean Junta's reply on March 7 conceded that "the rights to liberty have been restricted," but argued that "no arbitrary action has been or will be taken against any persons. . . . The Government cannot put an end to violations which it has not committed." The letter from the Junta contained no specific explanation for the various charges against it, nor any information about the persons mentioned in the Commission's telegram.

The texts of both the Commission's telegram and the Chilean government's reply were considered on May 9 at the 56th Session of the U.N. Economic and Social Council (ECOSOC). On this occasion, dissatisfied with the terms of the Chilean government's reply, the UK, Sweden, and the Netherlands, as an indication of their concern at reports of continuing violations of human rights in Chile, presented a resolution calling on Chile to "restore and safeguard basic human rights and fundamental freedoms." ECOSOC, which includes Chile and the United States among its members, adopted this resolution unanimously.

Below are the full texts of these three documents.

Telegram Sent to the Government of Chile by the Commission on Human Rights

From the Official Records of the Economic and Social Council, Fifty-sixth Session, Supplement No. 5 (E/5464), *Chap. XIX, sect. B.*

On behalf of the members of the United Nations Commission on Human Rights and as Chairman of the Commission at its thirtieth session, I have been authorized to send the following telegram to your Government:

"The Commission on Human Rights, while considering the obligation of all States under the Charter of the United Nations to promote universal respect and observance of human rights and fundamental freedoms, has considered with deep concern numerous reports from a wide variety of sources relating to gross and massive violations of human rights in Chile in contradiction with the Universal Declaration of Human Rights and other relevant international instruments ratified by a great number of countries, including Chile.

"The Commission on Human Rights, which has consistently deplored all violations of human rights, calls upon your Government for the immediate cessation of any kind of violations of human rights committed contrary to the principles of the United Nations Charter and other international instruments, including the International Covenants on Human Rights.

"The Commission expresses particular concern for the protection of persons whose lives are reported to be in imminent danger. These include such outstanding political, social and cultural figures as former ministers, senators, and heads and professors of universities, among others, Clodomiro Almeyda, Luis Corvolan, Enrique Kirberg, Pedro Felipe Ramires, Anselmo Sule, whose names have been cited as presently in the greatest danger for reasons of health or the conditions of their detention.

"The Commission insists that the above-mentioned persons and other Chilean citizens and foreigners in similar situations should not be prevented from leaving the country if they wish to do so.

"The Commission requests the Chilean authorities to inform its Chairman as a matter of urgency about the measures undertaken in pursuance of this telegram and about the fate and welfare of the above-mentioned and other persons being reported in dangerous conditions."

The Chilean Government's Reply

E/CN.4/1153, 7 March 1974. Letter dated 7 March 1974 from the Permanent Representative of Chile to the United Nations addressed to the Chairman of the Commission on Human Rights in reply to the telegram adopted by the Commission on 1 March 1974 and sent to the Government of Chile by the Chairman of the Commission.

I have received instructions from the Minister for Foreign Affairs of Chile to transmit to you the following communication:
Sir,

Firstly, because of the special regard in which the Government of Chile holds the Commission on Human Rights, those countries participating in it which are genuinely interested in such rights and you personally, I am replying to the telegram which you sent to me on behalf of the Commission.

Secondly, it is unfortunate, because it might lead to confusion, that this telegram should have been sent at a time when the Soviet Union has engineered a campaign to attack the Government of Chile, charging it with alleged violations of human rights. For this purpose the Soviet Union has made use of all its organizations which act as a front and other supporters and has instructed them to send to the United Nations hundreds of telegrams with the aim of artificially creating alleged world-wide concern for the situation in Chile. The Soviet Union cannot accuse anyone of violating human rights, because it has been systematically and grossly violating them itself for more than half a century. Even more, it is morally unqualified to do so in the present case, because its attempt to subjugate Chile through armed intervention led to the breakdown, three years ago, of our democratic institutions and to the suppression of fundamental human rights in my country. The country responsible for all the upheaval and suffering which Chile endured during these three years is the Soviet Union, whose aversion to the present Government of Chile is due precisely to the fact that this Government has succeeded in restoring our democracy and full respect for human rights.

Thirdly, it is unfortunate that this campaign of the Soviet Union should have distorted, in the Commission, the real picture of human rights in the world to the point of impressing it with a description of events which never happened in Chile, of diverting the Commission's attention from the problems with which it should really concern itself and of inducing it to practice unfair discrimination by addressing itself to the Government of Chile concerning a temporary situation which is fully in accord with the Chilean Constitution and the international covenants on human rights, while in the meanwhile overlooking the most persistent, gross and systematic pattern of violation of human rights of our time, namely, that presented by the Soviet Union and the countries subject to it.

Fourthly, the Government of Chile, after frustrating the armed intervention prepared by the Soviet Union in order to subject the majority of the population by force and set up a totalitarian dictatorship, was obliged to adopt some security measures so as to prevent further acts of intervention in that country, intervention which is to be feared because of the Soviet Union's repeated threats and massive campaign of slander. In accordance with provisions set forth in the Chilean Constitution, which are sanctioned by all the international conventions on human rights, the right to individual liberty has been restricted for the duration of this emergency. For reasons of public security these provisions authorize the detention of persons in places other than prisons. It is by virtue of these provisions that the persons mentioned in your cable are under detention. All of them are in good health, receive visitors and are lodged in a naval base where they enjoy the same comforts as officers of the navy. This was proved in a television programme broadcast last week in the United States and other countries. These persons will remain under detention for the duration of the present emergency, although many of them were released when it was established in some cases that this measure was no longer necessary. At the end of the emergency, all those under detention will be released by the Government and may leave the country, if they so desire, except for those who are prosecuted for common crimes punishable under laws antedating the acts with which they are charged and whose detention or liberty can be decided only by the ordinary courts of justice.

Fifthly, I reiterate that the Government of Chile steadfastly abides by the provisions of its Constitution and the conventions pertaining to human rights. We wish the protection of such rights under the conventions to be strengthened as much as possible, for which purpose our Permanent Representative has made some proposals in the Commission: Thus, respect for all human rights will be made more effective, starting with the right of self-determination of peoples, the violation of which brought upon Chile all the misfortunes we have suffered.

Sixthly, as the Government of Chile has strictly com-

plied, and will continue strictly to comply, with the above-mentioned provisions prescribing the respect of human rights, I must state, in reply to the specific points raised in the Commission's telegram, that the Government cannot put an end violations which it has not committed, nor adopt in favour of persons any measures other than those it adopted from the very day on which it assumed its responsibilities. The Commission can therefore rest assured that under the present Government of Chile no arbitrary action has been or will be taken against any persons, that their rights have been and will be respected and that the life of no person in the country is threatened.

Accept, Sir, the assurances of my highest consideration.

(*signed*) Ismael HUERTA DIAZ
Vice-Admiral
Minister for Foreign Affairs of Chile

Accept, Sir, the assurances of my highest consideration.

(*signed*) Raúl BAZAN DAVILA
Ambassador
Permanent Representative of Chile

Resolution Adopted by the Economic and Social Council

E/RES/1873 (LVI), 31 May 1974. Protection of human rights in Chile.

The Economic and Social Council,
Seriously concerned about the reported violations of human rights in Chile, particularly those involving a threat to human life and liberty,

Noting the concern of the Commission on Human Rights at its thirtieth session as expressed in the telegram from its Chairman to the Chilean Government, especially concern for the protection of persons whose lives are in imminent danger,

Noting also the reply dated 7 March 1974 of the Chilean Minister for Foreign Affairs,

Concerned that nevertheless violations of human rights in Chile continue to be reported,

1. *Endorses* the concern of the Commission on Human Rights;

2. *Calls upon* the Government of Chile to take all necessary steps to restore and safeguard basic human rights and fundamental freedoms in Chile, particularly those involving a threat to human life and liberty. ■

The Amnesty Report

Rose Styron is a member of the Board of Directors of Amnesty International (USA) and the author of a book of poems, Thieves' Afternoon. *Her article which appears below is reprinted from* The New York Review of Books, *Vol. XXI, Number 9, May 30, 1974.*

Amnesty International, an apolitical world organization dedicated to protecting nonviolent "prisoners of conscience" and basic rights for people in all countries, receives reports almost daily of kidnapings, closed trials, arranged deaths, summary executions, expulsions, barbaric torture, and government by intimidation throughout Chile.

AI's sources are numerous. They include leaders of the American clergy who have worked in Chile or visited there since the coup as well as members of a women's group, of a trade union, and of several university faculties who have gone to Chile on fact-finding missions; also the United Nations and its High Commissioner for Refugees, who have set up sanctuaries there; commissions of both French and American jurists; and Amnesty's own three-man mission to Santiago. The Junta rejected Amnesty International's January report as "biased and superficial" and "full of imaginary concepts about torture." But AI has compiled confirming evidence for all its charges.

Eyewitness Reports

Reports of torture have come from many eyewitnesses, for example the wife of an Argentine lecturer held in Estadio Chile. (This is the larger of the two sports arenas which have been turned into detention centers in Santiago; at one time it held as many as 5,000 people.) She was stripped twice, and abused, searched by soldiers for "dynamite in her vagina" while she listened to the cries of her husband being beaten nearby. At one point she saw him in a room, naked and hung by his arms and legs, being given shocks with an electric goad. Several witnesses to the death of folksinger Jara have testified to what happened to him in the same stadium: his captors gave him a guitar and commanded him to play while they broke, then cut off, his fingers; when he began to sing, they beat and then shot him. "As an example," one report states, they left his body "strung up in the foyer of the stadium."

Friends of Paulina Altamirano, wife of the leader of Allende's Socialist party—who was "the most wanted man in Chile" until he escaped to Cuba—report that she was forced to listen to faked tapes that led her to believe that she was hearing her children screaming.

The sophistication and systematic use of such methods of repression and revenge is the most depressing aspect of the current regime. A few weeks ago I was shown a crumpled piece of blue paper with minute writing edge to edge, smuggled out of the Santiago stadium. Its author is a very young man. I quote from it here:

In case this anguished message arrives soon in the hands of anyone in my family, I am going to tell what they did with us since Friday the week of January 18, 1974, when civil personnel in the presence of Sr. Guillermo Alvarez K., delegate from CORFO, "invited" four of us to take part in an interrogation which would last "two hours." We tranquilly got into vehicles, cream and blue. . . . They proceeded to put adhesive tape over our eyes and there we understood that it was a kidnaping. . . . In a closed truck, blindfolded and tied we traveled two or three hours. . . . I heard the noise of weapons which chilled me to my soul. I said goodbye to myself with my eyes full of tears for all my loved ones. I thought they were going to shoot us because they put us against wooden beams with our hands up and our legs spread behind. I didn't know what to think. My God, but why do they do this?

. . . Monday, they took us in a small truck, . . . we went down a stairway, . . . hooded, our hands tied behind. They made us undress, tied us again, put us in small cells . . . and the inferno of terror began.

The first one they took to the torture table did not emit screams, they were howls. My body trembled with horror, one could feel the blows and hear the voice of the torturer, "Who painted it? Who

went?" . . . I spent many hours there listening to the tortures. . . .

My turn came. They tied me to a table. . . . They passed cables over my naked body. They wet me and began to apply currents to all parts of my body and the interrogator did not ask me, he assured me, "You did this thing." I denied the monstrosities and the blows began to my abdomen, ribs, chest, testicles, etc. I don't know for how long they massacred me, but with the blows in my chest, my throat and bronchial tubes filled up and it was drowning me. I was dying. They were laughing but assured me they were not kidding and threw acid on my toes. They stuck me with needles. I was numb. They took me down. I could breathe.

They took us back to the camp. There no one slept because of our moans. The prisoners cried with us.

They took us another day and it was worse. They did things that cannot be told, . . . threats of death if we didn't sign what the interrogator wanted. "No one knows about you," he said, and he tortured us. He was making fun of us. We were no longer men. We were shadows. . . .

Eight days later we were transferred from Tejas Verdes, the place of our capture, to the Estadio Chile where we were isolated from the rest for being dangerous. . . . We signed the criminal declaration because we wanted to live and prove our total innocence. . . .

Why do they do this to us? . . . At the company all the workers that day saw the vehicles. Are they guilty by chance?

This is our ordeal. Why, my God, why? We trusted in justice.

—Estadio Chile, *February 14, 1974*

Prisoners and Camps

The real purpose of the torture seems to be not so much to extract confessions as to induce conformity by terror, dehumanization, and the destruction of the will by prolonged pain. Much has been learned from the regime in Brazil, and, more specifically, from the Brazilian officers who were invited to Chile to give courses in interrogation to the armed forces and police. Amnesty has received reports of torture from the following prisons and detention camps:

—Quiriquina Island, where 500 prisoners on meager rations have been building their own jail.

—Chacabuco, the mine in the northern desert of Antofagasta (temperatures 110 by day, 32 by night), where approximately 1,600 middle-level officials and professional men and the relatives of ministers are being held. Among them is the musician Angel Parra, son of the singer Violetta and nephew of the poet Nicanor Parra. (In spite of conditions of hunger and maltreatment a remarkable mass by Angel Parra was said to have been performed there at Christmas.)

—Three "detention ships," including the *Lebu*, docked off Valparaiso, where, according to Amnesty's sources, men are dropped into the dark hold and all but abandoned.

—The women's prison, called Casa de Mujeres el Buen Pastor, in Santiago. Here electricity applied to the gums produces hysteria; applied to the uterus of a pregnant woman, it produces brain lesions and abortions. Young girls are sent here pregnant from other torture camps, with their hair pulled out and their nipples and genitals badly burned.

—Tejas Verde, 250 kilometers south of Santiago, where paramilitary organizations have taken their victims.

—The concentration camp at Cerro Chena, where teenagers are subjected to sexual assaults, shock treatment, the burning of extremities.

—The Antarctic Dawson Island camp, not far from Tierra del Fuego.

In September, thirty-six members of Allende's government were taken to Dawson Island from Santiago after being interrogated. Nineteen had turned themselves in to the police as a radio announcement requested them to do, rather than take refuge in the embassies that offered it. They included José Tohá, Minister of Defense, a man six feet four inches tall, who, when last seen alive, was down to 112 pounds, and could hardly see, hear, or walk. The Junta has listed him a suicide, but there are convincing reports that he died by strangling. Daniel Vergara, one of two deputies who was shot in the back after he tried to negotiate with soldiers in La Moneda during the coup, was suffering from gangrene from his untreated wounds; it is feared that his arm may have to be amputated. His only son has been held for months in Chacabuco, for no other reason than being his father's son.

Before the Dawson Island camp was closed down in late April, the prisoners there suffered from extreme cold, hunger, lack of medical attention, and denial of privileges to read or write. They were forced to do manual labor too severe for them. Now they await trials being planned for prominent political prisoners—expected sometime in in May—and are being held incommunicado in secret locations near Santiago.

The "Public" Trials

Trials of the Junta's remaining enemies in the military services have already begun. Just before the coup more than a hundred officers and soldiers whose loyalty to the Junta was in doubt were murdered. Others were shot during the takeover. The regime not only cannot afford to have experienced military opponents at large but seems determined to make examples of them. On April 17, 57 Air Force officers and 10 civilians were put on trial for treason and conspiring against the regime—the group is described as *"Bachelet y Otros,"* ofter General Bachelet, who mysteriously died before the trial began.

The Air Force under the Junta, it is generally agreed, is the most brutal of the four branches of the military (the *carabineros* are the mildest), all of which have the power to arrest and interrogate. Some civilians have been arrested and then released by three of the military services and gloomily await arrest by the fourth. Such people may be given "conditional release" if they sign a statement that they were well treated and agree to return once a week to "cooperate." Arrested members of the military service, however, are not released at all.

The trials of allegedly disloyal Army and Navy officers and the Dawson prisoners will follow. Aside from the death sentence, the penalties being asked range from 18 months to life, 15 to 30 years being common for younger men. One military student is facing the death penalty because he protested flagellation. A 32-year-old officer named Patricio Carbacho, described as a model soldier, has been accused of conspiring with dissenters months before the coup, although he carried out all orders unhesitatingly when it took place. Unaccountably, he also faces a death penalty. At least two generals who supported the coup have recently resigned. One is General Baeze, whose own nephew died by torture while he tried helplessly to intervene.

The "Private" Trials

The military trials, though not discussed in Chilean newspapers, are "public." But secret trials and executions go on all the time throughout the country. In the province of Osorno for example, dozens of farmers and workers disappeared last autumn and were located only when their sentences were announced or their bodies found. On March 29, Senator Kennedy's office learned that two Osorno women had been condemned to death and 39 others given sentences of six to 20 years. At least 30 corpses of people who had been missing, some without arms, legs, or feet, were washed up on river banks in Osorno during the winter after relatives had given them up for lost.

In the "private" trials, the state-appointed lawyers usually have been given less than the legal 48 hours notice of trial, and frequently less than 12 hours, with no advance information about the charges, and only a few moments in which to see their clients. The prosecutors and judges are rarely lawyers and are frequently men with little education. A young school teacher was condemned to 30 years for allegedly instructing (*"conscientización"*) his elementary school pupils in Marxist doctrine.

Four young students from the University of Chile at Arica were arrested for nothing more than participating in political discussions at the university. One of them, 23-year-old Enzo Villanueva, received an arbitrary 19½-year sentence (although the prosecutor asked for five) after seeing his lawyer for five minutes. Another, Jorge Jaque, received 13 years. Suffering from a disease of the joints, he was both severely tortured and denied medicine by his captors. One hand and his toes were amputated. The other two men, Miguel Berton and Sergio Vasquez, received 25 and 18 years, respectively. They are all in La Serena jail with little hope of appeal.

Amnesty has extensive reports not only of persecutions in the colleges and among educators but of the torture and terrorizing of children in order to intimidate their families. Amnesty was informed in March that a nine-year-old girl and a four-year-old boy were tortured to death in front of their parents. There have been dozens of documented cases of kidnapings—particularly in the poorer districts—and of threats of kidnaping made to families whose children were at school. Kidnaped children have often been returned to their families after being maltreated by the police.

One of the regime's most feared instruments of terror is the paramilitary intelligence group called the DINA, which General Pinochet set up in December as a plain-clothes terror apparatus directly under his control. It is apparently modeled on the death squad in Brazil, where some of its leaders are known to have been trained. It specializes in brutal raids on factories and the houses of the politically suspect, sometimes kidnaping the inhabitants; it tends to be used in cases where the police and military forces want to avoid legal inquiries about missing persons.

Persecution of Doctors

Members of the medical profession have been selected for particularly vicious treatment. Since September 11 at least 65 doctors have either been shot or have died as a result of torture and untreated wounds. Seventeen psychiatrists were murdered in various parts of Chile the first day of the coup and psychiatrists in general have been persecuted, jailed, or kept under house arrest. Many doctors, nurses, and medical assistants have been arrested as potential threats to the Junta, apparently because they were much respected in working-class communities and therefore seen as dangerous. Those who did not take part in a strike against the Allende regime by doctors and other professionals last summer became highly visible. A large number of them have since been under attack and, if not imprisoned, refused the right to practice. Several sources have estimated that over a thousand have been dismissed from hospitals.

Silvia Morris, the head nurse at the children's hospital in Valparaíso, was condemned and tortured, for no greater offense than suggesting that her patients needed more nourishment and medical attention. Doctor Ernesto Luna Hoffer, a well-known neurosurgeon from Valdivia, was given a year in jail for raising the Chilean flag at half-mast as a sign of mourning for his fellow doctor, President Allende. Dr. Danilo Bartolin, a heart surgeon whose friends in Santiago despair now of his surviving, was taken to the Estadio Nacional in Chile in September, whipped and tortured, and taken to the mine at Chacabuco. Dr. Elana Galvez, after being removed from the Hospital Sotero del Rio, was abused in the stadium for refusing to take reprisals against hospital functionaries; she has just been released from jail.

On March 26, Amnesty International received a distressing new appeal from a group of Chilean doctors. Painstakingly documented, it lists 18 doctors now in prison. None has specific crimes charged against him. Nine have been condemned to death. Six well-known doctors were arrested January 13 (an ad in *The New York Times* and pressure from U.S. colleagues helped to bring about the release of one of them, Dr. Gustavo Molina). It is now feared that death sentences will be handed down in secret trials to Alejandro Romero, Patricio Cid, and Bautista von Schowen. Earlier in March Amnesty heard that von Schowen, 30 years old, picked up December 13 after police had kept watch on his parents' home for two months, had been so beaten and mangled that he was taken to a military hospital.

The Church

Catholic priests and other clergy have been doing more than anyone else to help the victims of terror in Chile and they have emerged as the only group that has been openly challenging the regime. At increasing risk to their immunity, they have been pursuing every legal means available to secure information on people who are missing and to arrange the release of prisoners or publication of charges against them. They give moral and financial help to the thousands of Chilean children who have recently become orphans, to families in which the wage earners are dead or jailed, and to those who want to emigrate. Much of their time is spent trying to find lawyers to defend the poor, weak, and ignorant. (In fact, because so many lawyers have been persecuted or disbarred, they are also helping to find counsel for the well-to-do.)

The Lutheran bishop Helmut Frenz has recently organized the "Committee for Cooperation and Peace" along with Fernando Ariztía, the Auxiliary Bishop of Santiago, and Fernando Salas, a young Jesuit priest. Prominent Jewish and Protestant clergymen support this committee, which is trying to help political prisoners and their families, as well as the unemployed. In the last few weeks Bishop Frenz's committee has sent 131 writs of habeas corpus to the Minister of the Interior, with no response.

Since the coup, Cardinal Raúl Silva, the highest-ranking Roman Catholic in Chile, has been walking a tightrope. A year ago he tried to hold off civil war by inviting the leaders of opposing political parties to meet with him privately in the hope that Marxism and Christianity could coexist in Chile. After the coup, he continued to try to keep his office neutral, and was criticized by Catholic and Protestant leaders abroad for defending to the Vatican a policy of accommodation with the Junta.

Since March, however, he has become openly critical of the regime. Over official objections he held a public mass for José Tohá—a symbolic refusal to accept the Junta's claim that Tohá was a suicide. In his Easter sermon delivered under guard because the Junta claimed that his life was being threatened by left-wing extremists, Silva accused the generals of ignoring the wishes of the church and continuing to violate "sacred human rights" ("We have said it in every voice and we have not been heard!"). On April 24, the Catholic bishops of Chile issued a strong statement accusing the Junta of arbitrary detention and the use of torture and of creating unemployment and economic havoc for the poor. Chileans, they declared, were "living in a climate of insecurity and fear." [See p. 124.]

Clergy Detained

The Junta has tended to be more careful in the pressures it applies to the clergy than it has been with other groups. As General Leigh put it, the regime has "great respect for the church, but like many men, without realizing it, they are vehicles for Marxism." Immediately after the coup, however, American and other foreign priests were herded into Estadio Chile. A Spanish priest, Juan Alsina, was assassinated in the hospital where he worked. Most foreign clergymen left the country.

At Christmas, Ulysses Torres, a Methodist minister from the southern city of Chillán, was jailed with several young people who, according to military intelligence, had used his machine to mimeograph anti-Junta remarks. He has not been released. Father Raul Hasbrun, a priest sympathetic to the right, ran the Catholic University's television station until April. He was fired when he refused to accept the directives of Admiral Swett, the new rector appointed by the Junta. Bishop Frenz was arrested and taken to the police to "talk about Marxism," and then sent home. On April 19 a Methodist minister, Samuel Araya (who had been fired from his post as head of Santiago's theological institute in February), was arrested while teaching an evening class at the seminary and taken to Estadio Chile. Father Joel Gajardo was taken to the stadium the same day and is still being held. Araya was released only after appeals were made by church leaders in Europe and the U.S. as well as by former Ambassador Nathaniel Davis, who had been Pastor Araya's parishioner.

A Prescription for Protest

William Wipfler of the National Council of Churches, who helped with the appeals on behalf of Samuel Araya and many others, has warned that "only the most intense and united pressures from outside Chile will be able to save the clergy and the laymen still in prison there." Indeed it should be clear that pressures from abroad, and particularly from the United States, are the principal hope (if a slim one) for the victims of terror in Chile. The Nixon Administration, having done much to undermine the Allende regime, now has been supporting the Junta with economic and military aid and remains silent about its atrocities and its absolute suppression of rights. It has refused asylum to Chilean refugees (by contrast with Canada, France, West Germany, Sweden, and other countries which have admitted thousands).

What is urgently needed is that American congressmen, lawyers, and other professionals visit Chile as observers of trials, prisons, hospitals;* that protests be made to General Pinochet in Santiago and to the Chilean Embassy in Washington; that Congress, the White House, and the State Department be brought under pressure to cut off all aid to Chile until constitutional rights are restored, and to allow the refugees from Chile to enter the United States.

Those who want to learn about such efforts (or contribute to them) can write to Amnesty International at 200 West 72 Street, New York, New York 10023, or to the National Council of Churches at 475 Riverside Drive, New York, New York 10027. ■

---

*Senators Kennedy and Abourezk and Congressman Donald Fraser of Minnesota have been the most active U.S. legislators on behalf of the victims of persecution in Chile. Recently the "Fair Trial Committee for Chilean Political Prisoners" has been organized and has been sending observers to the trials in Santiago and trying to assist Chilean lawyers.

CRITICS AND DEFENDERS

No other part of this book created so many problems for the editors as this section dealing with the Junta's critics and defenders. Of critics there was a superabundance. Usually the only issue was whether a particular statement belonged here or elsewhere in the book. The defenders were something else. In some cases, obvious invective took the place of argument. In others, as with the Junta's ambassador in Washington, General Walter Heitmann, the charges and denials were so blatantly in contradiction with known facts that to print them seemed merely to be setting up a straw man in order to knock him over. (We decided to include one sample of Heitmann.)

As we went to press, however, *The New York Times* obliged with a specimen that seemed for many reasons to merit reproduction at some length. The Sunday *Times* handed over almost a full page in "The Week in Review" (June 16, 1974) to Paul N. Rosenstein-Rodan, identified as a former adviser to Eduardo Frei, Allende's predecessor as president of Chile. This represented a double departure from standard procedure. Normally, in this section each page deals with half a dozen topics, with little more than a column for each. In addition, copy is almost always original, whereas this long piece was "in part" a summary of lectures and previously published material. The *Times* neglected to include among the sources the plea made by Mr. Rosenstein-Rodan before the Inter-American Council for the Alliance for Progress for stepped-up loan support for the Chilean Junta.

We reproduce a letter to the *Times* which reflects on some of the Rosenstein-Rodan allegations and claims, the *Times'* refusal to print it, and a further comment (still unacknowledged) to the *Times*. What remains a mystery is the editorial motivation of the *Times* in reproducing and giving such extraordinary prominence to this particular piece of partisanship. Perhaps part of the mystery is cleared up by John Pollock's article, the result of a long-term study of the values and assumptions of the U.S. press as exemplified by its coverage of the Allende regime and its aftermath. It shows that it is naive to imagine that the business-dominated and profit-motivated press is or can be objective. The single swallow of Watergate definitely does not make a summer.

Another last-moment inclusion is an article from *Maryknoll*, together with the flak it drew. The article defending the Junta has been around for some time. It took considerable journalistic jaw-boning, however, to obtain for the record various responses hitherto shrouded in diplomatic silence.

Allende "Incompetent"?

The article by Paul N. Rosenstein-Rodan which appears below was printed in The New York Times, *Sunday, June 16, 1974, under the title "Allende's Big Failing: Incompetence." In its introduction to the article, the* Times *identified Mr. Rosenstein-Rodan as an "adviser on development to the governments of Italy and India, as well as to that of Eduardo Frei in Chile. He is Director of the Center for Latin American Development Studies at Boston University. The article is in part a summary of two lectures he gave at the Center, and published in* Challenge, *a magazine of economic affairs."*

The death of Salvador Allende was a three-fold tragedy. It was a tragedy because it has been taken as a breakdown of socialism, and socialism is a great, perhaps the greatest, ideal of this century. It was a tragedy because it has been taken as proof that socialism and democracy are incompatible, that only a dictatorship can impose socialism, but the Chilean experience offers no proof of that. And it was the personal tragedy of a man whose hopes and dreams had been shattered, ending in suicide or murder.

Salvador Allende died not because he was a socialist, but because he was an incompetent. After he took office, he accomplished a major redistribution of income that dramatically increased demand, but he did nothing to increase production to satisfy that demand. Instead, he printed money. A breakdown was inevitable, and the resulting inflation not only destroyed the income distribution that had taken place, but lowered real wages below the level of 1970.

It is not inherent in socialism to be inefficient. Russia is also a socialist society, but it does not increase its money supply by 10 percent every month. Any undergraduate economics student would have known better. The question is why the economists in the Allende government allowed such obvious mistakes. The answer is that the program of the Allende government was not well worked out. The party was not prepared or perhaps did not expect to win and to govern in 1970. . . .

In the first year following Mr. Allende's election there was great division. Twenty percent of the people were in a state of revolutionary euphoria; 10 to 20 percent experienced a spasm of violent (un-Chilean) hatred; and the remaining 60 percent seems paralyzed by shock. The middle and upper classes lived in a *fin de siècle* mood: tomorrow we die. Instead of saving, everybody spent. One had to phone to find a seat in a luxury restaurant. Santiago almost became a swinging town whose ambience was reminiscent of the unreal atmosphere that pervaded Vienna in the midst of the despair and doom of the 1920s. During the first few weeks there was a run on the banks, a flight of capital, and an emigration of many technicians.

The panic subsided gradually and the Allende economic program began. It consisted of a short-run policy, which was vaguely Keynesian, and a long-run policy of transition to socialism, which was vaguely Marxian. The short-run program had three objectives: a substantial redistribution of income, full employment, and stabilization of prices. There was a recession in Chile in 1969-70, with some unemployment and considerable unused capacity. The Keynesian policy assumed that by raising wages substantially (they were raised on the average of 50 percent), the increased demand would lead to the absorption of excess capacity and the recovery would therefore be, in a way, self-financed. According to the plan, the main actors of the Allendista demonology—the imperialists and the landowners—were to be properly squeezed and eviscerated. Money, considered only a bourgeois veil, was increased at an unprecedented pace of 10 percent per month and price controls were imposed. . . .

The squeeze and reduction of profit in private enterprise led to decapitalization in the private sector and a fall in private investment. The redistribution of income to the lower income classes was not accompanied by any measure designed to increase the savings of the workers, which would have provided funds for investment. Last but not least, the price policy of public enterprises and of enterprises nationalized under the Allende government kept prices low, vastly reducing investment funds in the public sector. Output and employment increased, but investment fell by 20 percent in 1971.

Fidel Castro correctly pointed out that "Marxism is a revolution of production; Allende's was a revolution of consumption." During his first year, Mr. Allende won the battle of consumption but lost the war by not fighting the battle of production.

Production was also hindered by the nationalizations. Under Mr. Allende, the nationalization of Chilean enterprises proceeded partly by buying up all the banks (paying for them and for subsequent expropriations with freshly issued money), partly by nationalizing big industrial enterprises, and partly by invoking a 1932 law which allowed the government to take over an enterprise whenever a strike or a breakdown would be against the public interest.

Taking over the banks is not the main point. Whether or not it is a nationalized banking system does not matter half as much as what that banking system is made to do. The nationalization of the banks enabled Mr. Allende to prescribe credit irrespective of credit worthiness—or any other consideration. A policy that directed the banks to operate efficiently would have had a completely different outcome.

The Flight of the Experts

The question of compensation is complex. For example, copper is Chile's main source of foreign exchange. Had the Allende government promised adequate compensation for nationalization of the copper mines, Chile would have been able to run the mines more efficiently and to open new mines. It was a matter of just a few people: the emigration of two dozen experts meant that the plans to expand production were never implemented. These experts, most of whom were Chilean, are now employed in Australia and elsewhere by the same companies they worked for in Chile. The international experts later brought into Chile from Russia and Japan were unfamiliar with Andean conditions, and their advice was useless.

Adequate compensation to the multinationals could have been something like an annual payment over 40 years at a 3 percent rate of interest. Or the payment could have been in newly issued bonds. In either case, this sort of settlement amounts to a confiscation of 30 to 50 percent, an amount which is internationally acceptable.

Expropriation of the copper mines reduced Chile's major source of foreign exchange but, even more important, expropriation resulted in less production.

The case of agriculture is also instructive. Chilean agriculture was characterized by the conventional inequality: a small percentage of large units controlled a high percentage of cultivation. . . .

Under Mr. Allende's program, holdings above 250 acres were to be expropriated. For those farms already intensively cultivated, the effect on production was negative. Even this type of reform, if properly managed, could have been positive on balance. But seizures were completely haphazard, and many were illegal, and the effect of the uncertainty on production was enormous.

In the mining sector, nationalization was a popular and emotional issue. But viewed functionally, the Allende program was a disaster not only because Chile could not open new mines but because production broke down in the old mines. President Allende's government failed to induce labor discipline. The very same workers who loyally demonstrated with slogans of *"El gobierno es la mierda, pero es el nuestro"* (the government is terrible, but it's ours) said: "Now we have our government, let's celebrate." On Mondays absenteeism ran 20 percent. Thus the nationalizations failed in part because of the labor movement. . . .

If after the first or even the second year, Mr. Allende had said: "We have established the basis of social justice and we are building a new socialist society; the coming year must be a year of consolidation," he could have saved the situation. Lenin was not bourgeois, yet he proclaimed the New Economic Policy (N.E.P.) in Russia. Something similar was needed in Chile, but it didn't happen. The economy slowed to a standstill and then lost ground. Queues formed. Workers took off to stand in the queue; half of what they got, they sold in the black market—and their profit was more than a day's wages. There was a complete breakdown of labor discipline. Inflation reached one percent a day.

Beginning of the End

The collapse came with the truckers' strike. Those drivers employed by large firms had benefited from Mr. Allende's initial reforms, but many of the truckers were small, self-employed entrepreneurs. The strike began as a normal collective bargaining dispute, but rapidly acquired a political tone. The lower middle class was entering into a revolutionary euphoria of its own. The truckers wanted guarantees that the expropriations would not be applied to them. Eventually, their goal became President Allende's resignation.

It was not just the lack of adequate planning or the inefficiencies of democratic Marxism that caused Mr. Allende's downfall. It was also his personal leadership. Being a revolutionary is like being in love. The characteristic of people in love is that they do not believe that anybody else in their lifetime has also been in love. So they do not learn from other people's mistakes and repeat all the same errors. This was eminently true of Mr. Allende and may now be true of the Junta generals.

By August 1973, Mr. Allende's power was gone. My estimate is that had a plebiscite been held then, at least 60 percent would have voted for a new government. The people almost wished for a military coup.

Despite the excesses of the Chilean generals—and there is reason to fear these days for the state of human rights in Chile—I still suspect that their concept of the ideal leader is not Mussolini or Franco but de Gaulle. They have all read the memoirs of de Gaulle, they know what he did for France in the 1950s, and they admire him. Fundamentally, however, the Chilean generals (unlike the Peruvian or Brazilian ones) never planned to govern the country permanently. They are critical of the shortcomings of their society (both under Mr. Allende and before) but have no clear, positive ideas of what to do about it. ■

More "Incompetence"

The first of the three letters printed below was sent to The New York Times *for publication following the appearance of the Rosenstein-Rodan article. The response from Mr. Marlens explaining why the* Times *could not publish the letter was challenged by Mr. MacEoin in a further letter which, to date, has received no reply.*

To the Editor:

The alleged and belatedly discovered "incompetence" of President Allende explains for Paul N. Rosenstein-Rodan (*NYT*, June 16) the tragedy of Chile. If a president is incompetent, does that justify scrapping the constitution, killing thousands merely suspected of dissent, wholesale torture, indefinite imprisonment without charge or trial, and economic strangulation of the poor for the benefit of the rich? Should we do the same in this country when we have an incompetent president?

Allende, says Mr. Rosenstein-Rodan, lost the battle of production. That he did, because the majority in the Chilean Congress constituted itself a disloyal opposition and joined the U.S. Administration and the multinationals in cutting off the means required to win that battle.

A plebiscite in August 1973, says Mr. Rosenstein-Rodan, would have produced a 60 percent vote against Allende. The plotting generals did not think so. In local government elections in 1971 and congressional elections in March 1973, Allende had reversed the long-term trend to loss of support for an incumbent president. In fact, he told the generals on September 7, 1973, that he would announce a referendum in a message to the nation the following Tuesday. That was September 11, on the morning of which they led the troops into the streets "to kill" (in General Pinochet's vivid words)—and the President died.

Mr. Rosenstein-Rodan says the question of compensation for copper is complex. Not really. Competent or incompetent, Allende had no control over it. All Chilean parties had joined in approving the constitutional amendment which regulated the issue, and the law was administered by the Comptroller General, an official appointed by Frei and removable only by impeachment. Dedicated to absolute legality, President Allende invoked the 1916 treaty with the United States committing both parties to resolve by arbitration problems unsolved by normal diplomacy. The United States delayed an answer given by the generals September 11 last.

One is tempted to wonder if "incompetence" has not become a code word, a technique to distract from the facts in a process of justifying the elimination of constitutional rulers not subservient to U.S. interests by military dictators. Joao Goulart of Brazil was "incompetent." So was Juan Bosch of the Dominican Republic. So was Greece's Papandreou. Is there not here a double standard, horror at the slightest excesses of those struggling for social justice, tolerance of the monstrously greater excesses of those who fight for order without justice?

(signed)
Gary MacEoin, *Author*

Ralph Della Cava, *Associate Professor of Latin American History, Queens College, CUNY*

William Wipfler, *Latin American Director, National Council of Churches*

Joseph Michenfelder, *Trustee, IDOC/North America*

Wayne Cowan, *Editor, Christianity and Crisis*

New York, June 20, 1974

Dear Mr. MacEoin:

I appreciate your comments very much. Since *The Week in Review* does not have a letters section (the one that appears in the *Review* is simply the normal letters section of the daily *Times*, transplanted) I cannot consider your letter for publication, but I have forwarded it to Mr. Rosenstein-Rodan, and I hope he will communicate with you directly.

Our reason for running his piece was simply that in our judgment it was an informed analysis of an important subject by a writer not unsympathetic to the broad goals of the Allende regime. This section has, in the past, carried a great deal of editorial matter on Dr. Allende's downfall and on the behavior of the Junta that replaced him.

Sincerely,
(signed) Al Marlens
Editor, The Week in Review
June 29, 1974

Dear Mr. Marlens:

Re: *Your June 29 letter.*

Under what concept of journalistic ethics can an editor plead that the format of his publication prevents him from making amends for an injustice he has committed?

In fact, even that claim is not available to you. In open conflict with your assertion, *The New York Times* letters section to which you refer carried a letter on June 30 identified as a reply to "an article in your June 16 Week in Review section."

The quantity of *The New York Times* coverage of Chile is not at issue. What is at issue is its bias, a bias profusely documented by John C. Pollock, Director of the Latin American Institute, Rutgers University, and Assistant Professor of Sociology and Political Science at Livingston College (see *Worldview,* March and June 1974) [The March article is reprinted below.], and now further confirmed by the refusal to print a reasoned reply by a group whose knowledge and authority on the issue is a matter of public record.

I am bringing this correspondence to the attention of the Committee on the U.S. Press and Latin America of the Latin American Studies Association.

(signed)
Gary MacEoin
New York, July 5, 1974

Apologists for Terror

The U.S. press gave a badly distorted picture of Chile to its readers, according to John Pollock and Torry Dickinson. Writing in Worldview, *March 1974, they say that American coverage of the overthrow of the Allende regime and of the following "reign of terror with the professed purpose of purging the country of an entire political sector" reveals many of the same assumptions and values expressed by the Chilean Junta itself in its* White Book. *Pollock, who is Director of the Latin American Institute, Rutgers University, and Assistant Professor of Sociology and Political Science at Livingston College, Rutgers, heads the Committee on the U.S. Press and Latin America of the Latin American Studies Association. Dickinson is a student at Livingston. We reproduce below the part of their article that deals with the U.S. press.*

Although of little value in Chile, the message of the generals is nevertheless a warning for the United States. The significant lesson of the *White Book* lies not in the quality of its arguments but in the parallels between that argument and the reporting by several major U.S. newspapers in the weeks immediately following the coup. The overriding assumption of both appears to be that, if a government, however democratic, tries to widen significantly the distribution of economic resources and encounters financial difficulties, bloodshed and repression are regrettable but understandable in returning the country to "business-like" normality.

The point is not that U.S. reporting on Chile was necessarily "unbalanced" in terms of a pro-or-con measurement of paragraphs or column inches. The point is that several value frameworks shared with the generals are evident in postcoup reporting and comment by correspondents, wire services and editors in the six major U.S. papers concerned with Latin American affairs: *Los Angeles Times, Miami Herald, Washington Post, Christian Science Monitor, Wall Street Journal and The New York Times.*[1] In the first weeks after the coup these papers manifested three major perspectives supporting the new dictators, perspectives unchallenged by alternative or contrary viewpoints: (1) economic and social dislocation justified the coup; (2) threats to political stability were exclusively leftist in origin and justified repression; and (3) the military was (and is) essentially trustworthy, and the appropriate supreme authority, because it is "nonpolitical," intervened reluctantly and restored "normality."

The *White Book* asserts economic deterioration as an excuse for intervention. "The Chileans—their blood and their minimum necessities—were sacrificed by Mr. Allende and by the Popular Unity government . . . not for the profit of any business enterprise, but for the physical, economic, political, social, and gigantic moral destruction [of the country]." "[T]he country was thrown into the worst economic crisis of its national life, without parallel in the modern history of the world." Perhaps inadvertently, however, the Junta admits that the *gremios,* or occupational associates of the relatively powerful, were determined to sabotage the economy to bring down the government. "[The military decided to act] . . . stimulated by the state of [economic] *paralysis caused by new multiple strikes of gremios*—and by the repeated demands for President Allende to resign" (emphasis added). The Junta viewed its role as that of a sanitation engineer, cleansing society of a malignancy: "[T]he economic situation continued deteriorating in a catastrophic manner . . . [so] the military requested a *cleanup* in this area."

The U.S. press made similar assumptions about the sanitizing mission of the military in removing economic chaos, ignoring the alternatives of impeachment, referendum or new elections. Although the "middle" class constitutes no more than about 30 percent of Chile's population, the news media insisted on calling it a "majority," viewing its alienation as a legitimate pretext for a coup.[2]

---

[1]Photocopies of news clippings on Chile and other Latin American countries from these papers are available from the monthly *Information Service on Latin America,* P.O. Box 4267, Berkeley, Calif. 94704.

[2]Estimates of the size of the middle classes in Chile are based on interviews on October 4 and October 6, 1973, with, respectively, James Petras, author of *Politics and Social Forces in Chilean Development* (1969), and Dale Johnson, editor of *The Chilean Road to Socialism* (1973).

The *Monitor* claimed that "[T]he majority of Chileans were probably not sorry to see the end of the Allende regime [which] had only minority support . . . from the start" (September 14). The *Monitor* also apologized for the Chilean military on the grounds that officers had witnessed the "dramatic decline of the middle class as a result of an effort by the minority Allende government to impose irrevocable change on the majority" (September 18). William F. Buckley, Jr., appearing in *The Los Angeles Times,* invoked the image of "hundreds of thousands of people demanding an end to a regime that had brought repression, poverty, inflation, chaos, and fratricidal strife" (September 19). *The New York Times* viewed the coup as an act of majority will, picturing the middle class as a "mass force" involved in "mass action" which "virtually demanded military action against the constitutionally elected government of President Allende" (September 12; see also September 13 and 30). The *Times* also hypothesized that "[I]t was the progressive monopolization of economic power by the agents of a minority coalition, coupled with the gross mismanagement of that power, which so polarized the Chilean polity that democratic institutions could not be maintained" (October 21). *The Wall Street Journal* descended to the level of yellow journalism, saying Allende surrounded himself with "hard-eyed leftists intent on absolute power" (September 12). It even implied that Allende's death, declared a suicide by the military, was somehow posturing and insincere, done "with his eyes always on how history would record the events" (Everett Martin, September 25).

The second perspective shared by the Junta and the U.S. press is that a threat from the left made military intervention inevitable. According to the *White Book* the left welcomed the destruction of its own government. "It was [not the military institutions but] the Popular Unity government . . . [which] forced the ultimate decision [to intervene]. . . . All the previous events signaled that, from the middle of 1973, the government *had known* that its absurd political economy had placed the country in a swamp without a democratic exit. . . . They [Allende and his supporters] *preferred* a desperate attempt to take over the country by force . . ." (emphasis added). This view is not new to readers of the U.S. press. Throughout Allende's incumbency our major papers emphasized threats to democracy and stability from the left, failing to mention similar threats from the right (threats reported widely in the foreign press).

Reporting after the coup, like that which appeared during Allende's tenure, also portrayed the threatening left as bristling with "extremists." *The Miami Herald* reported "[I]t was an open secret that arms were being distributed to workers in an industrial ring around Santiago by extremists. . . ." (September 16). The *Herald* also expressed concern for the health of the military, urging that the "rise of extremists and armed para-military groups implicitly threatens the very existence of the armed forces" (September 23). *The Los Angeles Times* suggested that "They [officers] were alarmed by the formation of revolutionary factory militia cadres by some of the more militant groups for socialism" (September 19). *The Christian Science Monitor* was among papers which uncritically quoted the Junta in its contention that an "extremist apparatus was on the verge of launching a reign of terror in Chile aimed at eliminating the nation's military leaders, opposition politicians, newspapermen, and others, to give the Marxist-leaning Allende govern-

ment total control of the nation" (September 25). *The Wall Street Journal,* strongly supporting the Junta's claims, reassured its readers that the Junta would survive. "Armed attacks by extremists reinforced by more than 10,000 foreign revolutionaries from Cuba and other Latin countries are expected to continue for some time. But they aren't a serious threat to the Junta" (Everett Martin, September 25). The same reporter: "Chile's armed forces appear to have won the battle. . . . Now the military rulers face the much tougher task of trying to win the war—that is, rebuilding this nation's shattered economy and fulfilling their promise to lead Chile toward sustained economic growth" (October 4).

The New York Times is thought to represent not simply one paper's opinion but the "U.S. position" abroad, and thus exercises special influence. Early reporting by the *Times* after the coup minimized the importance of right-wing activity. Papers in Europe and Mexico's equivalent of the *Times, Excelsior,* regularly described the new regime as "right wing" or a "dictatorship." The *Times* spoke simply of the military "junta" or "government" and on several occasions said explicitly that the regime is "non-political." Not only was the *Times* loathe to speculate about the political orientation of the Junta, it also took pains to deflate widespread reports of terror and mass killings. Estimates of the number killed were usually taken from official military sources, and for the first week ran below a hundred. From the very beginning the foreign press reported deaths running into several thousands. As late as September 20, nine days after the coup, the *Times* reported repression as though it were directed mainly against foreigners in Chile. Echoing the official line, an editorial of the same day regretted that "lurid rumors of mass execution would circulate," adding that the "military *leaders* moved against Dr. Allende with great reluctance, and only because they feared a polarized Chile was headed for civil war" (emphasis added). This despite reliable reports of savagery and barbarism unprecedented in Chile's history, reports available from foreign news services such as Reuters and the Agence-France Press, many foreign papers, the academic community and, quite nearby, *The Washington Post. Times* readers scarcely knew that the presidential palace, La Moneda, had been almost razed by bombs, or, as the French moderately conservative *Le Figaro* put it, "torn out by the guts" (September 17). In Colombia, Bogotá's conservative *El Tiempo* lamented that a "river of blood had shipwrecked Chile" (September 17).

Toward the end of September evidence of terror and repression and the effective abolition of political parties began to receive serious attention in the *Times,* but even then it was "balanced" with items stressing the legitimate, acceptable qualities of the new rulers. Of the four editorials printed on Chile in September, three were apologies for the dictatorship and one warned that the praetorians were "Off Course in Chile." On September 22 and 26 Jonathan Kandell mentioned that Congress had been suspended, that no political rallies were allowed, that no plebescite would be asked for when the new Constitution was drafted (allowing for permanent military "participation"), that the Central Workers Confederation, Chile's largest labor group, was abolished, and that all mayors and city councilmen throughout the country were to be removed, their posts to be filled by men "appointed by the military Junta." The same reporter on September 26 blithely characterized these measures as efforts to merely "transform" Chilean institutions, to engage in their "remodeling" (September 28), and to replace all university rectors with military "delegates." As late as October 6, almost one month after the coup, no editorial opposition was voiced to the slaughter of thousands from the slums (where one-half of Santiago's population of four million lives), to the book-burning, the killing of U.S. citizens Frank Teruggi and Charles Horman, or to the destruction of universities by abolishing textbooks, teaching positions and entire disciplines.

The third perspective shared by the Junta and much of the U.S. press was that the coup was carried out reluctantly by a nonpolitical patriotic military. The *White Book* states that despite the economic deterioration, "the military continued cooperating, not with the [Allende] regime, but with the country, in a dignified, disinterested and patriotic manner." We are told that "actions of the armed forces cost minimal destruction and lives . . . and now the Junta is preoccupied with solving the terrible problems of all kinds which are the legacy of Allende and the Popular Unity government. Not the least of these is to seek new "institutions which will *block absolutely* the repetition in Chile of the sad days of [Allende's incumbency]" (emphasis added).

The U.S. press invited sympathy for the "reluctant" generals by emphasizing their cautious, non-political qualities, by humanizing them, and by suggesting rather quickly that the situation in Chile had returned to "normal" almost immediately after the coup. In a September 12 editorial *The Los Angeles Times* emphasized Chile's tradition of a "non-political" military, and the *Monitor* underlined the "reluctance even among the military to resort to unconstitutional means to get rid of [Allende]" (September 15). *The Wall Street Journal* reported that "the military leaders are sorry they felt obliged to stage a coup, but they don't really want to be in charge of the country" (September 17). Much of our press seems to accept the notion that the military should, as a matter of course, have considered formal intervention. The newspapers appeared to view Chile's political problems as a military problem. As the *Monitor* put it: "The real problem for them [the military] was political polarization and economic chaos into which Chile was drawn as a result of the movement toward socialism" (September 14).

The U.S. press has also emphasized the sympathetic personal qualities of the new dictators. *The Miami Herald* quoted Junta majordomo Pinochet: "I ascended the military hierarchy step by step, with no other ambition than to pursue my career. . . .We are a professional army" (September 17). The *Monitor* reported that "Pinochet . . . gave every indication of being disappointed he and his fellow officers felt it necessary to move against Allende" (September 20). *The New York Times* described General Pinochet as "tall and powerfully built," "quiet and businesslike," "disciplined" and "tough," and emphasized his "sense of humor" (September 15).

These reluctant, well-disciplined, concerned and virtuous men were returning the country to a "normal," "businesslike" situation. Those who continued to resist the dictators were often called "extremists" by *The Wall Street Journal* and "rebels" by *The New York Times* in the first few weeks after the coup. (Lovers of democracy who fought against dictators within their own countries were called "resistance fighters" in World War II). *The Wall Street Journal* solicited our understanding for the "thankless task of the armed forces. The discipline they will have to enforce throughout Chilean society will undoubtedly cost them some of the popularity they now enjoy among the majority of citizens" (September 25). *The Los Angeles Times* reported relief in Chile after the coup and quoted several citizens: "I'm sleeping better than I have in years"; "You feel safer when you hear the guns"; "I wish it [the dictatorship] would last forever" (October 12). The preferability of postcoup "normality" in Chile was emphasized by veteran correspondent Lewis Diuguid in a report in *The Washington Post* as late as October 21: "[T]he armed forces probably acted with majority support. . . . It may turn out that the military intervention was a substitute for civil war, forestalling large-scale death and destruction by use of violence that was cruel and arbitrary, but *limited*" (emphasis added). Terming the massacres in Chile "limited" violence, used to "forestall" "large-scale" death and destruction, is not entirely unlike "We had to destroy the village in order to save it."

But it did not have to be this way. The U.S. press had access to various materials documenting the holocaust. For example, early reporting on Chile's coup by *The Washington Post* far surpassed coverage by other major U.S. newspapers. Especially in articles written by Marlise Simons [see her article on p. 20 of this book], the *Post's* reporting was admirable for several reasons. The Allende government, the *Post* mentioned, had a clear plurality and was properly considered legitimate. Middle-class white-collar and truck owner-operators were identified by the *Post* as instigators of strikes. The *Post* expressed concern about repressive aspects of the military regime. Allende's death was labeled as a possible murder, and forthcoming trials by court-martial of jailed civilians, considered war criminals by the regime, were treated as the disturbing news it is. Censorship of dispatches from Chile was mentioned. Considerable speculation about American corporate intervention appeared in the *Post,* with an excellent article by Lawrence Stern, along with a definition of the Nixon-Kissinger low-profile strategy, a policy of withholding economic and humanitarian credits while military assistance increased to pro-United States armed forces in Chile and elsewhere. The *Post* made reference to alternative news sources such as Reuters, Agence-France Press, *Excelsior*, Prensa Latina (a Cuban news agency) and the North American Congress on Latin America (NACLA) employed in estimating ambiguous or conflicting information. Only *The Washington Post* mentioned the existence of Plan CENTAUR, described by Hugh Vigorena, Chile's former ambassador to Mexico, as an anti-Allende plot organized by the CIA, eventually contributing to the overthrow.

The foreign press and some exceptions in our own news media have expressed the outrage appropriate to Chile's situation. The performance of most of our major papers, however, is itself outrageous and a disservice to the protection of human liberty. In January 1973, months before the coup, several of us in the academy tried to relate our concern to journalists from major dailies at a conference at the Center for Inter-American Relations.

The response was generally hostile.[3] *The Wall Street Journal* and its correspondent Everett Martin seem particularly determined to prevent a relationship of greater trust between academics and journalists. In a November 2 article on Chile the *Journal* managed to attack the competence of *The Nation, Newsweek,* and practically every academic knowledgeable about Chile, arguing there "[is not] much that's accurate or useful in the colored accounts the U.S. academic community is currently putting out on the subject."

The national Latin American Studies Association (LASA), prompted by concern about reporting on Chile, has recently created a committee on the U.S. press and Latin America. The press has run the risk of alienating some important academics because of its unwillingness to help a genuine democracy survive in Chile while legitimizing sham democracies in other parts of the world.

Just prior to the coup Richard Fagen, Professor of Political Science at Stanford, spent eighteen months in Chile as social science consultant to the Ford Foundation. He is also president-elect of the LASA, which numbers over 1,700 professionals. Fagen described *The New York Times* coup coverage as "schizophrenic," ranging from some sensitive material by Marvine Howe to the editorials, which he described as "barbarous." "The contradictions between what the military Junta says and what it does are so clearly visible," he said in an interview several weeks after the coup, "that it is a complete violation of the trust put by people in the mass media to accept the edicts and press releases of murderers as if they constituted a legitimate government." Many of us in the academy have had to ask, and would encourage others to ask, whether a press that legitimizes incipient fascism abroad can be trusted to do a much better job at home ■

---

[3]For discussion of several themes in U.S. press reporting on Chile see John Pollock, "Reporting on Chile: What the Press Leaves Out," *The Nation* (January 29, 1973); Pollock with David Eisenhower, "The New Cold War in Latin America: The U.S. Press and Chile," in *The Chilean Road to Socialism;* with Torry Dickinson and Joseph Somma, "Did Eichmann Have a Sense of Humor? *The New York Times* and Militarism in Chile," *LASA Newsletter* (December, 1973). See also Jerry W. Knudson, "Allende Falls, the Press Reacts," *Masthead* (January, 1974); Pat Chain, "Press Coverage of the Chilean Coup: The Information Gap," *CALA Newsletter* (October, 1973); Joseph P. Lyford, "The 'Times' and Latin America," Center for the Study of Democratic Institutions, 1962; and Laurence Birns, "Chile in the Wall Street Journal," *The Nation* (December 3, 1973) [reprinted with a rebuttal and counter-rebuttal below].

Chile in *The Wall Street Journal*

Laurence R. Birns teaches Latin American politics at the New School for Social Research in New York. He has written extensively on Chile and edited IDOC's special issue No. 58 (December, 1973), Chile: The Allende Years, The Coup, Under the Junta. For the first half of 1973, he was a senior economic affairs officer for the U.N. Economic Commission for Latin America, located in Santiago, and was scheduled to return to Chile on behalf of a U.S. foundation on the day of the coup. The following article appeared in The Nation on December 3, 1973.

On November 2, *The Wall Street Journal* devoted some two thirds of its editorial page to the military overthrow of the constitutional government of Chile, its causes and its aftermath. It chose three lines of inquiry to develop its principal theses: the extent of the violence visited upon the nation; the quantity of public support that the Allende government had behind it immediately before its demise; and the achievements, on balance, of President Allende's tenure. Taken together, the three separate contributions which appeared on that page make up one of the most provocative ventures in American journalism of recent times.

One of the articles was "Those Horror Tales from Chile," by Pablo Huneeus. Several weeks earlier, Everett Martin, the *Journal*'s Latin American correspondent, had referred to Huneeus as "one of Chile's leading sociologists." At the time, I found this description puzzling since I had known several of Huneeus' family but had heard hardly any reference to him in Chilean intellectual circles. I have tried, therefore, to check closely into Huneeus' professional status, which I thought it important to establish, since the major thrust of his article is the contention that John Barnes, foreign correspondent of *Newsweek,* was inaccurate in his estimate of the number of bodies he had seen in the Santiago morgue ("Slaughterhouse in Santiago," *Newsweek,* October 8). Without question the Barnes piece was the most influential one on the Chilean coup to appear in the American press; it was a major factor in moving Senator Kennedy and the U.S. Senate to pass an amendment to the foreign aid bill which would restrict to humanitarian purpose U.S. assistance to Chile.

It has been established that Huneeus is a well-spoken, widely traveled and charming man who can hardly be called a leader of Chile's sociological community. He is himself of aristocratic background and has made two socially brilliant marriages. His first wife, Delia Vergara, is one of Chile's two female graduates of Columbia's School of Journalism and editor of *Paula,* the nation's foremost women's magazine. It was for this magazine, I've been told, that Huneeus had done some of his professional writing. *Paula* can be thought of as a more discreet cross between *Vogue* and *Cosmopolitan,* and Huneeus was something of its Joyce Brothers.

For part of the Allende period, he was out of the country on an extended honeymoon in the Spanish Mediterranean after his second marriage. Huneeus is part of the Zapallar set, frequenting Chile's upper classes. A member of the right wing of the Christian Democratic Party (PDC), he some time ago addressed a party meeting on the Allende administration's vulgarity and lack of culture. After watching him on television, one member of his own PDC faction described Huneeus' beliefs as being barely distinguishable from those of the rank and file in *Patria y Libertad,* the nation's most extreme right-wing movement.

The *Wall Street Journal* editors vouch for him as "a Chilean known to us as being objective and independent," an endorsement that would seem to strain the meaning of those adjectives. Huneeus emerges, rather, as a man who by breeding and experience would find Populist or Socialist politics anathema, and the *Journal*'s decision to use him as one of its windows into Chile casts reasonable doubt on its own objectivity. On September 20, Everett Martin introduced Huneeus to *Journal* readers as an intellectual whom he had sought out as part of his endeavor to supply a broad view of Chilean realities. By November 2, the association is closer: the editors identify Huneeus as a "journalist and professor of sociology at the University of Chile, who previously has assisted American correspondents, including those of *The Wall Street Journal* and *Newsweek*, in preparation of reports on Chile."

Presumably he did not assist John Barnes on his story of October 8. Huneeus is utterly skeptical of Barnes's account of his four visits to the Santiago morgue, raising even the possibility that he was never there at all. The accuracy of the *Newsweek* correspondent's body count at the morgue is important, because the military Junta that overthrew the Allende government on September 11 and now rules Chile has attempted to minimize the ensuing casualties and thus the magnitude of the violence to which the nation has been subjected. It has consistently issued unrealistically low figures—as late as September 16, the Junta was maintaining that only ninety-five people had been killed in the fighting. At about the same time, the CIA intelligence estimates were that some 2,000 to 3,000 people had been killed, and those were the minimum figures that the bulk of the European press was using; some reputable correspondents were claiming that scores of thousands had fallen. For the Junta, therefore, it was of pressing importance that the John Barnes article be discredited: it was playing havoc with the new regime's public relations abroad, particularly in the United States.

It is to this task that Pablo Huneeus vigorously directs himself. He questioned the morgue's resident doctors and staff as to the accuracy of the Barnes article. He was told that Barnes was lying when he said that he had seen fifty bodies strewn in a corridor. And as to the 2,796 bodies which Barnes says the daughter of a staff member told him had been processed through the morgue since the coup, the reactions are "what brilliant imagination!" "what an exaggeration!"

But supposing that Huneeus has reported accurately what he was told, what is the value of that evidence? He does not tell his readers that the Medical College of Chile (the equivalent of the American Medical Association) is an extremely conservative organization; that it was a mainstay of the massive anti-government middle-class strikes of October 1972 and immediately preceding Allende's overthrow; that it had stubbornly opposed the establishment of clinics in the poorer districts, insisting that medical services must be dispensed from hospitals (which are often many miles from the slums that ring Santiago), and that since the overthrow it had militantly supported the Junta.

Political bias aside, is it reasonable to suppose that anyone working as a public servant today in Chile would dispute official Junta statements? In the days immediately preceding Huneeus' trip to the morgue, books were being burned in the streets, machine guns were being held at the heads of children during nocturnal raids on private homes (including those of an American network correspondent and of the former rector of Santiago's Catholic University), people who disappeared from working-class districts were later reported killed while "attempting to escape." Barnes himself admits that he got into the morgue only because those on duty there were careless; it was scarcely to their advantage to substantiate his story. But Huneeus does not take such factors into account; as "one of Chile's leading sociologists," he strolls over to the morgue and has a chat with the people he finds there, as though Santiago were as relaxed a city as Geneva.

Friends in the European section of the U.N. Secretariat have given me a copy of a cable sent from Santiago to UNESCO, Paris, on October 5. It is signed by Luis Ramallo, at that time acting secretary-general of the U.N.-affiliated Latin American Faculty of Social Science (FLACSO). Among other matters, the cable refers to the abduction and subsequent violent death of a young Bolivian, Jorge Rios, who was a student at FLACSO. While Mr. Ramallo was recently in New York, I showed him my copy of the cable and he verified it. I also asked him about his observations at the morgue, which he visited on September 19 in search of Rios. Ramallo said that the room in which he had counted approximately 185 bodies was apparently not the one where Barnes saw the bodies that he described, but he confirmed Barnes's description of the entrance to the morgue and the physical surroundings of the anteroom through which Barnes had passed. [See the Ramallo cable in IDOC No. 58.]

After talking with Ramallo, I got in touch with *Newsweek*, and several hours later he and Barnes met me in my office where, using a makeshift diagram of the morgue's layout, they confirmed each other's account of the building and of what they both had seen. This encounter between Barnes and Ramallo became part of *Newsweek*'s response to the *Journal*'s attack on its accuracy, which appeared in the latter's issue of November 15.

When Ramallo made his morgue visit, he went first through the front door to get a pass, and then went out and re-entered the building through the ambulance entrance; he was accompanied by a Protestant minister. Passing along a hallway containing a number of coffins, he was shown into a large room to look for the body of Rios. Huneeus had quoted a Dr. Vargas, "an elderly experienced doctor," as dismissing Barnes's tally of the bodies he had seen, on the ground that he was suffering from "perception shock." To illustrate the effect of this reaction, Vargas said: "When there are ten bodies together many persons can't even recognize their wives or fathers." That, said the doctor, is what "must have happened to that correspondent, presuming he ever got into the morgue."

For Luis Ramallo, Huneeus and Dr. Vargas will have to provide another explanation, because he and his associate spent more than an hour in one of the morgue's rooms. And shortly thereafter he said in his cable that he had found his student's "bullet-ridden body with signs of multiple concussions and two large gaping wounds in chest and legs. Body was found among some 150 [he chose a figure lower than his actual count] similarly unidentified and wounded bodies in the public mortuary where it had been deposited by military."

Discounting the five children (three little boys and two little girls), one of whom, in death, was gripping his father's leg, and the small number of women, Ramallo had to peer into the face of almost every naked cadaver in the room, looking for his student. He noticed that the bulk of them appeared to be of working-class origin, that a number of them had mangled limbs, and that the majority of them had been shot. He guessed that they were all recently dead because attendants were mopping up blood after several bodies had been moved, and there was no smell in the room, even though it was not air-conditioned. He did not find Rios' body in that room and an attendant then told him it might be in an adjoining room. On entering, Ramallo realized that he was in the morgue proper, for he could feel cooling and noticed the sliding shelves common to such places. In this room, he found Rios' body. One of the things which Ramallo recalls from this visit was an offhand comment by one of the doctors that they no longer had time to make individual autopsies, and that many corpses received only visual certification of the causes of death.

Huneeus makes the point that the list of the cadavers on the door of the mortuary was consecutively numbered. He then says that the figure of 2,796 bodies cited by Barnes was actually the total for all of 1973. Mr. Ramallo saw a list of some 130 names posted on the door when he paid his visit, and of this number, two-thirds had the word "unidentified" next to them. He reports also the interesting fact that, under the column giving the source of the bodies, the bulk of the notations cited such authorities as the "Tacna Regiment," "naval patrol," etc. There is enough evidence in Mr. Ramallo's narrative to establish that during the period immediately after the uprising the morgue was being inundated with the victims of violent deaths, that the morgue itself was under military control, that there was no reason to believe that anyone would readily tell the truth, that the occasion when Mr. Huneeus visited the morgue was perhaps many days after Barnes had been there and that, whatever the accuracy of the statement made by the daughter of an official to Newsweek's correspondent, things were far from normal at the morgue, or for that matter in Santiago.

Given Mr. Huneeus' background, his complaint about the "journalistic imperialism" of Newsweek and his statement that this "rich American magazine sends from London a British correspondent a week after the coup" (Barnes has long journalistic experience in Latin America) because "he only wants to use us for a story that will sell" must be taken with a wry smile. It is a wonder that, with the dismembered ruin of his nation lying around him, a large number of his fellow journalists and academics in jail or dead; with many of the nation's newspaper and radio stations closed down (the remainder being censored); the universities purged; and the military acting as the praetorian overseers of national institutions, Huneeus can say with an almost palpable shrug that "it's sad so many died, but it's good so many survived."

While Huneeus does add, "Not that I am happy with the Junta," he mentions not one thing that causes him unhappiness. And his remark that "Every Chilean feels that, no matter how low the death toll, what happened is a tragedy," is patently untrue. The post-overthrow celebrations that occurred in middle-class neighborhoods suggest that a large number of political opportunists and those whose economic interests had suffered are perfectly content with the way things have turned out. At best, they deplore the death toll. And to offset the killings and the oustings, there is now more room in the university faculties, hospitals, media and professional life for those

who were, or thought themselves, slighted during the Allende years. (Unlike those now out of favor, they were able to voice their opposition to the government and their lives and those of their families were secure.)

For the Journal's editors, Allende got what he deserved—"The generals took care of him before he and his assassination crews could get to them." This apparently refers to "Plan Z," a document as well authenticated as the Protocols of the Elders of Zion. This alleged plot was trotted out several days after the coup, when a justification was needed quickly to placate the world outcry over the carnage. The Journal editorializes on November 2: "it is amazing there's been as little bloodshed as there has." Apparently, the minimum CIA figure (a more accurate figure might be from 7,000 to 10,000) is trivial.

Or does the Journal base its estimates on the reporting of Everett Martin, who has been their Latin American correspondent for several years, having previously been Newsweek's correspondent in Vietnam? Martin is a decent, well-meaning man, who has been far more ready than most U.S. correspondents to go out in the field for a story. The questions to be asked are what preconceptions does he take with him and how does he go about acquiring his information? Unfortunately, he is often unreliable as to facts and, although he is diligent, his insights are open to question. Since Martin began reporting on Chile, I have compiled a list of eighty-five of his most obvious mistakes of fact and interpretation.

Characteristic of such lapses were Mr. Martin's efforts in the piece he contributed to the Journal's November 2nd issue, entitled ". . . a Few Loud Echoes from Academia." Martin is troubled that ". . . so many misleading reports and analyses of the events surrounding the coup in Chile . . . have appeared in reputable" segments of the media. While slightly separating himself from Huneeus when he says that ". . . there have been killings and executions that certainly seem excessive," Martin is still convinced of Newsweek's "misrepresentation of the facts" and is distressed by the "presentation of much more insidious and subtle articles"—namely E. Bradford Burns' observations on the Chile coup which appeared in The Nation of October 29. Martin is specifically unhappy with Professor Burns' tally of a pro-Allende parade, but he is generally unhappy with the activities of the academics, for there isn't ". . . much that's accurate or useful in the colored accounts the U.S. academic community is currently putting out on the subject."

Since I'm a member of that community and since I'm on record as having said in the New York Review of Books (November 1) that Mr. Martin's reportage on Chile is helping to "construct a mythology designed to show that Allende was responsible for his own fall," I feel personally involved. In another publication, I hope to evaluate some of the economic statistics he has been providing since he began writing on Chile. I can say provisionally that only occasionally do they conform to generally accepted data.

In the Nation article which Martin attacks, Burns puts the number of people who participated in the pro-Allende parade of September 4 at more than 800,000. Martin, insists that at most there were 20,000. Both Martin and I know that, in the fervent atmosphere of Chilean politics, it has long been easy for both the government and the opposition to muster massive parades at short notice. Foreign observers have often marveled at this ability. In an article dated July 6, Martin himself noted that "... so far Chile's economic problems haven't apparently eroded President Allende's base of popular support." Yet a scant two months later, he is intent on establishing that it was difficult for the government to mobilize a large outpouring of supporters, and had to resort to tricks to bolster the crowd's apparent size. Says Martin, the Allendists chose the Plaza de la Constitución for their demonstration because its comparatively confined quarters would make it seem that more people were present. He and several colleagues (unnamed) "... noted that a large contingent marched around and around one block to make it look larger."

The facts are as follows: the plan was to have all the paraders (not just the group Martin mentions) march around the reviewing stands, which were in the Plaza. For six hours, four columns of marchers converged on the Plaza and then passed back to the Alameda, the city's principal thoroughfare and three or four times as wide as New York's Fifth Avenue. The crowd filled the Alameda from the Plaza Italia to the vicinity of the Moneda, the Presidential palace, a distance of at least ten city blocks. Conservatively put by the opposition, the crowd numbered 300,000. Others used figures closer to a million. Whatever Professor Burns' abilities as a crowd counter, they are superior to those of Mr. Martin.

Actually, it is possible that Martin got his demonstrations mixed up. In another article he says that "... at least 300,000 women gathered in Santiago to demand that President Allende resign." That demonstration, which occurred on September 5, extended the short distance between Catholic University and the UNCTAD building and, given the limitations of space, it couldn't possibly have numbered more than 15,000 to 30,000 people.

In his November 2nd article, Martin writes of "... mounting evidence that there was considerable fraud during the Congressional election for the government to achieve the 44 per cent total" of the vote which it won. This "mounting evidence" was actually the fabrication of one man, Jaime del Valle, dean of the Law School of Catholic University. Soon after he made this charge, he appeared on one of Chile's most popular television talk shows (having previously asked its director not to press him on the "fraud" issue), and in the presence of the director of the nation's electoral college, himself a member of the opposition Christian Democrats, was forced to reveal that he had no evidence. It should also be noted that the opposition-controlled Congress did not support the allegation of any sizable electoral fraud. Somewhat later, del Valle was overheard admitting to the rector of his university that he had invented the charge in order to provide the opposition with a little ammunition against the government.

Almost alone of foreign correspondents, Martin believes that "the armed forces were loyal to the government and were the last to turn against him." In that case, one might ask, who were the first? Jonathan Kandell of *The New York Times* wrote a long article on the plotting of the coup a number of weeks ago. His conclusion was that the military had begun to conspire almost a year earlier and that it soon reached the point of being determined to go through with the deed, whatever the circumstances. Rather than accept the official account, Mr. Martin might seek out interviews with Gen. Manuel Torres de la Cruz, Adm. José Toribio Merino, a Valparaíso right-wing priest by the name of Osvaldo Lira, and read back issues of a publication called *Tizona*. He might also explore the role of Jaime Guzman now the Junta's leading ideological mentor, and the ultra-montane "Movement for the Protection of the Family, Tradition, and Property." That group had close ties with similar groups in Brazil and elsewhere in Latin America, and was particularly active in proselytizing the navy (at its Valparaíso headquarters) against the government.

Furthermore, Martin's statement that the military's loyalty to the Allende government is evidenced by its having joined his Cabinet on three separate occasions somewhat obscures what actually happened. It wasn't, as Mr. Martin suggests, so much that Allende wanted the military to join him as that the opposition parties insisted that it do so as a precondition for settling economic and other difficulties. Nor does the record agree with Martin's contention that, far from advocating Chile's continuing to receive American military assistance, "... it was Dr. Allende's opponents who resent the U.S. aid to the Chilean military. ...." One would like to see one official or nonofficial statement from either of the two major opposition parties that would uphold this allegation.

And Martin seems to have recurring trouble with figures. In an article published a day after the coup, he gives the size of the Chilean army as 25,000 men; the navy, 5,000; and the air force, 5,000. In the 1973-74 listing by the prestigious London-based Institute of Strategic Studies, the figures are respectively, 32,000, 18,000 and 10,000. Martin also has trouble with chronology. Several paragraphs later in the same piece, he writes: "Last January, while the three chiefs of staff were still in the cabinet, Mr. Allende was pressured to allow passage of a bill. It gave the military the right to search for and to seize all illegal arms in the country." But that bill was passed the previous year and had gone unimplemented for many months. It can be persuasively argued that the military search squads began energetically to carry out raids (mainly against left-wing arms caches) only when plans for the military coup had matured and the need to strip potential adversaries was at hand.

Another issue raised by Martin is that "the professors want to forget" that back in April 1971, when the pro-Allende forces mustered 50 percent in the municipal elections (in the September 1970 elections their tally had been 36.2 percent), they pointed out that Allende was no longer a minority President. But after the March 1973 Congressional elections, when the government coalition received only 44 percent of the vote, they conveniently forget the slide from the earlier vote of 50 percent. But if Martin were conversant with modern Chilean history, he would know that almost invariably the Chilean electorate votes in larger numbers for the seated President in the first election after he has taken office than it has originally, and that also it invariably votes against him in the mid-term one. Allende's popular predecessor, President Frei, a Christian Democrat, experienced a similar precipitous rise and decline of support. The important feature of the March Congressional election was that, despite the dislocations, the food shortages and the dismal short-term economic prospects for the nation, the electorate voted in significantly larger numbers for the government candidates than it had in 1970. Considering the patterns of Chilean history, that was an exceedingly important achievement.

Martin speaks of corruption within the overthrown government. Of course there was corruption. But, given the difficult circumstances of the nation, and the basic middle-class background of most of the leftist administrators and managers, would Martin and the *Journal* maintain that corruption was at a level to justify the destruction of much of the civic decency that formerly characterized the Chilean nation? There were no political prisoners under Allende, and under his rule, the broad range of all the freedoms was maintained. Compare what existed then with what exists today. On a deeper level, there is implicit the inference that democratic procedures are only for good times and when a business-oriented regime is in power. When a regime committed to social justice and a redistribution of national wealth comes into office, different ground rules are apparently in effect. The *Journal* and Martin speak repeatedly of Allende's minority government, but in fact, except for the Frei years, every Chilean president in the 20th century has won office only with a plurality. And the fact that the opposition did win a majority vote during Allende's tenure does not justify Martin's conclusion that a majority of the public advocated the violent, bloody overthrow of the constitutional government.

The *Journal*'s staff could have approached the Chilean economy from a different direction. Martin dismisses those U.S. academicians who attribute Chile's economic difficulties to the fact ". . . that Chile has always had economic problems and anyhow all the difficulties were caused by the U.S. credit blockade." But is he prepared to deny that Chile had one of the most archaic and stagnant oligarchy-controlled economies in all of Latin America, or that Allende inherited one of the highest per capita national debts in the world? Granted that Allende's economic policies would win him no friends in the American business community, isn't it true that the cutoff of supplier credits from the United States and the aborting of development loans from the regional and international agencies, together with a falling market for copper through much of the Allende years, would have placed an insuperable burden on the best-managed of economies?

Martin goes on to say that in fact the Allende regime "received more international credit than any other Chilean government in history." He cites no figures, but even if his statement is accurate, what does it mean? For the most part, Allende's Chile received only bilateral credits, spaced over a period of years. (Supplier credits from the United States all but disappeared.) For any one year, the figure probably fell significantly under the inflation-adjusted credit flows which occurred during the Frei era. In any event, these credits were for specific goods from specific countries. They did not permit Chile to buy on the open market and were of little use in buying the replacement parts and components needed for industrial and transportation systems geared to equipment manufactured in the United States.

While I would certainly not blame all of the Allende administration's economic problems on the United States' systematic policy of economic denial, one cannot easily comprehend the *Journal*'s sardonic editorial statement that "We sympathize and understand why they [". . . armchair Marxists around the world . . ."] now blame the United States. . . ." Isn't the *Journal* struck by the fact that, although every year during the Allende period Chile asked the United States for grain credits, within a few days after its overthrow, the military Junta was awarded eight times the amount that Chile had received in the

preceding three years? And just the other day the flood of private credits began once again, with Manufacturers Hanover leading the file of U.S. banks that are providing the military Junta with $150 million of private credit. Another compelling fact is that the Inter-American Development Bank, which operates under a virtual U.S. veto, turned down every request made by the Allende government, but is now about to award the Junta a development loan almost five times the amount of IDB's disbursements to Chile during the entire Allende period.

Martin's Chile was a hermetic world, with its base in the American-flavored Carrera Hotel and largely cut off from the political realities of the nation about which he was critically reporting. Martin is a man of cheerful loquacity. He arrived in Latin America for the first time in 1971, and came upon a Chile under Allende. One of his early and consistent tutors there has been Orlando Saenz, president of the Chilean Manufacturers Association. His interpreters were at best members of the right-wing faction of the Christian Democratic Party. When he entered slums he was escorted by a militant of the same faction and talked to dissident PDC-leaning members of the community. When he went into the countryside, he was on occasion the guest of expropriated estate owners. To some degree that caricatures his actual performance, but during the time we were both in Chile, that tended to be his *modus operandi*. The whole of Chile isn't opened up by that type of scrutiny.

Martin's characteristic style is to relate anecdotally a series of interviews with unnamed people who are predominantly critics of the former government. From such sources he documents his impression that post-Junta Chile has "an almost unreal air of relaxed normality." A businessman tells him that the workers were showing up on the job even when they aren't scheduled, overlooking what he partially admits—that an atmosphere of fear and insecurity pervades the working classes. He then drifts over to Santiago's Cafe Haiti (a gathering place for businessmen and professionals), where he gets in conversation with an unnamed communist engineer who expands freely on the corruption and lack of discipline of Allende's Chile. Back at the foreign ministry, Martin discovers former staffers who are almost grateful for being fired by the new regime. As for the casualties at the Universidad Tecnico de Estado on the day of the coup, he discounts the "reports in the foreign press of mass killings," because "the death toll in this incident has since been revised to twenty, most of whom were reportedly foreign revolutionaries registered as students." But where, other than in a Junta press release, could one find these "revised" figures, and who reported that "foreign revolutionaries" were registered as students? A Chilean student who attended that university and who is a member of the Frei faction of the PDC has assured me that upwards of seventy-five students and others were killed in that incident. One of Martin's major shortcomings is that he finds it easy to believe Junta press releases, and equally difficult to believe statements from sources favorable to the former Allende government.

I do not dismiss that government's many errors of administration and conceptualization of policy. The record of such mistakes is substantial, and I have commented on it elsewhere. Nor do I want to debate Pablo Huneeus' thoroughly consistent opposition to the Allende government from its inception. Nor is it my intent to dwell on

Martin's careless and naive reportage (naive, certainly not conspiratorial), nor his inability to deal maturely and adequately with what he accurately calls "one of the most complex nations in the world."

What does concern me is the breezy way in which Martin and the editorial board of *The Wall Street Journal* have become militant apologists for a military regime that fulfills in every respect the definition of the word totalitarian, if not fascistic. I would have, for example, expected the *Journal* and its staff to display some concern for freedom of the press in Chile, some concern for civil liberties and civil rights and some ability to separate themselves from an attitude which tacitly assumes that the only segment of Chile worth concern is the middle class, and that the main yardstick of a nation's achievement is its GNP.

The quality of Everett Martin's reportage is particularly important because *The Wall Street Journal* is one of a handful of American newspapers that has a specifically designated correspondent for the Latin American area. It is essential, at a time when the region is experiencing a rising level of economic and political nationalism, that the U.S. business community be accurately informed of the problems and expectations of Latin America. Everett Martin's coverage of the Chile story patently fails in that respect. It would seem, also, that in a period of East-West detente, he reveals a certain lack of sophistication by constantly employing variants of the phrase, "the Marxist government of Chile." How would we respond if the left-wing press in other countries used the phrase, "the capitalist government of the United States?" Rather than mocking the effort being made by the U.S. academic community to grasp what has been occurring in Chile, it might be constructive if correspondents like Martin joined the scholars in a mutual learning process. The collaboration might improve our comprehension of a region which, when it receives any attention at all in the American press, all too often suffers from the biases of the reporters operating in the field.

Few recent international incidents have witnessed such a regrettable journalistic performance as *The Wall Street Journal's* coverage of Chile. Perhaps the phrase—"underlying contempt for Chile"—which Huneeus uses to score his opponents, should be redirected toward his employer: the *Journal's* treatment of the Allende years and the aftermath is almost a case history in distortion, ill will, condescension and amateurism.

Everett Martin Responds and Laurence R. Birns Answers

The following exchange of letters appeared in the January 19, 1974, issue of The Nation.

Professor Laurence Birns in his effort to discredit Chilean sociologist Pablo Huneeus and myself seems to have had considerable difficulty staying within the bounds of accuracy. Some examples:

Mr. Huneeus is *not* a member of the right-wing faction of the Christian Democrats. Although he held an appointed post in the Frei government, he's never been a member of any political party.

He has never criticized Dr. Allende on television. His last TV appearance was in 1970 on a panel discussion about youth while he was a U.N. employee.

Mr. Huneeus' so-called "extended honeymoon in the Spanish Mediterranean" was actually time spent working on a research project under the auspices of the sociological institute of Madrid University. He produced a book called *The Bureaucrats,* a look at how a state functions, and completed research for a second book on the Spanish younger generation.

Far from being a "Chilean Joyce Brothers" in a woman's magazine, at age 33 he has to his credit 17 papers for technical journals and three books: *Social Situation of Copper Miners* ('69), *Human Resources and Employment Policy* ('70), and *The Bureaucrats.* The first two, at least, are sufficiently dull to satisfy scholarly standards.

Rather than having contact with only the upper classes, as Mr. Birns claims, Mr. Huneeus is known for his field research. He lived for three months with miners for his copper study and the work brought about new laws to protect them from exploitation. For three years he was director of the National Employment Service, which brought him in close daily contact with the unemployed.

A fellow correspondent two years ago told me Mr. Huneeus was *the* best single source to contact in Chile. That correspondent was John Barnes of *Newsweek.*

I have never written or held the conclusion "that a majority of the public (in Chile) advocated the violent, bloody overthrow of the constitutional government," as Mr. Birns writes.

I've never been the guest of an expropriated landlord. I don't even know one and I consider this to be a shortcoming since I should have contacts at all levels of Chilean society.

Dean Jaime del Valle of the Catholic University Law School says he did not back away from his charges of election fraud, as Mr. Birns wrote. In fact, he reported on television that votes cast in the March election exceeded possible voters by 250,000, or 8 percent of the total vote.

In allowing Mr. Huneeus space to argue against the *Newsweek* story, "Slaughterhouse in Santiago," *The Wall Street Journal* is not supporting the coup, nor denying that there was killing nor approving of killing. But, as Mr. Birns notes, the *Newsweek* account was the most influential coming from Santiago; and by all that I and other correspondents could learn, it was gross overstatement.

Jonathan Kandell of *The New York Times* and Lewis Diuguid of *The Washington Post* each independently wrote stories casting substantial doubt on the *Newsweek* account. Mr. Kandell found that in Pincoya *población,* where Mr. Barnes reported that all males in one square block were killed, in fact only one person had died. He also found, as Huneeus did, that the morgue figures were for the period since January one and not for the first two weeks of the coup.

The difference between Mr. Birns and myself arises because I am only a reporter, not an advocate of any kind of ideology. What I found in Chile determined what I wrote. In defense of my stories I can only say that our readers were informed that the Allende government was heading into serious trouble and that the climax was likely to come this year.

Mr. Birns' central complaint against my reporting can be discerned when he quotes himself as having written in *The New York Review of Books,* "Mr. Martin's reportage on Chile is helping to 'construct a mythology designed

to show that Allende was responsible for his own fall.'"
The facts reported in my articles are uncomfortable to
Mr. Birns' romantic preconceptions. As a result, although
he was not in Chile during or after the coup, he sets out
to "correct" those facts through personal attacks which
are themselves laced with inaccuracies.

Mr. Martin speaks about my "inaccuracies," yet he is
reluctant about citing them. In my article I had listed a
number of major points and fact after fact where he had
erred. In his letter, he mentions not one of them, nor does
he refer to my support of Professor Bradford Burns, estimate of the size of a pro-Allende parade, which was the
very *raison d'être* of Mr. Martin's November 2nd *Wall
Street Journal* article. Even then I had decided not to quote
from Mr. Martin's column of October 24, 1972 because I
feared that his employer might start asking embarrassing
questions of him. This article included the sentence,
"And the President [Allende] himself isn't up for re-
election until 1976." Of course, the Chilean constitution
does not permit re-election of an incumbent President.

He contents himself to rebut what I myself had
described as symbolic conjecturings: that he had spent
his time largely in Chile with the middle class. I still
insist that this is the case. I agree with Mr. Martin that
he ". . . should have contacts at all levels of Chilean
society." But the question is, did he? As for the visit to
the expropriated landlord, he might never have reached
the *fundo* but it was certainly his intention to make the
trip.

In my article I made the claim that I can cite at
least eighty-five instances where Mr. Martin was factually
incorrect or produced distorted interpretations of events.
My claim remains. If the *Journal* will provide the space
to do this I will gladly oblige.

Concerning Mr. Huneeus, I stand on the account of
his professional and political evaluation that was developed in my article. To those who know him, Huneeus
always identified himself with the PDC and spoke as if
he were a member. The greater fact is that Mr. Huneeus
is a minor personality in Chilean national and intellectual
life and for Mr. Martin to suggest that he is a man of
the people is simply mirthful. For the *Journal* to peg so
much on Huneeus' analysis is in itself a reflection upon the
paucity of insight that it has shown regarding Chile.

Concerning the del Valle charges about alleged electoral fraud (I call them concoctions) in the congressional
election, my differences were not with the dean. I was
taking issue with Mr. Martin's original *Journal* report
that there was "mounting evidence that there was considerable fraud. . . ." A more professional way for Martin
to have presented his evidence would have been to have
specifically cited del Valle as his one source, characterize
the dean's position in the Chilean intellectual community,
and then present contrary evidence, if any existed. I say
that overwhelmingly the evidence was to the contrary. Mr.
Martin says that ". . . *The Wall Street Journal* is not
supporting the coup, not denying that there was killing
nor approving of killing." But isn't this statement testing
our gullibility? If the opposite isn't true then why did Mr.
Martin call those who opposed the Junta "resisters" rather
than constitutionalists, and why does he cite Allende as
the man who "defied" the military rather than the military
which was defying the lawful President.

But if the above contains something of interest, it
has to be subsidiary to Mr. Martin's suggestion that the
difference between him and myself is that "I [Martin]
am only a reporter, not an advocate of any kind of ideology." Mr. Martin would like to think of himself as "only
a reporter," an honest man in a dishonest world. But why
then does he title one of his articles "Wrecking Chile to
Build Marxism"? Ideology is not only the possession of
the left. Self-identified middle-roaders too have their ideology. During the period of his reporting, he consistently
ridiculed and denigrated the policies and institutions of
the Allende administration, in contrast to the image of
solidarity and efficiency which he attributed to those who
opposed it. As for his self-identified service in informing
his readers that things were in bad shape in Chile before
the overthrow, one needn't be a Pulitzer candidate to
have had this insight. There wasn't a newspaperman or
newspaper within or without Chile who wasn't saying
precisely this. Perhaps a more significant service to a
readership would have been telling why this was so, and
what were the constellation of forces producing Chile's
parlous state, and what were the options open to the
government and opposition leaderships, and what were
the external and internal constraints acting upon them.
Mr. Martin never provides us with this type of analysis.
In fact, he never analyzes, but merely presents a series
of semi-amusing, if tinted, vignettes, carefully constructed
to present a dogma out of which we are meant to extra-
polate major political judgments. As for the *Journal's*
editorials, its finding that "The generals took care of him
[Allende] before he and his assassination crews could
get to them" respects neither facts nor any pretense to
fairness.

The reason why I undertook this investigation of
Martin's reportage is not, as he states, because the "facts
reported in my articles are uncomfortable to Mr. Birns's
romantic preconceptions." After experiencing the realities
of Allende's rule, the quality of the opposition, and
scrutinizing the operation of the military Junta after the
coup, it is difficult to be romantic about Chile. What
troubles me is that Martin's "facts" often turn out to be
nonfacts, and that the language that he uses, the themes
that he selected to write about, the vignettes that he
presented, and the explanations that he provided *consistently* could have been straight from the manual of
arms of the nation's right wing. I am saying that his has
been poor reporting which falls apart once it is closely
analyzed and assessed. In my article, I had spelled out
my charges. Mr. Martin chooses not to respond to them.

Complete Freedom, Chile's Ambassador Insists

*On March 20, 1974, John R. Rarick (D.—La.), a member of
the U.S. House of Representatives, read into the Congressional Record the following radio interview conducted by
Fulton Lewis with General Walter Heitmann, the Chilean
military government's Ambassador to the United States.
Congressman Rarick introduced this material so that his
colleagues in Congress might have "the benefits of 'the
other side' of the story in Chile."*

Mr. Rarick. Mr. Speaker, the legacy of destruction that Salvador Allende bequeathed to the citizens of Chile will continue to plague that beleaguered country for years to come. Three years of Marxist misrule had brought Chile's economy to the point of total collapse.

In the rush of the mass media to discredit the new military government, Americans have been given a distorted, largely inaccurate picture of the situation in Chile. No one wants military rule. Aside from a total Communist dictatorship, which was the direction that Allende was taking Chile, military rule is probably the least popular form of government to we Americans. The new Chilean leaders obviously recognize this and are making attempts to return their country to civilian control as soon as possible.

In spite of our personal distaste for military rule, an accurate accounting of the activities, accomplishments and facts about Chile today should be expected from the U.S. news media. Unfortunately, this does not appear to be happening.

In order that our colleagues may have the benefits of "the other side" of the story in Chile, I ask that the interview of Ambassador Walter H. Heitmann, Ambassador of Chile, follow my remarks. The interview was conducted by Fulton Lewis, the highly respected radio commentator, on his syndicated program aired February 22 and 23 over the Mutual Broadcasting System. The interview follows:

Lewis. Last September the Marxist regime of Salvador Allende was replaced temporarily by a military government whose Ambassador to the United States, Ambassador Walter Heitmann, is my guest at this microphone now.

Mr. Ambassador, how long does the present Chilean government plan to hold the reins in Santiago?

Heitmann. Well that's a very difficult question to answer really, it's the same as if you would ask a patient in the hospital when he's ready to go home. It depends on how strong the medicine is that we get to heal our sick body. The sooner the government can return to complete freedom in the country, the better. And everybody wishes that.

Lewis. How much freedom is there now in Chile? The government now, of course, is predominantly military—but is it a military dictatorship as described by many of Chile's critics?

Heitmann. It is not a military dictatorship, it is a military government, and I think there is a big difference and everybody knows what the difference is. The Constitution is in effect in Chile, only in accordance with the laws and with the Constitution some of the liberties are limited or restricted right now because that is necessary for the recovery of the country.

Lewis. Such as—what kind of freedoms, what kind of liberties?

Heitmann. Well, there is complete freedom of the press again. The control was lifted last week, so every paper can write what they want to write and of course, if they write things that are against the law (the same law that we always had), then they have to go to court or are closed for a certain period. That's in accordance with the regulations we have and it's the same in every country.

Lewis. So the court system has not been suspended?

Heitmann. No, it has never been suspended, the judiciary system is the same as before, we have the same judges, the same courts, the same courts of appeal and the Supreme Court. And that has always been in effect. That's why we say there is no dictatorship and complete freedom. With a free judiciary system, that means we have freedom.

Lewis. What about the economy of Chile today? Of course this was one of the things that led to the downfall of Allende, the fact that the economy had fallen apart under his administration.

Heitmann. Well, the economy as many of the audience may have already known is completely wrecking the country. A fiscal deficit of a thousand, two hundred million dollars and that we have to cover through loans, through increased production and all the ways and means we have. Allende, when he came into power we had a superadd of four hundred million dollars, close to it. And when he left we had a deficit of almost a billion dollars. And we expect to get loans from the international loan institutions like the World Bank and the Inter-American Development Bank.

Lewis. So gradually Chile is recovering.

Heitmann. Is returning, yes.

Lewis. The previous government, the government of Salvador Allende, has been described as being anything from Marxist to Marxist/Leninist, and in different debates there is a difference. How do you describe it? Do you feel that Allende's regime was principally Communist, Marxist . . . ?

Heitmann. Well, it was Marxist/Communism, that, I would say was the exact definition of it. People might not agree on the meaning or the definition of it but that's the way it is. And he said it, even before he became president, but once he was president he never recognized it, he never wanted to tell it. He liked to give the impression that he was working towards a socialist regime, and never said what kind of socialism, but we found out what kind of socialism he was taking the country to.

Lewis. And the people he was affiliating with more and more were Fidel Castro, the Soviet Union. And as I understand it many of the arms that were used by Allende supporters were supplied by Fidel Castro.

Heitmann. Yes, I would say that Fidel Castro was his advisor, his supervisor, he told him what to do and how to do things and that's the reason Fidel Castro spent almost a month in the country. And that's when we met him and got to know him and we disliked him. Fidel Castro is solely responsible, I would say of sending all these weapons to the country, with the knowledge of Allende, of course, and that is against the law, because in Chile there is a very old law by which every arm that is taken into the country or bought outside has to go through

the customs and needs a special authorization. And they brought these arms, some of them, in boxes in the Cuban airline, and they were taken to Allende's house where later we found them.

Lewis. So these arms have been recovered, pretty much.

Heitmann. Most of them, we hope. There must be some hidden somewhere, but it's going to take a long time to find them all because many of the people who hid the arms, they left the country and we're never going to know where they are hidden really. But some day we're going to know the exact amount.

Lewis. Chile stands out alone among Latin American nations as a country who has been wedded to democracy; a country that has rejected and resented foreign interference. What was the reaction of the Chilean people to this sudden injection, not only of Cuban arms and Cuban influence, but also Soviet influence in their country?

Heitmann. Unfortunately all this information did not come to the knowledge of the people. It was handled secretly by the government and was very difficult to detect. We found the arms only after the military took control of the government. We never imagined how many arms we had in the country. We thought maybe a couple of hundred or a couple of dozen, we never realized that we had tens of thousands of arms in the country.

Lewis. All of which were coming from Cuba?

Heitmann. They were all coming from Cuba, yes.

Lewis. Initially Mrs. Allende declared her husband had committed suicide and then when she arrived a few days after Allende's death she changed her story and said Allende had been murdered. What is the truth about how Salvador Allende died?

Heitmann. Well, in the first place I would state very clearly that Mrs. Allende has not her own opinion. She is telling and she is saying what she is told to say. She is a machine of the international-propaganda now. So her statements and her words really have no meaning and have no value at all. And what really happened to Allende: he committed suicide. He was requested by the military to surrender and he was requested three times to surrender, and he thought he had control of the situation and that the popular militias would support him, and he would finally come out as the big winner. And when he finally found out that nobody was following him, that the imagined image he had of the guerrillas was artificially created by his followers, then he had no other recourse other than to commit suicide.

Lewis. In a sense it was a very sad thing because Allende, I think, probably believed throughout the last month or two that he still had the support of the people.

Heitmann. Yes, that happens most of the time with dictators; they never have the feeling of what the people think and feel about him, and it was the same with Allende.

He was told by some of his body-guards that he was very popular; that he had the support of the people and it was never true. He found it out too late, otherwise I think he would have quit the government before.

Lewis. On another controversial issue we get varying reports—some people say that there were only a handful of casualties during the brief skirmish that resulted in the ouster of Salvador Allende. Other people say it was a massive bloodbath. What is the truth about the number of casualties?

Heitmann. Well, there have been many figures in the papers and in the words of many people, but the official figures state around 2000 casualties, and not over it. Some people talk about 30 thousand, and if they realize that in the last war between Israel and the Arab countries the Israeli army lost (I think it was) 1800 soldiers, in a battle that lasted for a couple of days and with the most modern and effective weapons. So when people who talk about ten or twenty thousand casualties, they don't really know how many a thousand lives are. The figure is around 2000 and I think all the people who fled, who left the country and requested refuge in the embassies, they should know how many they killed.

Lewis. There is another controversy about the number of people—of Allende's supporters —who were imprisoned ... some people say that there were many murdered. How many were executed, what is the truth? How many were imprisoned and what legal rights do these people have?

Heitmann. Well, I don't know exactly how many have been executed, everything is registered in the files in Chile, but I don't have the figure. But I can tell you that all the prisoners that we had in the country came to 8000. Four thousand, four hundred and forty-two requested refuge in the embassies and the others were taken into custody into different places. At this moment there are only 300 prisoners in the country awaiting trial by the courts.

Lewis. So there have been trials, and as I understand it there are not just military trials but in some cases civilian trials when the offense is a civil offense.

Heitmann. Yes, every citizen has the same rights he ever had in the country. He can choose his own defendant and he goes to the court and has the regular time that everyone has to present his case with full rights available.

Lewis. Ambassador Heitmann, many liberal members of the U.S. Congress have backed legislation that would allow, if it were passed, literally thousands of pro-Allende, Chilean Marxists to enter the United States. Now you've had experience with these people in Chile. Were they to be allowed to come to the United States to live, what could we expect from them?

Heitmann. Well, I hope that your domestic system and your democratic life here will absorb them and will convince them that they were wrong, otherwise you are going to see what they will do. I cannot predict it, but I hope you don't have the experience we had.

Lewis. How militant were the Allende backers in Chile, during the period that Salvador Allende was president? Were they tolerant, were they understanding of people who disagreed with Allende or was there an attempt by them to suppress anti-Allende sentiment?

Heitmann. Yes. I am sorry this is not a television station, otherwise I would show you some pictures of Chileans who opposed the government of Allende were taken at night or at any hour of the day into the Civil Police for interrogation. And there they were beaten, they were tortured and there are many who never came back and some were crippled for the rest of their lives. So that is the tolerance they are preaching now!

Lewis. The United States gave credit, financial credit to the Chilean government when Allende was president, and that credit has been cut off now ...

Heitmann. Well, I wouldn't say it has been cut off now. We have the same credit, and we hope we'll get more credit than Allende got because everybody, in official circles, they have to realize how critical the situation is in the country. And if we don't get credit, that means that the Chilean population won't have enough food to eat, and I think that would be a crime against human rights.

Lewis. Ambassador Heitmann, what has been the Chilean government's response to requests by several international organizations for permission to inspect the prison facilities that have been set-up by the new government and to investigate the status of those supporters of the previous government who have been arrested?

Heitmann. Yes, that is a situation of which it is very unpleasant to tell. During the Allende regime they used Chile as a guinea pig—everybody looked and watched what was happening in Chile, and never did they try to help or avoid anything. And now everybody is going to Chile to see what the consequences were. But what they see they do not print and they do not tell. They only tell what has already been made up in their minds. Everybody is going to Chile to see what's happening. The United Nations Committee for Human Rights; the Red Cross and they all went to Chile and wrote their official reports—very favorable. These were never printed in the papers or mentioned in the media. And there are many small groups of liberal tendency or other left-oriented groups which go to Chile just to create problems, and when they come back they never tell what they've seen, they only tell what they were told to tell before they went to Chile to tell.

Lewis. But the International Red Cross Committee gave you a favorable rating?

Heitmann. Yes, all official organizations who have sent groups to study the Chilean situation are all favorable, but you don't read it in any papers or any magazines.

Lewis. One of the things that interests me is the economic experience that Chile has gone through, because socialism is not limited to Latin America, it's not limited to just Chile, the Socialists are trying to expand socialism throughout the entire world. When Salvador Allende took power he professed that he was going to have a government of the working people; it would preserve the Chilean economy and it would expand the economy and democracy. The record of Allende's government would suggest that it did just the opposite. I think the last year of Salvador Allende inflation went up between 300 and 400 per cent. And in his last days it was the working people themselves who took the lead in getting rid of Salvador Allende. What happened to Marxism in Chile? Is it a system, that in your view, is just bankrupt? It could never work? Or do you feel that the new government is going to "refine" socialism? Is socialism something that is just history now in Chile?

Heitmann. Well, Chile was always a socialist country and we have more advanced reforms and conditions than many socialist countries, in freedom. And that's the difference. And what Allende wanted to do in Chile was not a free socialism, a democratic socialism. He wanted to institute a totalitorian socialism—and that, we did not accept. And so I wouldn't say the socialist economy is a failure. Many countries have socialist economies, and we have it right now, and we call it "liberal socialist economy" —it's a different system, and I wouldn't say that socialism is not good. It's good for some countries, since every country has its own way of living; every country has ways of deciding how it's going to be governed by their certain system, but what is very clear and definite is that there is no "democratic communism"—it is totalitarian by origin and structure.

Lewis. Where does Chile go from here for the future, economically speaking?

Heitmann. We hope to recover the potential we had in 1970—that's three years ago—we hope to recover that in two more years. So it's a loss of five years in Chile's economic life and from then on, we hope in three years we might reach a national net product of around $5 billion. Right now it's close to $1.5 billion.

Lewis. What formula, do you intend, or rather does the government intend to use in developing the economy? Will the government believe in private ownership of property?

Heitmann. Yes, there is private ownership, and it has always been the same. The only thing we are going to increase now is the control of the State over the enterprises, over the organization and the industries. You see, we think the industries have a social meaning and content. The workers are not only money makers or machine tools for capital, but workers are human beings and they deserve the right to have participation in the earnings and the profits and also in the management of the organizations. And that is what they are doing now.

Lewis. So it's a kind of regulated free enterprise ...

Heitmann. Yes it is.

Lewis. Now, what about Chile politically? Now there is a military government there, the government leaders themselves have pointed out that they are old men, that if they were ambitious to be dictators they would have let young men take over the government. But they have declared that their intentions are to be in power temporarily. How long is temporarily, and what happens then?

Heitmann. Well, there is one thing I want to make very clear. Chile has always been a democratic and free country, basically democratic. And it's going to be that way. The Constitution is re-written right now, because we have to make some changes in accordance with the past experience. What I think has to change in Chile is the organization of the political parties, because during Allende's regime and afterwards we found out that the Chilean population does not accept any totalitarian system. They like and they love freedom, and they're going to stay that way. And political parties now have to recognize that it is useless to talk about Communism and other things. All the parties now have to reprint their contents, their philosophical content. They have to consider the wishes of the Chilean population made known to the world after September 11th.

Maryknoll's Doubletake

Maryknoll—officially, the Catholic Foreign Mission Society of America, Inc.—had at recent count 713 priests and brothers, 18 percent of all U.S. Roman Catholic missionaries working outside the U.S., with a major presence in Chile and other Latin American countries. Maryknoll Sisters, 611 in number, accounted for 20 percent of all U.S. missionary sisters abroad.

Over the years, Maryknoll sedulously projected the image of a dynamic organization, progressive in its mission philosophy, conscious of the need for social change in Latin America as a prerequisite to and concomitant of religious renewal.

For many people that image was clouded by an article in the April 1974 issue of Maryknoll, the slick, mass-circulation monthly magazine which plays an important part in Maryknoll's sophisticated fund-raising processes. Its author, Nicaraguan-born Miguel d'Escoto, is Maryknoll's director of communications. The article was a sweeping condemnation of Allende and of the "'emotional and ill-informed" liberals in the United States who continue to defend his memory. Frei, d'Escoto said, was correct when he said that "the military saved Chile"; and today Chileans "are enthusiastically collaborating with their new government."

The shock within Maryknoll was all the greater, because all Maryknollers had been strictly warned by their superiors not to express any views about the overthrow of Allende or the subsequent actions of the Junta, and almost everyone had fully observed that ban. One of the few exceptions had been The Reverend Charles Curry. Just back from five years in Chile, he said in a news interview in November 1973 that Chile was becoming "more democratic" under Allende, with the poor achieving some of the status and share of the national production which were their right, whereas the Junta was committing the kind of violations which it falsely attributed to Allende. And in February 1974, the Maryknoll missionaries of the Peru region urged the Maryknoll superiors to give public support to the protest against the repression of human rights in Chile just issued by the U.S. bishops.

Actually, Father d'Escoto was the victim of his own emotions and misinformation. A "confidential" document sent by a small group of Chilean bishops (backers of the Junta) in December to bishops in other Latin American countries was "leaked" to him as being the expression of the official stand of all Chilean bishops. Ignoring all contrary evidence, he followed its line slavishly, but without referring to it, and consequently assuming responsibility for all its distortions.

D'Escoto was further disserved by the time lag in Maryknoll's publication. By the time the article hit the newsstands, the Chilean bishops had broken their silence with the denunciation of the Junta's methods published in this issue.

Maryknoll was understandably embarrassed. The General Council had a new article prepared offering a different evaluation. D'Escoto himself also wrote a new article, in which he called the bishops' Easter statement "the most effective indictment to date of the conduct of the military leaders." Protests poured in from individuals and groups. Yet the General Council decided to publish neither the new articles nor the protests. The reason, as offered to IDOC by The Reverend Raymond A. Hill, Superior General, is that the original article was not "a statement of Society policy" and that "the magazine has proven its weakness in trying to serve as a current news (sic) magazine, and that we will try to avoid this in the future."

Response from Maryknoll Sisters was particularly vigorous. Part of the reason may have been the concern of the Sisters to stress that they are—in the words of Sister Barbara Hendricks, Community President—"distinct, financially and structurally" from the Maryknoll Fathers and that the magazine is a creation of the Fathers "and does not therefore necessarily reflect the experience and opinions of the Maryknoll Sisters." It is also probably true that the Sisters are more advanced theologically and emotionally than the priests, the former a sociological group recognizing the need for structural revolution, the latter still locked into the philosophy of developmentalism. This split has been widely evident in the U.S. church at home and abroad since Vatican II; the priests threatened by change, the Sisters—with nothing to lose—embracing it.

One Sister wrote d'Escoto that his article had caused "great sadness among some Maryknoll Sisters and other communities who work here in Santiago. We cannot be included among your 'best-informed sources,' . . . because those of us living in the marginal areas of Chile are not heard. We also know some of your statements are outright falsehoods. . . . The people who live there (in the poblaciones) are not all of the Chilean people, but they are many, and they are God's preferred children, his poor —his poor who suffer with no voice, underneath the white-washed daily news the press and radio present. . . . 'Tell them we are suffering,' one woman said. A simple request, to those who will hear."

A letter from two Maryknoll priests in Peru, reproduced below, puts the d'Escoto article in a broader perspective. One of its authors, The Reverend Darryl Hunt, has been head in Lima, Peru, of the Noticias Aliadas and Latinamerica Press, a news service in Spanish and English, for several years. The other, The Reverend John Wiggins, moved to Peru from Chile shortly after the Junta seized power.

This letter was discussed at a meeting of all regional superiors at Maryknoll, New York, in April 1974. No action resulted.

Miguel d'Escoto in Maryknoll

Politically and socially Chile is a unique country. The democratic election of Marxist Salvador Allende in 1970 and its subsequent ratification by a non-Marxist congress was a first in the world. Both the people who voted for him and the Christian Democrat Party—who decided to honor the majority which Allende had obtained at the polls by giving him their indispensable congressional confirmation—believed the campaign rhetoric: that Allende's was to be a different kind of Marxism.

Chile's alternative to capitalism was not to be a society fashioned after the example of Cuba or Russia for, as Allende claimed, true Marxism must take into account a people's cultural values and distinctiveness. His revolution was to have the taste of "beef turnovers and wine." To his constituency that meant it was to be genuinely Chilean: free, democratic, respecting always the right to dissent and criticize.

However, as often happens elsewhere, any resemblance between campaign rhetoric and the reality of the administration was accidental. Unidad Popular (the Marxist coalition which formed Allende's government) quickly realized that Chile's time-honored tradition of separation of powers did not allow the executive branch of government to turn its latest whims into the law of the land. Contrary to the case with Castro, Cuba's dictator whom we now know to have been Allende's idol and mentor, Chilean presidents have to deal with a congress, a supreme court and a *contraloria* (supervisory body on constitutionality of executive measures).

Thus Allende's only hope became the armed forces. He had hoped that this well-trained and traditionally highly respected body of men could be won over to his side in the fast-widening struggle between the executive and the other branches of the Chilean government. For months the future of Chile depended on whether Allende's well-known *muñequeo*, or ability to persuade, was greater than the sophistication and patriotism of the armed forces.

The outcome is by now known to everybody, but the interpretations given in this country to the overthrow of September 11, 1973, have largely been gravely mistaken, due mainly to the emotional and ill-informed liberalism which characterizes much of the information being produced in the media. Idealistic and sensitive people, who are understandably frustrated by capitalism's failure to produce a more humane society, often lack the insight and factual background needed to accurately evaluate the alternatives open to Chile. Thus many well-intentioned people continue readily to accept a Marxist interpretation of recent events in Chile and firmly deny they have been deceived, even after facts clearly demonstrate that this has been the case.

To Prevent Chaos

The action of the Chilean military against the Marxist government should not be confused with a rightist military coup, so common in other countries in Latin America. It was, according to Chile's best-informed sources, the only effective way to end the irresponsible adventures of a government that had all but led Chile into total national chaos.

The military were, if anything, almost too respectful of Chile's long-standing tradition of military nonintervention. They moved reluctantly but decisively when it was obvious that Allende's government had placed itself in direct opposition to constitutional legality and thereby threatened their country, which they had pledged themselves to defend.

With President Eduardo Frei, twice-elected predecessor of Allende, one can honestly say that "the military saved Chile"— saved it from the greatest threat to its national identity and sovereignty since the days of independence. According to Chile's best-informed sources, the military action of September 11, 1973, was dictated by Chile's past, present, and future, and not, as some would claim, the action of reactionary and/or irresponsible military who could no longer tolerate the "progressive" measures of Allende's government.

Hopes for the Future

As we look to the future, with great love and respect for the Chilean people, we can only hope that, just as the military did not succumb to the pressures of the Allende government, they will not now allow the well-organized forces of the right to turn a patriotically conceived government into a reactionary, repressive nightmare. This, unfortunately, is more than a remote possibility at this moment.

The Chilean people are enthusiastically collaborating with their new government in the arduous task of reconstruction. They are also patiently but anxiously waiting for the Junta to announce a date when free elections can once more be held in their great country.

The Junta has inherited a situation more difficult than that of any previous government and it is safe to assume that no political party could rationally wish to be in power at this moment. It will require a long time to put Chile back on its feet again. But even if it be three or four years from now, the Chilean people understandably want to have a date set for the next election. ■

The Hunt-Wiggins Letter

Rev. Raymond Hill, M.M.,
Superior General, and
The Maryknoll Regional Superiors
Maryknoll, N.Y. 10545

Dear Maryknoll Superiors:

We are addressing ourselves to you on an issue which may have profound effects on the future of the Society and Maryknoll policy for many years to come—the question of the present situation in Chile.

Since our office is a central source of news on Latin American trends and issues we feel that we would be remiss in our duty not to inform all of you to the best of our ability as regards the present Chilean scene.

1. We are convinced that many Church elements associated with the former Frei government and the Christian Democratic Party are engaged in a campaign which is clouding the issue of atrocities and fascism being employed by the ruling military Junta. Our analysis is based on the actions of Bishop Alfonso Lopez Trujillo and Fr. Renato Poblete, S.J. and their anti-marxist, pro hard-line (Frei) stand emanating from their related groups and agencies: e.g., CELAM statements, press conferences, the magazine *Mensaje*, etc. We also feel that the April 1974 *Maryknoll* Magazine article on Chile reflects the same kind of position.

This faction fought openly, and subtly, against the Allende government, aligning itself with the upper classes while opting closed-mindedly for an anti-socialist position. It is taking advantage of the present crisis for its own political aims and insists that it is *a-political*. Most Chilean bishops have belonged to this faction and still do. This is easily deduced from an analysis of Bishop Oviedo's letters, both the public and private ones, while he was

Secretary of the Chilean Bishops' Permanent Commission. It is also evident in the condemnation made of the "Christians for Socialism" movement by the Chilean hierarchy previous to the military coup and its subsequent release for publication after the coup.

2. News and information on the scope of the Junta's activities and atrocities are not available in the usual news media of Chile. Those living in Chile, especially if they were not aligned with the Unidad Popular of Allende before, are susceptible to the heavy influence of the press, radio and television that is now 100 percent controlled by the military. They were used to one of the finest free presses in the world up until September 11, 1973. Given this to understand, there is a great propensity to underestimate and play down the actual facts.

The real facts are that thousands of workers have been murdered, thousands of officers and enlisted men likewise, tens of thousands jailed without charges, many of them tortured brutally, many given 15-minute trials followed by death penalties or long jail sentences, many exiled or persecuted into exile. We ourselves are witnesses to at least 50 cases of refugees here in Lima, many of whom show signs of torture, and we know that there have been at least 3,000 more Chilean refugees channeled through Lima alone.

And the present facts should be considered within the whole context of what happened in Chile since Allende's popular election—the open conspiracy of the multinationals, especially ITT, and the CIA's involvement, just to mention some of the shameful ingredients.

In our opinion Maryknoll cannot, must not, stand silent in the face of such assaults on the human dignity of their fellow men in a region where it claims to be witnessing to Christ's liberation. The Society must make a statement denouncing these facts. They are undeniable.

Even the British government suspended military and economic aid because of them. A strong statement should be made even if it results in the expulsion of Maryknollers. For those men in the Chile region who would oppose such a statement, they should be given the opportunity to either leave the country beforehand or to make an opposing statement, if they deem it necessary. We enclose the Canadian missioners' manifesto [reprinted in "The Church and Chile" section of this book, p. 125] as an example of such a statement.

If it is said that a strong statement cannot be made because "the people need us to stay in Chile" and this could quite possibly result in expulsion, we say that the people need us more to denounce their mistreatment to the world. And they need us to be true to our own preaching of the Gospel.

We feel that the Church of Latin America needs this kind of strong statement and possible action. Other mission societies smaller than ours need the encouragement to speak out. Maryknoll can supply this help. Not to speak out is to widen the credibility gap that already exists among the masses who judge that we really are agents of our government and not of Christ.

Most of the background sources for a statement are available through the Social Communications Department's clipping service on Chile, our own *Latinamerica Press* bulletins since September and the U.S. State Department's reports.

Be assured of our prayers that you will have a very successful meeting in the Spirit,
(signed)
John Wiggins, M.M.
Darryl Hunt, M.M.
April 17, 1974

CHILE IN THE U.S. CONGRESS

The Administration of the United States has at no time wavered in its support of the Chilean Junta, no matter how gravely it has been embarrassed by the Junta's disregard of the conventions of civilized societies. In the U.S. Congress, on the other hand, significant elements of concern for human rights and elementary justice are on record. If U.S. policies are to be modified, this is where the process must be initiated.

One line of approach is the provision of aid for Chilean nonimmigrant residents of the United States. Their status and possible ways to improve it are indicated in proposals for legislation made by Representative George E. Brown, Jr. (D-Calif.).

Other areas in which alliances with a broad spectrum of interests are possible is in relation to the appropriations for foreign aid and foreign assistance. Below will be found proposals to introduce stipulations in such legislation that would bring pressure on the Chilean Junta to modify its activities.

Also noteworthy is the statement read into the *Congressional Record* of Senator Edward M. Kennedy (D-Mass.) on American policy toward Chile. As chairman of a Senate subcommittee on refugees, Senator Kennedy has played a leading role in keeping the problems of Chile in the public eye.

A National Legislative Congress in Washington in mid-July brought further grassroots pressure on senators and congressmen to support the amendments to the Foreign Assistance Act that would pressure the Chilean Junta to stop violating human rights. This Congress, sponsored by the National Coordinating Committee in Solidarity with Chile, brought together representatives of member groups from 30 states. The participation of the Women's International League for Peace and Freedom (WILPF) was particularly impressive.

Following a general survey of past and continuing efforts on behalf of Chile in Congress are four important statements: the opening speech of Representative Robert O. Tiernan (D-R.I.), and the ensuing debate, on his amendment to the Foreign Assistance Appropriations Bill, H.R. 11771 (December 11, 1973) with the voting line-up on that amendment; Senator Kennedy's challenge of U.S. policy toward Chile (February 5, 1974); two speeches by Congressman Brown on the plight of Chilean refugees (March 12 and 19, 1974); and the report by Representative Donald M. Fraser (D-Minn.) to the House on the International Commission of Jurists' mission to Chile.

U.S. Administration Stand Challenged

The Foreign Assistance Act of 1973, passed on December 5, 1973, contained a modified version of the Kennedy Amendment in Section 35[10], "Rights in Chile," which supposedly recorded, and outlined the methods for pursuing, a U.S. commitment to investigating and guaranteeing the preservation of human rights in Chile.

To several members of Congress, however, the flimsi-ness of this provision was obvious. First, the initiative for investigating violations of human rights was left solely with the President and the Department of State. Furthermore, Section 35 failed to check the flow of military assistance to the Chilean Junta, or expressly to deny further military aid unless and until human rights were guaranteed. Following is the text of that section:

SEC. 35[10]. It is the sense of the Congress that (1) the President should request the Government of Chile to protect the human rights of all individuals, Chilean and foreign, as provided in the Universal Declaration of Human Rights, the Convention and Protocol Relating the Status of Refugees, and other relevant international legal instruments guaranteeing the granting of asylum, safe conduct and the humane treatment or release of prisoners; (2) the President should support international humanitarian initiatives by the United Nations High Commissioner for Refugees and the International Committee of the Red Cross to insure the protection and safe conduct and resettlement of political refugees, the humane treatment of political prisoners, and the full inspection of detention facilities under international auspices; (3) the President should support and facilitate efforts by voluntary agencies to meet emergency relief needs; and (4) the President should request of the Inter-American Commission on Human Rights to undertake an immediate inquiry into recent events occurring in Chile.

The following article by Gary MacEoin includes a summary of the current challenges to the 1974 Foreign Aid Bill taking place in the Congress and a curious interview with a State Department spokesman on U.S. policy in Chile.

Pressure is building up in Congress for amendments to the Foreign Aid Bill of 1974 (S. 3394) that would cut off military aid to governments in violation of generally accepted international standards in their treatment of their citizens. Groups concerned for violations of human rights in Chile are leading the movement, gravely embarrassing the Administration which stubbornly identifies the interests of the United States with the Chilean Junta.

Amendments already introduced or being prepared would block aid to Brazil and Bolivia, the two countries scheduled for most military aid in fiscal 1975, as well as to Chile, for which the bill asks $20.5 million in military credit sales and $800,000 in grant military assistance. The Administration wants to increase total military credit sales from $325 million to $555 million.

Amendments Proposed

Senator James Abourezk (D-S.D.) has formulated in two amendments the minimum ingredients for a foreign policy that values human rights. They would make military aid contingent on a government's providing access to international humanitarian agencies; and they would end support for foreign police, paramilitary, internal surveillance, and prison systems.

1. No funds made available under this or any other law shall be used to provide military assistance, or to make military sales, credit sales, or guarantees, to or for any foreign government during any period in which that government does not allow such international organizations as the International Committee of the Red Cross, the International Commission of Jurists, Amnesty International and the Inter-American Commission on Human Rights free access into the prisons of the said country for the sole purpose of inspecting alleged violations of human rights.

2. None of the funds made available to carry out this or any other Act, and none of the local curren-

cies accruing under this or any Act, shall be used to provide training or advice, or provide any financial support, for police, prisons, or other internal security forces of any foreign government or any program of internal intelligence or surveillance on behalf of any foreign government within the United States or abroad.

Congressmen Donald Fraser (D-Minn.) and Michael Harrington (D-Mass.) are preparing similar amendments in the House, Fraser seeking a general restriction on all violators of human rights, Harrington concentrating on Chile. Senator Abourezk is also considering an amendment obligating the President to report to Congress on the status of human rights in any country requesting military aid, a report comparable to an "environmental impact statement."

Congressional investigative units have been concerned with human rights in Chile ever since the Junta seized power last September. First was a Senate investigation, headed by Senator Edward Kennedy (D-Mass.), of refugee and humanitarian issues. Then came a House study of human rights, under Donald Fraser, which established the fact of "widespread torture" in Chile and found "the response of the U.S. Government to be lacking in view of the magnitude of the violations committed."

Testimony Given

More recently, in May and June, an impressive roster of witnesses gave testimony, most of them just back from on-the-spot investigations, and all of them were unanimous in their condemnation of the Junta's continuing violations of human rights.

Several witnesses reported on the "show trials" now being conducted, the first public trials in the military courts since the Junta seized power. They included Charles Porter and Ira Lowe of the Fair Trial Committee for Chilean Political Prisoners; Covey T. Oliver, former Assistant Secretary of State for Latin America (International Commission of Jurists); former Attorney General Ramsey Clark; and Judge William Booth. The Clark-Booth study was funded by the National Council of Churches.

In other areas, Richard Fagen, incoming president of the Latin American Studies Association, testified on the violations of academic freedom in Chile, and Professor of Law Frank Newman, University of California (Berkeley), reported on the efforts of the U.N. Commission on Human Rights on behalf of refugees and political prisoners in Chile.

Ramsey Clark's testimony on June 11 acquired particular significance the following day when Harry W. Shlaudeman, Deputy Assistant Secretary of State, was examined by Congressman Fraser. Shlaudeman testified that the State Department position is that the Chilean Junta's declaration of a state of seige is in accordance with the Chilean constitution. The Clark statement had clearly established that the state of seige is illegal under the Chilean constitution, as are the measures taken by the Junta under it.

Shlaudeman has a reputation as a hatchet man. He was chief political officer in Santo Domingo from 1962 to 1965, playing a major role in negotiations with the Dominicans which led to the ouster of President Juan Bosch, the U.S. invasion, and the restoration of the dictatorship. He was deputy chief of mission in Chile from 1969 to 1973. Congressman Fraser questioned him aggressively and extracted some extremely revealing non-answers. The questions were related to an opening statement in which Shlaudeman stated that the U.S. government had "adhered to a policy of non-intervention in Chile's internal affairs during the Allende period."

Fraser: If it turned out to be a fact that the U.S. channeled money covertly to opposition political parties, would that be at variance with the policy of non-intervention?

Shlaudeman: Well, I am not sure. I am not sure that it would be, I would like to think about that. . . .

Fraser: Did the U.S. Government covertly supply money to opposition political parties following the 1970 election?

Shlaudeman: Well, I would like to postpone that question. . . .

Fraser: Are you prepared today to deny an assertion that the U.S. funneled money covertly to opposition political parties following the 1970 elections in Chile?

Shlaudeman: I am not. . . .

Fraser: You do agree that you have some knowledge of the facts?

Shlaudeman: Of course I do.

Fraser: You do know the facts?

Shlaudeman: Yes.

Fraser: On the basis of that knowledge you are not prepared to deny that the U.S. funneled money covertly to opposition political parties after the 1970 election in Chile?

Shlaudeman: I would like to be careful about what I say. . . .

Fraser: If money went through other political parties such as in Europe and came back to Chile, you would conclude that is a direct form of aid?

Shlaudeman: This is getting in a very complicated situation. . . . I would prefer to have the opportunity to make sure that I am precisely correct when I answer.

Fraser: Would you then be agreeable to returning to the subcommittee after you have rechecked the facts and responding as fully as you can to the question which I have put to you?

Shlaudeman: I would have to check that, too.

Further questioning elicited the information that the U.S. government is ignoring Section 35 of the Foreign Assistance Act of 1973. In this section, the Congress called on the President to urge the Chilean Junta to protect the human rights of Chileans and foreigners in Chile; to support international initiatives for the protection, safe conduct and resettlement of political refugees; and to ask the Inter-American Commission on Human Rights to inquire into the recent events in Chile.

The reason for ignoring this section, Mr. Shlaudeman testified, is that the Junta has assured the U.S. government that there are no "political prisoners of conscience" in Chile, that all prisoners are being held either for reasons of public security or to be charged with crimes under statutes dating from before the military seizure of power. At almost the same moment, the several hundred prisoners still being held in the National Stadium in Santiago were being told by General Oscar Bonilla Bradanovic, Minister of the Interior, that they would soon be moved to quarters more appropriate to their status as "prisoners of war."

The Foreign Aid Bill is still in committee in both the Senate and the House. The bill may be called on the floor of the House during the last week of July, and in the Senate probably early in August. ■

Excerpts from the *Congressional Record*

Rep. Robert O. Tiernan

On December 11, 1973, exactly three months after the military overthrow of the Allende government in Chile, the U.S. House of Representatives opened debate on the provisions of the foreign assistance appropriations bill (H.R. 11771), the enabling legislation for the Foreign Assistance Act of 1973, which had been passed on December 5.

During this debate, Representative Robert O. Tiernan (D-R.I.), a member of the House Appropriations Committee which had prepared the bill, appealed to the entire House to amend that bill specifically to prohibit financing foreign military credit sales to Chile. Following is the debate on that amendment, as

recorded in Congressional Record.

The other speakers whose remarks are included are Otto E. Passman (D-La.), Edward I. Koch (D-N.Y.), Robert A. Roe (D-N.J.), Samuel H. Young (R-Ill.), Garner E. Shriver (R-Kans.), George H. Mahon (D-Tex.), Michael J. Harrington (D-Mass.), Donald R. Fraser (D-Minn.), John B. Conlan (R-Ariz.), and Bella S. Abzug (D-N.Y.).

As the roll call shows, the amendment was soundly defeated, 304-102.

The Clerk read as follows:
Amendment offered by Mr. Tiernan: On page 13, line 25, insert "and none of these monies shall be used to finance military credit sales to Chile."
(Mr. Tiernan asked and was given permission to revise and extend his remarks.)

Mr. Tiernan. Mr. Chairman, in the conference report on the Foreign Assistance Act of 1973 past, which passed the House of Representatives on December 4 and is now before the President for his signature, section 32 of that bill reads as follows:

It is the sense of Congress that the President should deny any economic or military assistance to the government of any foreign country which practices the internment or imprisonment of that country's citizens for political purposes.

Now, my amendment would merely cut out the assistance to Chile, because it is clear that country is allowing that type of action, which we clearly set forth in the legislative enactment which I indicated had passed this House on December 4 and clearly since September 12 that government has held in Chile over 200 political prisoners.

Overwhelmingly, the Members of this House have indicated that they do not want to encourage any country to keep political prisoners within that country. The evidence is quite clear, and I am sure the Members of this House know the situation in Chile at this time. I think the amendment would be a very strong addition to this bill.

Mr. Passman. Mr. Chairman, I rise in opposition to the amendment.

Mr. Chairman, I want to say again that I have profound respect for my distinguished colleague from Rhode Island, but it is hard for me to believe that he is serious about offering this amendment. Chile was Communist. It had a Communist leader. No nation in the Western Hemisphere deteriorated as rapidly as Chile under the Communist regime.

They kicked out the Communist regime and they now have a friendly government, a government working towards democracy. Out of some 40 nations that we have in the military assistance program, we only provide $1 million for Chile for the training program and $10 million in credit sales.

We provided aid to the Communist regime in Chile. There were no objections last year that I know of to giving aid to Chile when they had a Communist regime, but now we have a friendly regime trying to develop a democracy, and to cut these funds out could conceivably turn them back the other way.

Mr. Chairman, I trust the members of the committee will vote this amendment down as we did the one offered a few moments ago. . . .

Mr. Koch. Mr. Chairman, first, I should like to say that I regret the calling of the quorum. It was not my doing, and I would want to have the amendment, which is not mine but Mr. Tiernan's, considered on the merits and not to have any irritability on the part of Members affect the final outcome. I will try as best I can to tell the Members why I rise in support of that amendment.

A young man who lived in my district and who went to Chile was, according to the reports available to me, killed by the Chilean Junta. That is why I am speaking tonight from this well in support of this amendment which would deprive Chile of further military aid. His name was Charles Horman. His wife, now a widow, and his father got in touch with me and told me what had happened. I will not give the Members the gory details, but I will tell you this: And it is in response to some of the comments that have been made by the opponents of the amendment with respect to Chile and the Allende government. I am not here to defend the Allende government. I disagreed with much that it did. There is no question but that Allende was a Marxist, a Communist, but the fact is that the Allende government was democratically elected, had a parliament made up of a majority of his opponents who were not Marxist or Communist, and there was a free press. It was a democratic government with an independent parliament and judiciary.

Today, as a result of the military Junta's activities, there are hundreds of people in jail, if not thousands. There are hundreds of people who have taken refuge in the various embassies. Indeed, the Swedish Ambassador was just expelled from the country because he was the only Ambassador to physically defend the refugees who had received his protection under international law and who, had they been picked up by the Junta, would have been slaughtered. He stopped them at the gate.

Why do I tell the Members this? I say this to the Members, not to praise the Allende government because I am not here to say praising things about the Allende government—many things that it did have got to be condemned—but what I am trying to convince them of is that it is not the role of the United States to involve itself in a civil war, because that, in fact, is what took place in Chile and what is taking place today.

There are many people who have written to me, and I believe many Members here have received similar letters, from those who believe that the CIA was in some way or other involved with the overthrow of the Chilean Government. Those suspicions have arisen by virtue of the fact that there were recent joint naval activities involving our Navy and the Chilean Navy. The suspicion comes out of the fact that many people believe we wanted to see the overthrow of that Government for good or bad reason. I have said to my constituents who have written that I hope and I want to believe we were not involved, that we learned our lesson.

But I know that if we continue to fund the Chilean Junta with additional arms so that it can engage in additional repression of its own citizens, that those suspicions will not be allayed but will be enhanced. So what I am saying in support of this amendment is that if we do not want to have the blood of the victims of the military Junta on our hands by virtue of their using our guns to shoot down their citizens, we should affirm the amendment. . . .

Mr. Passman. Mr. Chairman, will the gentleman yield?

Mr. Flood. I yield to the gentleman from Louisiana (Mr. Passman).

Mr. Passman. Mr. Chairman, I thank the distinguished gentleman from Pennsylvania for yielding.

I spoke on this amendment earlier but we have more Members here now. As we all know until recently we had a Communist regime in Chile and that country was deteriorating very rapidly. We now have a friendly government which is trying to form a democracy. There is a long way to go from communism to democracy.

In this bill for this friendly nation we have $1 million for military training and we have $10 million in military credit sales. I respect the distinguished gentleman from New York for his views but a little earlier the gentleman voted for $2.2 billion in military assistance and sales for Israel, and I did not hear any argument from the gentleman. I certainly hope that the Members will vote this amendment down.

Chile pulled away from communism. We have a democracy forming in a very friendly country and we would be flying in the face of this new government if this amendment were adopted. The military credit sales are short term and there is a favorable interest rate which will be applied to the loan. Only the $1 million is in the form of grant aid.

I hope the Members will consider this on the same basis as the earlier amendment and vote it down. . . .

Mr. Roe. Mr. Chairman, I rise in opposition to this amendment. I would like to call to the attention of Members of the House something I believe to be important.

One, there is no question that the Allende Government was a Communist government and a repressive government. I have facts which I know to be true which indicated that in one week's time, had the military not arisen, those revolutionaries who had infiltrated Chile would have joined with Allende and joined with that government and made it a totally Communist government. In one week's time that would have happened.

We ought to ask if the people of Chile have a right to self-determination. Of course they do. I think it is fundamentally wrong for us to say they have not when we founded our freedom in this country on a fight against oppression. Yes, we did. We based it on the facts and on the need and wants of our people. That does not mean I support bloodshed—I do not.

Chile has been a longtime friend of the United States. We have a temporary situation which has evolved. Our strength in this country and in our relationships with South America is critical. Our attitude toward Chile at this particular point could not be more critical as far as our whole Western Hemisphere relationship than it is now with Chile. It is wrong to say that we should not support Chile. The government has taken a friendly position and they are returning the expropriated land and expropriated industries and they are returning them back to private enterprise in those countries that had made the investment in the first place.

We should leave ourselves this one thought. If the Chileans were wrong, then why did the U.S.S.R. cut off their relationship with Chile?

They cut off their relations with Chile because they knew the jig was up and the game was over. We could be making the worst error in our Western Hemisphere relations by taking the situation we have today and supporting this particular amendment.

I trust the Members of the House will think clearly and concisely and recognize the strength of our country lies with our brothers in South America and let us not do something stupid that we cannot undo later on.

Mr. Young. Gentlemen, it was stated here a few moments ago that a certain citizen of the United States was killed in Chile, evidently from the State of New York. It was stated that if we did not vote to support this amendment that the blood of that particular citizen might be on our hands.

Well, I hope that that is not a correct statement. I represent the 10th District of Illinois in which Mr. Frank Teruggi was a resident. He was a citizen of the United States who was killed in Chile. I am going to vote against this amendment.

I do not think that if I vote against the amendment that I am going to have any blood on my hands, nor do I think the other Members of this assembly will have blood on their hands because they vote against this amendment.

I would also state that I am not here to defend the military Junta of Chile. I am critical of them. I tried to get information through the State Department about the circumstances of Mr. Teruggi's death. I have been trying for two and a half months. I have written a very caustic letter to the Secretary of State asking why we do not have better cooperation and better information about the death of Mr. Teruggi.

But I say that this foreign aid bill is an

entirely different matter. The tragic death of this young man has nothing whatsoever to do with the passage of this bill with respect to foreign military sales.

I think if this amendment is defeated or not defeated, it will not bring back these two young men who were killed in Chile.

I think the purpose of the amendment is wrong if it is going to be premised upon the argument advanced here today. I would not want to be a part of this body and vote against this amendment if I thought it would bring back either of these two citizens; it will not. I say, that is an irrelevant matter. Therefore, the amendment ought to be defeated. . . .

Mr. Shriver. Mr. Chairman, those of us on the subcommittee have been concerned with the results of cutbacks in making U.S. military equipment available to Latin American countries. It just does not work. They merely go elsewhere for their arms. They usually end up buying from some of our European allies who are only too happy to sell them whatever they want.

I do not see how it is in our national interest to antagonize our neighbor to the south, especially when we do not know what that government is about to do.

We must be reminded, these requests are illustrative and were made months and months ago. At that time Chile was under a Communist regime.

We have given assistance of this kind to every government of Chile, some rightwing governments, some Communist governments, a Populist government, a liberal government, and to this one; so it is certainly in our national interest to maintain our positions with our neighbor to the south.

Mr. Mahon. Mr. Chairman, I just want to say that the Committee on Appropriations approved the pending measure in its present form. It was considered in great detail. I agree it is not perfect but I hope the House will support the committee, and in my opinion, the best interests of the United States and the Western Hemisphere will be served by defeating this amendment by a resounding vote.

Mr. Harrington. Mr. Chairman, we have a rather clumsy, and I suppose awkward, doctrine that says we like to see nations in this world elect people freely. In 1970, after two or three less than satisfactory efforts, a fellow by the name of Salvador Allende was elected freely in Chile. He was a Marxist by definition, although I do not think he was much of a hard-line Marxist. He was a Socialist, and I thought that in the context of an era that has been called pluralistic—a word that has had currency on both sides of this aisle, and which recently led to the welcoming to this country as recently as last week of the head of the Communist state of Romania, and which has led to efforts to develop detente and rapprochement with both the Republic of China and Russia—we were finally going to rise above our usual compulsive obsession and concern with labels about countries in this world.

Obviously, listening to this debate, that is not the case—at least not in this instance. I was in Chile, and I do not have any particularly developed expertise as a result of about 48 hours of intensive conversations, but I visited a place called the National Stadium, which I would commend to the attention of those who tend to disparage the reports critical of the Junta which have appeared in the American press.

I saw a board on the wall which indicated that at one point in late September, some 5,000 individuals—some of them, perhaps, Americans—had been kept in that stadium. I am not here this afternoon to suggest that we defend Salvador Allende or that we offer eulogies for the Chilean people, who are sophisticated politically and who are concerned about the direction their country has taken and the degree of chaos that characterizes it.

Neither am I here to suggest that we refuse to aid the Junta by providing the Chilean people wheat, as we did within three weeks of the time the Junta took over, and by providing supplies of corn.

All I would suggest is that this Congress recognize that the Junta took over by force, whether we like it or not. They killed people, whether we like to admit to that or not. I do not think it important whether it was 1 million or 12 million; the point is, we have witnessed the destruction of a government freely elected by people three years ago, and we are now about to implicitly endorse that conduct. If we can aid the Chileans providing them with meals, because their economy is stagnated, and otherwise provide the sort of things that meet human needs, you will have no quarrel from me. But giving the Junta guns marked "made in the United States of America" or conducting training programs in the defense command school at Panama is hypocrisy of rank proportions.

Mr. Chairman, I think it is time to go on record and begin to reject the kind of obsessive concern we have had with things bearing the labels "Communist" or "Marxist," and to recognize that if we are going to do what we are doing in Russia; if we are going to do what we are doing in China; if we are going to welcome the President of Romania to this country, then—we can tolerate a regime like Allende's in Chile.

Mr. Chairman, I support in full the amendment offered by the gentleman from Rhode Island, and I hope we have the sense to design a foreign policy mature enough to suit the mid-1970's.

Mr. Fraser. Mr. Chairman, I rise in support of the amendment.

Mr. Chairman, I will not take the full five minutes.

The difficulty presented by the country of Chile today, if one sets aside the events of the coup, is that they have several thousand Chilean citizens who are in custody, whom they have acknowledged will not be brought to trial; will not be freed but will simply be kept in prison for an indefinite period of time. This treatment of Chilean citizens is in violation of the guarantees of international rights. It was violations of human rights which formed the foundation we accepted earlier today in denying to the Soviet Union credits and non-discriminatory tariff treatment. We acted on the grounds that the Soviet Union was violating its obligations under international covenants with respect to human rights.

Mr. Chairman, there is much to be said for the United States speaking out about violations of human rights, but for our position to be credible, we need to do it, whether it is occurring in the Soviet Union aimed primarily at Soviet Jewish citizens, or in Chile involving Chilean citizens who are in prison without the right to counsel, without the right to a trial, without any charges being brought, and with no prospect of release.

The past history of Chile, it seems to me, is not nearly so relevant as what the military Junta is doing today with respect to its international obligations. We lose credibility if we say in the case of one country we are going to stand firm in behalf of human rights and then say in respect to another country that we really do not care.

What I am able to tell the Members is based upon a statement by the Ministry of the Interior in Santiago, who acknowledges that these people will not be given a chance to have charges made against them, will not have a trial, and will not be represented by legal counsel.

Mr. Chairman, let us stand up for human rights. Let us stand up for decency. I believe we can show our concern by supporting this amendment, an amendment which, it seems to me, carries forward the same principles we expressed so clearly earlier today.

Mr. Conlan. Mr. Chairman, I rise in opposition to the amendment.

Briefly, there are just a couple of things that need to be rebutted, in answer to the statement made by the gentleman from Minnesota and the gentleman from Massachusetts.

There is a clear tendency to ignore the fact that the Allende government had only 38 percent of the vote; it had nowhere near the support of a majority of the population. Then, without any consent of the Congress of that nation, Allende and his Communist dominated regime moved in, using the entire patronage operation of the State, to deny housing except to those who supported the regime, to deny food and welfare except to those who supported the regime.

They used every instrument of power to clamp a dictatorship upon the people, and in the process, of course, there were some feelings and liberties deeply hurt.

The other point that has been raised here that detente is involved is a spurious one, and one that is not relevant. While we seek openings for trade, and while we seek openings for peace with the major Communist bloc countries, they are simultaneously training men and women through their activities in Cuba, and they are training men and women of all nationalities, through their apparatus worldwide, the techniques of subversion, sabotage and revolution in order to destroy democratic governments.

In this situation we have a responsibility to allow free world nations like Chile the opportunity to learn the techniques of self-defense.

I see nothing incompatible with our seeking detente with the major Communist bloc countries in the world and also granting the right, the techniques, and the tools of self-defense to a government such as that of Chile, which was able to reverse the activities in process before it went under a Communist dictatorship.

I think the amendment before us is most inappropriate and I urge its defeat. . . .

Mr. Roe. Just one more point. Is it not well documented that, yes, there were a good many people temporarily incarcerated, but it is well documented, also, and well known in Western circles that the bulk of those people were revolutionaries from up and down the whole Western Hemisphere, who were gathering in Chile to take it over and to deny the people the rights of freedom?

Let us talk about detente. We all agree on the point of human rights being respected. There is no one in this body who does not believe in human rights being respected. But let us not sacrifice human rights. However, we may be misguided by a lack of information and facts and in that way put the Chilean people back in chains, because that is what we would be doing if we voted for this amendment....

Ms. Abzug. Mr. Chairman, I rise in support of the amendment offered by Mr. Tiernan to strike U.S. aid to Chile.

On September 11, the legally elected, constitutional government of Dr. Salvador Allende was overthrown in a bloody coup d'etat.

What shocked people at that time were the daily reports of murder, arrest, torture, and imprisonment of thousands of individuals, members of the government and ordinary citizens, Chilean and non-Chilean alike. I was appalled as were the people of all democratic nations. In fact, I received pleas from the families and friends of some of the Americans who were arrested and held in confinement by the Junta, who I tried to assist. Their stories of brutality and deprivation of human freedom were overwhelming.

I am appalled today at the military aid this Congress is turning over to the military Junta of Chile. Just today *The Washington Post* reported that Harald Edelstam, the Swedish Ambassador to Chile, said "tortures, and arrests of people continue in Chile three months after the military takeover." Ambassador Edelstam also estimated that the Junta has been responsible for 15,000 deaths, the arrest of 7,000 people, and an additional 30,000 left homeless. On the same page in today's *Post* was a story reporting that there are several hundred people who remain inside the embassies of many nations, in asylum, unable to leave.

We cannot countenance American dollars going to repress the freedom of the individual. The present government in Chile remains in power by force. It took power through violence and reigns by violence.

It offends every notion of our concepts of democracy and defiles any meaning of foreign aid to use any money for this widely acknowledged repressive government.

The Chairman. The question is on the amendments offered by the gentleman from Rhode Island (Mr. Tiernan).

The question was taken, and the chairman announced that the noes appeared to have it.

Recorded Vote

Mr. Tiernan. Mr. Chairman, I demand a recorded vote.

A recorded vote was ordered.

The vote was taken by electronic device, and there were—ayes 102, noes 304, not voting 26, as follows:

[ROLL NO. 650]

AYES—102

Abzug	Gude	Reid
Adams	Hamilton	Reuss
Addabbo	Harrington	Riegle
Anderson,	Hawkins	Robison, N.Y.
Calif.	Hays	Rodino
Ashley	Hechler, W. Va.	Roncalio, Wyo.
Aspin	Hicks	Rose
Badillo	Holtzman	Rosenthal
Biester	Horton	Roush
Bingham	Hungate	Roy
Blatnik	Johnson, Colo.	Ryan
Bolling	Kastenmeier	St. Germain
Brademas	Koch	Sarbanes
Brasco	Kyros	Schroeder
Brown, Calif.	Leggett	Seiberling
Burton	Lehman	Stanton,
Carney, Ohio	Long, La.	James V.
Chisholm	Lujan	Stark
Clay	McCloskey	Stubblefield
Conyers	McCormack	Studds
Coughlin	Meeds	Teague, Tex.
Culver	Melcher	Thompson, N.J.
Dellenback	Metcalfe	Tiernan
Dellums	Mezvinsky	Udall
Denholm	Mink	Van Deerlin
Drinan	Moakley	Vanik
Eckhardt	Moorhead, Pa.	Vigorito
Edwards, Calif.	Mosher	Waldie
Esch	Moss	Wilson,
Ford,	Natcher	Charles H.,
William D.	Nedzi	Calif.
Fraser	Obey	Wolff
Gaydos	O'Hara	Yates
Gibbons	Owens	Yatron
Ginn	Pike	Young, Ga.
Green, Pa.	Rangel	

NOES—304

Alexander	Burlison, Mo.	Devine
Anderson, Ill.	Butler	Dickinson
Andrews, N.C.	Byron	Dingell
Andrews,	Camp	Donohue
N. Dak.	Carter	Dorn
Annunzio	Casey, Tex.	Downing
Archer	Cederberg	Dulski
Arends	Chappell	Duncan
Armstrong	Clancy	du Pont
Ashbrook	Clark	Edwards, Ala.
Bafalis	Clausen,	Eilberg
Baker	Don H.	Eshleman
Barrett	Clawson, Del	Evans, Colo.
Bauman	Cleveland	Evins, Tenn.
Beard	Cochran	Fascell
Bell	Cohen	Findley
Bennett	Collier	Flood
Bergland	Collins, Ill.	Flowers
Bevill	Collins, Tex.	Flynt
Biaggi	Conable	Foley
Blackburn	Conlan	Forsythe
Boggs	Conte	Fountain
Boland	Corman	Frelinghuysen
Bowen	Cotter	Frenzel
Bray	Crane	Frey
Breaux	Cronin	Froehlich
Breckinridge	Daniel, Dan	Fulton
Brinkley	Daniel, Robert	Fuqua
Brooks	W., Jr.	Gettys
Broomfield	Daniels,	Giaimo
Brotzman	Dominick V.	Gilman
Brown, Mich.	Danielson	Gonzalez
Brown, Ohio	Davis, Ga.	Goodling
Broyhill, N.C.	Davis, S.C.	Grasso
Broyhill, Va.	Davis, Wis.	Gray
Buchanan	de la Garza	Green, Oreg.
Burgener	Delaney	Griffiths
Burke, Fla.	Dennis	Gross
Burke, Mass.	Dent	Grover
Burleson, Tex.	Derwinski	Gunter
Guyer	Martin, N.C.	Satterfield
Haley	Mathias, Calif.	Scherle
Hammer-	Mathis, Ga.	Schneebeli
schmidt	Matsunaga	Sebelius
Hanley	Mayne	Shipley
Hanna	Mazzoli	Shriver
Hanrahan	Michel	Shuster
Hansen, Idaho	Milford	Sikes
Hansen, Wash.	Miller	Sisk
Harsha	Minish	Skubitz
Hastings	Minshall, Ohio	Slack
Heckler, Mass.	Mitchell, N.Y.	Smith, Iowa
Heinz	Mizell	Smith, N.Y.
Helstoski	Mollohan	Snyder
Henderson	Montgomery	Spence
Hillis	Moorhead,	Staggers
Hinshaw	Calif.	Stanton,
Hogan	Morgan	J. William
Holifield	Murphy, Ill.	Steed
Holt	Murphy, N.Y.	Steele
Hosmer	Myers	Steelman
Howard	Nelsen	Steiger, Ariz.
Huber	Nichols	Steiger, Wis.
Hudnut	Nix	Stephens
Hutchinson	O'Brien	Stratton
Ichord	O'Neill	Stuckey
Jarman	Parris	Symington
Johnson, Calif.	Passman	Symms
Johnson, Pa.	Patman	Talcott
Jones, Ala.	Patten	Taylor, Mo.
Jones, N.C.	Pepper	Taylor, N.C.
Jones, Okla.	Perkins	Teague, Calif.
Jones, Tenn.	Pettis	Thomson, Wis.
Jordan	Peyser	Thone
Karth	Pickle	Thornton
Kazen	Poage	Towell, Nev.
Kemp	Podell	Treen
Ketchum	Powell, Ohio	Ullman
Kluczynski	Preyer	Vander Jagt
Kuykendall	Price, Ill.	Waggonner
Landgrebe	Price, Tex.	Wampler
Landrum	Pritchard	Ware
Latta	Quie	White
Lent	Quillen	Whitehurst
Litton	Railsback	Whitten
Long, Md.	Randall	Widnall
Lott	Rarick	Wiggins
McClory	Rees	Williams
McCollister	Regula	Wilson, Bob
McDade	Rhodes	Wilson,
McEwen	Roberts	Charles, Tex.
McFall	Robinson, Va.	Winn
McKay	Roe	Wright
McKinney	Rogers	Wydler
McSpadden	Roncallo, N.Y.	Wylie
Macdonald	Rooney, Pa.	Wyman
Madden	Rostenkowski	Young, Alaska
Madigan	Rousselot	Young, Fla.
Mahon	Roybal	Young, Ill.
Mailliard	Runnels	Young, S.C.
Mallary	Ruppe	Young, Tex.
Mann	Ruth	Zablocki
Maraziti	Sandman	Zion
Martin, Nebr.	Sarasin	Zwach

NOT VOTING—26

Abdnor	Gubser	Rooney, N.Y.
Burke, Calif.	Harvey	Shoup
Carey, N.Y.	Hébert	Stokes
Chamberlain	Hunt	Sullivan
Diggs	Keating	Veysey
Erlenborn	King	Walsh
Fish	Mills, Ark.	Whalen
Fisher	Mitchell, Md.	Wyatt
Goldwater	Rinaldo	

So the amendments were rejected.

The result of the vote was announced as above recorded.

Sen. Edward M. Kennedy

Senator Edward M. Kennedy (D-Mass.), as chairman of the Senate Judiciary Subcommittee on Refugees and Escapees, has frequently focused the attention of the U.S. Congress on the need to respond to legitimate appeals for humanitarian aid from Chile. Following are his remarks of February 5, 1974, before the Senate and his presentation of the State Department's response of January 28, 1974, to questions submitted by him on October 18, 1973, as recorded in Congressional Record.

Mr. Kennedy. Mr. President, last October 18 I wrote to Secretary of State Henry A. Kissinger to inquire as to our Government's policy toward Chile, and our view of the continuing problems of political refugees and human rights violations. Last week I received a reply, which I would like to share with my Senate colleagues, because I believe it raises troubling questions about American policy toward Chile.

More than 4 months after the violent overthrow of the Allende government, the military junta in Chile apparently continues its gross violations of human rights. Reports in many quarters, including our Government as well as the most respected international humanitarian organizations, suggest continued repression, the denial of safe conduct passes to many political refugees, new waves of arrests, the torture of prisoners, and executions at an alarming rate.

Just a few weeks ago, Mr. President, the Congress expressed the view of most Americans when it resolved, in the foreign assistance authorization bill, that the President should make every effort to encourage the junta to respect human rights. The President signed this bill into law. But there is precious little evidence on the record to indicate that much has really been done.

In fact, the administration, in its growing support of the junta, has conveniently dismissed the continuing violations of human rights by labeling them as an "internal matter" of Chile. This despite the international presence of the United Nations High Commissioner for Refugees and the International Red Cross, and the appeals of many humanitarian organizations for American support in securing the junta's full cooperation in the humane treatment and relief of political prisoners, in the stay of executions among those convicted, in the granting of safe conduct to all refugees, and in the general lifting of repression and press censorship throughout the country.

Given Chile's long history of freedom and constitutional government—and our own claim to world leadership in this cause—the least our country should do is to support the appeals of these international organizations and expeditiously grant asylum to bonafide refugees. To do otherwise will be a serious default of international responsibility.

Mr. President, in line with the language of the foreign assistance authorization, I would hope we would see a sharp reversal in American policy toward the Chilean junta. The President should condition any U.S. military or general economic assistance on the junta's respect for human rights and progress in the restoration of constitutional government. We should respond to legitimate appeals for humanitarian aid, including a pending request from the Red Cross for emergency relief and medical supplies, but all general aid should be made conditional to the junta's response to the appeals of the Red Cross and the U.N. High Commissioner for Refugees.

Mr. President, I ask unanimous consent that the full text of my questions and the Department of State's reply be printed in the *Record.*

There being no objection, the text was ordered to be printed in the *Record,* as follows:

State Department's Response of January 28, 1974, to Questions on Chile Submitted by Senator Kennedy on October 18, 1973

1. Q. What is the Department's current assessment of allegations regarding: Widespread killing, executions, torture, etc.? What is the Department's current understanding of the cumulative total of persons killed, executed, arrested, detained, etc.? What is the Department's overall assessment of the impact of the overthrow of the Allende Government on political activities, civil liberties, and human rights in Chile?

1. A. "Some of the facts at issue in this question are as difficult to provide today as they were several months ago. Very few hard facts are available and unofficial estimates vary widely in range. [deletion] * A substantial percentage of these persons undoubtedly died during the skirmishing that took place the first day or two of the change of government. Approximately one hundred executions, usually of persons charged with engaging in armed resistance, have been acknowledged by Chilean authorities, almost all of them taking place in the month or so following the events of September 11. Some forty persons reportedly were killed attempting to escape military custody; again most of these took place in the

---

*Portions of the Department of State's reply were classified "confidential" and have been deleted at the Department's request.

September-October period. Although various interpretations could be given to the term "wide-spread killing," aside from the initial day or two of combat, some instances of curfew violations, the acknowledged executions mentioned above, a few skirmishes involving armed resistors and those announced as killed while attempting to escape, there are confirmed reports of only a few additional deaths. I would add, by way of illustration of the complexities, that the widely reported destruction of the Sumar textile mill by tank fire never took place.

We are unable to judge the validity of the charges of torture. We do note, however, that the Chilean Government has repeatedly denied that it is engaging in inhumane practices.

On the number of arrests, estimates are that some 7-8,000 persons were arrested and originally held in Santiago's National Stadium, the principal detention center following September 11. Of these, some 6,500 persons were released unconditionally, about 555 at last reports were being held in various jails and the rest are in some pending status or other. Figures for current detentions in Santiago and elsewhere are virtually impossible to verify but our impression is that the majority of those originally detained have since been released. The fact that some new detentions occur as others are released complicates any compilation.

In terms of the impact of the change of government on Chilean institutions, the new government has declared the legislature dissolved and, as provided in existing state of siege legislation, has suspended constitutional guarantees; Marxist political parties have been banned and the activities of other parties suspended; those newspapers allowed to publish are censored; and trade union activity has been circumscribed. While military courts have jurisdiction over all internal security cases, the civil court system continues to function. The authorities have promised eventual normalization, but have anticipated in public announcements that the extraordinary measures will persist at least until mid-1974."

. . . .

6. Q. Were any persons given asylum in the American Embassy? Were any persons refused asylum in the American Embassy, and, if so, on what grounds? Generally elaborate on United States policy towards granting asylum to an American Embassy or United States government office overseas.

6. A. "There have been no requests nor grants of asylum by the American Embassy in Santiago. In contrast to the Latin American Governments which practice diplomatic asylum, the U.S. does not recognize that such a right is sanctioned by general international law or by a regional rule of law. As a result, we are not a party to the following: Convention on Asylum signed at Havana, Feb. 20, 1928; Convention on Political Asylum signed at Montevideo, Dec. 26, 1973; Convention on Diplomatic Asylum signed at Caracas, March 28, 1954. Until 1972, U.S. policy on asylum—including diplomatic asylum— was carried out on the basis of long accepted general understandings and traditional U.S. conceptions and was not spelled out in any single place. The Kudirka Incident in 1970 resulted in a full, interagency review of asylum policy. This

policy closely follows that which has been historically followed by the U.S., though with some exceptions in execution.

The principal change in the 1972 policy was to provide granting of temporary refuge for humanitarian reasons wherein the life or safety of a person is put in danger, such as pursuit by a mob. The previous policy covered only imminent danger to the life of the individual. Both past and current U.S. policy on asylum strongly emphasize the temporary nature of the refuge provided. Enclosed is a copy of the U.S. General Policy for Asylum Requests. Part Three contains instructions for Asylum Requests. Part Three contains instructions for our overseas posts."

7. Q. Generally describe our Embassy's activities in behalf of the Americans present in Chile during and following the military coup? What specific activities were carried out in behalf of Americans detained, missing, etc.? Has the Department been satisfied by the response of Chilean authorities to official American inquiries and activities in this area of concern?

7. A. "The Embassy was involved in working to protect some 2,800 American citizens in Chile. As of mid-October, our Embassy had investigated the status of or directly assisted over 600 American citizens, ascertaining their whereabouts, informing relatives or friends in the U.S. about their welfare, obtaining the release of 17 American citizens under detention and obtaining safe conduct passes and arranging international transportation for more than 40 individuals. This was done in the midst of street violence, administrative disorganization in the Chilean Government, the absence of diplomatic relations with the new government until September 24 which occasioned difficulties in communicating, a rigid all-night curfew and severe restrictions on movement and activity of all civilians.

Unfortunately, two American citizens died during this period. An initial report has been received from the Chilean authorities related to the circumstances of these two deaths; we are pressing for more information."

12. Q. Define the considerations which led to United States recognition of the Chilean military government on September 24. Did any bi-lateral understandings, commitments, etc. accompany American recognition of the junta?

12. A. "Our Embassy received a circular note from the Chilean authorities on September 12, 1973, announcing the formation of a new government and requesting continuance of diplomatic relations. On September 24, after more than twenty countries, including Great Britain and West Germany, had resumed relations with the new government, our Embassy responded to the circular note indicating our desire to maintain relations between the two countries. By that time the new government was in clear control of Chilean territory and had pledged to respect international undertakings of previous Chilean administrations. As of this date, more than sixty countries including the People's Republic of China have either resumed or renewed diplomatic relations with the new Government of Chile, the main exceptions being some of the nations of Eastern Europe.

The continuation of relations *per se* implies neither our approval nor disapproval of a government's genesis or policies. This is in accordance not only with State Department practices in recent years but also with Senate Resolution 205 of 1969 which states:

That it is the sense of the Senate that when the United States recognizes a foreign government and exchanges diplomatic representatives with it, this does not imply that the United States approves of the form, ideology or policy of that foreign government."

No new bilateral understandings or commitments accompanied the normalization of relations with the new government."

13. Q. Describe any new United States aid or other commitments to Chile since the Allende government's overthrow by the junta. Describe any pending Chilean requests to and/or negotiations with the U.S. Describe any United States aid or other commitments to Chile as of early September 1973. Describe any pending Chilean requests to and/or negotiations with the United States, again, as of early September 1973. What effect did the Allende government's overthrow have on these commitments, requests and/or negotiations?

13. A. "As of early September 1973 the United States Government was conducting assistance and cooperative efforts with the Government of Chile. These included such activities as the Food for Peace and Peace Corps programs, technical training, community development, narcotics control and various forms of scientific research and collaboration. In addition, Foreign Military Sales (FMS) credits were provided to Chile in response to requests by the Allende Government. These credits, which are at near commercial rates, were within the range of similar credits provided to other Latin American countries and to Chile in previous years.

On several occasions in 1972 and early 1973, U.S. and Chilean representatives met to consider ways of achieving a mutually satisfactory resolution of the major issues between us, particularly the problem of compensating U.S. investors for expropriated properties and the Chilean Government's default of its foreign debts. The last such meeting was held August 16-17 in Washington. These continuing conversations were overtaken by the events of September 11.

In response to an urgent request from the new Chilean authorities following the skirmishing which accompanied the Allende Government's ouster, we provided emergency medical supplies to Chile under the disaster relief program of the Agency for International Development. To meet emergency food requirements in Chile, partially caused by the diversion away from Chile of grain shipments then en route from Eastern Europe, we provided commercial financing from the Commodity Credit Corporation (CCC) of the Department of Agriculture for export shipments of U.S. wheat and feed grains to Chile. Immediately after the change in government, wheat and flour stocks in Chile were down to a few weeks supply and the shipment financed by the CCC credit—equivalent to about one month's consumption—helped avert a serious bread shortage for the Chilean people.

The Chilean Government also has requested long-term financing for the purchase of U.S. foodstuffs under Title I of P.L. 480. This request is still pending.

Military assistance commitments made to the Allende Government continue to be met. New requests will considered on their merits.

In recent weeks negotiations have taken place for the rescheduling of unpaid Chilean debts to agencies of the United States Government which fell due in late 1971 and 1973. Agreement was reached between the two governments and an initial repayment installment of $16 million has been made by the Chileans. The Paris Club of creditors is to meet with Chilean representatives this February to consider the rescheduling of 1973 and 1974 debt repayments. The new government has also entered into direct talks with certain U.S. investors concerning ex-propriated properties.

14. Q. Was the overthrow of the Allende government in Chile in the best interests of the United States? Elaborate.

14. A. "In his testimony on September 20 before the House Subcommittee on Inter-American Affairs, Assistant Secretary Jack B. Kubisch stated:

We were not responsible for the difficulties in which Chile found itself, and it is not for us to judge what would have been best or will be best for the Chilean people.

I would add that observations made by President Nixon in his 1972 Foreign Policy Report to the Congress have continuing relevance:

In our view the hemisphere community is big enough, mature enough and tolerant enough to accept a diversity of national approaches to human goals. We therefore deal realistically with governments as they are—right and left. We have strong preferences and hope to see democratic processes prevail, but we cannot impose our political structure on other nations. We respect the hemispheric principle of non-intervention. We shape our relations with governments according to their policies and actions as they affect our interests and the interests of the Inter-American system, not according to their domestic structures.

15. Q. Regarding contacts between United States personnel attached to the Embassy and Chilean military personnel, list the names of the personnel involved, the dates of contact, and the subjects of conversation during the 10 days immediately preceding the coup.

15. A. "There has not been any reason to keep comprehensive records of U.S. Embassy contacts with Chilean military personnel, and none were maintained during the period in question. Normal social and professional contacts prevailed in the ten days preceding the coup, as they had at other times. These contacts took place in the normal course of the routine duties of our defense attache office, our military advisory group, and other Embassy personnel."

16. Q. The Senate Foreign Relations Subcommittee on Multinational Corporations concluded in its report: "ITT sought to engage the CIA in a plan covertly to manipulate the outcome of the Chilean presidential election," and that "the pressures which the company sought to bring to bear on the U.S. for CIA

intervention ... are also incompatible with the formulation of U.S. foreign policy in accordance with the U.S. national, rather than private interests." On the issue of whether American foreign policy should be highly influenced by the interests of private U.S. firms, have U.S. officials or Department of State personnel met with officials of U.S. firms which had been nationalized by the former Chilean Government since the coup? If so, when and who and which companies were represented? Elaborate on the purposes of the meetings and at whose initiative they were called.

16. A. "State Department officials have continued to meet periodically, including in recent months, with officials of the expropriated copper companies. Such meetings, as those with representatives of other U.S. private interests in Chile, are usually held at the request of the firms in question and are considered to be useful in keeping the U.S. Government abreast of private sector views and attitudes toward developments in Chile as they affect the individual company's interests. The U.S. Government has a particular interest in the treatment accorded to American investors as well as in specific cases where financial assistance has been extended by the U.S. Government."

17. Q. (a) From the ITT hearings of the Foreign Relations Committee, the Senate is familiar with a series of Forty Committee meetings in 1970 which dealt with Chile. The first meeting of which there is public knowledge took place in June 1970. At that meeting, the CIA was authorized to carry out a covert propaganda campaign against Allende. $400,000, was, in fact, spent for this purpose. Additionally, the testimony states that there was a further meeting of the Forty Committee which dealt with Chile soon after Allende was elected on September 4, 1970. The subcommittee was unable to get a clear answer as to precisely what transpired at this meeting. But it was subsequent to this meeting that Mr. Broe of the CIA made his proposal of September 29, 1970, to Mr. Gerrity of the ITT Corporation to create economic chaos in Chile. The testimony showed that this proposal was made with Mr. Helms' knowledge and approval.

How many times since has the Forty Committee considered the Chilean political situation and U.S. policy with respect to the Allende regime? When was the last Forty Committee meeting prior to the coup in which the subject of Chile was discussed? What were the conclusions regarding Chile?

Did the Forty Committee at any of these meetings authorize CIA assistance, directly or indirectly, in any form whatever, to any of the groups or individuals opposed to Allende?

(b) From Mr. Hennessey's testimony before the Multilateral Corporations Subcommittee it is clear that the U.S. Government used its influence in the multilateral lending institutions to prevail upon these institutions to cut off economic development credits to Chile, even before there was any expropriation of any properties by the Chilean government. Yet Mr. Hennessey also testified that the United States Government made available millions of dollars of credits for military purchases. Why were new military credits offered and new economic loans denied?

17. A. (a) These proceedings are classified and there has been no authorized disclosure of any of them by the U.S. Government. You will recall that Assistant Secretary Kubisch responded to your questions along these lines in executive session insofar as he was authorized to do so. I would not like our response to pass, however, without reiterating once again that the U.S. Government did not participate in any way in the overthrow of Allende.

(b) Regarding the implication that the U.S. Government pressured multilateral lending institutions to cut off credits to Chile, we would point out that these institutions are independent bodies with their own lending criteria and sufficient experience to formulate their own judgments about a country's creditworthiness. It may be recalled that no Chilean loan applications came before the IBRD Board during the Allende period, and that the only two loans which were voted on in the IDB were supported by the United States. The IDB loans came up early in the Allende period when economic conditions in Chile were much better. It should likewise be recalled that the IMF lent Chile over $80 million in 1971 and 1972 to offset declining copper prices, and that disbursements by the multilateral institutions on existing loans continued throughout the Allende period.

The decision of the Allende Government to request the extension of U.S. credits under the FMS program was one which only it could make. Our decision was whether or not to continue extending credits under the FMS program to military institutions which had, over the years, developed and maintained an inventory of items produced in the U.S. The fact is that the Allende Government undertook to meet its FMS repayment obligations due to other U.S. Government creditor agencies."

18. Q. In an article in *The New York Times* of September 27, 1973, a *Times* correspondent reports that the plotting of the coup which toppled Allende began as early as November 1972. In October 1972 there were a series of demonstrations by Chileans, primarily from the middle class who were opposed to Mr. Allende, the so-called "pots and pans" demonstration. This demonstration bore a striking resemblance to similar demonstrations which took place in Brazil in 1963 and early 1964 against the Goulart regime. Did the CIA play any role whatsoever, directly or indirectly, in the demonstrations which took place in Chile in October 1972?

18. A. "The CIA played no role in the October 1972 demonstrations."

Rep. George E. Brown

Following are the remarks of George E. Brown, Jr. (D.-Calif.) before his colleagues in the U.S. House of Representatives on Tuesday, March 12, 1974, as recorded in Congressional Record.

Mr. Brown. Mr. Speaker, increasing public outcry against the abuses of civil liberties in Chile makes it imperative that I once again formally protest. It is clear that abominable conditions exist; we learn of executions, mass imprisonment and exile even amongst former members of the Chilean congress. Many people are being detained and imprisoned without being informed of the charges against them. Civil courts are being circumscribed by military courts; justice is military justice. Human dignity and civil liberties have little meaning; redress of grievances is unthinkable. Americans certainly cannot be proud of the U.S. tacit consent policy with respect to Chile.

In a recent congressional conference, "Chile: Implications for U.S. Foreign Policy," an attempt was made to shed light on the political and economic situation in Chile since the military coup in September. I think the conference was instructive and informative in this regard —it underscored the urgency of the situation, a situation deserving immediate attention. It was the sense of the conference that hearings begin in the Senate to investigate the state of Chile, the extent and validity of the junta's control, and ultimately to determine what the official U.S. policy should be regarding Chile. I would now like to add my wholehearted support to this endeavor.

Spokesmen for the junta, including the Chilean Ambassador to the United States, Gen. Walter Heitmann, have stated that free elections will not be held for at least 5 years. This poses an additional moral problem to the United States that I would like to briefly address myself to. That is, Chilean citizens temporarily residing in the United States. Over 4,000 Chilean citizens are here temporarily on student or work visas, many of whom have visas that expire very shortly. We should now consider the possible persecution that many will face upon their return to Chile. It is my intention to introduce legislation to permit an extension of visas for a period of 5 years or until free elections are held, to those citizens now residing in the United States. It is my sincere hope and expectation that the broader question of asylum for political prisoners will be entertained in the Senate committee investigating the implications of U.S. policy toward Chile.

On Tuesday, March 19, 1974, Mr. Brown again addressed the House of Representatives, this time on the subject of aid for Chilean nonimmigrant residents. His remarks, as recorded in Congressional Record, *follow.*

Mr. Brown. Mr. Speaker, in the past months I have become increasingly aware of the plight of our nonimmigrant Chilean residents, and have found it difficult to answer such residents' pleading letters with the usual noncommittal phrases.

A nonimmigrant resident has a defined time period to his visa. At the end of this period, he may apply for an extension, which is usually given if he can demonstrate that his present pursuits are those he was admitted upon. Thus, a student may apply for an extension if he proves that additional study is necessary; he cannot transfer his choice of occupation.

Under the usual course of events, this practice is totally justified and supportable. But when such a nonimmigrant resident must be forced to return to a home that offers only danger and possible arrest upon arrival, a home that is in chaos due to a military coup while the resident was away is another matter entirely. I found it no longer possible to turn away from these people, and am, therefore, introducing legislation today that will alleviate the situation. My bill will allow an extension of 5 years for all temporary Chilean residents who are in this country at the time of enactment.

In 1973, the number of temporary Chilean residents who reported under the alien address program was 4,921. I estimate that this is the number we are and will be dealing with if this legislation becomes public law. There are additional Chileans in the country, in pursuit of a pleasant tour of our great land, but they are not the ones that will choose to remain on this 5-year visa program.

This bill's sole purpose is to aid those temporary Chilean residents that are in fear of returning to their home at the present time due to harassment they are receiving from Chileans at home. I hope my colleagues will face this issue and the facts concerning the present deprivation of human rights in Chile that pour into our office daily. These temporary residents should not be labeled, they are merely people in fear of their lives, and the instinct that reaches for survival has no connection with any political philosophy. It exists in all of us, and in similar circumstances we, too, would be pursuing similar courses of action.

This bill merely extends the visas of these aliens for 5 years; it grants no additional privileges, and they can still be deported if a crime is committed. But at least it gives them time to pursue other courses, time to find other means to attain immigrant standing, and time for the situation in Chile to regain order.

I ask my fellow Representatives to think of the position of these temporary Chilean residents, to put yourselves in their place, and then to join me in this endeavor.

Rep. Donald M. Fraser

On May 22, 1974, Donald M. Fraser (D-Minn.), a member of the U.S. House Foreign Affairs Committee, alerted the House of Representatives to the upcoming series of hearings on human rights in Chile to be held before the Subcommittees on Inter-American Affairs and International Organizations and Movements. Following are his remarks, as recorded in Congressional Record. *The International Commission of Jurists' report to which he refers is published in the section of this book entitled "Justice and Human Rights," beginning on page 70.*

Mr. Fraser. Mr. Speaker, I would like to insert in the *Record* the preliminary report of the observer mission sent to Chile by the International Commission of Jurists. The mission visited Chile from April 19 to 28. The members of the mission are listed below.

The report contains the following conclusions:

First, ill-treatment, sometimes amounting to severe torture is carried out systematically by some of those responsible for interrogation;

Second, due process is severely lacking in the military trials; and

Third, approximately 10,000 persons are being held as political prisoners—charges are often not filed against them and many are held "incommunicado" for long periods.

Foreign Affairs Subcommittees on Inter-American Affairs and International Organizations and Movements have been holding a series of hearings on the human rights situation in Chile. On May 23 the subcommittees will be hearing from one of the members of the ICJ observer mission—Mr. Covey Oliver, former Assistant Secretary of State for Inter-American Affairs. On June 11 the subcommittees will be hearing from a Department of State spokesman.

I believe these hearings are particularly timely in view of the administration's request to the Congress to provide Chile with nearly $85 million in bilateral U.S. economic assistance, military assistance, and credit sales. For Chile, the administration is requesting $800,000 in military assistance—grants—and $20,500,000 in military sales credit. Congress should, I believe, take a very close look at these requests. A government which is committing repressive acts against its people, as the International Commission of Jurists' report reveals, should not be entitled to American arms. As Members of Congress we run the risk of being accomplices in these repressive acts if these arms become the instruments of oppression.

THE INTERNATIONAL RESPONSE

Seldom if ever in the history of Latin America has world opinion been so aroused as by the brutal ending of the Allende experiment and the continuing reign of terror, wholesale use of torture, and other violations of human rights. Of particular interest and significance was the reaction of the United States. While the Administration used all its enormous power to minimize the events, spontaneous protests developed all over the country. Senator J. William Fulbright, chairman of the Foreign Relations Committee of the U.S. Senate, reported that his committee received thousands of telegrams, letters, and telephone calls. That, he said, was not unprecedented, but "what is unprecedented is their unanimity. Not one expresses approval, or even acceptance, of the coup. On the contrary, they express dismay, strong suspicions of United States involvement, and deep concern over the fate of Chilean supporters of the Allende regime and of the foreign exile community in Chile."

The late President Juan Peron of Argentina spoke for most Latin Americans when asked if he thought the United States were involved: "I can't prove it, but I firmly believe it." Many Latin American countries proclaimed national days of mourning, and everywhere there were demonstrations against the United States. As *The Christian Science Monitor* put it, Allende was hailed throughout Latin America "as a democratic martyr sacrificed to the United States."

In Europe, public reaction was equally strong, with the difference that in most countries the governments joined openly with the people in protesting. ITT offices in many cities were bombed, as were offices of other U.S.-based global corporations. "Down with the murderers and the CIA," read the banners behind which thousands marched in Paris. The University of Brussels conferred an honorary doctorate posthumously on Allende, an unprecedented tribute, calling him "a symbol of an ideal of political democracy."

Even more surprising than the first spontaneous reactions was the continued intensity of the response month after month. Rallies of solidarity with the people of Chile, teach-ins, and strategy meetings continue to be held widely both in the United States and in many other countries. Committees sponsored by lawyers, by religious groups, and by professional, academic, and labor organizations raise funds to defend accused persons, help refugees, and sponsor commissions of enquiry into violations of human rights. Many of the major efforts are reported in this volume. If one conclusion is clear from all of them, it is that the Junta is losing the battle for world opinion.

International Commission of Enquiry

United States intervention in Chilean affairs and commission of crimes against humanity by the Chilean Junta are charged in the report of the International Commission of Enquiry into the Crimes of the Military Junta in Chile which met in Helsinki, Finland, March 21-24, 1974. The

Commission consists of internationally known lawyers, scientists, and representatives of cultural life of Algeria, Argentina, Australia, Austria, Belgium, Cuba, Denmark, France, the German Democratic Republic, the Federal Republic of Germany, Great Britain, Greece, Guatemala,

Hungary, India, Italy, Portugal, Spain, the Soviet Union, Sweden, the Democratic Republic of Vietnam, the United States, Panama, Morocco, Ecuador, Finland, Norway, Venezuela, Poland, Switzerland, Japan, Sweden, and Canada. They included Nobel Prize-winner Miguel Angel Asturias of Guatemala; Mario Soares of Portugal; Nobel Prize-winner Philip Noel-Baker of Great Britain; K. J. Lang, former Minister of Justice, Finland; and Luis Beltran Prieto Figueroa, former chairman of the Venezuelan Senate. The Commission's conclusions follow.

On September 11, 1973, a handful of insurgent officers staged a coup d'etat against the legitimate government of Chile. This coup was the result of a conspiracy, which had been in progress since early 1972, and cannot be considered to constitute anything less than high treason.

The military Junta has attempted to justify the illegal take-over of power by accusing the government of President Salvador Allende of being involved in a plot to instigate a civil war in complicity with foreign-trained guerrillas. The Junta has not been able to present any proof of this allegation.

The government of President Allende was democratically elected and consistently maintained its decision to abide by the Constitution of the country, whereas the military Junta, which professes to uphold the Constitution, has in fact abrogated it and taken measures to impose a new Constitution which will most certainly suppress the democratic rights of the people.

It is quite clear that foreign interests exerted pressure on Chile with the intent to overthrow the government. Private and public financial institutions in the United States of America as well as U.S. corporations acted, with the approval of the U.S. government, to strangle Chile economically. The International Bank for Reconstruction and Development refused all financial assistance to Chile under circumstances which strongly suggest U.S. pressure.

Further, there is direct evidence that the ITT Corporation planned to create economic and political chaos to undermine the rule of the Chilean government. These plans were communicated to the Central Intelligence Agency of the United States (CIA).

There are also claims which appear to be well founded that the CIA was involved in infiltration, sabotage, acts of political violence and the coup itself.

In addition, the coup coincided with demonstrative maneuvers and movements by the U.S. Navy along the Chilean coast, separately and jointly with units from the Chilean Navy.

These circumstances suggest a rather consistent patter of U.S. involvement and collaboration in the military take-over in Chile. This conclusion can be supported by statements of high-ranking U.S. officials before and after the coup.

The purpose of such intervention was to prevent the government from gaining national independence in the economic field and making essential changes in the social and economic structure.

This type of interference in the internal affairs of Chile constitutes a serious violation of the political independence and sovereignty of the country according to general international law and the Charter of the United Nations.

The evidence considered by the Commission has clearly demonstrated the strategy and *modus operandi* by which the anti-democratic and neo-colonialist forces usurp power by either creating or exploiting difficult economic conditions or crises in the developing countries. These forces constitute a threat to the self-determination of nations and to world peace.

•

At the time of the coup, arrests and killings without trial took place on a massive scale. People were arbitrarily and indiscriminately executed for no other apparent reason than to terrorize and to subdue the population. The Presidential Palace, workers' quarters, factories and other installations were bombarded.

Large numbers of people, including many who were not engaged in political activity of any kind, were apprehended, interrogated and tortured, often with fatal results. Many people were forced to be present when members of their families were tortured. Wives and families of detainees were held as hostages and also abused. Women were raped; children were taken from their parents and placed under arrest.

Under the fictitious "State of Seige in time of war" later proclaimed by the Junta, military tribunals were set up to try and sentence persons accused of violating Junta orders. These courts martial maintain complete jurisdiction as long as the state of war exists. The principle of non-retroactive penalties has never been respected by these tribunals despite solemn assurances to the contrary given by the Junta's Minister of Justice. The entire manhunt of members and sympathizers of the Allende government is designed to try to sentence people for the acts and policies of the past.

The military sentences, which are without appeal, have been irrationally harsh and quite out of proportion to their alleged crimes, rendering as much as 30 years in prison or capital punishment. Such heavy sentences have now been demanded for members of the armed forces who refused to participate in the coup. The defendants have been offered no defense guarantees whatsoever when subjected to these extreme summary proceedings.

The dictatorship of the Junta has completely destroyed all democratic structures and procedures with their correlated rights and freedoms. Thus, the Junta has banned political activity and branded all political organizations associated with the government of President Allende illegal, thereby abolishing the fundamental rights to freedom of peaceful assembly and association. Further, freedom of information has been totally suppressed by closing down papers and imposing very heavy censorship. The mass burning of books stands out as a symbol of the Junta's utter contempt for culture.

The suppression of the working class is a fundamental feature of the regime. The workers' right to organize has been eradicated by banning all free trade unions. Exploitation of the workers has been accelerated by means of wage freezes and demands for extra work without pay. Even the very right to work is taken from them by massive dismissals for political reasons only.

The military Junta has been characterized by xenophobic outbursts against foreigners. Purely racist tendencies can be discerned in the prosecution of certain ethnic minorities such as the Mapuche Indians and gypsies.

The total picture which emerges from these facts is reminiscent of the rise of German fascism. In conclusion, it is then overwhelmingly obvious that the military Junta has never intended to fulfill its solemn pledges before the United Nations to respect human rights and their obligations under international law. On the contrary, it has made a mockery of such authoritative international instruments as the United Nations Universal Declaration of Human Rights, and the International Covenant on Civil and Political Rights of 1966 approved and ratified by Chile and the American Convention on Human Rights of 1969.

•

An extremely large number of political prisoners and detainees is still held in prisons, concentration camps and other places. Estimates of their number vary since the Junta releases no information and it does not permit any international inspection.

In general, the conditions for all of these prisoners are extremely harsh. Brutal treatment and torture are commonplace. Many of them have been provoked to escape and then shot as fugitives. Besides being physically terrorized, they are forced to live in continual uncertainty by their undefined legal position and the lack of contact with spouses, families and lawyers. A major part of them are held in complete isolation. Only seldom are formal charges filed and a great number are admittedly held for indefinite periods for purely preventive reasons. The imminent threat of execution is ever present as demonstrated by the fact that it was recently announced that certain political leaders might be put to death.

Ever since the coup the situation of the foreign refugees residing in Chile has been very serious. At the time of the take-over large numbers of them were tortured and killed. Despite assurances given by the Junta's Foreign Minister, many of them have been forcibly repatriated to their countries of origin. International humanitarian organizations such as the United Nations High Commis-

sion for Refugees have been permitted to operate to some extent on terms laid down by the Junta, which has totally disregarded its obligations under the Geneva Refugee Convention of 1951 and the additional Protocol of 1967.

Though many Chileans and foreigners have been granted diplomatic and territorial asylum by courageous governments and embassies, Junta policy has been in poor agreement with long-standing practice and conventions in Latin America with respect to granting of diplomatic asylum. Contrary to normal procedure, safe-conducts have been refused to a large number.

In spite of the fact that the granting of diplomatic asylum is a peaceful and humanitarian action, Junta authorities have not even hesitated to attack and intimidate members of the diplomatic corps who attempted to take such action. In flagrant violation of the Vienna Convention on Diplomatic Relations of 1961, Junta troops opened fire on the Cuban Embassy and shot and wounded persons under the protection of the diplomatic missions.

The International Commission shall not be regarded as a Court. It has neither the power nor the competence of a court. The only sanction at the disposal of the Commission is the moral verdict of humanity.

Therefore, the Commission now urgently appeals to all individuals and organizations, to all government and international bodies: to denounce the crimes against humanity committed by the Junta and U.S. intervention in Chilean affairs; to work for the isolation of the military Junta from the international community; to end all support for the Junta; to give active support to the struggle of the Chilean people to restore the legitimate government; to put pressure on the Junta to lift the state of war, to stop the terror, definitely close all concentration camps and release all political prisoners. ■

A European conference of Communists, Socialists and Social Democrats meeting to discuss Chile closed here this afternoon with a resolution calling for the restoration of civil and political rights in that country.

Beatriz Allende, daughter of the late Chilean President, Salvador Allende Gossens, who was deposed in a coup on September 11, 1973, told the more than 300 delegates and guests at the Pan-European Conference for Solidarity with Chile yesterday that a resistance movement was now being organized there. She was joined at the conference by a number of Mr. Allende's former associates, including Carlos Altamirano, the Chilean Socialist party head, who is being sought by the Chilean police, and Orlando Millas, a former minister of economic affairs in the Allende government.

The conference brought together members of Eastern European Communist parties and of social democratic, Socialist and Communist parties and trade unions in Western Europe, including the Social Democrats in Italy and the British Labor party. Other parties represented included those from Belgium, Denmark, Spain, Sweden, Finland, Luxembourg, the Netherlands and Portugal.

Francois Mitterrand, the head of the French Socialist party, said the meeting was the first time "that so many organizations rallied for a just cause."

—"Special" from Paris
The New York Times
July 8, 1974

WILPF Mission to Santiago

The Women's International League for Peace and Freedom (WILPF), based in Philadelphia, Pa., sent six members to Chile on a fact-finding mission from January 29 to February 10, 1974. On their return, they testified before the U.N. Human Rights Commission and the congressional conference cited in the succeeding article. Following is the report by Katherine Camp, WILPF International Vice President, published in the League's newsletter, Peace and Freedom, *Vol. XXXIV, No. 3, March 1974.*

"In every soldier there is a Chilean. In every Chilean there is a soldier." In signs and posters everywhere, the *Junta Militar* strives to impose itself as the spirit of the new Chile. It conforms with the existing "state of war" which serves as the official excuse for the wholesale denial of basic legal and human rights: searches, detention, interrogation with compelling physical inducements, secret tribunals, and outright murder.

The WILPF investigating team confirmed that the violence and bloodshed which followed the September 11, 1973, coup continues today, though diminished in scale. While in Chile we learned of the death sentences imposed on the young, popular former Senator Erich Schnake and the former vice-president of the State Bank,

Carlos Lazo. Their executions could herald the elimination of the remaining officials of the Allende regime, most of whom are imprisoned on Dawson Island near the Antarctic Circle.

Women Prisoners Tell of Torture

We asked to visit Dawson, Chacabuco and other detention centers. After persevering we did see the women's "House of Correction", El Buen Pastor, for an unforgettable 20 minutes. We were swamped by women of all ages eager to tell of their mistreatment. Some have been held incommunicado since September, many were tortured at previous centers, some had been raped. They were not physically abused here under the nuns' care, but a doctor who knew their histories had been put into isolation for our visit.

The Director of Prisons himself escorted us to the Estadio Chile, so the conversations with the three "prisoners" produced were restrained. But from the 200 or so captives who saw us high above them from the ground on which they stayed came the poignant, quiet call, "Come down, come down."

Workers' Clinic Demolished

With an unemployment rate of 25-30%, inflation topping 1000%, and government assistance only for those who "qualify" politically, massive numbers of Chileans face starvation when the tomato-potato season ends this month. Rice which cost 7 escudos a year ago and 16 just before the coup is now 360 escudos. We heard of one family that has bread and tea for dinner six days a week. Although the Minister of Health told us the Allende milk program now includes cereal and vitamins, it is clear that they are not available to all children. We were taken to a city clinic that was apparently functioning well, but the one we visited on our own in a workers' district has been completely demolished, the doctors dispersed or in jail. A doctor told us that 1500 physicians had been detained, thrown out of work or killed.

General Pinochet admits that 100,000 persons have been fired from their jobs and 20,000 students expelled. The universities are in disarray. The Junta told us they are being reorganized and will open later. Books have been burned and Chilean popular folk music cannot be found in the shops. Martial books and music are on display. Military conscription has been expanded from three months of service to two years.

We spoke with a young widow whose husband had been executed two days before the date of his announced military tribunal. Thousands more (we have reason to believe 12,000) are being detained without charges or due legal process. Hundreds have disappeared and are presumed dead. We have names and documented cases of twenty-five.

In Talca province we learned that there had been some strikes of railroad and construction workers. But with labor and the opposition party leadership killed or in jail, there is virtually no organized resistance. Labor unions have been dissolved, the right to strike nullified. The free press has been abolished and many journalists imprisoned. Congress has been dissolved; political parties are banned. We were told that there would probably be no elections for five years.

The U.S. shares with Britain the shame of being the least generous of Western countries in admitting Chilean refugees from fascism. Two hundred or more face indefinite detention in foreign embassies, while the government refuses to grant safe-conducts and is charging criminal violations against those detained.

Our members in Santiago are working very hard where it counts most: helping families victimized by having the breadwinner killed, detained or forced out of work; helping to obtain lawyers and funds; and giving moral support in many other ways.

Team Has Credibility

The credibility of our team rests largely on the fact that we interviewed both sides. Countering the 78 woman-hours with government officials were the first-hand reports of the many contacts brought to us by all members of our team, plus Chileans who risked coming on their own despite fears of government retaliation. Three members of our group were fluent in Spanish and three had lived or stayed in Chile before. Kay Cole combined sensitivity to people with sensibility about converting currency. Evelyn Mauss disciplined our diet and pace. Peg McCarter's charm and fluency in Spanish brought us valuable new contacts. Pearl Shamis' voluble Spanish and good humor eased some tense moments. Charlotte Ryan's knowledge of the language, culture and geography proved invaluable.

As I saw seared into the flesh of Chilean prisoners the same small, round cigarette burns that I had seen on Vietnamese, I knew that we must oppose tyranny wherever we find it. One immediate and urgent need is to write the Junta on behalf of the people in Chile who are facing military tribunals. Write *Senores Junta Militar, Edificio Diego Portales, Santiago, Chile.* ∎

"What happened you could see coming. From the very first moment you could see it: those bourgeois women with their pots out in the street, the disobedience of authority, open conspiracy against Parliament, an apolitical army whose essence consisted in keeping itself in reserve to take care of things from the inside. It was a very difficult situation! The legal means could have been taken further. Now I'll tell you the truth: the marxist principle of a dictatorship of the proletariat is valid . . . without a revolutionary dictatorship there is no revolution, no social change. The old social system is maintained not only by the State's control, but also because it has created a culture, the culture of the dominant class. To transform that culture, the revolutionary apparatus must have the means of educating the people in its hands, and must deprive the reactionaries of those means. I don't know if at the end of this historical process of such a change in Humanity many countries may be able to change through parliamentary ways. That may be possible at the end, when the balance of power is leaning greatly towards socialism. But in the present situation, and in countries like ours, it is very hard to change by those means."

Q: "Do you believe that the situation is favorable for the Chilean people?"

"The Chilean people that I saw were a patriotic people, enthusiastic, a fighting people. I am sure that the Chilean people will not stand for that system very long. Those people of the Junta don't have the slightest chance of maintaining that reign of terror that they have established and the Chilean people will stand up to them sooner or later. I imagine that first they will have to recuperate from the blow, that was very hard. The fascist dictatorship in Chile is one of the most ferocious that has existed in the world. And the dictatorship has isolated itself. Yes, terror has an objective, it can intimidate the people, but only for a short time. In the long run terrorism has the effect of creating an antidote to itself: people adapt to the worst and the most incredible repressive situations, they organize themselves, and start to collaborate with one another and become immune to that terror. There is nothing worse for that terror than when people stop being afraid. In Chile the people are beginning to be unafraid. They are already moving; we know that they are moving. The dictatorship has treated Chile like an occupied country. And Chile is not Indonesia. . . ."

—Fidel Castro, in an interview conducted in Havana by Luis Suarez, editor of the Mexican magazine Siempre, *and printed therein February 20, 1974*

The Swedish Ambassador's Report

Countless innocent lives were saved in Chile by Harald Edelstam, Ambassador of Sweden. At great risk to his own life, he protected many Chileans and foreigners, giving them asylum in the Swedish Embassy and arranging passage out of the country, until he was finally declared persona non grata by the Junta and forced to leave. During World War II, he had performed similar feats of daring and bravery on behalf of victims of the Nazis in Norway.

What follows is his testimony at a Congressional Conference on Chile: Implications for United States Foreign Policy, held in the United States Senate Office Building on February 28, 1974. Sponsored by 25 members of the U.S. Senate and 53 members of the House of Representatives, this forum was arranged with the assistance of the Fund for New Priorities in America, which published the edited transcript of the conference from which this statement is reprinted.

The brutality of the Junta shown during and after the coup stands in sharp contrast to the methods of President Allende. The repression and the killings are still going on, five months after the coup. Many members of the government were taken prisoner when they left the burning Presidential Palace. Some of them were taken to Dawson Island in the Straits of Magellan where the climate is very difficult, cold, and unhealthy. Among the prisoners there are the respected Foreign Secretary, Clodomiro Almeyda, and former Chilean Ambassador in Washington, Orlando Letelier, to mention only two. Six hundred political prisoners are kept in a closed salt mine in the desert in northern Chile where the temperature reaches 110 degrees Fahrenheit in the daytime and goes down to 32 degrees at night. Six thousand more political prisoners are in other camps. About two hundred prominent Chileans have taken refuge in different foreign embassies, such as Luis Figueroa, President and leader of the United Trade Unions and former Minister of Labor,

and Rolando Calderon, Secretary General of the Trade Unions and former Minister of Agriculture. Mr. Calderon was shot by an unknown sniper when he was standing in the courtyard of the Cuban Chancellery, which has been under Swedish protection since the 12th of September when Chile broke relations with Cuba. Fortunately he survived. Other names which could be mentioned are the Minister of Industry, Pedro Vuskovic, and political leaders such as Luis Corvalan, Anselmo Sule, and Oscar Garreton. Their only crime is that they have served their President and their country. The Junta is trying to accuse them of common crimes which they never committed.

According to reliable estimates, between 10,000 and 15,000 people were killed during and after the coup, and some 35,000 people were interned in camps and prisons. It is also necessary to mention 30,000 children who were made orphans; 200,000 people who have lost their jobs for political reasons; and 25,000 students who are no longer allowed to study and who cannot get jobs. Many have been tortured and maltreated. There are thousands and thousands of people who are beaten, slain, and forced to be silent. You find them mainly among the industrial and rural workers and among the mine workers.

During the time of President Allende, not less than 13,000 refugees from other Latin American countries, mainly from Brazil, Uruguay, and Bolivia, were generously and hospitably received in Chile. Some 8,000 of these refugees desperately wanted to leave Chile after the coup. Several thousand of them were arrested and put in camps and prisons. Others sought protection in various embassies and in United Nations centers established in different parts of the country. These refugees are now

"I personally believe that the record is well established that the present government in Chile has gone beyond what is tolerable under the Human Rights Convention. . . . I also believe that we should discontinue all deliveries of military assistance until such time that there is a restoration of some minimum requirements. . . . Finally, one thing that is very easy to do is to have an authoritative statement out of the executive branch of this government as to precisely where we stand on human rights. . . ."

—Ralph Dungan, Chancellor of Higher Education, State of New Jersey; former U.S. Ambassador to Chile (1964-67), addressing the Congressional Conference

spread all over the world, mainly in the European countries. The great majority of them want to go back to their homelands when it is possible.

President Allende was legally elected by the people and the Congress. His government was lawfully appointed. The efforts of President Allende and his government to create a better society in Chile with more equality, social justice, better education and nutrition were appreciated and admired in many countries. His programs for the development of agriculture, economic life, trade, and industry were praise-worthy. He made great efforts to uphold the independence of his country and to oppose foreign influence and intervention.

President Allende certainly made his share of mistakes in the economic and political field, but his goals were noble and his methods were legal, democratic, and just. The enormous economic forces that his opponents controlled were, in the long run, a formidable contribution to his downfall. ∎

Bertrand Russell Tribunal II Provisional Verdict

"Serious, repeated and systematic violations of human rights" on a scale that constitutes "a crime against humanity." Such was the verdict issued last April by the Russell Tribunal II on Latin America on the present regimes in Brazil, Chile, Uruguay and Bolivia. The jury was headed by Italian Senator Lelio Basso. It included Juan Bosch, former president of the Dominican Republic; author Gabriel García Márquez, since deceased; Latin American trades union leader Emilio Maspero; Protestant theologian George Casalis; and Catholic theologians Giulio Girardi and Johannes B. Metz.

As soon as it was officially constituted on 6 November 1973, the Russell Tribunal II made the following statement concerning its own investiture: "It does not reject the idea that a tribunal is necessarily the emanation of an authority. A society as little organized as that of international society is governed by an authority that is diffuse, embodied not by the moral authority of state, or by governments responsible to the peoples but residing in those peoples themselves. The only rational and real foundation of international law is the desire for peace of men and women who share the conviction of their mutual solidarity."

Until now, governments have claimed to be the only institutions qualified to represent the international community. Such a claim is patently unjustified, especially when it is considered that the action of governing bodies at the international level has impeded rather than encouraged the development of law and the growth of international solidarity. The Russell Tribunal II will endeavour to express the aspirations of the international community. In order to acquire this legitimacy it needs the active support of public opinion: to help all men and women to develop a more active and enlightened awareness of world problems, as well as to obtain the support and assistance that legitimize its activities.

Procedure

From 30 March to 5 April, 1974, the Russell Tribunal II on repression in Brazil, Chile and Latin America held 13 sessions in Rome, during which it received a considerable amount of documentation on the violations of human rights and fundamental liberties, of which four governments of the South American continent are accused: the governments of Brazil, Chile, Uruguay and Bolivia.

The Tribunal, having heard the accusations made by qualified representatives of the peoples of these countries, listened to reports, interrogated numerous witnesses and experts and examined written and audio-visual information materials.

In Respect of the Law

These governments are accused of serious, repeated and systematic violations of human rights and fundamental liberties. Three categories of human rights may be distinguished: civil liberties and political rights; economic, social and cultural rights; the right of peoples to self-determination and to be responsible for their own future, as well as the right to economic independence and cultural autonomy.

The preamble of the United Nations Charter, adopted 26 June, 1945, and six articles of this Charter* contain an express reference to the "universal and effective respect for human rights and the fundamental liberties of all."

According to the International Court of Justice "a denial of the fundamental rights of the individual is a flagrant violation of the objectives and principles of the Charter."†

On 10 December, 1948, the General Assembly of the United Nations proclaimed the Universal Declaration of Human Rights.

The American States are also bound by Articles 5 and 13 of the Charter of the Organization of American States (The Bogotá Treaty of 30 March-2 May, 1948).

Both the United Nations Charter and the Charter of the Organization of American States contain legally binding clauses which affirm respect for human rights. Both of them are reinforced by a Declaration which defines the extent of these rights.

But while the Universal Declaration followed upon the United Nations Charter after an interval of three years, the American Declaration of Human Rights and Obligations was adopted in the Final Act of the Bogotá Conference of 1948, during which the same States had signed the Charter of the Organization of American States. Therefore, when in articles 5 and 13 of the Charter, which are legally binding, the contracting States "proclaim the fundamental rights of the individual" (Article 5.1) and undertake to respect "the rights of the individual and the principles of universal ethics" (Article 13), we may interpret these provisions in the light of the Declaration that was adopted during the same conference.

Although this Declaration is not itself legally binding, it is of great value in the interpretation of the concepts used in the Convention which is legally binding on the contracting states.

In view of the great number of facts that have been established before the Tribunal and of the proof that has been gathered, in both written and oral reports given by the witnesses, only the most serious and most typical actions have been taken into consideration by the Tribunal.

After having carefully verified their authenticity, the Tribunal has sought to identify those which constitute a real serious and systematic violation of human rights, such as to justify the condemnation of the governments concerned.

The violations of human rights may come under either of two headings: either they take the form of institutionalized violence, which has been given the semblance of formal legality, or they consist of acts of violence that are illegal but perpetrated by agents of the government or tolerated by it. In each of the two cases, the condemnation of the government demands two conditions to be satisfied.

The case of institutionalized violence or the transgression of human rights resulting from a legislative act or statutory regulation would appear, without any doubt, to be the responsibility of the States. These actions are the most serious insofar as technicians and jurists have participated in the violation of international law, somewhat in the same way that doctors and psychologists have put

---

*Articles 1, 13, 55, 56, 62, 68
†Consultative advice of 21 June, 1971, No. 131

their expertise at the disposal of the torturers. In both cases, it is necessary to condemn the complicity of those who, by their very vocation, should have protected that which they have helped to destroy.

The Tribunal feels that the principle of the sovereignty of States does not prevent serious, systematic and repeated violations of human rights from being judged in the name of the international community. Articles 55, 56, and 62 of the UN Charter stipulate that such violations, which are a threat to peace, justify the intervention of the appropriate organs of that community.

The Tribunal also rejects the idea that respect for formal national legality is a shield against verification that the contents of legal or statutory regulations do indeed conform to international law.

As for illegal acts of violence, it is not enough that reprehensible acts or tortures have been committed on the territory of a government, for the government to be responsible. It is necessary that the government has ordered these actions to be carried out, or at least that it has tolerated them, in circumstances in which it is clear that it had political reasons for doing so.

The attention of the Tribunal has thus concentrated on the actions which show the systematic nature of these violations of human rights, the material means put at the disposal of their executors by the government itself, as well as the arbitrary actions carried out by the people accused of serious violations of human rights.

The reasoning on this point is different to that which applies to jurisdiction dealing with war crimes and called upon to judge the *individuals* who are under accusation.

The Nuremberg Tribunal, in particular, decided that an order given by a superior did not absolve the individual who had carried it out from personal responsibility.

In judging the governments only, the Russell Tribunal II in no way wishes to dismiss the personal responsibility of their agents, but keeping within the limits of the task that it has set itself, it has concentrated on the facts that prove the direct responsibility of the governments themselves.

Furthermore, it considers that it should publicize the names of all those, the governors or the executors, who are personally guilty of serious violations of human rights. It thus proposes to publish the list of these guilty persons.

Summary of the Evidence
Brazil

Since the *coup d'état* of 1964 in Brazil, the violation of human rights has been developing with a rare technical perfection, reaching its culminating point in the Constitutional Act No. 5 in the new Constitution of 1969 and through the institutionalization of arbitrary actions through various decrees. All this soon took on the form of a perfectly orchestrated repression, the pieces of various machinery managing to deprive individuals, organizations, trade-unions of any possibilities of expressing independent political ideas. This is shown in the record of only 10 months of dictatorship, during which 521 people (among them 58 federal deputies) have been shorn of their political rights. Very soon even the legislative assemblies of the states of Rio de Janeiro, Guanabara, São Paulo, Pernambuco and Sergipe were dissolved. In 1969 there was a new *coup d'état*. The executive was given by decree the power to exile the political enemies of the regime. The law of national security, which was already in operation, was brutally reinforced by a definition which hardly merits comment, in that it affirms that such a law "constitutes the guarantee necessary for carrying out national objectives against opponents both internal and external." It is the usual story: vague and abstract terms which can be applied, as convenience dictates, to concrete cases.

Most of the legal system was destroyed through a decree in 1971. The President assumed the power of dictating secret or confidential decrees for internal use. It is scarcely necessary, given the type of regime, to emphasize the significance of these secret measures.

Brazil had once been able to pride itself on having the most advanced social legislation in Latin America. Suddenly, the most elementary rights in this field were brutally denied the Brazilian workers. Any union actions decided by the workers were forbidden. The workers and the peasants have become the object of severe repression, immediately whenever there is a sign of the least protest. All union and strike action is forbidden, salaries are blocked and cannot be negotiated through the unions, the holdings of the small farmers have been given to the big landowners, in striking contrast to all agrarian reform principles. One particularly revealing and hateful provision is that the minimum age for young workers is now 12 years, while the American Charter of 1948 fixed the minimum age at 14 years.

In such a context, it is hardly a surprise that one of the basic rights, that of habeas corpus, has been suspended in order to give the government every possibility of preventing any activity that it holds is contrary to its interests, without the judiciary being able to exercise its power of control. Even worse: the authorities soon withdrew the application of the law of national security from any control by the judiciary which goes beyond the scope and provisions of this law. In this way, the right of the police to detain a person for 30 days, renewable for another 30 days, has been systematically extended to periods which, according to the declaration of some witnesses, have been as long as 12 months in some cases.

It is in this detention period, almost always a state of isolation, that the most repugnant violations of human rights are committed. We mean, of course, the systematic use of torture as a means of extracting confessions or destroying the spiritual and physical personality of people considered to be enemies of the military regime.

The Tribunal possesses a list of more than a thousand people who have been tortured in Brazil. It also has a list of the torturers and a description of the very refined means that are used, as well as detailed information about the public offices (commissariats and barracks) where torture is practiced.

It is difficult to describe in a few phrases all the atrocious systems used to create maximum suffering in the victims. All the possible means of pressure—physical, psychological and moral—are used, with increasing sophistication, by specialists whose imagination surpasses that of Dante. This is no exaggeration. As far as we know, no children were tortured in the poet's "Hell." In Brazil, there was a case of a one-year-old baby who was given electric shocks and was immediately killed. One witness referred to the case of a lawyer who was tortured together with his six-year-old daughter and that of a child of three tortured in the presence of his mother.

Besides this, everything else pales into insignificance. However, one cannot but mention the practice of collective torture, during which some prisoners are forced to martyrize their own companions. This usually happens inside the prisons, but sometimes it is done publicly in order to sow terror among the population. In the state of Bahia there was the case of peasants being crucified in a stadium, as an appalling example for the others present.

If someone asks: "What is the responsibility of the government in such practices?", suffice to say that torture occurs in a restricted number of public buildings (barracks and police stations), that the torturers dispose of highly perfected technical means, not to mention the help given by doctors in scientifically controlling the limits of the physical endurance of the tortured. One witness confirmed the presence of a foreign technician who spoke Portuguese with an Anglo-Saxon accent and others have described torture machines that have been very highly perfected— one of them made in North America. Another witness declared that her son had been used as a guinea-pig in a course on torture for some 70 army officers, some of whom had to retire because they could no longer stand it.

However, torture is not even the worst aspect of a regime that uses all means to eliminate its adversaries. In Brazil, violence reigns at all levels and this violence is prepared and implemented with the same cold-blooded efficiency shown in torture. With such antecedents, the emergence of the so-called "death squads" can hardly come as a surprise. Organized soon after the *coup d'etat,* the squad began by assassinating delinquents and "emarginated" people, whose bodies were left in the streets with notices and slogans aimed at terrorizing those who saw them. From this, they went on to political assassination. The notorious head of the squad, delegate Fleury, boasts shamelessly of the number of assassinations that he has personally committed or that his men have committed. When a judge dares to accuse him of a crime and orders him to be put in prison, Fleury very soon gets his liberty back, thanks to a law that was voted hurriedly by the national congress especially to help him gain his freedom.

One could say a lot more. But, after what has been said already—is it really necessary?

Chile

Leaving Brazil and going to Chile means passing from a slow process of destruction to a savage eruption of violence that has tried to accomplish in a few months what other dictatorial regimes have sought to do in the course of many years. It is unnecessary to emphasize the illegitimate nature of the military Junta which took over power, overthrowing a government that was not only constitutional, but was also respectful of the Constitution. And it carried this out with a brutality that is unlike anything that has been known in the annals of Latin American history.

It would be equally useless to show to what extent the coup of 11 September of 1973 violated the many constitutional provisions that aimed at preventing such actions. The rebel military not only trampled on juridical and moral principles: their troops launched the attack on Moneda Palace where President Allende heroically resisted until finally overcome by the concentrated attacks of infinitely superior forces.

At first, the Junta, presided over by General Augusto Pinochet, tried to show that they had taken the initiative because of the danger of the government implementing a plan that was supposed to liquidate the Chilean army. In spite of this, an interview with General Viaux, filmed in prison where he was put after the assassination of General Schneider, which was projected during the Tribunal sessions, proves decisively that the military had

planned a coup from the beginning of the Popular Unity government and that their arguments claiming legitimate defense are without any foundation. More recent declarations by General Pinochet have confirmed this.

It is thus difficult to talk in a detached way about the Chilean case, when the whole country is running with blood. However, we shall begin by mentioning the suppression of political rights, as this is a weapon as efficient as machine-guns in destroying the Junta's adversaries. The National Congress has been dissolved, thus all possible aspirations of the people. All political parties have been disbanded as, according to one of the Junta members, "political silence is necessary." The judicial powers have been put to one side, thanks to vulgar subterfuges, to which, however, there is no appeal. War councils have become the only ones that can judge and condemn, even if in thousands of cases, there has been no need of their services, which are substituted by assassination or mass execution.

The international press has fully reported on the horrors of the repression in the whole Chilean territory— operating with the same violence against both nationals and foreigners. Episodes like the bloodbath in the National Stadium are but a microcosm of the general situation prevailing in the country. It is impossible today to calculate the number of deaths, of prisoners, of tortured people, concentration camps, the "suicides" or the "death through illness" of important personalities of the Popular Unity government. The climate of violence continues, maintaining the people in a constant state of anguish. All these are but the aspects of a general violation of the most elementary human rights.

Added to this orgy of physical violence, a number of coercive measures has been accumulating, suppressing the most important social rights and creating a climate of insecurity in all sectors of public and private life, in jobs, in union organizations, whose leaders have been systematically arrested. To these must also be added the serious violations of international law: the attacks against the embassies and the assassinations of people who had taken refuge in them have been so widely reported in the international press as not to need repeating here. But perhaps most repugnant of all has been the way in which the Junta, in defiance of all rights, has expelled political refugees from other Latin American countries—in many cases (as for that of the Bolivians) handling them over directly to their own countries, which was tantamount to condemning them to prison, to torture or to death.

The cultural repression has been particularly savage: the university system has been destroyed, due to the suppression of its autonomy, the closing of numerous study centres, the elimination of professors and students, the burning of books considered subversive and the revision of study programmes in order to eliminate all ideological content considered dangerous.

Again, as we asked about Brazil, need one say more? We do not believe so and yet it does seem necessary to emphasize the presence and the assistance of foreign elements, accomplices of the Junta in the carrying out of the military coup and in the brutal repression against the Chilean people. The Tribunal knows about the presence of Brazilian police who collaborated in the National Stadium, in the torture of refugees from that country. On the other hand, this foreign assistance had started long ago, with the brazen intervention of the ITT maneuvering to overthrow the Popular Unity government, as well as the support given by the CIA to the strikes that paralyzed the Chilean economy, preparing a more favourable climate for the coup of 11 September.

Uruguay

In February of 1973, the Uruguayan military took power, dissolved the Parliament, disbanded the various political parties and began a systematic silencing of the information media. Arbitrary detention became more and more frequent. There is an implacable advance in repression and violence. The proclaimed law of the state security gives a semblance of legality to the fact that civilians are subject to the military penal code and to the military tribunals.

At the same time, there is a continual increase in the denunciations against torture and the inhuman detention conditions of many political prisoners. The rapporteur estimates that the number of people arrested is about 20,000, many of whom have been and are being tortured. This is a significant number when one recalls that Uruguay has a population of 2,800,000.

Torture has many of the refinements that are practiced in Brazil but also has its own characteristics. For example, the systematic use of a hood, aimed at isolating the prisoner psychologically and physically creating a state of anguish that can result in hallucinations and madness. The accounts of the witnesses show that the regime has lost all sense of respect for human rights and will stop at nothing in order to terrorize the population and make them passive towards the bullying of brute strength. The contempt for culture has been demonstrated by the arbitrary detention of the great writer Juan Carlos Onetti and of other writers and journalists. This, in essence, masks the intention to liquidate the only publication that had a different ideology from that of the regime, the magazine *Marcha*.

In Uruguay, too, the foreign intervention is more than proved. Who has not heard of Dan Mitrione? Who needs further proof?

Bolivia

As for Bolivia, the facts denounced reveal a clear and disquieting similarity to those described in the other countries: destruction of the legal system, re-establishment of the death penalty, adoption of a law on state security which subtracts those crimes that are defined as political from the jurisdiction of ordinary judges.

But these laws, as in the case of the other countries being considered, do not seem to satisfy the implacable desire for repression of General Banzer's regime. This accounts for the very bloody happenings, of a cruelty that often reaches the monstrous, that have been denounced by witnesses: bestial assassinations, tortures of such violence that they seem, rather differently from those inflicted in the other countries under examination, to be almost exclusively aimed at provoking the death of the tortured person after atrocious sufferings and humiliations.

The repression is clear in the social field. The Bolivian Workers Centre has been dissolved, union leaders have been imprisoned and popular demonstrations have been bloodily repressed. The most recent episode, which happened in January of this year, was the massacre of peasants in the region of Cochabamba. The foreign presence, as far as repression is concerned, seems to have found its own symbol, according to various witnesses, in the figure of Colonel Rafael Loayza, head of the secret service of the Ministry of the Interior, whose permanence in that post, in spite of various changes of government, is due to his links with the North American secret service.

Therefore

The Tribunal sees, in the systematic destruction of the legal system and in the violation by the dictatorships of their own legality, not only the negation of human rights but above all a means of liquidating all the gains that have gradually been achieved by the workers' and peasants' movements.

When arbitrary government becomes a rule of law it serves to reduce the workers—in a period of advanced industrial civilization—to a system of oppression and poverty that harks back to the early days of capitalism.

The Tribunal has indeed observed that, in these countries, wages are not sufficient to allow workers to exist and to reproduce the work force. The armed soldiers that ensure the attendance of the workers in some Chilean factories or of the peasants at work in some regions of Brazil, the offers of work that in Brazil remain unanswered because the wages are so low—all these represent the final phase of a system which, in the name of a model of economic development, ends up by denying the very basis of any industrial society.

Only ever-increasing violence has allowed this historical regression—a violence that finds its most visible expression in bloody repression and in the use of torture as an instrument for managing society.

In fact, as far as torture is concerned, the Tribunal has observed that this has developed in a remarkably similar way in all the countries being studied.

The documentation and the witnesses that have been gathered together show that the original objective of torture—to obtain confessions for mounting trials or for extracting information that would lead to arbitrary arrests—has already been superseded. From being a means of investigation, torture has become an additional and gratuitous means of punishment. Apart from the judgments and the penalties, it is used to neutralize the democratic and revolutionary forces, causing physical suffering, annihilating individuals—making them feel guilty and artificially inducing them to commit treasonable acts. But even apart from those who are actively struggling, torture is essentially aimed at the population as a whole, to intimidate it and to reduce it to the submissiveness of a depoliticized society.

The Tribunal is thus convinced that, far from being the result of arbitrary action, it is deliberate and consciously guided, whether by the national governments that organize torture, or by the foreign governments that inspire it, in particular Brazil—and beyond Brazil, the United States of America. Torture is one of the elements of a political design that aims at submitting the workers to the national oligarchy and to foreign imperialism.

From the individual to the collective, from the physical to the spiritual, from the private to the public: torture has thus become a means of government.

The Tribunal's condemnation of this system of government is based above all on the struggle of those who, all the world over, are fighting against this form of human degradation and, in particular, on the will to resist of those who, even having been tortured, continue to fight. In this connection it should be recalled that the preamble of the Declaration of Human Rights states that man, as a last resource, may have recourse to rebellion against tyranny and oppression.

The Tribunal is driven to the conclusion that the facts that have been revealed—the assassinations, the tortures, the arbitrary detentions, the degradation of those who have been deprived of work, of medical assistance and of food—consist both of crimes committed against each of the victims as well as of attacks against the inalienable right of peoples to decide for themseves their own future—political, economic and social.

This is the Tribunal's concept of human rights.

The proceedings of the first session have been dedicated to the defense of the martyred people of Chile, Brazil, Uruguay and Bolivia.

From these proceedings it would appear that the multinational companies and the upper classes that obey them have been the beneficiaries of the fascist regimes that have been installed in many Latin American countries.

A further session will have as its aim a detailed analysis of the role that is played by the Government of the United States, by the international agencies that depend on this government, and by the multinational companies responsible for the establishment and maintenance of such regimes in power.

Sentence

In view of the foregoing evidence,

The Tribunal declares the authorities that exercise power in Brazil, Chile, Uruguay and Bolivia to be guilty of serious, repeated and systematic violations of human rights.

The Tribunal also declares that, given the scale of these violations, taken in their entirety, they constitute a crime against humanity committed in each of the four countries in question by those same authorities that exercise power.

Appeal

The Russell Tribunal II on Repression in Brazil, Chile and Latin America has just pronounced its first sentence, condemning those responsible for serious, repeated and systematic violation of human rights in four countries of Latin America.

We believe that it is more than a question of the violation of human rights. It is a question of the crushing of the human being, of his body, of his interior strength, of his dignity, of the strongest ties of family and friendship. It is a question of a plan that is being carried out with scientific refinement and unbounded sadism. We have heard the witnesses with feelings of indignation, oppression and nausea.

It seems to us that in the name of "Western and Christian civilization" crimes are being committed that are the negation of any civilization, that are the expression of barbarism. To the extent that these crimes go beyond individual responsibilities and become a governmental operative, or more exactly an imperialist imperative, they form an unprecedented menace to the future of the Latin American continent and the whole of mankind.

The Tribunal appeals to the conscience of all people. It joins with all the democratic forces in the world in order:

1. To publicize what is going on in Latin America by all possible means, keeping interest in these problems by organizing meetings, demonstrations, articles, etc.

2. To raise funds.

3. To ask all governments to stop all military and economic assistance to the authorities that have been condemned by the Tribunal.

4. To launch a massive campaign for the liberation of political prisoners in Brazil, Chile, Uruguay and Bolivia.

5. To exercise pressure on the Junta of the Chilean regime so that it gives safe-conducts to the political leaders that are still refugees in the embassies.

6. To boycott the sending of arms to governments whose repressive character has been shown up.

The Tribunal appeals to the highest moral and spiritual authorities. It is transmitting its work and its conclusions to the Secretary General of the United Nations and to the international agencies such as UNESCO, ILO, WHO, OAS, and the Justice and Peace Commission, the World Council of Churches, the International Confederation of Workers (CMT, Brussels), the World Federation of Trade Unions (FMS, Prague), the International Confederation of Free Trade Unions (CISL, Brussels), Amnesty International, the International Association of Democratic Jurists, The International Association of Catholic Jurists, the Permanent Secretariat of the Organization of Non-Aligned States, the international youth organizations, the Leagues for the Defense of Human Rights, to all governments, to members of the Senate and the House of Representatives of the United States of America.

At the conclusion of this session, we would like our last words to be a message of hope. The courage of the martyrs in front of their executioners, singing before the execution squads, refusing to speak under torture, resisting in their cells and in concentration camps, enduring weeks of obscure and solitary detention without flinching —all these are examples for the rest of the world and an augury of the future. The fury of the regimes of oppression and of their international and local agents is a consequence of the growing resistance of peoples who refuse to remain in bondage and continue to struggle for their liberation.

Our Tribunal has learnt a lesson never to be forgotten; man cannot be overcome by exploitation, sadism and terror. The crimes of today herald the defeat of the executioners and the victory of the victims. Everything is still possible. The story of tomorrow is yet to be written. The future belongs to those who refuse to resign themselves.

Among the words that have struck us most, we recall those of two women, both horribly mutilated in body and spirit. One of them said to us: "I resisted under torture because it is necessary that people outside know what is going on in the secrecy of our cells and because we must fight right to the end so that our children will know another world than that in which we are living today."

The other said: "If you ask me how I have survived —well, I can only say that it is because the desire to live is so great in those who know where the truth lies."

Composition of the Jury

President
Lelio Basso, *Senator of the Italian Independent Left*

Vice-Presidents
Wladimir Dedijer, *Yugoslav historian, former partisan leader, university professor in the United States*
Gabriel García Márquez, *Colombian writer (since deceased)*
Francois Rigaux, *professor of international law, Catholic University of Louvain, Belgium*
Albert Soboul, *professor at the Sorbonne University, Paris*

Members of the Jury

Omar Abu, *representative of the Palestine Liberation Organization, professor of political science in the United States*

Juan Bosch, *former president of the Dominican Republic, President of the P.R.D.*

Louis Cabral, *President of the Council of the Democratic Republic of Guinea-Bissau (absent)*

George Casalis, *Protestant theologian*

Julio Cortazar, *Argentine writer*

Giulio Girardi, *Catholic theologian, lecturer at the Catholic Institute*

Uwe Holtz, *member of the S.P.D. and of the Parliament of the Federal Republic of Germany*

Alfred Kastler, *French Nobel Prize Winner in Physics*

Emilio Maspero, *Secretary General of the C.L.A.T. (Confederación Latinoamericana de Trabajadores)*

J. B. Metz, *Catholic theologian, professor of theology at the University of Munster in the Federal Republic of Germany (absent)*

John Mølggard, *of the Danish Social Democratic Party, trade union leader (absent)*

Joe Nordmann, *Secretary General of the International Association of Democratic Jurists*

Andreas Papandreou, *Secretary General of the Pan-Hellenic Movement*

James Petras, *professor of sociology at New York University*

Pham Van Bach, *president of the commission for U.S. war crimes in Vietnam, Vice-President of the Lawyers of the Democratic Republic of Vietnam, and President of the Supreme Court in the D.R.V. (absent)*

Laurent Schwartz, *mathematician, professor at the Sorbonne University, Paris*

Benjamin Spock, *pediatrician in the United States*

Armando Uribe, *professor of international law, former Chilean Ambassador (under Allende) to Peking, member of the executive of Izquierda Cristiana*

George Wald, *Professor at Harvard University, Nobel Prize Winner in Biology (absent)*

THE CHURCH AND CHILE

For several months after the military take-over, Raúl Cardinal Silva Henríquez of Santiago, as head of the Catholic church in Chile, "pursued an agile policy of riding several horses at once," in the words of *Latin America* newsletter. A moderate progressive, he recognized the polarization within the ranks of the clergy and also the threat of expulsion of foreign priests who number 60 percent of the total. Many of these foreign priests worked and lived in the *poblaciones,* while Chilean priests preferred a more traditional ministry in a higher social and economic category. The Junta ordered all foreign religious personnel eliminated from the *poblaciones,* and several were killed in the searches.

After an appeal for respect for those who had fallen in the struggle, especially the President of the Republic, the Cardinal kept quiet for several months. He made no public protest when the Junta expelled many priests and nuns, or when it put its nominee in charge of Catholic University. Meanwhile, around him, reactionary elements in the church openly defended the Junta. Chile's Catholic welfare organization distributed a letter to parallel organizations in many countries denigrating the Allende regime. In December, a letter was sent in the name of the central committee of the conference of Chile's bishops which sought to justify the actions of the Junta, claiming that it was acting with utmost moderation, that there were no shortages, and that unemployment was falling.

Meanwhile, however, a committee headed by Catholic bishop Fernando Ariztía Ruiz, Lutheran bishop Helmut Frenz, and High Rabbi Angel Kreiman was trying to protect the lives of thousands of Chileans held without charge or trial. In March it filed a habeas-corpus action on behalf of 131 people who had been arrested and subsequently disappeared, people who "in their vast majority are innocent, poor and humble, lacking any social status, without well-known names and without important influence." When the Chilean bishops met at Easter, this committee submitted a dossier on widespread physical and mental tortures and other abuses. The result was a strong public protest from the bishops, the main elements of which are reproduced below. Also reproduced are major segments of the confidential documents in the dossier, as translated from the Mexican daily *Excelsior.*

Three of approximately 30 Chilean bishops reportedly opposed the statement. It is understood that one of them notified the Junta before the document was released, and that pressures from the Junta caused the Cardinal to preface the dossier with a statement that "it reflects the thinking of the majority of the Chilean bishops" and that "the Chilean situation cannot be understood without bearing in mind the chaotic state of things and the enormous and passionate tensions that existed under the previous government" and without realizing "that armed resistance still exists on the part of certain individuals opposed to the present government."

Response among Protestants has been as ambivalent as that among Catholics. A few leaders known for sympathy to the Allende regime have been expelled. Those who remain maintain a low profile. Protestant reaction in Europe is expressed in the powerful article of a German theologian, Helmut Gollwitzer, whose struggles during the Nazi era convinced him that the church must relate to political and economic life.

Chilean Bishops Speak Out: The Easter Statement

Released by the Secretariat of the Chilean Episcopacy under the title "Reconciliation in Chile" (Ref. No. 144/1974), the statement abstracted below was signed by Raúl Cardinal Silva Henríquez, Archbishop of Santiago, "for all the bishops of Chile" on April 24, 1974. That the bishops may be playing "the role of international Marxist agents without realizing it" was the Junta's response, as formulated by General Gustavo Leigh.

We know that the Lord has entrusted to us, the bishops in union with the Holy Father, the task of guiding his people. . . . Conscious of this inescapable and untransferable responsibility, we want to share with you the hopes and anxieties that have arisen among us as we reflect, in the light of the gospel, on the challenges of this present hour.

We feel this is particularly urgent because certain other voices are being raised, which though they do not have the authority granted by Christ, seek to guide the people of God and succeed only in sowing confusion and anxieties among them. . . .

There are two basic attitudes that cannot be absent in those who believe in the gospel, two attitudes that by restoring lost confidence make possible a future of peace, two attitudes that give back to the man who has them his full stature: (a) We must ask pardon, an inescapable attitude in anyone who knows he has defrauded his brother, not only by some positive offense, but also through a love that he did not extend when it was needed. (b) We must know how to pardon those who have offended us. Pardoning an enemy, praying for those who persecute us, and blessing those who curse us (cf: Lk. 6:27-28)—these are not just beautiful words written to move those who read them, but the only possible way to get along together.

We Christians must not only be reconciled, each one with his enemy of yesterday or today. We must also be peacemakers (cf: Mt. 5:9). Out of love for our country, we must help re-establish a pattern of coexistence in which all of us Christians can live together and feel that we are brothers. Let us briefly explain what are, in our view, the conditions for achieving this goal. But first, each one should ask himself sincerely if he really wants to reach that goal. For without that honest and effective desire, it is useless to make statements or even take steps.

The basic condition for getting along together peacefully is the full observance of human rights, so that the Constitution and the law will be a guarantee for all. Hence we are extremely interested that a new constitutional text is rapidly being drafted. Hence too we judge it opportune that the government has published a Declaration of Principles. Its explicitly Christian tenor is praiseworthy, and we believe that despite certain inadequacies in stating the Christian ideal for social and political life, it offers a basis for guiding civic and social life in this emergency situation. We hope that all, both rulers and people, will faithfully abide by its spirit in the search for the common good. But we are the first to hope that Christian principles will be incorporated into our country's Constitution, in view of our people's free acceptance of them and after a discussion in which all citizens can participate actively and knowledgeably.

We recall, and the Declaration of Principles we mentioned above asserts it, that it is licit to disagree with this or any government, but the country's peace and welfare demand that we collaborate with the authorities in all that is manifestly for the common good.

We do not doubt the honest intention or the good will of our rulers. But as pastors, we see objective obstacles for a reconciliation among Chileans. Such situations can be overcome only by an unrestricted respect for the human rights enumerated by the United Nations and by Vatican Council II, which the Declaration of Principles correctly describes as "natural, and both prior to and higher than the state." A respect for man's dignity is not genuine without respect for these rights.

We are worried, first of all, by a climate of insecurity and fear, the root of which we think we see in delations, false rumors, and a lack of participation and information.

We are also worried by the social aspects of the present economic situation, among which can be pointed out the rise in unemployment and the firings for arbitrary or ideological reasons. We fear that, as economic development is accelerated, the economy is being structured in such a way that wage-earners are being burdened with an excessive amount of sacrifice, without having the desirable amount of participation.

We are worried, too, that the educational system is being completely restructured and reoriented, without sufficient participation by parents and the school community.

We are worried, finally, in some cases, by the lack of effective juridical care for personal security, which shows up in arbitrary or excessively prolonged detentions in which neither those held nor their relatives know of the concrete charges that prompt them; by the interrogations with physical or moral pressures; by the restrictions on access to legal defense; by unequal sentences for identical causes from place to place; by restrictions on the normal use of the right of appeal.

We realize that particular circumstances can justify a temporary suspension of the exercise of certain civil rights. But there are rights that touch the very dignity of the human person, and they are absolute and inviolable. The Church has to be the voice of all, but especially of those who have no voice.

We must not forget that it is God who is calling us to reconciliation; and it is he too who offers it to us as pardon in the sacrament of penance. Hence we make our own the words of St. Paul: "We beg you in the name of Christ: let yourselves be reconciled with God" (2 Cor. 5:20) . . . ■

An official Soviet broadcast from Moscow praised the Catholic bishops of Chile, particularly Cardinal Raúl Silva Henríquez of Santiago, for aiding Chileans "persecuted" by the current military regime, and warned that the Junta is trying "to split the Catholic hierarchy from within."

—National Catholic Reporter
July 19, 1974

"We Cannot Remain Silent"

Bishop Carlos Camus, Secretary of the Chilean Bishops' Council, made the following comment on the bishops' statement on Chile's national television network during an interview on April 26, 1974.

In Chile the Carabineros and the Church are the institutions that permeate the whole country, that is, the human tapestry. Normally priests are the ones who receive the intimate, personal and private confidences of the people; medical doctors do also but they do not dare to speak out. We priests have nothing to lose and can speak with complete freedom. The information we have is generally confidential; nobody wants to go into details and give his name because he is afraid. But when information is given to us we always filter it because there are emotional people, people who exaggerate—there is great exaggeration—and there are campaigns by people who utilize and even want to infiltrate the Church. So it is that we do not speak lightly. But when we have heard of suffering we cannot remain silent. We should have preferred not to have to speak out. ∎

U.S. Bishops Charge Junta

The 28 bishops who comprise the Administrative Board of the U.S. Catholic Conference (USCC) issued in April 1974 the following public statement protesting human rights violations being committed by the Chilean Junta. The Administrative Board is the decision-making group of the U.S. Catholic Conference which functions as the national-level agency of the U.S. Catholic Conference. Observers in Washington report that this is the first time the bishops have spoken so directly and forcefully on a specific violation of Christian social justice.

We are deeply distressed by the violations of human rights taking place in Chile. We associate ourselves in solidarity with the Church of Chile during these troubled times. We are also concerned that in the face of these violations our government is escalating its financial aid to the Chilean Junta.

Therefore, with the exception of humanitarian aid, we urge the United States Government to condition its financial aid and military assistance to Chile upon the demonstration that human and civil rights have been restored in that country. . . .

[The bishops stressed that moral principles should be applied to foreign policy and quoted from the resolution authored by the U.S. bishops celebrating the 25th anniversary of the United Nations Universal Declaration of Human Rights.]

The pervasive presence of American power creates a responsibility of using that power in the service of human rights. The link between our economic assistance and regimes which utilize torture, deny legal protection to citizens and detain political prisoners without due process clearly is a question of conscience for our government and for each of us as citizens in a democracy. ∎

Canadian Missionaries Indignant

The following are excerpts from the Manifesto by Canadian Missionaries Expelled from Chile by the Military Junta.

We priests and laymen of Quebec and Canada who were expelled and forced to leave after the military takeover feel a duty to join the workers of the world who will be celebrating this anniversary [of the inauguration of Allende as president of Chile] in mourning. We also feel obligated to tell what convinced us to support Salvador Allende and the Popular Unity Party, namely that at that moment in Chilean history the Popular Unity Government became the most adequate and competent instrument to achieve the liberation of the Chilean workers and peasants.

We are still indignant over what happened in Chile and by virtue of our experience there we are asking the Church of Canada to be alert to the campaign undertaken by the military Junta through different spokesmen—businessmen, churchmen and military officers—in an effort to justify the military coup. For anyone who lived in close contact with the common people it will be difficult to discover the positive aspects of the present fascist dictatorship. We hope that the Canadian Church, which we have represented in Chile, will trust us as witnesses to the situation and as worthy of faith as any bishop or dignitary of the Church.

We deeply regret the silence of the Chilean bishops regarding the injustices of the fascist regime and the support some of them have given to the Junta. We understand that it may be difficult to speak out. At the same time, our hearts are saddened when we see that the Church seems to be directed by military chaplains and at the service of the Junta.

We ask the citizens of Quebec and Canada to be alert to the activities of the multinational corporations (we mean the international companies of the United States) which impose their own laws without rendering account to anyone, except to their more important stockholders. They arbitrarily make and unmake governments, even those that are democratically elected.

We condemn the attitude adopted by the Minister of Foreign Relations who stated before the House of Commons that he was willing to take the necessary steps for immigration of Chileans and other refugees but who made access to the Embassy difficult if not impossible.

Finally, we ask international organizations to be more astute and not let themselves be seduced on their visits to Chile by the smooth language of the military Junta. In effect, thousands of people suffer unjustly and are constantly deprived of their rights. Thousands of people have been tortured and an unknown number executed in a true Nazi style. These facts must not be ignored either by the United Nations, or the World Council of Churches, or international organizations such as the Red Cross, International Labor Organization, and others.

We ask for the creation of an International Tribunal to judge the crimes committed by the Chilean military Junta, similar to the one in Stockholm that judged those committed by the American armies in Vietnam.

In the name of justice we call for the doors of our country to be opened wide for Chileans and foreigners persecuted by the Junta.

We call upon the Canadian people to receive the Chilean refugees with Solidarity, as brothers unjustly oppressed.

Our manifesto is intended as an homage to the Chilean people, as a compensation for all that we learned in their country. We went there to give, but we now find ourselves richer than when we left here. We owe this to a people who wished, in a democratic way, to build a more just and fraternal society, one which would give to rural and urban workers the place that belongs to them in the construction of society. ■

Ecumenical Aid for Victims Through the CCP

EPICA, a church-related group devoted to information and documentation on Latin America, published the following account in Lucha: Christians' Response to Military Repression in Chile, *June 1974.*

Amidst the political and social repression since the military seized power in September, a small ecumenical group has been doing more than anyone else to help the victims of terror in Chile. In the early days of October, the Lutheran bishop Helmut Frenz, along with Don Fernando Ariztía, the Auxiliary Bishop of Santiago, and Fernando Salas, a young Jesuit priest, organized the Committee of Cooperation for Peace. Prominent Jewish and Protestant clergymen have also given their support to this committee which is dedicated to helping political prisoners and their families as well as the unemployed.

The Committee has centers in Santiago and in 12 provinces throughout Chile. Each center is staffed with lawyers, social workers, and volunteers. In Santiago alone, 17 lawyers work full time defending political prisoners who could not otherwise afford legal assistance.

Among specific tasks taken on by the Committee are: legal assistance for political prisoners and workers arbitrarily fired from their jobs for political beliefs; material assistance for the families of those who have been killed, imprisoned or fired from their jobs; relocation of those who must leave the country for political or economic reasons; aid to students and professors suspended from the universities for political beliefs; and economic and technical aid for projects to create new jobs for the unemployed.

The source of much pain and anguish for many Chilean families today is the lack of information concerning the whereabouts of loved ones who have been missing since the bloody days of the military coup. In their maddening search for information, hundreds of mothers, wives, children, relatives and friends have pounded on countless doors. These humble families without money or influence have begged military officials for information and rarely have they been heard. In desperation they have come to the Committee that they might plead their case before the government officials.

The Committee has pursued every legal means available to secure information on people who are missing and to arrange the release of prisoners or the publication of charges against them. Of the 1300 families who have come to the Committee for such help, over 600 have been able to find out where and when their relative or friend disappeared—most of them having been killed, some of them imprisoned or exiled.

Firings for political or economic reasons have left about 20 percent of the Chilean work force unemployed. Informed sources estimate that 100,000 Chileans have been fired for their political beliefs. Those who have been fired have been blacklisted and generally cannot find other jobs.

In response to this situation, the Committee has provided economic and technical assistance to workers who are organizing to create new sources of employment—in cooperative workshops or small businesses run by the workers themselves. Some 120 groups of workers fired from their jobs have solicited technical and economic aid from the Committee for the formation of their own workshops. Many of these groups have already received the support necessary to start these new endeavors.

Human rights are still being trampled on in Chile by men who claim to be inspired by Christian humanism. . . . Unemployment grows. . . . Collapse of purchasing power hits the poorest hardest. . . . The government's encouragement drives people to become informers in the hope of keeping their jobs or getting them back. . . . The military court decisions are arbitrary. . . . All of us in France can contribute to creating international opinion in favor of change in a country that is our friend. . . . Oppression takes many forms in every continent, and such contempt for men calls everyone to "spiritual resistance" and that applies first of all to Chile.

Statement of the Justice and Peace Commission of France's Catholic Bishops and of the Social and International Commission of France's Federation of Protestants

July, 1974

The maintenance of the Committee of Cooperation for Peace is extremely difficult. The ordinary expenses of the Committee centers throughout Chile are approximately $13,000 a month. Added to the financial burden of the Committee are the growing threats of reprisals from the forces of the right. The conservative daily, *La Segunda*, a semi-official newspaper closely identified with the most right-wing groups in Chile, recently published headlines accusing Bishop Ariztía and the Committee of "calumnies" against Chile. It also called for "logical and severe reaction on the part of the Chilean Government" against Bishop Ariztía and Jesuit Father Fernando Salas, the executive secretary of the Committee.

"Neither should be allowed to continue to attack the government and the country with total impunity under the protection of the Church," the paper said.

In response to such attacks the Committee of Cooperation for Peace continues to reiterate that its task is that of providing "spiritual, social and legal aid" to the poor and needy. ■

An Interchurch Group Reports on Torture

The most incontrovertible of the many reports on torture, firing squads, assassinations of suspected opponents of the Junta, shooting of prisoners in pretended escape attempts, massive firing of workers, use of informers, and other types of repression is that of the Committee of Cooperation for Peace in Chile whose composition and activities are described above.

On May 15, 1974, the Mexican daily Excelsior *published what it called the most startling of the eight sections into which the confidential document was divided: those dealing with torture, with the institutions involved in search and seizure, with the development of the Junta's actions against political dissidents, and with the situation of women in Santiago.* Excelsior *reported that the Commission had hundreds of volunteer workers in its central office in Santiago and 12 regional offices and that in May it still had a daily turnover of 200 to 300 people seeking its help. What follows is translated from* Excelsior *by Barbara Durr and Gary MacEoin.*

Torture

After describing some shocking experiences, for the accuracy of which it vouched (for example, how "a 15-year-old girl was stripped, her body covered with excrement, then left to be attacked by rats") the section on "torture" continues:

1. Only those tortures are listed here that are fully confirmed. They are testified to by the people who either suffered or witnessed them. In some cases, the kinds of tortures which caused death could be deduced from the corpse in the absence of any other cause of death. In one case, a 17-year-old prisoner told a visitor that he was maltreated in jail. Two days later, the authorities said that he was dead because he had "tried to escape." There are similar cases, such as the report in the news daily *La Prensa*, December 22, 1973, that four persons had died in a confrontation with the military. Witnesses claim that the four persons in question had been arrested four days earlier and that at least one of them died during interrogation on December 20. To sum up, this report does not include all cases that deal with deaths for "trying to escape" or "confrontation with the military," when the real cause of death may have been maltreatment. The report includes only those cases documented by testimony.

2. Forced nudity, the most common of all abuses, has been mentioned only when it was used in combination with some other kind of maltreatment.

3. The majority of those arrested and almost all of those interrogated were blindfolded. The blindfolding, referred to in this report, was used during and after interrogations. It continued at times for a few hours, at times for days, at times for a whole month. Sometimes it was alternated with confinement in dark rooms.

4. A considerable number of witnesses testify that, before release, they had to sign a declaration stating that they had been well treated. In some instances, before signing this document, other means, such as hypnosis and threats to prisoners and their families, were used to secure the silence of the tortured. The state of desperation and anxiety of those interrogated often defeated attempts at hypnosis. This difficulty was overcome, however, by not allowing prisoners to sleep the night before.

The torture section covers six months in detail, distinguishing three periods: September 11 to October 31, 1973; November 1 to December 31, 1973; January 1 to March 11, 1974.

Here is a summary of the frequency and kinds of physical tortures used in the first period: electrical shocks in various parts of the body, usually the gums, genitals and anus, 7 cases; beatings, 15; blindfolding, 3; burns with acid or cigarettes, 14; immersion in oil or water, 3; random flagellation, 2; confinement in unsanitary or insect-filled cells, 2; forced witness or performance of sexual activities, 2; dragging over stones, 2; forced witness of torture, 1; ingestion of excrement, 1; stocks, 1; hanging by the neck, 1; depriving of water for one week, 1; deliberate fracture of an already injured arm, 1; throwing blindfolded prisoners into pits, 1; insertion of two-edged, curved blades under fingernails and toenails, 1; cuts in hands, 1; and nude exposure to the sun, 1. Psychological tortures used in the first period: frightening with threats to family, simulated shootings, and simulated beatings.

The identified locations of torture were the municipal headquarters in Los Angeles, School for Military Engineers in Tejas Verdes, Infantry Headquarters in San Bernardo, Cavalry Headquarters in Viña del Mar, municipal headquarters in Guias, Telecommunications School in Valparaíso Naval Academy of War, third precinct police station in Bulnes, and the National Stadium.

The verified consequences of torture were: Need for intense psychiatric treatment, insomnia, headaches and eye pain, memory failures, recurrent symptoms of abortion in which the fetus is born with genetic defects, broken ribs, internal injuries, concussions, rib-cage collapse, broken pelvis, and a crushed foot. Corpses of four persons tortured to death could not even be dressed.

During the second period there were: electrical shocks, 10 cases; beatings, 9; blindfolding, 5; burns with acid or cigarettes (caused death), 1; random flagellation, 1; castration (caused death), 1; crushed skulls with missing encephalic mass (caused deaths), 2; forced witness of flagellation, 1; cold water baths (caused death), 1; sexual abuse of women, 1; keeping awake by kicking, 1; rifle shots next to ears, 1; asphyxiation (caused death), 1; extraction of fingernails and toenails, 1; arm fracture, 1. Psychological tortures included frightening with threats to family, photographs in different positions, simulated rape, simulated shooting. Verified results of torture included burned fingers, permanent depression and withdrawal, and serious nervous disturbances.

Identified locations of torture were the Chile Stadium in Santiago, military base in Maipú, municipal headquarters in Tacna, military base in Cerro Chena, Investigations Headquarters, the Buin regiment, and the El Bosque air base.

Recorded for the third period were: electrical shocks, 10 cases; beatings, 10; blindfolding, 4; burns with acid or cigarettes, 2; unspecified tortures, 7; stocks, 2; hanging, 1; forced witness of tortures, 1; pricking and jabbing, 1; dragging across the ground, 1; tied nude to a chair for two days, 1; and shackled on wet concrete with an ultraviolet light shining on the victim's head, 1.

One simulated shooting was verified as a psychological torture in the third period, and the following consequences of torture were established: pulmonary edema (excessive accumulation of serous fluid in tissues), separated shoulder, burned hands, hemothorax (blood filling the thorax area), psychological disturbances, fractured jaws, immobilized arm, punctured legs, bruised back, symptoms of epilepsy, serious difficulty distinguishing sound intensity, neurosurgical treatment, disjointed arms, and lameness. Six deaths resulted from acute anemia. Two bodies were incinerated before they could be identified, and therefore without the families' consent. Another had a leg missing, and the extremities of yet another were completely burned off.

Identified locations of torture were Tejas Verdes, Concón, National Police base at Maipú, El Bosque air base, Londres Street No. 38, and the third precinct police station.

Information concerning minors: Young children did not escape. A 16-year old boy was locked in a box and fed through a small hole. A 15-year-old girl was stripped naked and covered with excrement.

Organization of Search and Seizure

Concentration camps, designed to hold large numbers of persons in military custody and under conditions similar to those of prisoners of war, were established at Putre, Province of Tarapacá, near Arica (available information

---

An ecumenical group here is providing legal aid and other services to thousands of Chileans affected by last September's military takeover, according to statistics just released.

The Committee of Cooperation for Peace (CCP), headed by Catholic auxiliary Bishop Fernando Ariztía and Lutheran Bishop Helmut Frenz, reports that as of June 26 it has attended 15,564 requests for aid.

The CCP has given legal assistance to 4,136 persons dismissed from their jobs for political reasons. It also has provided legal defense for 3,655 persons on trial in military courts.

Assisting 1,120 students expelled from universities, the Committee claims it tries to award scholarships as well as reinstate students into their schools.

Half of CCP's 2,003 requests for relocation are still pending, but it has helped 904 people leave the country.

The Committee has distributed food, clothing, books and money to the families of detainees, prisoners, the missing or the dead. The CCP also reports it arranged transportation for 580 women to visit their husbands in the Chambuco political detainee camp, located some 900 miles from Santiago.

Finally, in an effort to help those areas of Chile hit hardest by unemployment, the CCP has created 250 small business projects. To date 50 have been financed, giving work to about 510 persons.

—Latinamerica Press
July 11, 1974, Vol. 6, No. 18

---

indicates existence of a prisoner camp, but first-hand testimony is lacking); Chacabuco, Province of Antofagasta; Piragua, Province of Tarapacá; Diesco Island, Province of Valparaíso; Quiriquina Island, Province of Concepción; and Dawson Island, Province of Magallanes.

Detention centers in the Province of Santiago, as of March, 1974, were the Buin regiment, the Tacuna regi-

ment, the Telecommunications regiment, the 2nd Armored regiment, El Bosque air base, the Polytechnic air academy, the War Academy of the Armed Forces, the Quinta Normal naval base, the basement of the Ministry of National Defense, the area underneath the Plaza de la Constitución, General Headquarters of the Department of Investigations and its centers at Nuñoa, Quinta Buin, Renca, Barrancas, Paine and Puente Alto, the Tejas Verdes regiment, the Bucalomu regiment, the Puente Alto regiment of Rail Workers, the San Bernardo infantry school, the Cerro Chena military base, the Colina air base, the School for Parachutists at Colina, the National Stadium, Londres Street No. 38, precincts of the National Police, Agustinas Street No. 632, police units in Melipilla and Talagante, Polytechnic School for Minors in San Bernardo, and the School for Specialized Activities of the Armed Forces.

The regular prisons and penitentiaries, as well as the House of Correction for Women, were also utilized.

In the provinces, other locations were operated as detention centers, for example, in Antofagasta, the Investigations Headquarters, Cerro Moreno Air Force base and the National Police Training School. Suspects were frequently tortured in these three locations.

Other provincial locations of imprisonment and torture are the naval base in Playa Ancha (Valparaíso), Buque Lebu (during the early months after the coup), Marine War Academy (Valparaíso), municipal headquarters in Tucapel de Temuco and Los Angeles, and Investigations Headquarters in Puerto Montt.

New Organs of Control Created by the Junta

SENDET (National Executive Secretariat of Detentions) was created December 31, 1973, for the following official reasons. (a) A variety of problems has arisen because of the large number of detentions that result from the State of Seige in force in Chile. (b) The advantage of SENDET is having a way to centralize and coordinate all the elements needed to solve these problems.

SENDET performs the following functions (according to the legal regulations under which it was established). It coordinates with other ministries the necessary information concerning persons detained. It advises the Ministries of Interior and National Defense regarding the same information. It coordinates the activities, control and information of all detention centers in Chile. It maintains up-to-date statistics on those arrested and records of their legal situations and state of health; keeps watch on the public attention and assistance to prisoners in general; and attends to situations that do not come within the competence of other authorities or are so complex that other authorities cannot solve them. SENDET is located in the National Congress building.

DINA (Department of National Intelligence) was also created. It is one of the four departments of the National Executive Secretary of Detentions. Its objective (according to official definition) is to establish standards for interrogations and reinterrogations of prisoners, determine the dangerousness of prisoners, and maintain a permanent coordination with Military Intelligence services.

Women in Santiago

This appendix deals with the "situation of women in Santiago," particularly with the Women's House of Correction, on the basis of the reports confirmed up to the early days of April. At that time there were between 80 and 90 women political prisoners, though in normal confinement, placed in the "patio of political women" (separated from the common criminals), and about four or five women in solitary confinement.

The treatment in this facility was normal: two meals a day, weekly visits, and preferential care by an order of nuns that usually worked there. The women in solitary confinement were kept in special cells.

Nevertheless, at least half of the women were forced to submit to interrogations with torture, done principally in Tejas Verdes and at Londres Street No. 38. Formerly they were brought to the National Stadium, the Ministry of Defense, and other locations. It is important to note that in the part of Tejas Verdes used for torture, there is a special section for women.

The tortures most frequently inflicted on women were threats to their children, beatings, electrical shocks, interrogations while naked, and sexual abuse. There were two women whose pregnancies were the result of torture, and a few others were waiting for medical examinations to determine possible pregnancies.

For the medical care of women prisoners there are doctors in the institution who attend to them when necessary. Several attempts were made to obtain permission from the authorities for these women to have private medical consultations outside the institution or be treated in hospitals by doctors contacted by the Committee. Those requests were refused, and the women were obliged to go to only one hospital.

Generally, the principal health problems that afflict these women are psychological. Some who have been released have had to have psychological treatment. One of them—her name cannot be released—suffered a complete psychological breakdown, which is probably irreparable.

There were also some problems with women who were pregnant before being arrested. Five were pregnant at this institution including two pregnancies which were pathological because they were the result of torture.

The husbands of at least seven women in the Women's House of Correction were arrested, indicted, or sentenced to jail (in Chacabuco or public prison), and their children thus had to live with relatives or neighbors.

Six women have already been sentenced: one, from Arica, to 26 years; one, from Talca, to 20 years; the others, to 15, 10, six and three years. On the other hand, approximately 12 women had been there since September without benefit of either the beginnings of a trial or the assignment of a public attorney to them.

These women began to experience a new problem; they were transferred to different locations. The reason for their transfers, according to SENDET, is that there was very little discipline in the Women's House of Correction. On April 5, 12 women were transferred to the Chile Stadium (at least that was where they were officially supposed to go). Among them were three 16-year-old girls.

Junta Action Against Opponents

The section entitled "The Development of the Military Government's Actions Against Political Dissidents" concentrates on examining the character of the military government's actions in the area of human rights from September 11, 1973, to the present. This interval is broken down into four time periods. The first is from the day of the coup to October 31, 1973.

This period includes the seizure of power by the Junta and extends to the establishment of the first forms of more systematic organization for dealing with political prisoners, an intelligence apparatus and Military Justice in Wartime.

Repression was carried out principally by the military, which set out to achieve and later secure what it called a "military victory."

A great number of people died, some by chance, others in the resistance. Others were executed summarily. Thousands sought asylum in foreign embassies. There were massive arrests. On the radio, a call was heard for all persons in higher levels of the government and politics to present themselves before the military. Huge search-and-destroy operations were performed in residential neighborhoods, *poblaciones* (slums), factories, estates, and public buildings. There were many cases of *ley de fuga* (formally, the right to shoot an escaping prisoner b.. often used as a cover up for summary executions).

The general characteristics of this period were rapid and massive repression directed at those who had appeared to be in leadership positions, the object being to destroy any political organization or opposition social base. Many people died. (It is not possible to give an exact figure, nor even an approximation.) Excessive numbers of arrests were made relying on later clarification, and this resulted in a piling up of prisoners. Torture was customarily part of interrogations. There was a complete lack of legal defense. The information of the Intelligence Services was not sufficiently processed or centralized. The first steps for creation of a system of Wartime Military Justice were taken.

More Deaths, More Torture

In the second period, from November 1 to December 31, thousands of prisoners were released. Projections of official data from various parts of the country—consistent with indications from direct sources and unofficial information—put the number of persons detained at over 19,000 in the entire country, in mid-December.

The apparatus of Military Justice in Wartime began to develop and organize. Instructions were given to lawyers and judges, and hearings began in the War Councils more regularly, though slowly. Of all people detained, only one in five was granted a trial, and only a small number of these trials reached completion in this period.

Lawyers found insuperable difficulties in presenting adequate defenses. Access to the defendant was almost impossible. The preparation of the defense was limited to 48 hours or less. Defense lawyers could not present evidence or challenge the evidence of the state's attorney. The possibility of questioning the tribunal did not exist; consequently, any possibility of appeal to a higher court was precluded. Provisional liberty could not be obtained. The judgments of the state's attorneys were almost always the basis of sentences, and many of these attorneys lost sight of fundamental juridical principles. The average sentence in these cases was unusually long.

It was evident that the military attorneys operated on the basis of the statements and other previous data from the Intelligence Services. The seclusion of prisoners and defendants was prolonged for weeks and months. The detentions and arrests—almost exclusively the result of leads by informers—were frequently carried out directly by intelligence personnel, without a warrant.

Many petitions for pardons were presented. The legal processes were extremely slow, and very few favorable verdicts were made. Generally, the conditions of prisoners, except in a few places, were abominable. Prisoners were often taken from detention centers and brought to other locations for interrogation by the Intelligence Services. Constant and repeated use of intense torture was characteristic of these interrogations. A tendency was observable towards uniformity of the kind of torture used in all of Chile.

Many persons died, some from torture. There was publicity about the application of *ley de fuga* (see above note). Relocation of foreign refugees was organized and developed by the churches and the United Nations. Although nearly 5,000 persons were relocated, more continued to seek asylum outside Chile. Characteristics of this period included repression more clearly directed from above, transfers and relocations of prisoners, release of many persons detained since September or October, better organization and more systematic functioning of Military Justice in Wartime, control of interrogations and detentions by the Intelligence Services, better systemization and coordination among the Intelligence Services, constant use of torture, the beginning of uniformity of technique and forms of torture, serious difficulties in preparing legal defenses, and fewer deaths.

State of Siege Prolonged

The third period covers January 1 to March 11. On January 3, Law 288 was decreed. Through this law, all the arrests made since September 11 were legalized. It also established that future arrests could only be made by decree of the Minister of Interior in the name of the military Junta.

More than 300 persons were released from Chacabuco, and several thousand others were released throughout the country. (Toward the end of this period, according to Red Cross reports, the number of prisoners was estimated at 10,000.)

Despite the intentions of Law 288, arrests continued without any decree, with the exception of a few cases. The arrests were made by plainclothes intelligence agents who did not identify themselves and drove unmarked vehicles.

A large number of persons was arrested again without any apparent redress, but it is for periods varying from a few days (more common) to three to six weeks. There was often either no way of knowing that the arrest had been made or no way of finding out the whereabouts of the arrested. Hundreds of reports about missing persons were received by the churches. Many persons reappeared after a few weeks and testified that they had been imprisoned in torture camps, usually Tejas Verdes, during that time. They also said that the interrogations seemed to have no clear objective.

SENDET officially announced that no notification of arrests would be made until after three weeks.

During the third period, various locations were fitted out for torture. The courts of Military Justice in Wartime were operating in a more organized way, though still very slowly, making the same errors, judgments, and verdicts as in the previous period. Although many prisoners were taken out of seclusion, many more remained under heavy security. The lifting of seclusion often meant only permission for the family to visit. No other person, not even the prisoner's lawyer, was allowed.

A few cases of provisional liberty began to be granted. Two petitions for pardons were accepted by the Appellate Court of Santiago, but did not secure the prisoners' release (one was subsequently revoked by a Supreme Court decision).

Just over 20 percent of the tried prisoners were sentenced by the end of this period. An examination of the sentences shows, in addition to a constant number of serious errors, a great disparity in the criteria of the District Attorneys and War Councils in different parts of the country.

The work of the Committee for Refugees reached its highest point. A large number of persons left Chile, especially the unemployed who had been prisoners. It was hoped that the State of Siege would be concluded at the end of this period, which coincided with the close of the maximum duration of a state of siege allowed by the Constitution. The end was postponed, however, until September 11, 1974.

Characteristics of this period were an increasing coordination of Intelligence Services which succeeded in getting the repressive activities under their control, observable signs of increasing autonomy of the Intelligence Services with respect to government authorities, and the tendency of agents of repression to "institutionalize themselves." The government decreed more laws and established organs for the specific purpose of regulating the treatment of political dissidents.

A Rest Pause at Tejas Verdes

During the fourth period, from March 11 to about April 10, the number of prisoners remained stable and, unlike during the previous period, there were no releases from Chacabuco or other prison camps. The leading members of the Allende government were transferred from Dawson Island, but were still incommunicado.

State attorneys were instructed to speed up the trials, which could mean a stay of proceedings, shorter sentences, or sentences based on time already served. A few important trials were being prepared, in particular against officers of the armed forces. (*Excelsior* has had access to some of the claims of the defense attorneys, which include, among other things, evidence of torture.)

Arrests continued to be made by Intelligence agents in the same manner as described in the previous period. Many people still seek asylum. People continue to pour out of Chile. Torture continues in the way described. ∎

In a July editorial Santiago's *El Mercurio* asks for the elimination of the Committee of Cooperation for Peace which was organized by Chilean churches. The Committee has given aid to detainees, helped many to leave the country whose lives were in danger and continues to aid their families by providing legal counsel, visits from social workers, distribution of food and clothing, finding jobs, etc. Catholic Bishop Fernando Ariztía and Luthern Bishop Helmut Frenz have been frequently questioned by government officials, most recently when the Committee was accused of giving lists of torture victims to Mexico's *Excelsior*. *El Mercurio* praised the helpful spirit of the Committee and then deplored the fact that "when so many were persecuted" during Allende's regime no such committee functioned nor were churches concerned about human rights. It asks that the Committee be eliminated since it is "superfluous in a country like Chile where law and right have dominion."

—Latinamerica Press,
Vol. 6, No. 21, August 1, 1974

An Open Letter to ITT

Mr. Harold Geneen
Chairman of the Board of Directors
International Telephone and Telegraph Corporation
New York, New York

Dear Mr. Geneen:

We write as people in the Churches deeply concerned about the recent events in Chile and the demise of democracy there. We write because we are particularly dismayed by the role ITT has played in attempting to influence events in Chile.

We are aware that the Christian Church (Disciples of Church) filed a stockholder resolution early this year requesting that ITT disclose information in response to five questions:

1. Details on how the decision was made within the company to offer the CIA $1 million to intervene in Chile.

2. A statement of the company position explaining the rationale for this decision.

3. A summary of public reaction in Chile and in the USA to this decision.

4. A summary of the reasons of the CIA for rejecting this proposal.

5. A summary of any actions the corporation took to influence U.S. government agencies or U.S. banks or companies to isolate Chile.

In response ITT offered to make available to any interested stockholder the report by the Senate Subcommittee on Multinational Corporations entitled "The International Telephone and Telegraph Company and Chile, 1970-71" and a statement by ITT on its policy regarding interference in other countries' internal affairs.

We have read that report carefully and are urging the American public to take the time to read this detailed account of ITT's attempt to influence the course of history in Chile. Among the principal facts revealed are these:

1. In July, 1970, ITT, through you as Chairman of the Board, approached the CIA and offered a substantial fund for the purpose of opposing Salvador Allende in the upcoming elections in Chile.

2. In September, 1970, ITT offered $1 million to the CIA in support of any U.S. government plan designed to form a coalition in the Chilean Congress to prevent Allende from becoming president.

3. In September, 1970, ITT management considered a plan proposed by the CIA to create economic chaos in Chile but rejected it as "unworkable."

4. In October, 1971, after the Chilean government announced plans to nationalize ITT's operations, the corporation management approached the U.S. government with an eighteen-point action plan designed to guarantee that Allende would not "make it through the next six months." These plans detailed ways of economically boycotting Chile, thereby exacerbating the Chilean economic situation.

5. Once these plans were publicized in the media, negotiations on compensation between ITT and Chile were broken off.

We are aware that ITT publicly defended these actions at the 1973 stockholders meeting when you, Mr. Geneen, replied to Church questioners:

> The Chile Hearings, long delayed, showed only that we strived through our government to protect our shareholders' properties, worth $153 million, which actions were entirely within our legal rights. . . . I'm sorry we were not able to persuade the U.S. government to take a stronger stand in Chile. (*Kansas City Times*, May 10, 1973)

Our reading of the Report of Hearings does not support your claim to the appropriateness of your action. We believe the evidence is clear that ITT management was willing to use political subterfuge and economic sanctions to subvert the legally elected government of a foreign country.

We are not aware of any occasion on which ITT management has apologized for its behavior, or admitted (in the words of the Senate Subcommittee report) that "the company overstepped the line of acceptable corporate behavior." We have seen no admission of wrongdoing, no intention not to repeat this same pattern of events should similar situations arise.

We are shocked by these actions and urge ITT to immediately repudiate them and pledge itself not to interfere in the political processes of another country either directly or through an agency of the U.S. government.

Furthermore, ITT equated its economic interests with American national interests, arguing through former CIA Director McCone that the United States should intervene in Chile since the Overseas Private Investment Corporation (OPIC) would have to compensate ITT if nationalized and the cost would have to be borne by the U.S. taxpayer. We reject this argument of convenience. OPIC guarantees are certainly not provided by our government so that they can be used later as justification for covert military or political interference in Latin America.

We believe that ITT's actions in trying covertly to intervene in the political process in Chile is unacceptable to persons of conscience. We further believe that the Overseas Private Investment Corporation should not repay ITT for its losses in Chile. In our opinion, ITT forfeited any right to these insurance guarantees by its actions.

We urge the corporation to admit its error in this case and to pledge publicly that ITT will never again seek to subvert the course of history in Latin American or anywhere else for its own economic benefit.

(signed)   Very truly yours,

Rev. William L. Wipfler, *Latin America Mission Director*
    National Council of Churches
Rev. Paul McCleary
    Assistant General Secretary, Latin American Affairs
    Board of Global Ministries, United Methodist Church
Rev. Ben F. Gutierrez
    Liaison for Latin America and the Caribbean Program
    Agency, United Presbyterian Church in the USA
Father Placide Bazoche, *North American Secretary*
    World Student Christian Federation
Rev. W. Sterling Cary
    President, National Council of Churches
Dr. William J. Nottingham
    Executive Secretary for Latin America
    Christian Church (Disciples of Christ)
Joyce Hill, *Executive Secretary for Latin America*
    Board of Global Ministries, United Methodist Church
Dr. Howard Schomer
    World Issues Secretary, United Church of Christ
Rev. Merle Crouse, *Latin America Representative*
    World Ministries Commission General Board
    Church of the Brethren
May 4, 1974

WCC Report on Refugees

Following the coup, a number of concerned groups responded to the World Council of Churches' international appeal for emergency aid to victims of the Junta. A summary of their recent work on behalf of Chilean refugees follows.

In the five months following the military take-over, approximately 5,500 non-Chilean refugees left Chile under the auspices of the National Committee for Assistance to Refugees (CONAR), according to a June 1974 report of the World Council of Churches (WCC) to institutions, churches, and groups which contributed to its appeal for emergency help.

Some 150 refugees are still under the care of the CONAR staff, awaiting the opportunity to leave Chile, and some 200 have opted to stay in Chile. CONAR is also working with several hundred others who are relatives of refugees who have left and are consequently eligible to join them in their country of asylum.

Church committees in Argentina, Peru, Costa Rica, Honduras, Ecuador, Colombia, and Panama have worked and continue to work with CONAR to facilitate the temporary needs of refugees from Chile while they wait for permanent asylum.

The Argentine group, CAREF, has under its care about 3,500 of the estimated 10,000 refugees (mostly Chileans) now in Argentina still awaiting a permanent solution of their problems. The inflow of Chileans to Argentina continues. The WCC has given CAREF $150,-000 and pledged a further $135,000 for care and maintenance, legal and health needs, internal travel, and permanent-solution schemes. Total estimated needs for these purposes in Argentina in 1974 are $1,400,000.

The Peruvian committee is working with 800 of the estimated 3,500 Chileans who have fled to Peru since September by plane, car, boat, train, and on foot across the northern Chilean desert. Peru is not granting any permanent residence to Chilean refugees, and many are in extreme need. About 500 have been resettled elsewhere.

Over-all figures indicate that 4,500 non-Chilean refugees have left officially for countries of asylum, mostly in Europe, and that 350 foreign refugees are still in Chile. An estimated 800 family members of persons who left for asylum are still in Chile. The number of Chileans in Argentina is estimated at 10,000, and in Peru at 2,300. Foreign embassies in Santiago gave asylum to 4,200 people, almost all of whom have left Chile.

The Committee of Cooperation for Peace (CCP) set up under church auspices in October has concerned itself with the protection of Chilean nationals. By mid-May it had received requests for help for 3,400 persons in the military courts, prisons, and places of detention, including nearly 200 who had simply disappeared. It also helped nearly 4,000 people—most of them peasants and bluecollar or whitecollar workers—in labor courts, succeeding in getting pay retroactively from date of dismissal to date of trial for three-quarters of them and having nearly one in five reinstated in jobs. It also helped to get nearly a thousand of them out of the country.

WCC expenditures for Chilean relief to date total more than $650,000, and the projections call for nearly $400,000 immediately and an equal amount later in 1974. Special contributions to date total about $750,000, most from Europe and only six percent from the United States.

Learning from Chile

The following article, reprinted from Christianity and Crisis, *May 13, 1974, is a reflection by the German theologian Helmut Gollwitzer on recent events in Chile. It was given as an address to the "House of Church" in West Germany three days after the September coup. Translated here by Gerald Williams, a graduate student in German Studies at Stanford University who studied with Gollwitzer, the essay first appeared in* Das Argument, *October 1973.*

At least by now everyone can see what class struggle is all about: The class struggle always comes from above. It is the struggle of the privileged who are resolutely prepared to commit any brutality, any transgression of the law, any massacre, even to destroy democracy itself, whenever they are no longer able to guarantee their rule. The class struggle is never begun by malevolent ringleaders or by socialists; it comes from above, is always in progress and uses widely varied methods—including the shedding of blood when need be. *The class struggle from below is the counterviolence of the oppressed.* When someone asks you your position on violence ask him first about his position on the violence from above; and then, when he begins to stammer, laugh in his face!

(1) "He who says capitalism must also say fascism," Max Horkheimer said in his more lucid days. This does not mean that capitalism unavoidably leads to fascism; rather: Capitalism of necessity resorts to fascism when its position is endangered. Two years ago Leo Guiliani wrote in *Lo Mondo* (July 25, 1971): "Liberal democracy is the mask the propertied classes wear when they have nothing to fear; fascism is the mask of fear." The "gentlemen" of property and culture in our land . . . get all excited about the difficulties of a few intellectuals in the Soviet Union. They are even prepared to see their basic principle of nonintervention—which is held holy with respect to Thieu or Portugal—suspended in Sacharow's case.

Actually, in taking this position they are only cooking up another anti-Communist brew, as can be seen by their total indifference toward the intellectuals and workers in the prisons of the NATO countries such as Greece and Turkey. This is all the more clearly revealed now by their approval of the coup in Chile. Whenever the ruling "gentlemen" of property and culture have the choice between a parliamentary democracy that leads to socialism and a fascist dictatorship that can prevent it, they choose the latter. That is the true parallel between today and 1933. For this reason everybody ought to know where the true loyalty of the capitalist "defenders" of the Constitution lies.

(2) The military machine, which transforms the sons of the people into its compliant, weak-minded tools, is the most dangerous instrument of class rule. One unsolved problem of the socialist movement is this: How can the military and police in a bourgeois democracy be so trained that they are prepared to defend the commonwealth against foreign enemies and internal crime, but are unwilling to turn their weapons against a popular movement for socialism?

"Unity Comes Before Clarity"

(3) The capitalists exercise international solidarity—the people of Chile fight on alone. One of the weaknesses of the socialist movement is that it has remained national: Its internationalism is still only verbal. In the European Economic Community (EEC) there is still no international counterweight within unionism to place against the power of the multinational corporations, still no international strike solidarity. Our task is easily ascertainable in this situation: The present awakening of class consciousness among German workers must be directed towards international class consciousness from the very beginning. The workers of the industrial nations, who have allowed themselves to be fattened up into a workers' aristocracy, must recognize that their interests are also being decided in Chile, in South Africa, in Angola.

(4) Such catastrophes as the one in Chile demand that the divisions within the socialist movement be surmounted. This demand is often heard, but most people only mean by it that "other" groups should join theirs. However, instead of the motto "Clarity comes before unity" I propose "Unity comes before clarity." Differences of opinion with regard to strategy must no longer be allowed to hinder the common battle. Fidel Castro said in Chile two years ago: "Revolution is the art of uniting diverse forces in order to achieve a common goal . . ."

(5) During the past few years Christians and Marxists in Chile have found a common meeting ground. Christians have become Marxists without ceasing to be Christians, and through this partnership Marxists have come to see that Christianity can have revolutionary potential; it does not necessarily have to be reactionary. This realization must have some effect upon our society. Only the capitalists have profited from the quarrels between Christians and Marxists. Ideology must no longer be allowed to divide us.

(6) The coup in Chile has *not* disproved the thesis once and for all that parliamentary democracy can be utilized in the transformation to socialism. On the contrary, without Allende's attempt the consciousness of the masses would not have grown so strong. But the dangers of using parliamentary democracy for this transformation have become clearer, and they require further analysis.

In order to function with even modest success, parliamentary democracy needs a developed middle class. Yet in the moment of decision the middle class sides with the counterrevolution, especially when the counterrevolution, which in fact created the chaos in society, presents itself as the savior of the hour. For this reason a process of educational enlightenment is necessary within the middle class. This is no less important or difficult than the educational work still to be done among workers.

This process had already begun in Chile, but time ran out. When in the transition to socialism such an educational process is insufficient and dictatorial measures become necessary (such measures were not possible for Allende due to lack of power and time), we are presented with the following questions: How can one prevent these measures from leading to a permanent party dictatorship? How can one assure the realization of democracy and freedom within socialism? (*Die Zeit*, in an article on September 14, 1973, used the Chilean coup as proof to the "educated" German that "radical socialism obviously cannot function without dictatorship.")

It seems to me we can learn the following from Chile: The parliamentary democracy phase is the best opportunity to develop the strength of the socialism movement, until the point is reached that coup-planning generals become powerless against it. In this situation the peaceful transition to socialism will be possible; the army will no longer be in the hands of the coupists, and dictatorial measures against a few groups (if they are necessary at all) will not diminish the new democratic achievements. Our present task follows from this argumentation: to utilize parliamentary democracy to the hilt and to make it secure against those who wish to reduce it to the mainstay of capitalism.

A Matter of Life and Death

(7) Whether Allende was murdered or took his own life is not decisive. Even supposing he took his own life—and that is the less likely of the two possibilities!—it would have been the exact opposite of Hitler's desertion through suicide. It would have been the last service that Allende could have given his movement and his people at that moment—and I say this consciously as a Christian theologian. It would have been the signal for the fact that it is a life and death matter. It is a matter of life and death for the Chilean people and all the people of Latin America who have been pushed more deeply than ever before into the catastrophe of hunger and slavery by the coup.

In Latin America more people will starve during the 1970s than during the decade of the 1960s; the experts are in agreement about that. The hunger catastrophe is one part of the catastrophe of all mankind that is now in progress. Every setback for socialism is a step towards the downfall of mankind, a downfall for which capitalism in its blindness is preparing us. Mankind can no longer afford capitalism; we are dying of it. This situation demands of us discipline, devotion and selflessness.

Much of that which we think we can still afford has become too costly. It is no longer possible to advocate socialism while blithely satisfying our daily needs and desires on a capitalistic basis. Socialism has application to life in its totality. Today we can be sure of the rightness of the socialist cause, but not of its success. Each of us must seek the strength for courage and sacrifice. Christians have something to say here. But every person will be able to discover for himself that this struggle is an opportunity to live life meaningfully.

(8) We will have to be inventive in our solidarity. The fact that we have done shamefully little in earlier situations, and have therefore accomplished little, should not hinder us now. Rather it should lead us to demonstrate our solidarity with more creative imagination and selflessness than ever before. We can now expect the worst possible fate for all the persecuted fugitives from other Latin American dictatorships who had found refuge under the Allende government; there are more than ten thousand of them. In addition to that there will be Chilean emigrants—those who succeeded in fleeing. Then there are the thousands already starving and being tortured in Chile.

Amnesty International has new tasks and needs our support. We must demand of the Government that it open the Federal Republic as an asylum for the persecuted from Latin America. And we must make the same demand of ourselves. The case of Chile is revealing the hypocrisy, cynicism and brutality of the reactionaries in our country —and perhaps also our own indifference and lethargy. This is our schizophrenia: the gap between words and deeds. We cannot do very much. That is all the more reason why we should do what we can. ■

THE ECONOMIC DIMENSION

Dependency has characterized Chile's economy for at least a century. Foreign capital and management have controlled the production of copper and other raw materials sold in foreign markets. Inflation has been almost continuous, with a succession of booms and busts. Particularly since 1940, agriculture has been stagnant. In the 1960s, foreign indebtedness rose to a higher per capita level than that of any other country in the world in peacetime.

Allende's economic policies sought to establish national control over the basic means of production, to increase production in industry and agriculture, and to redistribute the national product more equitably. All these objectives were achieved in the first two years of his regime. By the third year, however, the combination of external and internal sabotage (as recorded in IDOC/International Documentation No. 58 and in this volume) induced galloping inflation and interfered seriously both with production and distribution. In spite of the sabotage, nevertheless, impressive gains were recorded. Total food availability in Chile during the Allende years was up by about 25 percent per capita, the poor receiving a far higher share than ever before.

The Junta's economic policies are designed to reverse the directions taken by the Allende regime. By freeing prices while holding down wages, the Junta assured that the benefits won by the workers were wiped out overnight and driven to a level significantly below that enjoyed in 1970. Unemployment soared. Most of the nationalized industries were returned to the previous ownership and management. Foreign firms were welcomed back, and oil firms were invited to write their own terms for exploration contracts.

These policies were designed to help the rich at the expense of the poor. They have succeeded indeed in imposing inhuman burdens on the poor, but they have failed to benefit more than possibly a small segment of the very rich. Only nominal amounts for expansion of the economy have been obtained from international sources, public and private. Most loans merely serve the purpose of stretching out the repayment period for earlier loans, and their effect is to increase the already excessive dependence of the economy on foreigners. While high copper prices are beneficial, the benefit is more than wiped out by the spiraling price of petroleum products. And the battle against inflation staggers from defeat to defeat. Spurred in the first eight months of 1973 by the "invisible blockade" and domestic sabotage, it rose sharply in the final four months to more than 700 percent for the year, and the projection for 1974 is at least 500 percent. In these circumstances, one can only anticipate increased squeezing of the poor to maintain the privileges of the rich and a corresponding rise in the level of institutionalized violence to maintain order without justice.

The Political Economy of Military Fascism

In its May/June 1974 issue of Latin America & Empire Report, *NACLA published a number of important articles documenting the resurgence of the popular resistance movement in Chile today. Among the articles is a trenchant analysis of the political economy of the Junta by Ruy Mauro Marini, which is reprinted below.*

During the decade of the Sixties, a silent battle raged within the Chilean ruling class. A period of industrial growth, occurring after the Forties, and the increased penetration of foreign capital, in the following decade, helped to crystallize a sector of the bourgeoisie with an increasingly narrow field of interests. Because this sector was tied to the increased production of luxury goods and because of the specific nature of Chilean industrial development (in durable consumer goods and chemical and electronics industries, principally), this sector began to seek a reorientation of credit lines in its favor, to foster the entrance of foreign capital and technology, to remold foreign commerce (in terms of imports as well as, and most importantly, exports, with the creation of the Andean Pact of particular importance in this field), and restructure the internal market. In this last aspect, the objective of this bourgeois sector was a regressive redistribution of income which would increase the purchasing power of the high-income groups, the slightly more than five percent of the consumers capable of purchasing their products. To accomplish this, they proposed a wage policy which harmed the immense majority of the workers.

The greater part of the measures proposed by this national and foreign big bourgeoisie was detrimental to the mass consumer market and negatively affected the industry producing these goods. The industry was almost totally in the hands of medium and small entrepreneurs. It was inevitable, then, that intra-bourgeois contradictions would sharpen. Furthermore, these contradictions would become more important in the measure that the big bourgeoisie was increasingly able to influence the determination of the nation's political economy.

By 1967—during the second half of the government of Christian Democrat Eduardo Frei—the policies of the big bourgeoisie had produced a recession in the mass consumer goods industry and worsened the workers' and semi-proletarian masses' living standards as well as those of the lower sectors of the petit bourgeoisie. Salaries fell at the same time that prices and unemployment rose.

All this helped generate a powerful advance in the level of the mass movement in the city and the countryside which, besides provoking immediate economic demands, gave rise to their growing political radicalization. At the same time, the contradictions between the big bourgeoisie, on the one hand, and the medium and petit bourgeoisie, on the other, increased, creating deep fissures in the system of class rule on which they all rested. The ruling class' incapacity to unite its forces and present a single candidate for the 1970 presidential elections was largely a product of this situation. And, in the same framework, one can better understand the victory obtained by the coalition of worker and petit bourgeois parties, the Unidad Popular, which elected Salvador Allende to the presidency of Chile.

Three years after its election, the UP government was swept out of office by a military-fascist movement which destroyed the institutions of bourgeois democratic parliamentarianism, unleashed an incredibly savage repression against workers and peasants, outlawed union organizations, leftist parties and—under the euphemism of placing them "in recess"—the very parties of the bourgeoisie, suppressed the most elemental liberties, took over the universities, and imposed a regime of torture and terror throughout the country. This tragic unfolding of what used to be called the "Chilean road to socialism" represents but another stage in the Chilean class struggle beginning in the Sixties, and it cannot be understood if we do not use this period as our point of reference. The military Junta which took over the government in September 1973 revealed its class character by handing over the formulation of its political economy to Fernando Léniz, ex-president of *El Mercurio* who is closely tied to infamous North American and Chilean financial groups. In other words, the "economic reconstruction" of Chile, much hailed by the military-fascists, has therefore been openly given over to the big national and foreign capitalists.

But it is not only this which demonstrates the class character of the military-fascist regime. Their class character is also demonstrated when they apply, with an iron fist, the economic measures demanded (in the pages of *El Mercurio*) by the big bourgeoisie. Eager for revenge and emboldened by the bare sword placed at their disposal, the representatives of monopoly interests no longer place any limits on their exploitation of the workers. The working day in factories and offices has been lengthened without a corresponding wage increase. In the basic industries controlled by the state, such as the coal mines of Concepción and Arauco, they have imposed a system of forced labor which goes so far as to prohibit workers from leaving the zone without permission from the military authorities. In factories and farms, which have been returned to their former owners, they prohibit the creation of any type of organization which can uphold the workers' rights. Wages and salaries have been re-adjusted by approximately 300 percent, but the Junta itself foresaw, for 1973, an inflation of close to 600 percent.

It is evident that the principal objective of the big bourgeoisie's political economy is the rapid accumulation of a high rate of surplus value at the cost of inexorably squeezing the workers. This spells super-exploitation for the workers. And, in this sense, Chilean military-fascism does not present any innovation on those fascist regimes which have preceded it in history. Nevertheless, it does do more than simply reproduce a general aspect of fascism. It expresses the concrete necessity which the Chilean bourgeoisie, as a class, feels to re-orient its investments toward productive activities; in other words, to re-activate the process of capital accumulation. In order to understand the causes of this situation and, consequently, the political economy of Chilean military-fascism, it is necessary to begin our analysis in the period before the *coup d'état*.

The Economic Crisis

During the government of the Popular Unity and especially in its last months in office, the characteristic aspect of the non-public Chilean economy consisted in the systematic conversion of productive capital into speculative capital. Obviously, political reasons alone could explain this, because the Chilean bourgeoisie (and this is still more evident for foreign groups) consistently refused, from the start, to collaborate with the Allende government.[1] Nevertheless, there were also purely economic reasons to explain why the bourgeoisie abstained from any type of productive investment, and these reasons have much to do with the political economy of the Popular Unity government.[2]

In its first year of government, the UP's results in the economic field filled it with optimism. In effect, by making use of idle capacity in the plants and stocks accumulated in the pre-1970 period (characterized, as we pointed out, by a recession in the consumer goods industry), industrial production was able to expand markedly. The motor force behind this change was the UP-promoted redistribution of income in favor of wage workers. This produced a notable increase in the internal demand for goods and services. Nevertheless, given the conditions under which this occurred—the absence of investments which would assure a real growth in installed capacity—industrial expansion would quickly reach its limits. This was caused, on the one hand, by the exhaustion of idle capacity and accumulated stocks, aggravated by a decline in production which resulted from the employment of less efficient machinery as well as by the sabotage of the entrepreneurs; and, on the other, by the relative inelasticity in the supply of intermediary goods and equipment. This second point is the more important in order to understand the economic crisis which took place at the end of 1972.

It is important to keep in mind the fact that the Chilean industrial economy does not have at its disposal a real capital goods sector. Rather, it has a reduced productive base of intermediary goods (steel, etc.) and durable goods which are directed almost totally towards luxury consumption. To accompany the growth of demand, production of mass consumer goods would therefore have to count on the importation of raw materials, intermediary goods and capital and, above all, investments which would increase the productive capacity and, in a certain measure, permit the conversion of a part of the luxury goods industry into a capital goods industry. Nothing like this took place.

We do not have to recall the basic fact that the bourgeoisie withheld new investments. We will point out only that the government did not apply the necessary measures to capture and then reinvest the earnings which economic expansion placed in the hands of private enterprise. The government proceeded in this manner for the same reasons that it did not actively promote the transformation of the luxury goods industry.

The UP's economic orientation called for nationalization of basic industries (copper, coal, steel, etc.) and the large firms producing consumer goods (textiles, food). It left untouched the firms producing luxury goods (automobiles, durable consumer appliances). The fact that, when pressured by the workers in these latter firms, Allende's government expropriated many of them does not change the picture since, when they became state property, they maintained their traditional lines of production.

The Popular Unity government had its reason for acting in this manner. Of course, its search for an agreement with certain sectors of the national bourgeoisie influenced its decision. Thus, for example, in respect to the auto industry: the government only proposed the nationalization of production, opening up the field to the bids of foreign capital and, in passing, simplifying the models produced. It did not pretend to substitute the models for vehicles with a greater social utility. One should also consider the UP's preoccupation with not alienating the middle sectors who consumed these products. This had to be a fundamental point in a strategy which, by proposing the modification of socio-economic structures inside the framework of parliamentary institutionality, had to count on middle-sector votes. Finally, the UP was profoundly convinced that, by increasing the state's participation in the field of production, the government would be able to direct the activity of private entrepreneurial groups by employing the normal instruments of political economy.

Nevertheless, what is important to remember is that the government did not try to expand or convert existing industrial capacity in order to guarantee an increase in the supply of intermediary goods and capital. Satisfaction of this sector's needs, therefore, came to depend essentially on the external sector, in other words, on the availability of foreign exchange in order to import these products. And yet it was here the UP encountered its greatest difficulties, because it faced a serious balance-of-payments crisis. Various factors led to this situation: the withdrawal of private foreign capital and the financial boycott established by the U.S. government and the international agen-

cies under its influence.[3] Other factors also intensified the shortage of foreign exchange such as the rise in the international prices of foodstuffs (an item of considerable weight in the Chilean import structure) and the fall of the world-market price of copper, alleviated only in the last year of the government.

All this slowed down the production of mass consumer goods and was, in itself, sufficient to generate a serious disequilibrium in the economy given an increased demand for these items, a product of the income redistribution policy. This problem was aggravated by an early type of speculation: the illegal shipment of merchandise abroad where, thanks to the accelerating devaluation of the escudo, these items could be sold at a greater profit. In short, this resulted in the increasing lack of mass consumer goods on the internal market.

Speculation and Fascism

After an initial period, the bourgeoisie took political advantage of this shortage in its campaign against the government. The infamous December 1971 "march of pots and pans," which joined a sector of the petit bourgeoisie with the fascist-prone lumpenproletariat for the first time in the streets of Santiago, demonstrated this point. Soon the bourgeoisie no longer limited itself to taking advantage of the shortage: it helped create the shortage. Having large sums of ready capital at its disposal, due to its decision not to invest in production, it turned to hoarding and black-market operations in goods from cars to cigarettes. In this way, it neutralized the government's policy of income distribution and also realized enormous profits.

What the Chilean example demonstrates—and an analysis of the behavior of the bourgeoisie in other countries under similar conditions will reveal the same—is that, in a moment of crisis, capital can halt its process of accumulation and provoke the degeneration of the whole economy through its transformation into speculative capital. And it can do this while at the same time increasing its economic power and tilting the class struggle in its favor. In this respect speculation arises as the political economy of fascism during the phase of the struggle for state power. And, in the absence of a revolutionary response by the working class, it is through this mechanism that capital can unite the basic conditions for the victory of fascism: the cohesion of the bourgeoisie, the opposition of large sectors of the petit bourgeoisie to the working class, and the winning over or neutralization of popular sectors who, in other circumstances, would be certain allies of the proletariat.

With respect to the bourgeoisie (as well as the property-owning sectors of the petit bourgeoisie), the speculation unleashed by the big bourgeoisie achieved its results in two ways. On the one hand, it lessened the intrabourgeois contradictions over the appropriation of profits. In effect, thanks to their economic and technological base, the large enterprises operate with smaller production costs while (if competition does not cause them to function in another manner) they take advantage of market prices equal or superior to the rest. Now, by turning to speculation, the weakest capitalist sectors began to charge superprices (at the consumers' expense) which not only compensated them to a large degree but even began to threaten the big bourgeoisie's appropriation of some of their earnings because speculation was most pronounced in the area of mass consumer goods (where, as we saw, the participation of the medium and small enterprise is greatest). On the other hand, in the measure to which its practical opposition to the government's political economy increased its earnings, these bourgeois sectors, initially neutralized by the Unidad Popular, became increasingly more hostile to it. And, for a bourgeoisie, there is no political opposition better than that which can be done not only with impunity but also for the benefit of its own pocketbook.

Under these circumstances, the most efficient method of defending the poor's level of consumption rested not in rationing, as a certain sector of the government believed,[5] but in the creation of a system of distribution which would curtail the possibility of established commerce acting as a center of hoarding and speculation. Popular organizations capable of exercising mass control over distribution would be given control of this new system. It was for this reason alone that the bourgeoisie fought with such rancor the centers of supply and price (Junta de Abastecimiento y Precios, JAP), the popular stores, the communal commands of food supply and other organizations of this nature. For its part, the government, faithful to its plan for winning over the middle sectors, continually gave the merchants guarantees and refused to expropriate the large private distribution houses (a condition *sine qua non* for the control over distribution), limiting itself to the operation of a state center which accounted for only 33 percent of wholesale distribution.[6]

The struggle for the appropriation of income thus was moved into the stores and markets, which became the scene of a daily confrontation between the petit bourgeoisie and the popular masses who fought over bread, shoes, or matches. For the petit bourgeoisie, the worker, and the slum dweller (*poblador*) were physically identifiable competitors, beings of flesh and blood who had to be combatted and defeated. With the development of the black market, the highest-income groups could avoid this struggle in the stores and markets, and thus they won their first victory over the workers. But the long lines which formed at dawn, and at times during the night, were daily gathering points for the popular sectors, where they began to feel hostility towards their neighbors, indignation against those who provoked the situation (the bourgeoisie, the bureaucrats, or the government, according to their political tendencies), and an increasingly painful sensation of impotence.

Thus, by unifying the capitalists, polarizing the petit bourgeoisie, and sowing depression in the midst of the people, speculation was converted into the weapon *par excellence* of fascism. It is clear—although space will not permit a lengthy analysis here—that in the end this mechanism could not triumph of its own accord. The big bourgeoisie had to reach out to the armed forces. But it is no less certain that the victory reached by the bourgeoisie on September 11 would not have been possible without this systematic offensive in the economic field.

The Politics of the Big Bourgeoisie

As succulent as were the profits from speculation for the bourgeoisie and as much as speculation corresponds to a normal activity of the capitalist economy, it cannot indefinitely displace capital accumulation in the field of production. Thus the overthrow of the UP government has created a central task for the bourgeoisie: the reorientation of capital toward productive activities.

We have already seen how this presupposes an increased exploitation of labor or, what amounts to the same thing, the generation of a higher level of surplus value for the capitalist. But the situation generated by speculation in terms of the circulation of merchandise also obliges the capitalists to worry about the reorganization of the structures of distribution and consumption which were used to undermine the previous government. In this case, pricing policy—which aids in the super-exploitation of labor—represents a fundamental element once the purchasing power of the masses is restricted (by devaluing salaries via prices) and they are no longer able to compete in the consumer-goods market.

It is in this second aspect that one discovers the clearest stamp of the big bourgeoisie on the political economy of the military regime. In effect, the increase in the working day and the decrease in salaries are measures which interest all the bourgeoisie. Through such measures, the large, medium, and small capitalists are benefited, because they all receive a greater rate of surplus value. On the other side of the coin, these measures harm all salaried groups equally, whether proletariat or petit bourgeoisie.

The situation is different with regard to the measures adopted in the area of consumption, particularly concerning pricing policy. Here, those who suffer most from ill-effects are the low-income groups, particularly unskilled workers and low-level white-collar workers (*empleados*) as well as the poor sectors who do not have a regular income. Quite simply, the lower the wage level, the harder it is to get by. We should add that the restriction of the market which results from such a policy particularly affects the mass consumer goods industry, especially the production of low-quality goods, generally controlled by small- and medium-sized firms.

It would be an error to think that this political economy has only a temporary character, as some would have us believe. In this economy we see a return of the tendency which dominated the Chilean economy before 1970 and which we pointed out at the start of this essay: the restriction of the market for mass consumer goods, which depends on the purchasing power of the low-income sectors, in benefit of an expansion in the area of luxury goods production which is buttressed by the high-income groups.

A dependent economy has its laws, and the big bourgeoisie understands them perfectly. Since they stand at the head of the capitalist forces and orient the development of the system as a whole, their politics tend to coincide with the objective tendencies pushing dependent capitalism ahead, converting it into an increasingly exploitative system as well as one which excludes ever greater numbers of people. Super-exploitation of labor and its most immediate result, the break between production and the consumption needs of the broad masses—this is the pivot of dependent development, the same which today orients the actions of the big bourgeoisie in Chile.

From the viewpoint of the class struggle, it would seem that Chilean society is preparing to return to a point previously reached in 1970. In effect, while the contradictions between the ruling class and the workers grow sharper, the policies of the big bourgeoisie tend to split the bloc of classes which supported the military coup, causing the divergent interests of the various bourgeois sectors to smash against each other as well as against the interests of the petit bourgeoisie.

Nonetheless, this does not represent a return to the

past. For many reasons the class struggle is developing in Chile today in a radically different framework from that of 1970. First, the big bourgeoisie has reinforced its position, resolving in its favor the conflict which provoked a crisis in the earlier period. And it is ready to make its interests prevail over the remainder of society at any costs. In this sense not only are the workers the objects of its violence but also sectors within the bourgeoisie. Thus, it is likely that, through a policy of accelerated concentration of capital, new signs of intra-bourgeois violence will emerge.

A second reason is that the petit bourgeoisie has been forced to occupy a subordinate political position in the country. This conglomerate of social sectors whose leading group retained for three decades, even during the UP government, a privileged position within the state apparatus has experienced a bitter defeat. The Chilean process demonstrates clearly the incapacity of the petit bourgeoisie to solve the problems of capitalist development once a sector of large capitalists with perfectly defined interests emerges. This incapacity became evident when, as the class struggle increased, bringing society to the brink of a total breakdown, the petit bourgeois sectors had only two alternatives. They could have placed themselves behind the working class—the only class, after October 1972, to present a revolutionary solution to the contemporary crisis—or behind the big bourgeoisie and its military arm, thereby becoming a manipulated mass lending itself as a social base for military-fascism. Its attempts at autonomy, either through Allende-style reformism or as the institutional opposition headed by the Christian Democrats, resulted in a resounding failure, causing it to lose even those positions which, regardless of its ups and downs, it was able to conquer and maintain during the last decades.

The third and most important reason is due to the huge development in consciousness and organization which occurred within the mass movement during the period of Popular Unity government. The incorporation of less-advanced sectors from the city and the countryside into political life; the emergence of a constellation of middle-level worker cadres, uncompromised by reformism; and the organic expression of these phenomena in the creation of Industrial Belt (Cordones Industriales) and Communal Command (Comando Comunales) organizations: these are irreversible facts. And it is upon the base of this renovated and strengthened mass movement, in spite of the setback suffered in 1973, that a revolutionary vanguard without precedent in the history of Latin America is coming into being.

All this means that the class struggle is developing in Chile today without camouflage and, in a certain sense, in a simplified form. This is caused not only by the destruction of the democratic veil with which capital had disguised its domination. It is also due to the fact—and this is how one can understand why parliamentary tradition could be broken—that within the bourgeoisie a hegemonic faction, represented by the big bourgeoisie, has arisen, thus closing a stage of intra-bourgeois struggles which began, as we have seen, during the 1960s. But it is also due to the growth of the mass movement which has revitalized the working class. This class, on experiencing in its own flesh and blood the limits of the reformist program put forth by the Unidad Popular, is now in a privileged condition to throw off the yoke of reformism placed on its neck by the petit bourgeoisie nearly 50 years ago.

The polarization in the class struggle does not imply, however, that the contradictions which affect other classes or sectors of classes are going to diminish. On the contrary, they will tend to become more profound precisely because the hegemony conquered by the big bourgeoisie will permit the latter to impose its interests upon the other bourgeois sectors as well as the petit bourgeoisie in a much more brutal manner. If it is certain that the big bourgeoisie embodies the interests of the bourgeoisie as a class, it is no less certain that it can grow only at the expense of the great majority of the capitalists. Its hegemony carries along with it, therefore, the sharpening of intra-bourgeois contradictions as well as conflicts with the petit bourgeoisie. For this reason, the polarization of the class struggle will mean its intensification on all levels. For the working class, this represents a greater possibility of establishing alliances with new social groups, thereby broadening the bloc of classes which it leads, and of isolating more and more its principal enemy: the large national and foreign capitalists.

What the working class needs to carry out this task is to translate its class interests into revolutionary politics and to implement these politics on the basis of objective conditions created by the new level of the class struggle. It is obvious that, if the working class does not fulfill these conditions, it will risk again being held back by political gradualism. Incorrigible left-wing reformism already is attempting to assign to the working class, as its *exclusive* task, the reestablishment of democratic liberties, as if with this things could return to what they were before the military coup, in other words, the easy game of bourgeois parliamentarianism. Only then, say our reformists, can we talk of the problem of the conquest of power.

Unfortunately, for them, things are not like that. The military coup does not constitute a small hitch in the road to nonviolent revolution. It expresses the decision of the large national and foreign capitalists not to permit that revolution in Chile. There is no way to re-live, under these circumstances, the experience of the deposed Unidad Popular government. It has been buried under the debris of the Moneda [presidential palace], drowned in the blood of thousands of workers and revolutionaries whom military-fascism murdered and still murders in Chile.

Only in the measure in which the working class, by placing itself at the head of all the people, prepares itself to destroy by force the regime of force imposed by the bourgeoisie and imperialism, only in this way can it now move beyond the reestablishment of bourgeois parliamentary democracy to construct a true democracy, proletarian and socialist. It is this challenge which today confronts the Chilean vanguard.

There is no reason to doubt that it will be able to give this response. The organic capacity and the strategic and tactical ability of the revolutionary left, both before and after the coup of September, demonstrates this. And those who have erected a praetorian guard in the capital know it well.

Under the blanket of terror which military-fascism has thrown over Chile, the old mole, of which Marx spoke, untiringly continues its labor.

Footnotes

1. It should be noted that at least one major Chilean financial group attempted to work with the Unidad Popular government for at least a short period. This group, the "Grupo Banco Hipotecario" (commonly

nicknamed the "piranas"), controlled approximately 11 financial corporations and four insurance companies as well as important industries. Interestingly, when this group changed its initial policy of selling its stocks to the government, it shifted rapidly to the right, even passing the highly conservative "Edwards Group" in the process. Its members are now some of the Junta's top economic advisers. [NACLA editor's note]

2. In general, this was analyzed by Cristian Sepulveda and myself in "La politica economica de la 'via chilena,'" *Marxismo y Revolucion* (Santiago), No. 1 (July-September 1973), 106-123.

3. See, in particular, "Facing the Blockade," *New Chile* (Berkeley: NACLA, 1973), 178-208. [NACLA editor's note]

4. Only in its last period did the UP government try to establish a differential readjustment of wages and salaries which would benefit those with a lower income. Nevertheless, the corresponding legislation presented to the parliament was furiously diverted by the bourgeois opposition.

5. The Communist Party, MAPU, and the left wing of the Socialist Party. The government, through Fernando Flores, Minister of the Economy and a member of MAPU, went so far as to announce the adoption of rationing, at the start of 1973, a measure which was never concretized.

6. See *Chile Hoy* (Santiago), No. 31 (January 12-18, 1973) and No. 32 (January 19-25, 1973). [NACLA editor's note]■

Economic Stagnation in Chile

James Becket, an international lawyer who works for Amnesty International in Switzerland, analyzed the economic outlook for Chile at the International Conference on Lessons from the Coup d'Etat in Chile held in Amsterdam, Holland, February 22-24, 1973. Following are the major points of his presentation, in which he sought to highlight the pecularities of the Chilean economic climate in contrast to Spain, Greece, and Brazil.

Chile has a long and strong corporatist tradition dating from the 1930s going through Ibáñez groups like PADENA and finding a congenial audience in the Christian Democrat Party. Frei's writings indeed are strongly corporatist, and the new regime can be the logical extension of this conservative tradition in Chile. "Hierarchy, Discipline, and Nation" will have considerable resonance.

On the other hand, however, Chile has the tradition of a highly politicized working-class movement which is accustomed to democracy from below, choosing its own leaders and following independent action through such means as strikes. Furthermore in Chile other sectors of the population have experienced mass popular movements of a type contrary to that of corporatism. In fact, it is difficult to think of a country falling under this type of regime in the post-war period which has a more politicized population and a population which has had more experience with organized independent pressure groups.

Another relevant factor in Chile is the large size of the public sector of the economy. This sector will give considerable power to the state and provide leverage in the hands of the military against the capitalists if they conflict over certain issues. Generally, however, under regimes of this type, and in Chile of the past, the public sector essentially aids the private sector and takes on the tasks not attractive to the private investor.

What about the foreign factor that has rescued other corporatist regimes? Chile cannot export its unemployment problem and be paid for it in remittances the way the Southern European countries have done with Northern Europe or Mexico with the United States. Likewise, tourism, despite Chile's beauty, is out as a major foreign exchange earner, especially in a period when the tourist industry is in decline. Other invisibles such as shipping are out for Chile. The exploitation of a skilled local labor force through runaway factories is not open to Chile either, given its distance and other factors. Foreign investment also has drawbacks. The local market is limited, and using Chile as an export base for the rest of Latin America does not seem so attractive. This leaves Chile back where it has always been—dependent on foreign investment for export. And on the export of raw materials. Chile has minerals of various kinds. Exploration for oil by foreign companies might well take place under some contract with the state oil company. Chile also has a natural advantage in the growth of pine forests, which are a source of cellulose and newsprint. It would appear, then, that the Junta is closed off from many of the means used by other similar regimes, and it must face an organized labor force with high political consciousness (unlike the Brazilian situation which was also favored by a broader range of riches and exports).

Some Speculations on What to Expect

1. Given that Chilean democracy is dead and buried and the whole delicate system of compromise, so "Chilean," has been shattered, any evolutionary return to a system of free elections is illusory. The Junta will certainly attempt to institutionalize military dictatorship through some kind of constitution, probably corporatist in concept. They will try to enlist ex-politicians in a show of "national unity," drawing from the conservative wing of the Christian Democrat Party, the National Party, and a few leftist apostates. These regimes try the impossible trick of getting back to the "good old days" while at the same time excluding half the population from any rights. It is a trick that cannot be managed, and the nature of these regimes makes a "return to democracy" impossible. In fact, such regimes generally have to retract that most timid move toward liberalization, as they do not have the resilience to absorb criticism and cannot risk any independent organization.

2. Repression will continue to be severe, and the regime will rule by martial law, or state of siege. Torture as a means of breaking up opposition will become endemic and refined. Persecution of those suspected of leftist sympathies will continue. One can only anticipate the worst here, as so far no internal or external influence has appeared to influence the Junta to any effective degree in humanitarian matters. The repressive apparatus will garner larger and larger chunks of the budget, and there will be competing security forces, but there will be considerable foreign aid both financially and technically.

3. The economy will stagnate. Inflation will continue as it has in the past at high rates. The regime will have to expand credit to stimulate economic activity, and Chile will be affected by inflationary trends outside Chile. Despite controls on capital movement, capital flight will go on as in the past. There will be a redistribution of income generally from lower classes to higher classes, though certain groups such as the armed forces, technicians, and some workers will do better than average.

4. The economy will be increasingly foreign-dependent. It will be at the mercy of international commodity prices. Chile already has a large foreign debt, and although this regime will benefit from postponements and renegotiations, it still must meet compensation payments that it will take on and it must service new debts that it will incur. Despite the trend in the Third World now toward nationalization of basic resources, it is hard to see how Chile could manage this in its highly dependent position.

5. The regime will make a special appeal to two groups outside its natural constituency (the armed forces and the bourgeoisie). These two groups are the industrial working class and technicians. It will try to assure good wages in the Gran Minería and other key industries. Copper will be basic for the regime, and it must keep production going, strikes being a threat to its survival. The regime will try to put all workers into state-controlled syndicates. Judging from the past behavior of the miners in the Gran Minería, the regime could have success with an economist policy. Technicians will be the other privileged sector as they are mobile and can leave the country. The regime needs them to keep production going.

6. There will be thorough purges of the church and universities. Just as investment in police and defense will rise, so education will receive less and less of the budget. Intellectual Dark Ages.

7. The military will form a new ascendant class, inserted into institutions and enterprises in commissar-type roles. There will be ever-increasing corruption among this new class, especially because there will be no control over it. Lying about statistics, etc.

8. American bread and circuses, PL 480 and Hollywood. There will be an attempt to recapture "normality," the 1950s, but both PL 480 and Hollywood are dead, so the regime will have to rely on football and pray for a good harvest. It could get lucky from a good harvest and, from what one gathers, could reap what the Unidad Popular sowed in the way of progress in the agrarian sector during three years.

Experience over the last years has shown that such regimes have been more successful economically than this prognosis would indicate for Chile; but given the current world economic conjuncture, Chile's lack of exogenous escape hatches, and the static nature of the system, it is difficult to see how Chile will grow. Recent experience has shown that regimes of this kind have been very successful in holding onto power. Part of this has been due to their successes in buying off some sectors of the population; part of it has been due to the strength of their repressive systems enjoying unlimited funds, equipment, and manpower; and part of these regimes' success has been due to the weakness of the left, its factionalism,

and the extreme difficulties of organizing under these repressive conditions—which puts the left constantly on the defensive, concentrating on survival.

Chile will once again be an important test case. Can an American-sponsored regime of this type survive in a country like Chile with little or no economic growth? It is possible to conceive of Chile over the next few years characterized both by acute poverty and acute repression. (GNP down, torture up). ■

Class and Group Expectations

Upper

Capitalists	Retention of privileges; some compromise with military
Landholders	More power, more credit, more discipline over workers
Officer corps	Occupation of key posts in state institutions, economy; social ascension; economic betterment from salaries and corruption
Managers Technocrats Bureaucrats	Beneficiaries of system as servants of elite
Church	Purge of those not favorable to Junta; less emphasis on social action; Opus Dei technocrat style

Middle

Small businessmen Professionals State functionaries Employees	Little change; will be hit by inflation if salaried
Intellectuals and students	Targets of merciless repression if politically oriented; will endure Intellectual Dark Ages
Petit bourgeoisie (shopkeepers, transport workers)	Potential source of trouble for regime; will be left out of system, but will go fascist, not socialist; look for man on white horse
Industrial workers; copper miners (Gran Minería), steel, coal, and textile workers	Privileged sector; will receive wage and social benefits
Nonindustrial and service workers	Exploited without protection

Lower

Armed Forces and Police enlisted personnel	Better salaries, gain from system, increased privileges
Peasants	Return to peasant-lord relationship; will be highly exploited by landowners, even small ones, as state will need low food prices for urban areas
Lumpenproletariat	Super-exploitation, occasional charity, constant repression

Make the Poor Pay

Reprinted from Latin America, *October 5, 1973.*

With the cancellation last weekend of the 200 percent wage "adjustment" which had been decreed by the Allende administration for 1 October, the full impact of inflation will now be felt by that sector of the population that can least bear it—the poorest. The late President Salvador Allende had always publicly maintained that wages must keep pace with inflation so that it would not be the poorest who had to take the strain, as it always had been in Chile (and the rest of Latin America). This policy has now been reversed, and the middle classes, which were bearing the brunt before, will doubtless breathe a sigh of relief. What will particularly please them (and by the same token be of concern to the working classes) is that the military government has also decreed a return to "normal" methods of distribution. In other words, state distribution networks of food and consumer goods (through which adequate supplies of rationed, low-price goods were maintained in working-class areas) are to be abolished, and free-trade competition is to be restored. ■

Orthodox Market Economy

Reprinted from Latin America, *October 26, 1973.*

On the economic front, the new team led by economy minister Fernando Léniz, and his chief adviser Raúl Sáez, once finance minister under the Frei administration and one of the Alliance for Progress' "nine wise men," took the country further back from Allende's "road to socialism" into an orthodox market economy. Léniz announced at the end of last week that some 200 private firms nationalized without congressional approval, or "intervened" (in effect managed without a formal change of ownership) by the state, would be returned to their proprietors. In about 40 cases U.S. capital is involved. This will at least help to reduce the massive budget deficit, since a good few of these firms were running at a loss. Their owners are apparently to be assisted into profitability by being allowed to dismiss workers they regard as surplus (the more politically militant have already gone) and to increase the working week from 44 to 48 hours without extra pay until the end of the year.

The massive price rises which had been announced came into force at the end of last week, with petrol the most notable at about ten times its previous cost. These increases more or less bring all prices into line with the black market rates prevailing under the Allende government. But of course the Junta has ended the distribution of rationed goods to poorer districts at low prices described by Léniz as "laughable, political and demagogic." The slight consolation for industrial workers is a monthly minimum wage of 12,000 escudos—equivalent to 43 or 14 dollars, depending on which exchange rate is selected. ■

Churning Out Money

Reprinted from the Andean Times, Latin America Economic Report. *November 16, 1973.*

Despite the criticism of the Allende government's practice of finance via the printing press, the Junta has quickly resigned itself to the fact that it will have to go on using exactly the same method for the foreseeable future. The increase of 70 percent in the money supply, between September and the end of the year, will be higher than for any period under Allende before May this year. The financial resources that the central government will need to meet its commitments to the end of the year are in the order of 130,000 million escudos. Deficits for state companies (such as the railways, electricity and petroleum companies), and for companies taken over by the Allende administration and not yet returned to their former owners, are expected to reach an additional 40,000 million escudos, approximately, bringing total government requirements to 170,000 million escudos.

Anticipated income for the period is, however, only about 112,000 million escudos. The government has therefore got to find a further 58,000 million escudos by the end of the year. Officials have indicated that at least part of this deficit may be financed through credits from abroad. Unofficial sources suggest, however, that even if credits are forthcoming in the near future, it is unlikely that funds will be made available before the end of the year to finance budgetary deficits.

On top of central-government and other public-sector deficits, the private sector is also going to need an increase in the money supply, due to factors such as price increases, permitted increases in production costs, and wage-compensation allowances. A figure in the order of 10,000 million escudos has been mentioned in this connection as the amount of credit expansion needed for the private sector to the end of the year. Most of these increases will have to be in the form of inorganic emissions, though a certain amount will be credits on the books of the Central Bank.

The increase in the total money supply will probably, bankers say, be of a substantially higher order due to the multiplier effect of Central Bank increases when they hit the commercial banking system. Official predictions, however, are more conservative and suggest that the expansion rate of money outside the banking system (70 percent) will be only matched by increases in demand deposits of the private-sector, central-government, and public-sector institutions. ■

Debts Pile Up

Reprinted from the Andean Times, Latin America Economic Report, *March 17, 1974.*

While the final outcome of the Paris renegotiation of Chile's debts with the "Paris Club" countries is not expected to be known for several months, the government has meanwhile been confidently signing up hefty sums in new loans. The Central Bank said at the end of last month that the total since last September was $294 million, but in fact the loans and credit lines opened since the coup add up to around $570 million.

Money committed from the United States, Brazil, Argentina, the International Monetary Fund (IMF), the World Bank, the Inter-American Development Bank (IDB), and the Andean Development Corporation (CAF) amounts to $468.8 million. On top of this a group of U.S. banks—Bankers Trust, Franklin Trust, and Schroeder Trust—has opened a $100 million line of short-term credit. A small group of new credits is also about to be made effective, officials say. One is from the Banco de Colombia, for $10 million, and another, also for $10 million, will be made available by the Swiss foreign trade financial commission to finance the installation of sulphur-processing plants in the north. The only other credit on record is a U.S. military loan of $11 million—$10 million of which is for equipment and $1 million for officer training. Additionally—though this is refinancing rather than new money —a group of U.S. banks, with which Chile has maintained an undischarged debt since 1971, granted a refinancing in the amount of $124 million shortly after the coup.

Out of all this, one of the most important is the group of loans approved last month by the IDB, for $171 million, on soft terms: 30 years with seven years' grace, at 2 percent a year. Most of the loans included in this are for major development projects: $70 million for the Antuco dam and electrification scheme, $45 for the Convento Viejo and Digna-Mayle irrigation projects, $15 million for re-afforestation, $25 million for agriculture, $10 million for assorted CORFO projects, and $6 million for housing and related projects in "marginated areas." This group, added to an earlier IDB loan of $30 million, brings the Bank's contribution to Chile since September to $201 million— though it is not known how much of this will actually be disbursed this year. The World Bank has so far approved loans of $18.3 million—$13 million for "technical assistance to the public sector," approved last year, and $5.3 million approved last month for preinvestment studies.

The willingness of these international banks to give loans to Chile—without, as yet, any definite signs of an improvement in its economic situation—is based partly on the confidence of the IMF report of late last year on the effectiveness of the measures the government has been putting through, to control inflation and "normalize" the economy. This resulted directly in the IMF stand-by arrangement for $95 million.

Meanwhile, the government has lost only $25 million in loans which had been committed to the previous administration—a credit from Sweden for 40 million kroner (approximately $10 million) and a $15 million loan from Finland for forestry projects—which appears to have been replaced by the $15 million from the IDB for reafforestation. But Chile is unlikely to receive much of the balance of the $395 million committed by the Soviet Union, other COMECON countries, and China, of which only $91 million had been disbursed by 11 September.

At the Paris meeting at the end of last month Chile was seeking a rescheduling of the $700 million, approximately, in foreign debt repayments and service due during 1973 and 1974. Chile was asking that it should only have to pay 10 percent of this amount this year. An arrangement was reached with the most important of the creditor countries—the United States, West Germany, Britain and France—and this is expected to release supplier and other types of credit for specific projects, like the smelter to be built at Chañaral by British Smelter Construction with financing from Lloyds & Bolsa.

The terms on which Chile is to be allowed a generous rescheduling of debt will, however, also involve the country in some major payments. A condition of the refinancing is that Chile pay compensation for the Kennecott, Anaconda and Cerro mines expropriated in 1971. Negotiations with Kennecott were already well advanced by the end of last year, when a Chilean delegation—headed by Julio Phillipi, former finance minister under the Alessandri administration—travelled to Washington to negotiate; the negotiators, however, were unable to bridge the difference of $300 million between Chile's $300 million offer and Kennecott's demand for $600 million. Raúl Sáez, the Junta's economic adviser—who in 1969 negotiated the terms of the purchase by Chile of 51 percent of the copper companies' properties—did not clarify the situation when he said in Paris that the payment to Kennecott would be between $300 and $600 million.

It is also expected, though, that once the amounts have been agreed on, Chile will be given a further series of loans through which to make the payments—along the lines of Peru's agreement last month on compensation for expropriated U.S. companies. Meanwhile, in a related move, Chile has made the first payment of $1.6 million to the Overseas Private Investment Corporation (OPIC) for two similar debts: $3 million paid by OPIC to the Bank of America for unpaid instalments due from a paper mill in Chile partly owned by Parsons and Whittemore and $4.8 million, plus interest, covering instalments due on promisory notes originally held by Kennecott's Braden Copper. ■

Foreign Debt Renegotiation

Reprinted from the Andean Times, Latin America Economic Report, *May 10, 1974.*

The government is treating the successful renegotiation of the 1973-74 foreign debt as a major victory. Officials have not been prepared to give details on the nature of any guarantees that had to be provided, apart from those formally stated in the agreement reached in Paris at the end of March. But they believe that although the final issue was never really in doubt following the International Monetary Fund's (IMF) granting of the $94.8 million stand-by credit at the end of last year, the settlement nevertheless marks an important psychological step in clearing the way for new credits for Chile.

General Eduardo Cano, president of the Central Bank, said: "We will now be able to act with greater liberty. This opens possibilities to us in all economic fields and in foreign trade." A British financier who expects to be supplying mining equipment here added: "Bankers are like sheep; they all feel a lot better now that the [Paris] Club has formally said okay."

Although detailed arrangements for rescheduling debt payments now have to be negotiated bilaterally with each of the creditor nations—and this can take time, as the Allende government discovered to its cost—the Paris Club agreement should give the Chilean authorities a vital breathing space to pay back the $750 million in principle and interest falling due for payment in 1973 and 1974. Of this figure, 20 percent will be paid during the next three years in quotas of 5 percent each for 1974 and 1975, and 10 percent for 1976. In other words, Chile will have to pay $150 million over the next three years ($37.5 million each in 1974 and 1975 and $75 million in 1976). The remaining $600 million will be paid off in 14 six-monthly quotas (roughly $86 million a year) starting in 1977.

The 12 members of the Club—basically the world's richest nations—agreed in addition that they would meet again in November to talk about the payments due to mature in 1975—about $300 million—and to make decisions on this in the light of economic and financial developments between now and then. The Paris agreement contains a clause identical to the one attached to the similar 1972 agreement reached with the Allende government.

This clause has confirmed Chile's intention to "accept the principle of a just indemnization" for all nationalizations "according to Chilean and international law." This last phrase does not of course mean much, as the critical factors are not so much legal as political and financial. The reference is mainly to Anaconda and Kennecott's expropriated copper mines and related installations. ■

Payment for Copper to Cerro

Reprinted from The Wall Street Journal, *March 13, 1974.*

After almost three years of negotiations with two Chilean governments, Cerro Corp. said the South American country has agreed to pay it at least $41.9 million for its copper interests that were seized in 1971.

Under an agreement announced jointly in Santiago by the company and the military Junta that took power in Chile last September, Cerro has already received $3.2 million in cash. The remainder, nearly $38.7 million, is to be in the form of 17-year notes bearing an interest rate of 9.165 percent, free of Chilean taxes, the company said.

The settlement, which had been anticipated for some time, appears to entail repayment of most, or perhaps all, of Cerro's interest in Companía Minería Andina S.A., the nationalized company. According to Cerro's 1972 annual report, the company's investment at the end of that year totaled $39.7 million, including equity, notes, and interest. Thus, the settlement, which was effective at the end of February, would give Cerro all of its investment, plus about $2.1 million of interest for the 14 months since that report.

Of the three big U.S. copper companies whose Chilean properties were nationalized by the government of former Chilean president Salvador Allende, Cerro was the only one to maintain cordial relations with the government there. While the Allende government charged both Anaconda Co. and Kennecott Copper Corp. with taking "excess profits" that more than offset the value of their holdings, it agreed in September 1972 to pay Cerro all but $1.5 million of what it claimed. Cerro also continued to provide technical assistance to the Chilean operators of Andina's Rio Blanco mine.

The company was reportedly near agreement with the Allende government on the exact terms of payment last fall when Mr. Allende died in the military take-over of the government.

Neither Anaconda nor Kennecott has agreed on compensation for its properties. Both say they have held preliminary talks with the new Chilean government. In Santiago, Julio Phillipi, a former finance minister named by the Junta to negotiate with U.S. companies, said talks with Anaconda and Kennecott are continuing. ■

Junta Deal with Anaconda

Reprinted from The New York Times, *July 24, 1974.*

The Anaconda Company announced yesterday that it had reached a settlement with the new Government of Chile over the expropriation in 1971 of two of its subsidiaries, the Chile Exploration Company and the Andes Copper Mining Company.

These companies operated the Chupuicamata and El Salvador mining properties in Chile prior to their take-over by the Government of the late Dr. Salvador Allende Gossens.

Under the settlement agreement, Anaconda's subsidiaries were to receive here yesterday a cash payment of approximately $65 million. They were also to receive about $188 million in promissory notes of Corporación del Cobre, dated Aug. 1, 1974, and guaranteed by the Central Bank of Chile. The notes bear interest of 10 percent a year, subject to the Chilean income tax at a rate of 40 percent. They are payable in equal installments semi-annually over a 10-year period with the first payment due Feb. 1, 1975.

Spokesmen for Anaconda said that in arriving at these precise amounts, consideration had been given to the time elapsed between the 1971 expropriation and the settlement.

The Anaconda spokesman said that as a result of the settlement, all prior claims and controversies between Chile and the American company had now been resolved. This includes disposal of all claims for Chilean taxes and other matters, all legal actions in Chile and this country and all claims with respect to notes previously issued to Anaconda's subsidiaries at the end of 1969.

However, the settlement leaves Anaconda free to continue arbitration of its claim against the Overseas Private Investment Corporation with respect to the 1971 expropriation. The company said that if it is awarded a settlement from OPIC, the amount involved, which cannot be determined pending arbitration, would have to be shared with the Chilean interests.

Anaconda said it would treat the fair-market value of the settlement as taxable income for United States income tax purposes this year, which would have the direct effect of reducing the company's consolidated tax-loss carryforward.

Industry observers said that representatives of Anaconda had been meeting with the new Chilean Government for some weeks, working toward the settlement.

At the end of February both Anaconda and the

Kennecott Copper Corporation indicated their desire to come to terms with Chile for their expropriated properties. Both denied then that any agreements were near.

At the same time the Chilean Government announced that it would "shortly conclude a compensation agreement worth hundreds of millions of dollars" with the two companies and with the Cerro Corporation. Yesterday a spokesman for Kennecott said his company had been "engaged in conversations in Washington with representatives of the Chilean Government regarding compensation for Kennecott's expropriated El Teniente property in Chile." ■

Pie in the Sky

Reprinted from Latin America, *June 21, 1974.*

The long-suffering Chilean economy, after many years of comfortable state protection culminating in a tepid move towards socialism, has been plunged since last September into the icy waters of free competition. The economy minister, Fernando Léniz—high priest of financial orthodoxy aided by innumerable acolytes schooled in the tough discipline of the University of Chicago—was then given *carte blanche* by the military to put Chile back on the capitalist road, *cueste lo que cueste.* Two months ago, however, there were signs that his policies were leading to such confusion in the ranks of the Junta's supporters—reflected in the declining euphoria at the Santiago stock exchange—and to such increasing bitterness among the poor and unemployed in the shanty towns, that some change or rectification would be politically necessary.

But Léniz is still unrepentant, and the latest economic measures, announced this month, indicate that things will continue to get worse before they get better. As Professor Paul Rosenstein-Rodan, the U.S. economist and long-time observer of the Chilean scene, observed in *The New York Times* last week, the Chilean military have a critical attitude towards the deficiencies of Chilean society, "but they do not have clear or positive ideas about what should be done." Faced with their own incoherence and inexperience in economic matters—which they freely admit—they are not going to change horses in midstream. So Léniz plunges on, blaming the still dangerously uncontrolled inflation on external factors, and agreeing with his former employer, *El Mercurio,* that his measures are the price that has to be paid "for saving Chile from the worst threat in its history: Marxist dictatorship."

The situation at the end of last month was bleak. A pessimistic report from the Oficina de Planificación Nacional (ODEPLAN) was published at the same time as figures from the Instituto Nacional de Estadísticas (INA) indicated that inflation for the first five months of 1974 had reached 102.3 percent. Admiral José Toribio Merino, the Junta's economic expert, has always claimed that it would be possible to confine inflation to 100 percent for the whole year. Unemployment at an official 9.2 percent is the highest for 15 years and, as in all Latin American countries, this disguises a much larger figure for the underemployed. Allende's not inconsiderable achievement of bringing unemployment down from 8 percent when he took over to 3.6 percent in December 1972 has now been wiped out. Raúl Sahli, president of the Sociedad de Fomento Fabril (SOFOFA), estimates that half a million people will be out of work by the end of next year—16 percent of the working population of just over three million. The government thinks it can be kept to 300,000. Unemployment will certainly help to keep labor costs down, but the social and political cost—even just the inevitable increase in petty crime and violence—will be hard to bear in a country which has prided itself on its law-abiding citizenry. Chile, as the economic policy-makers need to remind themselves from time to time, is not Brazil, and in any case this is a strange moment to follow in Brazil's footsteps.

Underlying uncertainty about the future has generated other problems. Foreign credits have been hard to come by, and foreign private capital is still hesitating, nervous about the international situation in general and the Chile situation in particular. The Chilean Ambassador in Washington, General Walter Heitmann, admitted during a "routine visit" to Santiago last month that the "foreign Marxist campaign" was causing problems. He said that, although the White House was excellently disposed towards the Junta, new lines of credit would have to be approved by Congress, where the Junta's supporters are rather thinner on the ground.

Some of the uncertainty should be dispelled by this month's economic measures, indicating that Léniz continues to go on as he originally began. On 6 June prices of a number of essentials went up 100 percent—bread 79 percent, cooking oil 90 percent, milk 100 percent, cigarettes 115 percent. To mitigate the immediate impact, a bonus of 10,000 escudos was authorized, in anticipation of a *reajuste* or wage rise, to be paid by the private sector by 14 June, and by the public sector *"lo antes que sea posible."* The following day General Augusto Pinochet announced the new plan to deal with inflation. Firstly, employment in the public sector is to be cut by 20 percent, which is likely to throw 100,000 people out of work by the end of the year—in addition to the existing high number of unemployed. From the beginning of this month no fresh personnel are to be recruited, which will cause difficulties for school leavers. Secondly, all government agencies are to cut spending by 15 percent, and no new public works are to be started. Thirdly, the universities and their attendant television channels are to be self-financing after 1976.

Last week, on 13 June, Léniz appeared on television to announce the new wage increases. There is to be a *reajuste* of 20 percent at the beginning of July coupled with a family bonus of 5,000 escudos, and there will be a further 15 percent *reajuste* in October. In addition the minimum monthly wage is to be raised to 34,300 escudos. This week the escudo was devalued by about 4½ percent, with the tourist rate going from 790 to 825 and the commercial rate from 720 to 750.

The economy minister claimed that the stabilization envisaged for the second half of the year would bring the "effective recovery of the inevitable loss in purchasing power." A new social security mechanism is also promised, and, to mitigate the immediate effects of unemployment, the newly unemployed will receive a subsidy for a year, instead of two months as a present.

Having delivered the medicine, Léniz then painted a rosy picture of the future: a growth rate of seven percent between 1976 and 1977, reaching 10 percent by 1980, and a doubling of the GNP by 1984. In the meantime, the Chilean worker can look forward to a 16 percent increase in income per head by 1977. After the alarums of the past decade it is doubtful whether the Chilean worker is taken in by such promises, but the minister is trying to impress the foreign investor, rather than the Chilean work force, that the future is bright. ∎

Taming the Workers

Reprinted from Latin America, *March 15, 1974.*

A revealing passage in the report of the Comite Interamericana de la Alianza para el Progreso (CIAP) on Chile suggested that the government's economic strategy could fail if workers were not prepared to accept a cut in their living standards. This cut would leave them worse off than they were in 1969. Their situation would be worse still if businessmen did not exercise some discretion in setting prices. Acceptance of the new rules by both sides was said to be a crucial factor in the economic equation. The CIAP report was written by economists who were basically favorably disposed to the military Junta, and it is likely that their worry is shared by Chile's economic planners.

Until now worker acceptance of the reduced standard of living has been obtained by the use of naked force: the Central Unica de Trabajadores (CUT) was dissolved; as many as 100,000 workers may have lost their jobs for political reasons; and thousands of known militants have been imprisoned or killed. But this is not a long-term solution if the Junta is to achieve success on its own terms.

Various approaches are being tried. The Confederación Nacional de Trabajadores (CNT) is being pushed as an alternative to the CUT. The CNT was founded a little more than 10 years ago with funding from the American Institute for Free Labor Development (AIFLD) in the United States. It has remained almost entirely a paper organization except for brief months in 1965, when the United States poured money into the seaman's union (COMACH), the only effective member of the CNT, in an effort to break the CUT. The new president of the CNT, Eduardo Rojas, is also president of COMACH, which has been singled out by the North American Congress on Latin America (NACLA) as "a very useful conduit for funds" from the United States to extremist groups in Chile during the years of Unidad Popular. The AIFLD was founded in the early 1960s as part of the general response to the Cuban revolution. AIFLD officers have never made any secret of their part in fighting communism in such countries as Brazil, the Dominican Republic, and Guyana.

In Chile, some 10,000 workers have attended AIFLD seminars, and there was a sudden surge in the number of Chileans attending courses at the Institute's Front Royal headquarters in Washington following the first truck owners' strike in October 1972. According to Peter Grace, AIFLD's dynamic president, who also heads his family firm, "its objectives in Latin America are to promote democratic free trade unions; to prevent communist infiltration and where it already exists to get rid of it. . . . It teaches workers to help increase their company's business . . . the AIFLD urges cooperation between labor and management and an end to class struggle."

These sentiments are very close to those expressed by members of Chile's military government. Democratic and free trade unionism—rather like democratic and free elections—seems unattainable for the time being, so all emphasis has to be on teaching workers to increase their company's business. General Sergio Nuno, vice-president of the Corporación de Fomento de la Producción (CORFO), has said he is extremely keen on the idea of participation by workers, but he emphasized that what he had in mind was quite different from the participation referred to in the agreement between the CUT and Unidad Popular, in December 1970. This agreement stated bluntly that participation was a political matter and should involve worker participation in economic planning decisions taken by the government and the management of companies.

General Nuno was less specific and confined himself to the general feeling that participation involved an acceptance of discipline by workers, and perhaps a share in the rewards of greater productivity. He said that the participation envisaged under Unidad Popular had led to a breakdown of authority and the placing of people with nothing to recommend them (beyond political influence) in key jobs. The government promised an *estatuto social de la empresa* some five months ago. Its non-appearance is a further cause of disaffection for the Junta's former supporters among the Christian Democrats. It is not that anyone expects anything very spectacular from the promised law, but its non-appearance leaves those trade unionists who might be interested in cooperating with the government in a precarious situation. Prices have risen faster than the government had expected, and this is increasing the desperation of workers. There have already been a number of short-lived strikes in Santiago, and the government is anxious to find some formula which allows it to pursue its cherished goal of "economic recovery." General Augusto Pinochet expressed the sense of the CIAP analysis very graphically when he said recently that if "we do not manage to take control of the economy this year, we will lose the war." ∎

U.S. Trade Union in Chile

The information which follows on the role of the American Institute for Free Labor Development (AIFLD) in Chile was excerpted from "An Analysis of Our AFL-CIO Role in Latin America or Under the Covers with the CIA," a pamphlet by Fred Hirsch, pro tem chairman of the Emergency Committee to Defend Democracy in Chile (San Jose, California), and appeared in the May 8, 1974, issue of Tricontinental News Service. TNS commented that Hirsch's pamphlet ". . . does more than detail AIFLD's involvement in Chile. It shows, through historical example, how the class collaborationist policies of the AFL, now AFL-CIO leadership, have led it to spawn an organization that has participated in overthrowing a government which represented the aspirations of several million Chilean workers."

The mechanism of the AFL-CIO in Latin America is the American Institute for Free Labor Development (AIFLD).

This organization was formed as a non-profit corporation in 1962. Its president is George Meany. Chairman of the Board of Trustees is J. Peter Grace, chief executive of W. R. Grace & Company, a multinational corporation with extensive interests in Latin America. The AIFLD Board of Trustees is largely made of leading labor officials and corporate executives with enormous holdings in Latin America and the Caribbean countries.

Originally an educational project, AIFLD now operates in several other fields—social projects, credit facilities, social action, and "community development." The educational phase of the operation is massive. In Colombia and Peru it has trained as much as 5 percent of the union membership—far exceeding any AFL-CIO training program offered to unionists in the United States. In local seminars, people are chosen to participate in area-wide or nationwide seminars; from these are selected the most likely people (often they are not even unionists), who are offered a three-month course in AIFLD's training center at Front Royal, Virginia. The trainee gets a per diem payment in excess of what he or she would earn on the job. When the trainees return home they continue on the AIFLD payroll for at least an additional nine months.

The ABC's at AIFLD School

The courses are heavily larded with material similar to that dispensed in the '60s by the Christian Anti-Communist Crusade (one of the first Directors of AIFLD was listed as a speaker for that group). They do not deal with problems created by multinational corporations, American or European neo-imperialism, oligarchic national control, land redistribution, or the fascist patterns of military governments. They do not mention any courses relating to strike strategy. The basic premise of the educational program is that all solutions will come to working people through collective bargaining and opposing communism in collaboration with management and government.

The U.S. government expectations of AIFLD are best expressed in the 1966 State Department contract which handed over $645,600 to AIFLD for use in Chile:

"The target of this activity is to strengthen and develop a trade union leadership that is capable of organizing a democratic labor movement in Chile which can participate and contribute to national development . . .
and to develop and implement

". . . small impact projects intended to meet the needs of workers' groups and develop a friendly attitude to the United States."

It takes more than a fair share of arrogance to assume that Chileans have not or cannot organize their own democratic labor movement. The labor movement in Chile began as early as our own, with effective general strikes as far back as 1890, and Chileans have organized a higher percentage of the working class than the AFL-CIO here at home. The difference is that the democratically elected leaders of the majority of Chilean workers are oriented toward socialism and against collaboration with the corporations which exploit their labor, many of which are to be found in the membership and directorate of AIFLD.

Zeroing in on Chile

AIFLD first appeared in Chile in 1962 in the form of one William C. Doherty, Jr. [listed by *The Washington Post* as a man "closely identified with CIA operations"]. Doherty led an AIFLD delegation to Chile where he met with labor leaders in the Pan American Hotel, offering loans for cooperatives, housing, and small impact programs. Doherty's moves were like a tank that opens the way for the infantry.

Next came John Snyder and Ester Cantu. Their object was to organize telephone workers away from the militant Union of Telephone Employees. They opened an office in Santiago, were given a list of employees by the company, and launched a campaign of wining and dining. Those workers who didn't buy the line and had influence found themselves fired for various reasons. When Doherty's people won the next election, the company saw to it that the former militant leaders no longer had jobs in the industry. To the credit of the workers, by 1967 the situation was reversed and the company had to deal once more with militant union representatives.

Through the '60s AIFLD had unusual difficulty in Chile for several reasons. The Christian Democratic minority of unions kept vacillating in its alliances. Open collaboration with U.S. money was unthinkable—it would invite rejection by the rank-and-file. The long and militant history of organized labor in Chile placed economic exploitation by American companies high in the consciousness of the workers. CUT (Central Conferation of Workers) presented a militant program and the strength to win immediate gains while keeping an eye on a socialist future. This kept AIFLD at bay, especially after 1970 when CUT —as part of the Popular Unity—elected Allende president.

With the election of Allende, tensions grew between Chile and the U.S. State Department. Most credits and economic aid were cut off with two exceptions: U.S. military aid and training programs continued to the tune of $12 million. Though Allende controlled the executive branch of the government, the military operated with a certain amount of independence. Judging by the events of September 11, 1973, the $12 million was a fine business investment for the expropriated U.S. copper companies. The other exception was $1 million of AID money set aside for "technical assistance." Much of this was for the continued operation of AIFLD, which receives 92 percent of its funds from AID.

AIFLD Intensifies Its Work

Robert O'Neill [AIFLD program director for Chile] reported that through October of 1969, 5,963 Chileans had participated in AIFLD seminars in Chile. It is impossible to tell whether or not the figures are based on reality or puffery, but the 10-year report of AIFLD in 1972 puts the Chile seminar total at 8,837. Between '69 and '72 the continuing seminars involved 2,877 more people . . .

For a reason never explained or mentioned in public reports, the Chilean AIFLD staff was suddenly in a big hurry in the short time prior to the coup . . .

We get some clues to the reason for the speed-up in activity from the multinational corporation chairman of AIFLD: "The AIFLD urges cooperation between labor and management and an end to class struggle. It teaches workers to help increase their company's business . . . promote democratic free trade unions; to prevent communist infiltration and where it already exists to get rid of it." [An Address by Peter Grace, AIFLD Booklet, 9/16/65]. Salvador Allende was a Marxist, CUT was leftist, and Chile was viewed by ITT, the copper companies, and the U.S. State Department as a communist menace. We can be certain that the State Department did not continue special AID funding for an AIFLD speed-up without specific purpose.

Maritime Union Gets AIFLD Attention

The 10-year report says that COMACH (Chilean Maritime Federation) was the "major labor organization with which AIFLD cooperates." . . . According to Jorge Nef, a Chilean Christian Democrat and professor of political science at University of California at Santa Barbara, COMACH is not a typical Chilean union. "Its membership is largely maritime officers, many of whom served as officers in the Navy: even those without a naval background spend their first year of training in classes with naval officers." The naval officers in Valparaíso were prominent in the leadership of the September 11 coup, and whether they were working with the coup leaders or not, there was the unusual presence of U.S. Naval Intelligence personnel in Valparaíso at the time. Off the coast of Valparaíso on September 11, 1973, U.S. vessels were standing by in manuevers with the Chilean Navy (*The New York Times*, September 14, 1973). It would seem that the AIFLD activity with COMACH offered one excellent opportunity to live up to past practice and doctrine by intervening to destroy the Allende government.

AIFLD Promotes Truck Owners' Strike

Though there had been professional employee associations for some time, in May of '71 AIFLD assisted the formation of the Confederation of Chilean Professionals (CUPROCH). CUPROCH was started in the copper industry but became an important national force quickly, when it supported the truck owners and merchants strike in October of '72. The former secretary general of CUPROCH says that the federation was suddenly flooded with funds toward the end of the strike. This may account for the sudden drop in the black market rate for U.S. dollars. It could also account for a story by *Time* correspondent Rudolph Rausch, who interviewed some striking truckers near Santiago one mealtime. Despite serious shortages, they were having "a lavish meal of steak, vegetables and empanadas." He asked them where the money for the meal came from; they replied, "From the CIA." (*Time* Magazine, September 24, 1973)

. . . In those countries where AIFLD intervention has aided the overthrow of governments which threatened the continued economic domination by the multinationals, it has followed a pattern. AIFLD tries to promote its influence in the transport and communications industries. The *Readers Digest* (AIFLD member and contributor) issue of December 1966 carries an article describing the influence of AIFLD graduates in Brazil. There, graduates saw to it that communications workers kept the lines open to facilitate the military takeover, even though it meant scabbing on the general strike called by the Brazilian labor movement.

The list of recent Front Royal graduates from Chile shows 37 of 108 people to be from the communications and transport industries.

The organization which directed the "strike" of truck owners and merchants is called the National Command for Gremio Defense. The word *gremio* makes for convenient confusion in English; it is often translated as "union," but actually means "guild" or "society." In Chile a *gremio* is usually an association of employers, professionals or tradespeople, but it can include both workers and employers. The word *gremio* embodies the AIFLD

concept of labor-management solidarity moreso than any word in our language.

In December 1972 Jorge Guerrero, secretary of the National Command for Gremio Defense, was invited to attend one of the advanced courses offered by AIFLD in Washington . . .

. . . Such are a few of the allies of AIFLD in Chile. These forces, with the aid of the AFL-CIO, will build "free and democratic" unions on the ashes of the left-oriented CUT and of the 10-15,000 workers slaughtered by the Junta . . .

After the Coup

In a new development the first week of January '74, the Junta arranged for and approved a meeting of 26 small AIFLD-connected unions. The group, the Chilean National Workers Confederation, led by Eduardo Rojas, president of AIFLD's prime client union, COMACH, claims to be the "new alternative" to CUT. Its vice-president is Luis Villenas, another AIFLD graduate. The fascist Junta knows which side its "bread and butter" is on. ■

Foreign Capital Still Holds Back

For the Junta, no development has been more disappointing, and potentially more threatening, than the failure to attract new foreign capital. Through mid-1974, its spokesmen blamed worldwide protests against violations of artificially organized by the "international forces of communism."

More recently, however, it has become clear that other major obstacles exist, primarily, as Latin America newsletter *reported on June 28, 1974, ". . . the Junta's own failure to agree swiftly enough on an investment code that will spell out the financial advantages of investing in Chile. In particular, the Junta's plans have been held up by the failures of technicians to find a way around Decision 24 of the Andean Pact [Regimen Comun de Tratamiento a los Capitales Extranjeros], which limits the percentage of foreign ownership in any new concern in the area to 49 percent [and profit remittances to 14 percent]. The Junta has been happily waiving this and other clauses to companies that are prepared to jump into Chile now, but it cannot put it into black and white without offending its partners [Peru, Bolivia, Ecuador, Colombia, and Venezuela] in the Pact."*

Finally, after the formal investiture of President Pinochet and the elevation of Admiral Merino to the No. 2 post in charge of the economy, Chile's foreign investment statute was published, as Decree Law 600. But on the substance of Decision 24, it was extremely ambiguous, and the result, extremely disappointing, as the following article reprinted from the Andean Times, Latin America Economic Report, *August 9, 1974, explains.*

The Junta's foreign investment statute was expected, perhaps unreasonably, to clear the air about investing in Chile and to herald a flood of offers from foreign companies. Instead, it has been met with caution and even skepticism by foreign businessmen, because it leaves so much undefined. Foreign businessmen here feel that the law will not in fact make much difference to new investment, though a number of likely investors, who have been holding back while waiting to see what the statute's promised benefits would be, will now go ahead and sign up. This will primarily be in fields which are attractive anyway, such as mining and forestry. The law is not expected to attract investment in manufacturing industry—which is what the government had hoped. . . .

Details such as the level of profit remittances, taxation rates, customs duties, depreciation rates, and exchange controls are not defined in the new law: these are to be spelled out in the contract which all new investors must sign with the government's foreign investment committee which is to be set up under the terms of the statute. In this way a number of key aspects are left open to negotiation by a prospective investor, and—since the Junta has established that it is keen on foreign investment—this could turn out to be an attraction. Contracts will normally be for 10 years from production start-up, extendable to 20 years or more 'if justified.'

The law—issued as Decree Law 600—establishes a series of guarantees to protect the foreign investor. These include:

—a guarantee that foreign investment will get the same treatment as local investment on taxes, tariffs, depreciation and exchange controls; no legislation will be issued that discriminates against foreign investment; and

—a guarantee that, should the rules subsequently be changed in any way which prejudices or causes a loss to a foreign investor, he has the right to compensation. A special tribunal, independent of the executive, is to be set up to decide on any claims under this guarantee.

An additional guarantee is given to investors in natural resources—mining, fishing, forestry, and so on—which can be written into their contract, to the effect that the taxation rates and any other special incentives in application at signature of the contract will not subsequently be altered.

No specific reference is made anywhere in the law to the Andean Group's Decision 24 or its limitations on profit remittances, and the whole question is left undefined. Since Chile is trying to get some of the provisions of Decision 24 changed (LAER II, 28), but could not hold up publication of the law until the question of changes is settled, this vagueness was inevitable. However the law does state (article 3) that the contracts signed by foreign investors must be in accord with any international obligations which Chile has undertaken: these would automatically include any decisions of the Andean Group which have formally been ratified by Chile, including Decision 24.

The new law also specially confirms (article 19) the Andean Group ruling that foreign-owned companies in Chile cannot claim tariff reductions on trade with the other Andean countries unless they comply with Decision 24. One other important point left unclear—though the Andean Group has rulings on it—is how much access foreign investors will have to both short- and long-term local credit. This is to be decided by the 'competent authority' in consultation with the foreign investment committee. On credits obtained abroad, the law sets the following limits:

—contracts for such loans must be approved by and registered with the central bank, which will issue regulations on terms, interest rates and commissions for foreign loans;

—the state will only offer a guarantee on foreign credits up to the proportion of local investment in a company.

The law introduces an important tax modification on profit remittances: on foreign investment from countries which have no double taxation agreement with Chile, the government can lower the tax on profits remitted abroad. Officials say this will not make a tax haven for investors, but will bring the present tax structure to 'internationally acceptable levels.' They add however, that a general tax reform is in the works—probably to come into effect next year—to 'rationalize and reduce' taxes.

Apart from profit remittances, a company is also allowed to use export earnings to cover costs incurred abroad, provided it gets the unanimous approval of the committee to do so; such costs are loosely defined as those of 'operation, maintenance and replacement,' and this seems to allow a potential loophole to any limitations on remittances. A further incentive is that companies which are at least 20 percent foreign-owned can get total or partial exemption from import duties on capital goods—again with specific approval.

Foreign companies already operating in the country have two choices: to continue under the legislation in force at the time the investment was made; or to apply to come under the new system, in which case the application will be treated in the same way as new investment. Foreign investors cannot buy out more than 20 percent of an existing privately owned company, unless the government decides that foreign participation in a particular operation is of 'national importance.' They can, however, buy out any proportion of an existing state company—an incentive to acquire the large group of companies that CORFO is trying to get rid of—provided application to do so is made by the end of 1975. Reinvestment, or additional new investment, of more than 10 percent of the original foreign investment, must be covered by a separate contract negotiated with the government.

The foreign investment committee is to be headed by the economy minister. It will negotiate individually with bidders for large investments, while setting specific guidelines to be met for small-scale investment projects. According to the statute, it will give priority to labor-intensive projects and those involving a high degree of local value added, while projects whose capital input depends largely on credits requiring a state guarantee will get a correspondingly low priority. Other members of the committee are the finance minister, the foreign minister, and the minister in whose sector the project falls (mining, agriculture, and so on), together with the executive head of CORFO, the head of the national planning office [ODEPLAN], the president of the the Central Bank and, as representative of the local private interests, the president of the Confederación de la Producción y del Comercio. ∎

"As U.S. executives see it, the crucial competition in the years ahead will be the contest between Latin America's two very different approaches to development. Naturally enough, they will be cheering for the Brazilian version. If Brazil's boom continues, they say, neighboring countries will feel tremendous pressure to try to match the results by copying the methods. . . . If foreign investment won't come in under those [i.e., Andean Pact] investment laws, then the prideful countries of Spanish America may in time change the laws."

—Fortune
August 1974

THE PHOENIX AND THE ALBATROSS

"The Chilean people are fighting back. Resistance to the Junta, sporadic at first because of heavy losses and initial disorganization, now grows daily. When the mass movement was most weakened by the murders and terror, resistance to the Junta was isolated, uncoordinated, but no less courageous. By the end of last year, however, mass discontent with the military dictatorship had spilled out into the streets in a hundred different ways: wildcat strikes and slowdowns at construction and industrial sites; sabotage in the factories, sand poured into delicate Air Force jet engines, postage-stamp size leaflets plastered onto bus seats, refusals to be conscripted into the armed forces, revolutionary slogans painted on the car doors of the military. And, beneath this, the slow work of reorganizing and regrouping the workers' parties and organizations has been going on." (NACLA's Latin America & Empire Report, *May/June 1974)*

Outside Chile, the exiled left is also regrouping and reorganizing. The need for unity has swept away doctrinal debates among the pre-coup groupings of the Chilean left as they join to create a broad political front of resistance. On February 12 of this year, the parties that composed the UP coalition, the MIR, and the progressive sectors of the PDC joined hands in Europe and signed the following declaration of common purpose and tactical goals in the name of the workers of Chile.

For five months now, the people of Chile have lived under a cruel fascist dictatorship. Invaded by its own armed forces, Chile today is a long strip of blood-soaked land where thousands of patriots are assassinated, tortured, deprived of their liberty, expelled from schools and universities, implacably persecuted, and deprived of the right to subsist by means of a dignified job. The armed Junta that has usurped the government thinks with its brutality it can destroy the people and silence the voice, always generous and brave, of a Chile that is suffering.

They will not achieve their objective. The people of Chile have a long and heroic history of struggle and unity. With their blood and their social combat, Jose Manuel Balmeceda, the anti-imperialist patriot; Luis Emilio Recabarren, working-class leader; Pedro Aguirre Cerda, democratic teacher and visionary; and Salvador Allende, first authentically popular President of Chile, consistent revolutionary, and hero of the struggle for the peoples' independence, wrote the pages of that history.

This tradition is today embodied by those fighting against the dictatorship—challenging the repression and the terror. The struggle of our fatherland against those that want to raze it is being organized and is increasing. The militants of the Chilean left who are temporarily on the outside, are an active part of this struggle, whose leadership is found within the country. We have met and agreed to make this declaration public on the date of another anniversary of the founding of the CUTCH as an homage to our working class and to all Chilean workers.

(1) Significance of the Popular Government

The three years of the Unidad Popular government represented a profound and historical change for Chilean society. The nationalization of the property of the transnational monopolies and the development of a truly sovereign and independent international policy brought the Chilean people ·face to face with Northamerican imperialism. The expropriation of the large private landholdings developed the peasantry as a social and productive force. The formulation of an area of socially owned industrial property and the placing of the financial system under state control displaced the monopoly bourgeoisie from their leading role. The encouragement of numerous forms of popular participation in the productive and administrative apparatus and the rise of new popular mass organizations permitted the development of a social movement characterized by a high political consciousness of the masses.

The large bourgeoisie and imperialism were hit hard by these advances of the people. Their answer was the fascist coup of last September 11. The military dictatorship is their last recourse.

(2) The Eruption of Fascism: Its Criminal, Exploitative, Dependent Nature

The fascist Junta smashes the very institutionality that the bourgeoisie created and claimed to defend. It assassinates the President of the Republic; closes the Parliament and the Municipalities; militarily controls the universities; decrees the dissolution of all popular political parties without exception, confiscates their funds and all their means of expression, and even submits the parties of the right to control; suppresses the freedoms of the press, of meeting and of petition and the right to strike, ignoring all previously sacred legal norms.

The workers are deprived of their most elementary rights, the dissolution of the CUTCH is decreed, and there is the attempt to prohibit the functioning of the trade unions. They must carry the burden of an economic and political repression that is growing in a synchronized way—carrying social decay, misery and uncertainty to wider and wider sectors of the population.

The official economic policy is to re-establish the monopoly character of production and finance to make it possible for the large national and foreign corporations to resume their process of accumulation based on an even greater level of exploitation. This task of destruction is carried out by reducing real salaries and generating, whether by ideological persecution or by means of economic recession, the highest level of unemployment known to date. The redistribution of profits in favor of large capital, at the cost of the working masses and of the broad middle sectors, is inexorable. The desperate action of seeking external financial mechanisms to ease the situation of foreign revenue payment is developed by coming to an understanding with international monopolies, by denationalizing various industries and by searching for some disguise by which to hand over the real control of Chilean copper to the large Northamerican corporations.

The working day is arbitrarily lengthened, establishing a true system of forced labor. Under the threat of death, torture, imprisonment or unemployment, new "productivity" norms are imposed on hundreds of thousands of miners, farmers, workers, technicians and professionals. Nevertheless, this brutal system does not achieve any substantial increase in the production of exportable minerals. In the fields, the worst grain harvest in the country's history is produced.

In a cynical public declaration, the Junta announces that 1974 will be "the worst year in the history of Chile," declaring with the backing of their guns that the whole population should perform "sacrifices." At the same time they squander the small resources that the country commands, directing the highest percentage of the national budget ever known to military expenditures, that is to say, to the maintenance of the apparatus of terror and the acquisition of new and modern armaments that permit them to repress the people in the most brutal way, to strengthen the new axis formed with Brazilian sub-imperialism and to justify the geo-political fantasies of the Chief of the Junta.

The Junta isolates Chile from traditionally friendly nations and hands itself over to Northamerican imperialism. It opens the doors of the country to the hunger of transnational conglomerates. It disregards the right of asylum and protection, violates diplomatic immunity, shoots murderously into diplomatic missions accredited in Chile. It cannot prevent its fascist character from projecting its bloody image into the world outside.

(3) Imperialism Organized the Coup

From the moment of the popular triumph in 1970, by means of plans prepared by the CIA and financed by the transnational companies, the sinister conspiracy that culminated in the assassination of President Allende in the bloody military coup of last September 11 was put into play.

A part of these plans were the economic blockade and sabotage, the financial boycott and the concerted action of the transnational corporations, which constituted a new form of intervention by imperialism.

Chile's economic strangulation, destined (as verified in ITT documents) to create favorable conditions for sedition and subversion, was corroborated by the cable sent by Northamerican [U.S.] Ambassador Davis in which he advised the State Department to create "a discontent large enough to stimulate majority support for military intervention."

The military coup in Chile fits the model of the reactionary counter-offensive by imperialism in Latin America, whose object is to crush with blood and fire the development of popular struggles on the continent.

The action of the traitor generals is, therefore, determined by the global strategy of large international capital

—of which they are merely the policemen, put in charge of repressing the Chilean people.

(4) The Consequences of the Fascist Barbarism

There is no doubt that at this level of development of the fascist policies of the dictatorship, it cannot count the majority of the country on its side. Fascism is beginning to reap the fruits of its policy of cruel exploitation of the working class, of the plundering of the weakest sectors of the bourgeoisie, of the criminal repression of the workers' and popular organizations, of the silencing of all expression of political life in the country.

The Junta is trying to consolidate the terror and turn it into a permanent way of life for the people of Chile. They announce the establishment of a "new order," which is nothing more than the way the Junta tries to justify its determination to remain in power forever with the object of constructing a society in which the most elementary forms of democratic life, culture, the freedom to think and to determine the destiny of the country are forgotten. In their feverish eyes they perceive the church, the United Nations, the governments of Europe and even the Northamerican press as "marxist."

The fascists have been given the job of destroying every democratic vestige that allows the people of Chile to express their protest and struggle.

(5) The People Are Present

The working class and the Chilean people feel today in their own flesh the effects of a policy based on their exploited labor, on the violent decrease in their living standard and on generalized repression, the object of which is the recuperation of economic power by the groups fascism represents.

With each day the workers and popular masses are dragged further into misery, unemployment, to jail, torture and death. Each day the necessity to shake themselves free of a domination that crushes and attempts to muzzle them becomes clearer. Each day conditions ripen for the development of a popular resistance that confronts the fascist regime, corners it and ends by hurling it from power.

Neither exploitation, nor repression, nor crime can smother what the working class has won in experience, in consciousness and in organization and what the dictatorship is not capable of destroying.

Expressions of resistance to the policy of fascism arise and multiply. The working class, overcoming the terror that the usurping Junta has imposed, confronts it in the copper and coal mines and in many industries, in defense of its living standard, its trade union and essential rights. It is becoming a clear truth for all that the repression can not act with impunity or without response and that with each step new contingents are added to the active resistance against fascism.

The brutal and massive repression has not only failed to break the combative spirit and organization of the workers, but it has also failed to erase the parties that express and lead the combat of the masses. In the midst of difficult conditions imposed by fascism and surrounded by the solidarity of the masses, the popular parties increase their level of organization and leadership. Placing unity as a task of the first priority, these parties have applied themselves to leading the struggle of the people of Chile that will culminate in the overthrow of the fascist gang that has usurped the government.

It is not only in the working class and its parties that the conditions for struggle and victory mature. Among the peasantry it becomes increasingly evident that the demagogic policy of giving away a few individual titles of property is nothing but a cover for a policy of returning the expropriated estates and restoring economic power to the landlords. The peasants' years of struggle for the land and elimination of the *latifundios* have not been in vain; it is not possible to erase with the stroke of a pen what the peasantry has gained in difficult and prolonged combat. Nothing can detain the struggle against the return to misery and exploitation to which fascism would drag the masses of the countryside.

The *pobladores* who have known the crimes, massive raids and the razing of entire neighborhoods are reorganizing and lend their support to the struggle against the dictatorship.

Evidence of opposition to the dictatorship is also appearing among wide sectors of small proprietors, businessmen and industrialists. Even those who actively collaborated with the fascists before the September coup today discover with desperation that the government they helped to create attacks them as well, ignores their interests and places on their shoulders as well the cost of accumulation of economic power by the monopolies that yesterday flattered and deceived them.

In this way, then, conditions are created to isolate the dictatorship, organize the majority of the country against it and place its power in growing danger.

(6) Unity Against Fascism

Fascism has forced the country to return to a state of barbarism. As a result, there has been created among the Chilean people conditions for the coming together of vast sectors, including persons and groups that did not identify with the Popular Unity government.

The task of destroying fascism grows out of the profoundly democratic tradition of the proletariat and of the rest of the sectors of the people.

This also coincides with the real interests of middle sectors made up of professionals, small and medium merchants, etc. Many of them were not able to understand how their objective interests coincided with the Popular Government and its program. Today they discover that in addition to the inhuman and murderous character of the fascist dictatorship, it submits them to the exploitation of monopolistic national and foreign capital, deprives them of political freedom and, with the return to barbarity, impedes their human development. All democrats are today against the dictatorship, whatever their ideological, religious or cultural definition. Everyone has a place in the task of isolating, containing and defeating fascism.

The popular forces observe with interest the strengthening of the tendency of growing sectors of Christians to actively join the anti-fascist movement. Many of the pastors have avoided compromising themselves with the fascist crimes and have endeavored to defend the trade union rights of the workers and public freedoms. This position has brought them into conflict with fascism and earned them attacks from the Junta's mercenaries. Even greater potential exists in the Christian masses. The development of the values of solidarity and fraternity must bring a large number of them into the anti-fascist struggle.

Furthermore, within the Armed Forces themselves there are soldiers, non-commissioned officers and even officers who are acquiring growing consciousness of the criminal and bestial role that fascism demands them to play. Many of them discover that they are being used by the minorities that represent big capital, and by imperialism, for anti-national and anti-patriotic purposes. To apply such a policy, the fascist generals have implanted a brutal repression within the Armed Forces. Many members of the Armed Forces will join the patriotic and national work of combatting fascism. All of those who develop this democratic and popular consciousness and who are not stained with the bloody bestiality have a place in the anti-fascist movement.

The Christian Democratic Party again finds itself at a critical juncture. Many of its leaders have collaborated with the fascists. Eduardo Frei and his supporters, who led the party in the recent period, encouraged the coup, conspired with the fascists and today negotiate with them for positions of power.

This contrasts with the role of many of their leaders, who since the beginning condemned the coup and joined the great anti-fascist task. But above all, many sectors of their membership and social base of support have already resolved this contradiction or are on the way to doing it, individually or collectively. Before the bare exploitation and criminal repression that they are the object of, the people have affirmed their solidarity, joining in the struggle against the dictatorship or collaborating in the tasks of the moment.

(7) Broad Front of Struggle

This broad anti-fascist front is made possible by the alliance of the proletariat with the rest of the popular sectors. To it the people and sectors whose democratic and humanistic consciousness is bringing them to the struggle against the dictatorship are being incorporated. It will grow until it becomes the broadest movement in the history of the Chilean social struggle.

Its principal task is the defeat of fascism in all its expressions. It proposes, then, to defeat the dictatorship, liquidate its present instrumental bases of domination, root out the ideology at its foundation and the pathologies that it stimulates in the social character. But above all, the interests of the true dominators of the system—national monopoly capital and imperialism—have to be destroyed.

All vestiges of fascism should be eliminated in order to build the authentic democracy that the country needs—so that this spectre can never again materialize over the Chilean people.

To accomplish this task the people are reorganizing their political and social forces under severe conditions of repression. Today the popular and anti-fascist forces are in a better situation than in the first moments of the criminal repression. We should work to permanently improve this organization and make use of the weaknesses and mistakes of the dictatorship.

The ideological confrontation with fascism, the popular economic demands to stave off the dramatic effects of super-exploitation, the winning back of social and political gains—these are chapters in the present struggle that come before the more decisive stages of the fight.

The choice of each method of struggle and the initiation of each phase of combat will be determined by the correlation of forces and of the organization that the people and revolutionaries achieve at each point.

The survival of the popular forces and their reorganization under new conditions were the first achievements. The formation and securing of the alliance between the proletariat and the other sectors of the people and the incorporation of anti-fascist democrats are tasks presently in development. In practice, the struggle of the masses to regain their political and social rights has already been initiated. Its deepening and extension are the order of the day. The preparation for higher phases of struggle and confrontation with fascism is in force.

(8) International Solidarity: An Essential Factor for the Victory of the People

The peoples of the world have been profoundly moved by the military coup in Chile. The immense majority of humanity has condemned with indignation the crimes of the fascist Junta. A vast and powerful massive movement of solidarity has been developing on all continents.

Solidarity with Chile has become a factor unifying broad ideological, political and social sectors in the different countries, expressed in huge numbers of mass actions, in public statements, in permanent campaigns demanding the end of the terror, freedom for the political prisoners, and the closing of the concentration camps.

Worldwide personalities, heads of governments and political parties, church leaders, and even the Secretary General of the United Nations have taken part in these actions.

The attitude of firm and resolute solidarity in almost all the socialist countries constituted a hard blow against the fascist dictatorship on the international front. Many other governments of Western Europe, Latin America, Asia, Africa and the Middle East have taken positions that in one way or another have contributed to the world-wide isolation of the military Junta.

Governments and friendly people have opened their embassies and countries to receive hundreds of politically persecuted individuals.

International solidarity has been a powerful moral endorsement for the Chilean people in their fight against brutal repression, has had repercussions also in the internal isolation of fascism, and has been able to stop, on many occasions, the hand of the executioners.

The Most Urgent Tasks of Solidarity

The forces that represent the popular and revolutionary Chilean movement have made efforts from the beginning to put into practice the imperative of this unity. This process of strengthening unity has also had its expression among the Chileans outside the country. As far back as last December, in a declaration from Rome by all the parties and movements of the left, they made public their decision to combine forces to realize the tasks destined to guarantee and develop the broad movement of solidarity with the struggle of the Chilean people that has arisen all over the world.

Now we are taking a step forward. Advancing on the road of unity, we have decided to establish a permanent coordination of the Chilean left on the outside. In this way, we place in the hands of the workers and people of Chile and in the hands of the revolutionary and progressive forces all over the world a more effective instrument to face the requirements of the present moment.

Freedom for the Dawson Prisoners before the Winter

We again call upon international public opinion to intensify even more the massive campaign for an end to the repression, respect for human rights, the closing of the concentration camps, freedom for political prisoners and the repeal of the State of Internal War.

In particular we urgently ask for a tremendous world effort demanding the freedom of Luis Corvalan, Clodomiro Almeyda, Anselmo Sule, Pedro F. Ramirez, Bautista von Schowen, Vicente Sotta and the rest of the prisoners on Dawson Island.

Dawson Island has been converted into a true experiment camp. Its climactic conditions, the regime of seclusion and forced labor and the lack of medical attention, all aggravated by the nearness of the Antarctic winter, mean that the Junta has condemned, in fact, the highest Chilean popular leaders and personalties at this concentration camp to a slow but certain death.

The world can mobilize with urgency to save the lives and liberty of all of them.

In the name of the workers and people of Chile, we are grateful for the solidarity that has been given us. We are certain that it will continue to grow, that it will take root in the popular masses, that it will be felt with even greater force in each factory, in each school, in each home, encouraging, from all points of the globe, the resistance that is developing in Chile and that will end in victory, opening for our people the doors of a new, truly democratic society.

Socialist Party of Chile   *Communist Party of Chile*
MAPU Workers and Peasant   *Radical Party*
Christian Left   *MIR*
MAPU   ■

Pablo Neruda delivered the following address to his fellow writers at the fiftieth-anniversary celebration of the American Center of P.E.N., April 10, 1972. We reprint it from The Chilean Road to Socialism, *edited by Dale L. Johnson (Anchor Press/Doubleday).*

Neruda was then Chile's ambassador to France and the 1971 Nobel Laureate for poetry—both honors symbolic of his two-fold identity as spokesman for his people and poetic voice of people everywhere. Uniquely Chilean, he remains uniquely universal. His total identification with the Chilean people, his active participation in their revolution, and his death in the wake of the September coup seem all of a piece. Like Whitman, "his patent nationalism forms part of a total and organic universal vision." His speech, prophetic and poignant in light of the Chilean tragedy, is a fitting, resonant close to this small offering to the struggle which he embodied and ennobled—and which goes on.

In the course of my roving life, I have attended quite a number of strange meetings. Only a few days ago, however, I was present at what seems to me to be the most mysterious of all the meetings in which I have ever taken part. I was seated there with a handful of my fellow countrymen. In front of us, in what looked like a vast circle to my eyes, sat the representatives of banks and treasuries and high finance, the delegates of numerous countries to which—so it would seem—my country owes a very great deal of money. We, the Chileans, were few in numbers, and our eminent creditors—almost entirely from the major countries—were very many: perhaps 50 or 60 of them. The business in hand was the renegotiation of our Public Debt, of our External Debt, built up in the course of half a century by former governments.

In this same half century, men have reached the moon complete with penicillin and with television. In the field of warfare, napalm has been invented to render democratic, by means of its purifying fire, the ashes of a number of the inhabitants of our planet. During these same fifty years, this American Center of the P.E.N. Club has worked nobly for the cause of reason and understanding. But, as I could see at that relentless meeting, Chile was nonetheless under the menace of an updated version of the garrote, namely the Stand-By. In spite of half a century of intellectual understanding, the relations between rich and poor—between nations which lend some crumbs of comfort and others which go hungry—continue to be a complex mixture of anguish and pride, injustice, and the right to live. . . .

For my part, I, who am now nearing 70, discovered Walt Whitman when I was just 15, and I hold him to be my greatest creditor. I stand before you, feeling that I bear with me always this great and wonderful debt which has helped me to exist.

To "renegotiate" this debt, I must start by recognizing its existence, and acknowledging myself to be the humble servant of a poet who strole the earth with long, slow paces, pausing everywhere to love, to examine, to learn, to teach, and to admire. The fact of the matter is that this great man, this lyric moralist, chose a hard path for himself: he was both a torrential and a didactic singer—qualities which appear opposed, seemingly also more appropriate to a leader than to a writer. But what really counts is that Walt Whitman was not afraid to teach—which means to learn at the hands of life and undertake the responsibility of passing on the lesson! To speak frankly: he had no fear of either moralizing or immoralizing, nor did he seek to separate the fields of pure and impure poetry. He was the first totalitarian poet: his intention was not just to sing, but to impose on others his own total and wide-ranging vision of the relationships of men and nations. In this sense, his patent nationalism forms part of a total and organic universal vision: he held himself to be the debtor of happiness and sorrow alike, and also of both the advanced cultures and more primitive societies.

There are many kinds of greatness, but let me say (though I be a poet of the Spanish tongue) that Walt Whitman has taught me more than Spain's Cervantes: in Walt Whitman's work one never finds the ignorant being humbled, nor is the human condition ever found offended.

We continue to live in a Whitmanesque age, seeing how new men and new societies rise and grow despite their birth pangs. The Bard complained of the all-powerful influence of Europe, from which the literature of his age continued to draw sustenance. In truth he, Walt Whitman, was the protagonist of a truly geographical personality: the first man in history to speak with a truly continental American voice, to bear a truly American name. The colonies of the most brilliant countries have left a legacy of centuries of silence: colonialism seems to slay fertility and stultify the power of creation. One has only to look at the Spanish empire, where I can assure you that three centuries of Spanish dominion produced not more than two or three writers worthy of praise in all America.

The proliferation of our republics gave birth to more than merely flags and nationalities, universities, small heroic armies, or melancholy love songs. Books started to proliferate as well, yet they too often formed an impenetrable thicket, bearing many a flower but little fruit. With time, however, and especially in our own days, the Spanish language has at last started to shine out in the works of American writers who—from Rio Grande to Patagonia—have filled a whole dark continent (struggling toward a new independence) with magical stories, and with poems now tender, now desperate.

In this age, we see how other new nations, other new literatures and new flags, are coming into being with what one hopes is the total extinction of colonialism in Africa and Asia. Almost overnight, the capitals of the world are seen studded with the banners of peoples we had never heard of, seeking self-expression with the unpolished and pain-laden voice of birth. Black writers of both Africa and America begin to give us the true pulse of the luckless races which had hitherto been silent. Political battles have always been inseparable from poetry. Man's liberation may often require bloodshed, but it always requires song— and the song of mankind grows richer day by day, in this age of sufferings and liberation.

I ask your pardon, humbly, in advance, for going back to the subject of my country's trouble. As all the world knows, Chile is in the course of carrying out a revolutionary transformation of its social structure with true dignity, and within the strict framework of our legal constitution. This is something which annoys and offends many people! Why on earth, they ask, don't these pesky Chileans imprison anyone, close down newspapers, or shoot any citizen who contradicts them?

As a nation, we chose our path for ourselves, and for that very reason we are resolved to pursue it to the end. But secret opponents use every kind of weapon to turn our destiny aside. As cannons seem to have gone out of fashion in this kind of war, they use a whole arsenal of arms both old and new. Dollars and darts, telephone and telegraph services: each seems to serve! It looks as though anything at all will do, when it comes to defending ancient and unreasonable privileges. That is why, when I was sitting in that meeting in which Chile's Ex-ternal Debts was being renegotiated in Paris, I could not help thinking of *The Ancient Mariner*.

Samuel Taylor Coleridge drew upon an episode which took place in the extreme south of my country for the basis of his desolate poem.

In Chile's cold seas we have every kind and species of albatross: wandering, gigantic, gray, and stormy, and supremely splendid in its flight!

That is, perhaps, the reason why my country has the shape of a great albatross with wings outspread!

And in that unforgettable meeting, in which we were striving to renegotiate our External Debt in a just fashion, many of those who appeared so implacable seemed to be taking aim in order to bring Chile tumbling down, so that the albatross should fly no more!

To mention this may be the indiscretion of a poet who has only been an ambassador for a year, but it looked to me as though it was perhaps the representative of United States finance who concealed an arrow underneath his business papers—ready to aim it at the albatross's heart!

And if he would take the trouble to reread the poets of former times, he might learn from *The Ancient Mariner* that the sailor who perpetrated such a crime was doomed to carry the heavy corpse of the slain albatross hanging from his neck—to all eternity. ■

SOURCE LIST

Amnesty International
P.O. Box 1182
Palo Alto, California 94302
or
200 West 72nd Street
New York, New York 10023
A worldwide organization collecting information on torture of political prisoners and other violations of basic rights and developing world opinion in favor of all oppressed people. A new publication called *Matchbox* is published quarterly by the Western Regional Office of AI in the U.S. at the Palo Alto address. It is sent to all AI members, contributors, and concerned individuals and "free to prisoners on request."

American Friends of Brazil
P.O. Box 2279
Station A
Berkeley, California 94702
Publishes *Brazilian Information Bulletin* irregularly (available by donation); best information available on torture and economics.

BARTOC
388 Sanchez Street
San Francisco, California 94114
Publishers of *Learning from Chile: Resources for Teachers and Students,* a collection of graphics, poems, bibliographies, and other resources on Chile.

**Bertrand Russell Tribunal II on
Repression in Latin America**
Formed in 1972 to investigate causes and consequences of the repression in Brazil and expanded to expose repression in Chile and four other Latin American countries. For more information, write: COFFLA, P.O. Box 8685, Washington, D.C. 20011.

Center for Cuban Studies
220 East 23rd Street—8th floor
New York, New York 10010
Makes available a comprehensive collection of documents, study materials, films, and graphics about revolutionary Cuba. The Center has a library and reading room and sponsors film showings, poster and painting exhibits, lectures, discussions, and language classes. Provides information and general resources for Latin America. The Center has published the speeches of Beatriz Allende and Fidel Castro on the events in Chile in a pamphlet entitled "What Happened in Chile . . ."

Center for Information on Latin America
P.O. Box 576
Station N
Montreal 129, Quebec, Canada
Publishes documents and a newsletter, *Grito y Fusil*, in French, Spanish, and English available at $3.00 yearly.

Center for the Study of Development and Social Change
1430 Massachusetts Avenue
Cambridge, Massachusetts 02138
Materials on Paulo Freire; information on problems of poor countries within a framework of scientific analysis.

Center for Intercultural Documentation (CIDOC)
APDO 479
Cuernavaca, Mexico
An intercultural center, co-founded by Ivan Illich, which serves as a library for Latin American history and sociology (housing excellent materials especially on Camilo Torres and the Tupamaros) and offers both intensive Spanish and English language courses and encounter seminars for North and South Americans. Catalog of courses and publications available. Newest commercially published series is *Ideas in Progress*.

Centro Nacional de Communicacion Social (CENCOS)
Medellin 33
Mexico 7, D.F.
Contributor to CoDoC's Bibliographical Notes on Chile (See CoDoC below).

Chicago Area Group on Latin America (CAGLA)
2546 North Halsted
Chicago, Illinois 60614
Publishes an irregular newsletter available for $3.00 yearly; helps operate the New World Resource Center, a bookstore and storefront, which hosts films, lectures, and seminars.

**Chicago Commission of Inquiry into the Status of
Human Rights in Chile**
A loose coalition of individuals and groups who joined forces following the military takeover to focus the attention of public opinion on the plight of political prisoners and victims of persecution in Chile. The Commission members have produced a major report based on their fact-finding mission to Chile and gathered an impressive body of raw documents. The full report, including the documents and other supporting evidence, can be obtained by writing to Joanne Fox Przeworski, 1320 East Madison Park, Chicago, Illinois, 60615, or Doris Strieter, 1600 South 14th Avenue, Maywood, Illinois 60153. Cost: $1.50 plus fifty cents for mailing.

Chile-Canada Solidarity Newsletter
Box 6300 Station A
Toronto 1, Canada

Chile Monitor and Chile Fights
c/o Chile Solidarity Campaign Co-operative Centre
129 Seven Sisters Road
London, N. 7, U.K.

Chile en la Resistencia
Insurgentes Sur 1160-601
Mexico 10, D.F.

Chile Research Team
Department of Sociology
Livingston College
Rutgers University
New Brunswick, New Jersey 08903
Professors and graduate students involved in continuing in-depth studies of contemporary Chile and its international relations, including U.S. press coverage of Chile.

Common Front for Latin America (COFFLA)
1500 Farragut, N.W.
Washington, D.C. 20011
A radical group, in the NACLA tradition, with input from missionary sources and strong religious motivation. Prepares packets of articles and booklets and works primarily in the D.C. area.

Community Action on Latin America (CALA)
Madison Campus Ministry
731 State Street
Madison, Wisconsin 53703
An independent research/action collective of students, clergy, and Latins working together to promote the cause of liberation in Latin America and of Hispanic people in the United States. Publishes a newsletter available for $2.00 yearly. Held an important conference on Chile out of which the national committee for Non-Intervention in Chile (NICH) emerged (see below).

Consejo Latinoamericana de Ciencias Sociales (CLACSO)
Callao 875, 3⁰ Piso E
Buenos Aires, Argentina
att: Enrique Otieza, Executive Secretary
The Latin American Social Science Council includes more than 60 research centers and other agencies which promote transnational and interdisciplinary research, both theoretical and applied. Fosters collaborative research by working committees on such topics as science, technology and development, education, "dependency," rural studies, and economic history. Has roster in its Buenos Aires office of displaced scholars it seeks to relocate, primarily in Latin America, and has reciprocal relationship with ECALAS in the U.S. (see below).

Cooperation in Documentation and Communication International Secretariat (CoDoC)
1500 Farragut Street, N.W.
Washington, D.C. 20011
CoDoC coordinates the documentation of groups seeking to promote a world of justice, participation, and liberty by sharing information on issues of oppression. It published the *CoDoC Common Catalogue No. 1, Bibliographical Notes for Understanding: The Military Coup in Chile,* March, 1974. Contributors include the following: Centro Nacional de Communicación Social, IDOC International, Institute on the Church in Urban Industrial Society, Latin America Documentation, MIEC-JECI Centro de Documentacion, and Third World Reader Service (see addresses under individual entries in this list).

Cuba Resource Center (CRC)
Box 206
Cathedral Station
New York, New York 10025
Funded by Protestant and Roman Catholic Church groups, it publishes the *CRC Newsletter.* The CRC seeks to: 1) circulate information on life in Cuba, and on the churches in Cuba; 2) effect a more positive understanding of the Cuban Revolution; 3) end measures taken by the U.S. government to isolate and undermine the Cuban Revolution; 4) build understanding of revolutionary movements elsewhere in Latin America; 5) expose and combat Church involvement in, and support for, U.S. domination of Latin America, with Cuba as historical background.

Division for Latin America-U.S. Catholic Conference
1430 K Street, N.W.
Washington, D.C. 20005
Approximately every three weeks publishes articles which have been translated into English. It conducts an active humanitarian campaign against torture in Brazil and elsewhere. It has published a $2.50 packet entitled: "Puerto Rico: Showcase of Oppression."

Ecumenical Program in Inter-American Communication and Action (EPICA)
1500 Farragut Street, N.W.
Washington, D.C. 20011
Publishes newsletter, coordinates action in Washington, D.C., stimulates development of other groups, works with Interaction Coalition on the Third World Reader Service, and runs Third World workshops.

Edition Latin America
P.O. Box 218
Station N
Montreal 129, Quebec, Canada
Publishes booklets such as "The Political Economy of Population Control" and a recent work on Brazil.

Emergency Committee to Aid Latin American Scholars of the Latin American Studies Association (ECALAS)
Ibero-American Center
New York University
24 Waverly Place, Room 566
New York, New York 10003
Created November 1973 as a clearing house for information on displaced graduate students and professors driven from teaching posts and barred from academic pursuits in their own countries. A network of regional coordinators and international collaborators, ECALAS has helped to place some 50 students and faculty members, representing about $250,000 in tuition waivers, student assistantships and stipends. Funds urgently needed to continue administrative activities and for travel of academics to U.S. to teach or study.

Emergency Committee to Defend Democracy in Chile
(San Jose Committee)
316 South 19th Street
San Jose, California 95116
Activities include publication of a pamphlet on the American Institute for Free Labor Development (AIFLD).

Emergency Committee to Save Chilean Health Workers
c/o The Physicians' Forum
510 Madison Avenue
New York, New York 10022
A membership group of U.S. physicians concerned with issues of social medicine. Protested Junta's violent acts toward Chilean doctors and health workers following the coup.

Friends of Haiti
P.O. Box 365
Hopewell Junction
New York, New York 12533
Publishes newsletter denouncing oppression in Haiti.

The Fund for New Priorities in America
156 Fifth Avenue
New York, New York 10010
A nonprofit educational organization devoted primarily to organizing Congressional Conferences on subjects affecting American priorities, such as "Chile: Implications for United States Foreign Policy" in February 1974. (Five-part edited transcript available for $7.50.)

Goff, James and Margaret
Latinamerica Press
P.O. Box 5594
Lima, Peru
The couple translates material into English, often on Christian thrusts toward liberation. To be put on their mailing list, send $3.00.

Guardian
32 West 22nd Street
New York, New York 10010
This weekly publication carries the most consistent news on Latin America of any of the radical publications and has a special supplement on Chile.

IDOC International
Via Santa Maria dell' Anima, 30
00186 Rome, Italy
International Center of Documentation on the Contemporary Church, established in Rome in 1965 and reorganized on an ecumenical basis in 1968. The documents published or listed in the monthly *IDOC Bulletin* form part of an ever-growing collection of texts . . . largely "fugitive documents" . . . catalogued and filed in the IDOC documentation department in Rome. The IDOC working group of 250 experts represents some 40 countries.

Institute on the Church in Urban Industrial Society
800 West Belden Avenue
Chicago, Illinois 60614
Contributor to CoDoC's Biblographical Notes on Chile (see CoDoC above).

Latin American Working Group of the National Council of Churches
475 Riverside Drive
New York, New York 10027
Major source of information on human rights in Latin America. Supports other groups in both North and Latin America and receives and distributes some publications.

Latin American Documentation (LADOC)
1430 K Street, N.W.
Washington, D.C. 20005
Contributor to CoDoC's Bibliographical Notes on Chile (see CoDoC above).

Latin American Forum
983 Columbus Avenue
New York, New York 10025

Latin American Program
Antioch College
Yellow Springs, Ohio 45387
Directed by Karl Lenkersdorf, this is a good program for undergraduate socialists.

Latin American Policy Alternatives Group (LAPAG)
2205 San Antonio Street
Room 190
Austin, Texas 78705
This collective has a weekly radio news program and shows films, among its many projects.

Latin American Project (LAP)
c/o Shepherd Bliss
Cambridge-Goddard Graduate School
5 Upland Road
Cambridge, Massachusetts 02140
A new group focusing on Chile and Puerto Rico; some members are earning the M.A. for working with the collective. It publishes a directory on groups doing radical work on Latin America.

Latin American Strategy Committee
1500 Farragut Street, N.W.
Washington, D.C. 20011
Coordinates activities of religion-related groups, sends out occasional mailings offering progressive evaluations of Latin American developments and issues.

Latin American Working Group
Box 5
Station B
Toronto 2B, Canada
This group comes and goes, but does produce a good publication, "La Banda," on the Dominican Republic.

Los Angeles Group for Latin American Solidarity (LAGLAS)
P.O. Box 24921
Village Station
Los Angeles, California 90024
Publishes *Notas del Metropoli*, designed for Peruvians.

MIEC-JECI Centro de Documentacion
Apartado 58
Lima, Peru
Contributor to CoDoC's Bibliographical Notes on Chile (see CoDoC above).

Monthly Review
116 West 14th Street
New York, New York 10011
An independent socialist monthly edited by Paul M. Sweezy and Harry Magdoff.

Non-Intervention in Chile (NICH)
Box 800
Berkeley, California 94701
A group formed in 1972 to study United States involvement in Chile; started in November 1973 to publish a monthly report, *Chile Newsletter,* offering radical interpretations.

North American Congress on Latin America (NACLA)
P.O. Box 57, Cathedral Station
New York, New York 10025
and
P.O. Box 226
Berkeley, California 94701
A closely-knit, ideologically homogeneous team of political scientists, sociologists, and cultural historians clustered around (but independent of) Columbia University in New York and Berkeley, California. NACLA is the pioneer in offering a radical challenge to conventional scholarship in the United States and a radical re-evaluation of the U.S. impact on Latin America. Publishes booklets such as *Research Methodology Guide* and *New Chile,* as well as the monthly newsletter *Latin America & Empire Report,* available to individuals for $6.00 and to institutions for $12.00 annually.

Noticias Aliadas
Apartado 5594
Lima 1, Peru
A news service with progressive religious orientation; appears several times a week in both English and Spanish.

Pacific Studies Center
1963 University Avenue
East Palo Alto, California 94303
Formed in 1969 in an effort to halt war research and counterinsurgency studies at Stanford University and the Stanford Research Institute. A resource center with a library of books, hearings, reports, and leftist periodicals. PSC publishes the *Pacific Research and World Empire Telegram,* a scholarly magazine focusing on U.S. foreign policy, multinational corporations, and the political economy of Asia and the Pacific.

Peoples Information Center on Latin America (PICLA)
Box 1165
Taos, New Mexico 81571

Puerto Rican Revolutionary Workers Organization
352 Willis Avenue
Bronx, New York 10454
Formerly known as the Young Lords. Publishes *Palante.*

Puerto Rican Socialist Party (PSP)
106 East 14th Street
New York, New York 10003
Favors Puerto Rican independence, publishes a weekly bilingual newspaper, *Claridad,* from 30 East 20th Street, Room 602, New York, New York 10003.

Third World Cinema
P.O. Box 4430
Berkeley, California 94704
or
244 West 27th Street
New York, New York 10001
Distributes revolutionary films, such as "Blood of the Condor" (Bolivia) and "The Hour of the Furnaces" (Argentina).

Third World Reader Service
1500 Farragut Street, N.W.
Washington, D.C. 20011
Provides articles of significance on a regular basis to subscribers.

Tricontinental News Service
30 East 20th Street, #303
New York, New York 10003
A news service/magazine reporting on political and social news of the developing countries of Asia, Africa, and Latin America. Most articles are from direct sources in these countries—journalists, wire services, newspapers, radio broadcasts, eyewitness accounts, internal documents, and actual-participant reports.

Union of Radical Latin Americanists (URLA)
c/o Joel Edelstein
College of Community Science
University of Wisconsin
Madison, Wisconsin 54302
This group, mostly social scientists, broke off from the professional organization of LASA and seeks coordination of the research efforts of its own membership.

Union of Radical Political Economists (URPE)
2503 Student Activities Building
University of Michigan
Ann Arbor, Michigan 48104
Group of Marxist economists with various local chapters. Publishes booklets and a newsletter.

U.S. Committee for Justice to Latin American Political Prisoners (USLA)
150 5th Avenue, Room 737
New York, New York 10011
A Trotsky-influenced group; publishes the *USLA Reporter* ten times yearly for $2.00, has local chapters, and organizes demonstrations.

Women's International League for Peace and Freedom (WILPF)
1213 Race Street
Philadelphia, Pennsylvania 19107
Oldest international peace organization, now with national Sections in 20 countries, 150 U.S. branches. Current priorities: finding alternatives to the profit system; ending U.S. militarism, particularly in Chile and Indochina. Published *Chile: State of War Eyewitness Report* ($1.50 each); monthly newsletter, *Peace and Freedom,* available for $3.00.

It is in the dynamic nature of some of the constituents above to be open to the winds of change, and although we'd like to, we cannot attest to the absolute accuracy or completeness of some of the information given. Any additions, corrections, or up-dating from our readers will be received gratefully.

It is our hope to expand and enrich this list periodically and make it available as a separate entity to all those concerned with Chile and Latin America. The usefulness of such a list in the continuing struggle for justice everywhere is obvious, and we hope you will help.

SELECTED BIBLIOGRAPHY

Allende, Salvador. Chile's Road to Socialism, ed. Joan Garces. Harmondsworth: Penguin Books, 1973.
Competent and representative collection of Allende's political theories and social goals.

Angell, Alan. Politics and the Labor Movement in Chile. New York and London: Oxford University Press, 1972.
Valuable statistical and other empirical evidence of growth of labor movement and long struggle for its control between Communist Party and Socialist Party, and later efforts of Christian Democrats to get a foothold.

Anonymous. Torture in Chile. USLA Reporter, July-August, 1974.
Summarizes reports of major international investigations; also surveys the world reaction to the revelations.

Arroyo, Gonzalo. Le coup d'etat au Chili. Paris: Seuil, 1974.
Jesuit political economist, leader of Christians for Socialism in Chile and staunch supporter of Allende, concludes from Allende's experience that "the liberal style of democracy is a fiction," ready to develop into "the most brutal fascism" when the capitalist system of which it is a function is threatened by people "who dare lift their heads in pursuit of freedom, justice and truth."

Birns, Laurence, Editor. The End of Chilean Democracy. New York: The Seabury Press, 1974.
A slightly expanded version of IDOC/International Documentation No. 58. (See IDOC/North America below.)

Cockcroft, James D., Andre Gunder Frank, and Dale L. Johnson. Dependence and Underdevelopment: Latin America's Political Economy. New York: Anchor Books/ Doubleday, 1972.
This collection of radical analyses by leading social scientists includes several chapters dealing specifically with Chile, with particular attention to class structures class attitudes.

COFFLA. Chile: Unmasking Development. Washington, D.C.: COFFLA, 1973.
Packet of informative articles from many sources intended as an organizing tool and resource kit for group discussions. Challenges the "American Way" as a model for Third World development.

Debray, Regis. The Chilean Revolution: Conversations with Allende. New York: Vintage, 1972.
French journalist, a Marxist, recently released from a Bolivian prison in which he had been held as an associate of Che Guevara, argues at length with Allende that socialism cannot be established in Chile or anywhere by peaceful means.

Evans, Les, Editor. Disaster in Chile: Allende's Strategy and Why It Failed. New York: Pathfinder Press, 1974.
Contributors to this Marxist-Trotskyist symposium include: Jean-Pierre Beauvais, Hugo Blanco, Peter Camejo, Gerry Foley, Joseph Hansen, Dick Roberts, David Thorstad.

Feinberg, Richard. The Triumph of Allende: Chile's Legal Revolution. New York: Mentor, 1972.
Sympathetic overview of Chilean situation which led to Allende's 1970 electoral success and optimistic description of the period immediately following. Fails to recognize depth of United States resistance to the experiment and consequently makes projection which events have hopelessly negated.

IDOC/North America. Chile: The Allende Years, The Coup, Under the Junta, ed. Laurence Birns. IDOC/International Documentation No. 58 (December 1973).
Collection of documents sketching a broad canvas of Chile before, during and after the coup. Includes material on political and economic intervention in Chile, cultural and religious realities, and the political responses to the coup from many factions. Material on role of U.S. in the coup, purges in universities, manifestos and party declarations, etc.

Johnson, Dale L., Editor. The Chilean Road to Socialism. New York: Anchor Books/Doubleday, 1973.
This symposium surveys many aspects of work of the Allende regime from the viewpoint of admirers, including land reform, nationalization of copper, and politicizing of workers and peasants. Much excellent material, but some of minor value.

Joxe, Alain. Las fuerzas armadas en el sistema politico de Chile. Santiago de Chile: Editorial Universitaria, 1970.
Important particularly because it explodes the widely held view that the armed forces have been traditionally and consistently outside politics. English summary in Monthly Review, New York, January, 1970.

Kaufman, Robert R. The Politics of Land Reform in Chile. Cambridge, Mass.: Harvard University Press, 1972.
Evaluates the new forces brought into play by land reform, including ideological and political conflicts between different categories of peasants encouraged by landowners seeking to frustrate reform.

Lau, Stephen F. The Chilean Response to Foreign Investment. New York: Praeger, 1972.
Detailed analysis of attitudes of different political groups to Chilean policy governing foreign investment.

MacEoin, Gary. No Peaceful Way: The Chilean Struggle for Dignity. New York: Sheed and Ward, 1974.
Places Allende regime in historical context. Shows why it met such deep-seated opposition from Chile's proper-

tied classes, the transnational companies, and the U.S. administration. Documents role of CIA, ITT and others in fomenting internal conflict and creating economic crisis that led to military takeover. Projects long and grim period of counterrevolutionary "reconstruction."

MacEoin, Gary. Revolution Next Door: Latin America in the 1970's. *New York: Holt, Rinehart and Winston, 1971.*

An overview of hemispheric pressures and counterpressures which brought Allende to power only to overthrow him.

Morris, David J. We Must Make Haste—Slowly: The Process of Revolution in Chile. *New York: Random House, 1973.*

A United States graduate student in Chile, impressed by UP regime's effort to progress without violence, gives the nonscholar the elements he needs to make his own judgments.

Moss, Robert. Chile's Marxist Experiment. *London: David and Charles, 1973.*

A staff writer for the *London Economist,* a publication as reactionary as Chile's *El Mercurio,* Moss formulates the oligarchy's version of the rise and fall of Allende.

Mutchler, David E. The Church as a Political Factor in Latin America, with Particular Reference to Colombia and Chile. *New York: Praeger, 1971.*

Valuable data on the part played by Chile's church leaders in bringing the Christian Democrats to power in 1964, and their embarrassment when the UP coalition triumphed in 1970.

NACLA. Latin America & Empire Report, *"Chile: Special Issue," March 1971; "Secret Memos from ITT," April 1972; "There Will Be Work for All," September 1972; "Chile: Facing the Blockade," January 1973; "Chile: The Story Behind the Coup," October 1973; "Chile: The People Will Not Forget . . ." May/June 1974.*

The North American Congress on Latin America, a closely-knit and ideologically homogeneous team of political scientists, sociologists and cultural historians, clustered around (but independent of) Columbia University, New York, and Berkeley, California, has pioneered in offering a radical re-evaluation of the United States impact on Latin America. Solidly documented, logical in analysis.

NACLA. New Chile. *New York: North American Congress on Latin America, 1973.*

Tables and articles which help identify the patterns and processes of United States influence in Chile as expressed in the military, trade-union and business spheres. Brings out the overwhelming dependence of Chile on external decision-makers and thus offers background for understanding the dynamics of the counterrevolution.

Petras, James. Politics and Social Forces in Chilean Development. *Berkeley: University of California Press, 1969.*

Documented analysis by informed social scientist of political parties and developments in political activity in Chile during the 1960s.

Petras, James, and *Hugo Zemelman Merino.* Peasants in Revolt: A Case Study, 1965-71. *Austin, Texas: University of Texas Press, 1972.*

Sweezy, Paul M., and *Harry Magdoff, Editors.* Revolution and Counterrevolution in Chile. *New York: Monthly Review Press, 1974.*

Collection of articles from the independent socialist magazine, *Monthly Review,* tracing the history of the Allende regime.

Touraine, Alain. Vie et Mort du Chili Populaire. *Paris: Seuil, 1973.*

A French sociologist's diary, written in Chile, July 29 to September 24, 1973; a day-to-day analysis of forces and events.

Zammit, J. Ann, Editor, with cooperation from Gabriel Palma. The Chilean Road to Socialism. *Austin, Texas: University of Texas Press and Institute of Development Studies at the University of Sussex, England, 1973.*

The proceedings of a major conference organized in Santiago in March 1972 by the Chilean National Planning Office and the Sussex Institute of Development Studies. The sections cover macroeconomic and industrial policy, land policy, foreign policy and external sector problems, participation and socialist consciousness, prospects for the UP government, the Chilean road to socialism. Also included are papers on experiments in socialist transformation in Tanzania, Yugoslavia, Cuba, and Hungary. Excellent reference and bibliography.

INDEX OF NAMES

Special Notes

General Augusto Pinochet Ugarte, commander-in-chief of the Chilean armed forces since August 1973 and head of the four-man Junta since September 11, 1973, proclaimed himself the President of the Republic of Chile and was formally invested in a 12-minute ceremony on June 26, 1974.

The other members of the Junta were relegated to "an advisory and legislative role," ranked as follows: Navy Admiral José Toribio Merino occupies second position, in charge of the economy; Air Force General Gustavo Leigh Guzman is third in line, dealing with social policy; and General Cesar Mendoza, the independence of whose Carabineros has effectively been neutralized, is fourth, in charge of agriculture.

On July 11, President Pinochet announced sweeping cabinet changes, replacing eight ministers and leaving only four in their same positions. The Chilean cabinet now comprises 17 ministries, occupied by five representatives from the Army; three each from the Navy, Air Force, and Carabineros; and three civilians.

Because of these changes, readers will find in the foregoing documents and analyses some discrepancies in the specific titles attached to officials in the Chilean government. Thus, the editors listed below, as a reference, the incumbent ministers (as of press release date, September 13, 1974) and the names of their immediate predecessors (pre-July 11). Letters in parentheses indicate service branches: (A), Army; (AF), Air Force; (C), Carabineros; (N), Navy.

Throughout the basic index, asterisks are used to indicate pages on which the person or publication indexed is the author, translator, or major source of the information on those pages.

Ministry	Incumbent Minister	Immediate Predecessor
Agriculture	General Tucapel Vallejos (C)	General Sergio Crespo (Ret. AF)
Defense	General Oscar Bonilla Bradanovic (A)	Admiral Patricio Carvajal (N)
Economic Coordination	Raúl Sáez	(none; newly created post)
Economy	Fernando Léniz	(same)
Education	Admiral Hugo Castro Jiménez (N)	(same)
Finance	Jorge Cauas	Admiral Lorenzo Gotuzzo (N)
Foreign Affairs	Admiral Patricio Carvajal (N)	Admiral Ismael Huerta Díaz (N)
Housing	Admiral Arturo Troncoso (N)	General Raúl Viveros (A)
Interior	General César Benavides (A)	General Oscar Bonilla Bradanovic (A)
Justice	General Hugo Musante (C)	Gonzalo Trieto Gandara
Labor	General Nicanor Díaz (AF)	General Mario Mackay (C)
Lands and Colonization	General Mario Mackay (C)	General Diego Barba Valdes (C)
Mining	General Augustín Toro Dávila (A)	(same)
Public Health	General Hugo Herrera (AF)	(same)
Public Works*	General Sergio Figueroa (AF)	General Arturo Yovane (C)
Secretary General	Colonel Pedro Ewing (A)	Colonel Dr. Alberto Spoerer (AF)
Transportation	General Hector Bravo (A)	(none; new position since Public Works was split into Public Works and Transportation)

* Now split into Ministries of Public Works and of Transportation

Volk, Steven, 16, 38, 40, 59
Vuskovic, Pedro, 9, 15, 18, 115
Wald, George, 116-121°
Wall Street Journal, The, 86, 87, 88, 89-95, 142°
Washington Post, The, 20-22, 23, 26, 51-52,° 86, 87, 88, 94, 106, 146
Werner, Dr. Asbalon V., 66
White Book (Junta Militar), 24, 74, 86, 87, 88
Wicker, Tom, 28°
Wiggins, Reverend John, M.M., 98, 99-100°

Williams, Gerald, 131-132°
Wipfler, William, 81, 85,° 130°
Women's International League for Peace and Freedom (WILPF), 47, 101, 113-114°
Woodward, Michael, 55
World Bank (International Bank for Reconstruction and Development), 17, 23, 26, 96, 141
World Council of Churches, 68, 120, 124, 131°
World Court, 59

World Federation of Trade Unions (FMS), 120
Worldview, 86-89°
W. R. Grace and Company, 145
Young, Samuel H. (U.S. Representative), 68, 103, 104-105°
Zamora, Riquelme, 54
Zarate, Gilberto, 56
Zeitlin, Maurice, 16
Zimbalist, Andy, 16
Zucchino Aguirre, Jorge, 55

RECOMMENDED

" 'A silent Vietnam' is what Allende called Chile when he spoke before the United Nations. Silent because low-profile economic warfare commands no footage on the evening news. Undramatic, more subtle than bombs, its weapons can easily be disguised as legitimate international finance, a subject seldom discussed and little understood by non-economists. So Nixon, free of the constraint of an informed public opinion as well as any War Powers Act, could launch a devastating and largely invisible war against Chile.

"Making those tactics visible and understandable is the greatest strength of . . . *The End of Chilean Democracy.* The book moves beyond rhetoric to provide well-documented evidence accessible to readers who would not plow through tedious economic tracts by using articles by such excellent journalists as Pierre Kalfon of *Le Monde* and Tad Szulc of *The Washington Post,* as well as by less leaden scholars like Joseph Collins and Laurence Birns.

"It is likely that in a time that will no longer tolerate the landing of U.S. marines to determine a foreign country's politics, low-profile economic warfare will become an increasingly popular tactic. Although the public is still a long way from a national debate on the moral, legal, and economic ramifications of nationalization, or teach-ins on U.S. economic policy in underdeveloped countries, this book makes an excellent start on the consciousness-raising that will be needed to counter our new style of war. . . .

"One can find valuable things here. . . . *The End of Chilean Democracy* gives readers an accurate idea of what really went on in Chile and provides a much-needed corrective to the myths promoted by the Nixon administration."

—*The Village Voice*

A slightly expanded version of No. 58 in the monographic series IDOC/International Documentation. Available from your bookstore or from The Seabury Press, 815 Second Avenue, New York, N.Y. 10017. Cloth, $8.95; paper, $3.95.

No Peaceful Way: The Chilean Struggle for Dignity

By Gary MacEoin

Offering an excellent broad perspective on Chile's past, this "somber, factual study"* sketches Chile's socio-economic history from the first awakening of its people in the 19th century through the end of 1973. Drawing on original sources (detailed in extensive textual notes), interviews with high-level officials, and the expertise of scholars in the field, MacEoin makes clear that the Allende experiment was not an isolated interlude in the life of Chile, but "a logical step in the upward thrust of a people."

He also shows the logic—from their viewpoint—of the exploiters, both within and outside Chile, of its resources and people, a logic which caused them to trample the democratic institutions of which they had previously boasted.

* "Right-wingers may come up with a counterblast to this book, but it's not likely they will as convincing: MacEoin has got at the facts," says *Publishers Weekly.* Professor Richard R. Fagen, President of the Latin American Studies Association (LASA), concurs: "*No Peaceful Way* is a fine book—very successful in communicating what the Allende government was all about, and why it met such deep-seated opposition both in the propertied classes of Chile and from the United States. It deserves wide readership, for the mark of the tragic overthrow of the Popular Unity government will be on this hemisphere for many years to come. There are important lessons to be learned, and this book helps make those lessons clear." "Terse and convincing," add Patrick Breslin in *The Washington Post Book World.* "MacEoin provides both the historical context and many of the crucial facts for understanding them." **Sheed and Ward, Inc. /cloth, $6.95**

"When the Chilean coup occurred, it was front-page news in the United States for about three weeks. As predicted, once the imposition of a fascist state was a *fait accompli*, political concern in the United States virtually vanished, just as it had already vanished over Indochina."*

Then, on September 8, 1974, Seymour M. Hersh disclosed, on the front page of *The New York Times*, evidence confirming the role of the Forty Committee and the CIA in pouring $8 million into the effort to "destabilize" the government of Salvador Allende, a campaign which Allende himself had called "a silent Vietnam." Hopefully, this disclosure will open meaningful public debate that can at last be elevated above paranoic obsession with the spectre of Marxism in the Western hemisphere and endless philosophical wrangling over Allende's "competence"—and, even more hopefully, America's attention will finally focus on the realities endured during this long year of silence by human beings suffering in the wake of an orgy of savagery unparalleled in Latin America's recent history.

For today, one year after the violent coup of September 11, 1973, the Chilean people continue to be victimized by the institutionalized violence unleashed by the Junta in collusion with exploiters both within and outside the nation who have made democracy a shambles and human rights a sham. Thousands of citizens languish in prisons awaiting trial—or even formulation of charges against them. Wages are frozen, while prices rise astronomically. The work days are arbitrarily lengthened, medical services are eliminated. Millions are denied jobs, while the Junta proclaims that whoever does not work does not eat. Universities are destroyed, children's minds "scrubbed."

And the Chileans can opt for neither redress nor escape: free emigration is denied, prisoners are refused access to defense lawyers, and all rights to freedom of association and expression have been eliminated.

These are not idle charges, but facts confirmed and analyzed in this volume. Recorded also are the elements of international protest, which to date have proved only marginally effective in reversing the policies of the Junta. As Mr. MacEoin says in his introduction, "Power in Santiago is arrogant, as it is in Washington, confident of its ability to beat into the ground all who do not voluntarily lie down. . . . [Yet though] the arrogance of power flouts public opinion, [it] fears it. Witness the vast expenditure of effort devoted to distorting and confusing people's minds. The first objective must be to counter this by searching out and proclaiming the truth, by developing in the minds and hearts of courageous people a commitment to human solidarity and a repudiation of inhumanity no matter how clothed. This volume is offered as a modest contribution to that long struggle."

*Richard J. Barnet, in his article "The Nixon-Kissinger Doctrine and the Meaning of Chile," from this volume.

An original paperback compiled, edited, and produced by
IDOC/North America

Printed in the U.S.A.

ISBN 0-89021-027-6